That Blue Sky Feeling

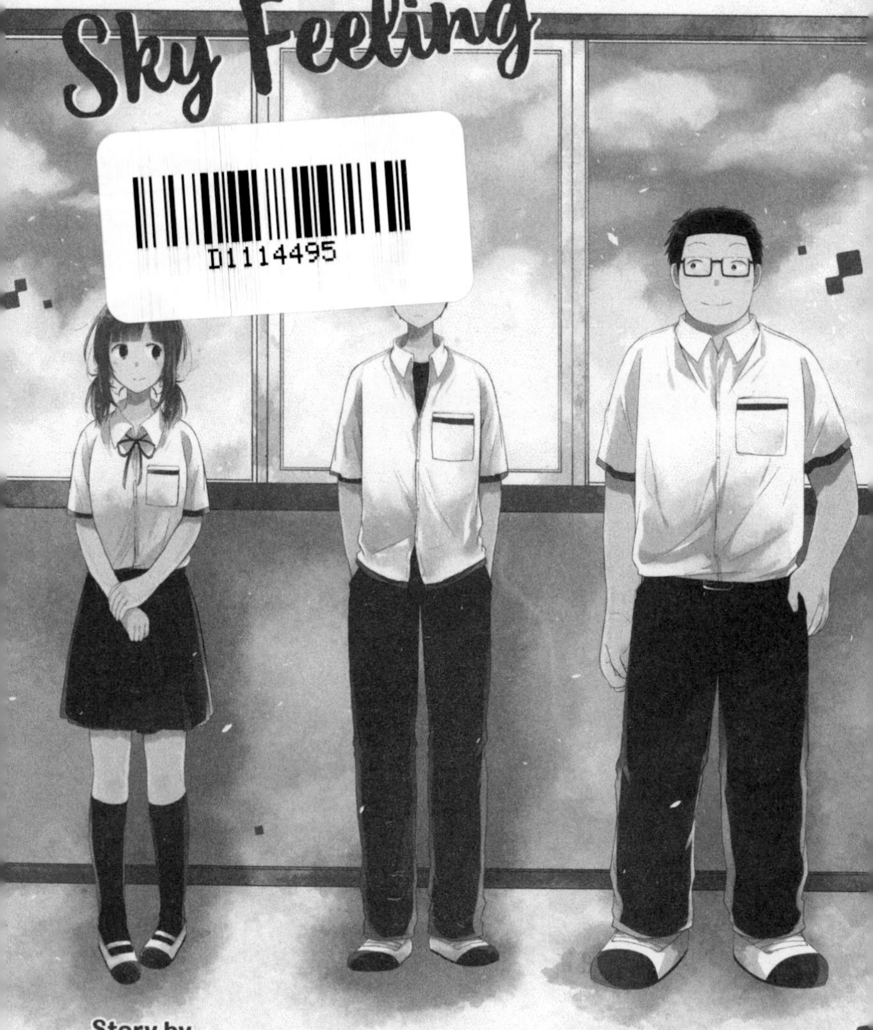

Story by
Okura

Art by
Coma Hashii

2

CONTENTS

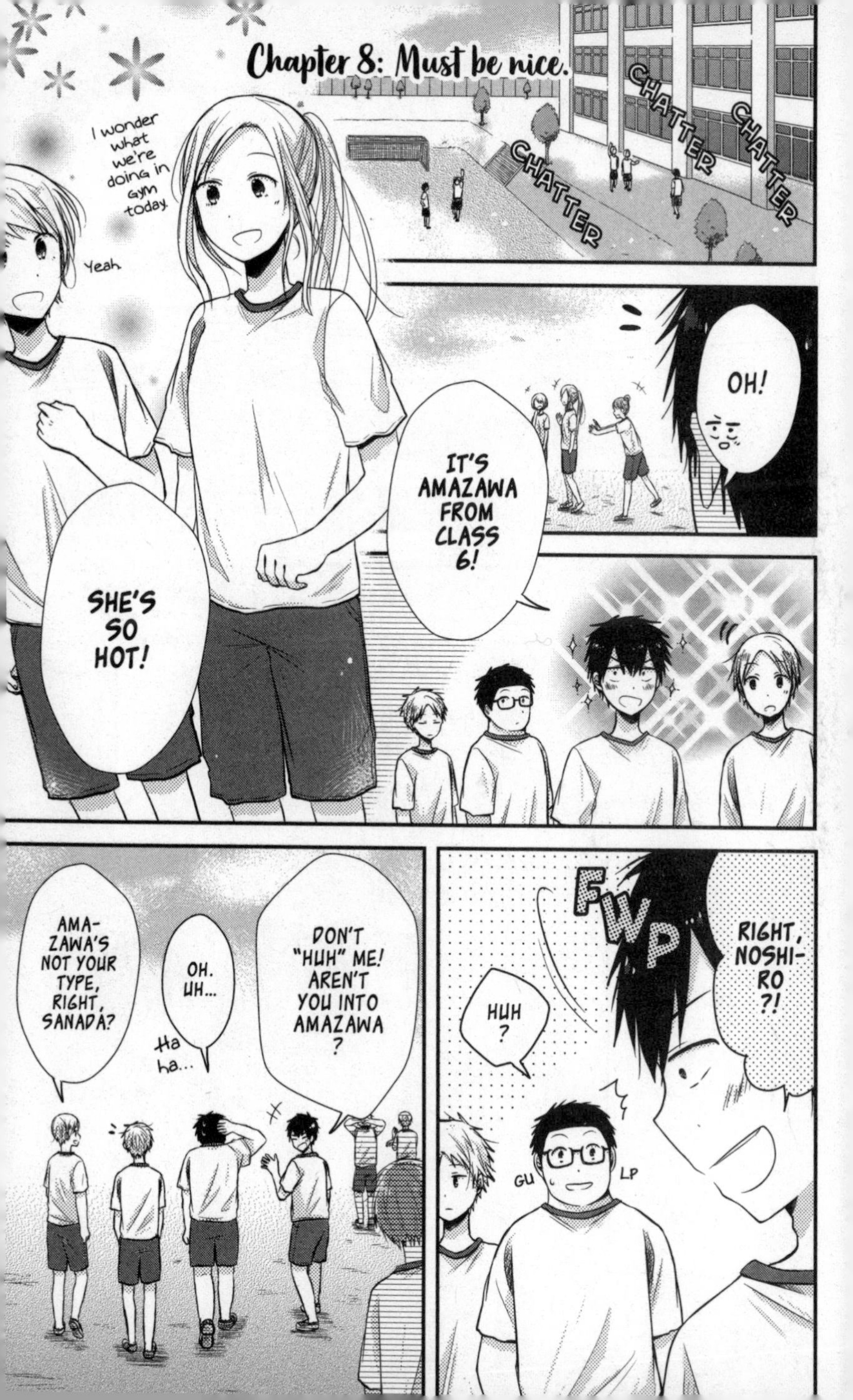
Chapter 8: Must be nice.
CHATTER
CHATTER
CHATTER
OH!
IT'S AMAZAWA FROM CLASS 6!
SHE'S SO HOT!
I wonder what we're doing in gym today.
Yeah.
FWP
RIGHT, NOSHIRO?!
HUH?
GULP
DON'T "HUH" ME! AREN'T YOU INTO AMAZAWA?
OH. UH...
Ha ha...
AMAZAWA'S NOT YOUR TYPE, RIGHT, SANADA?

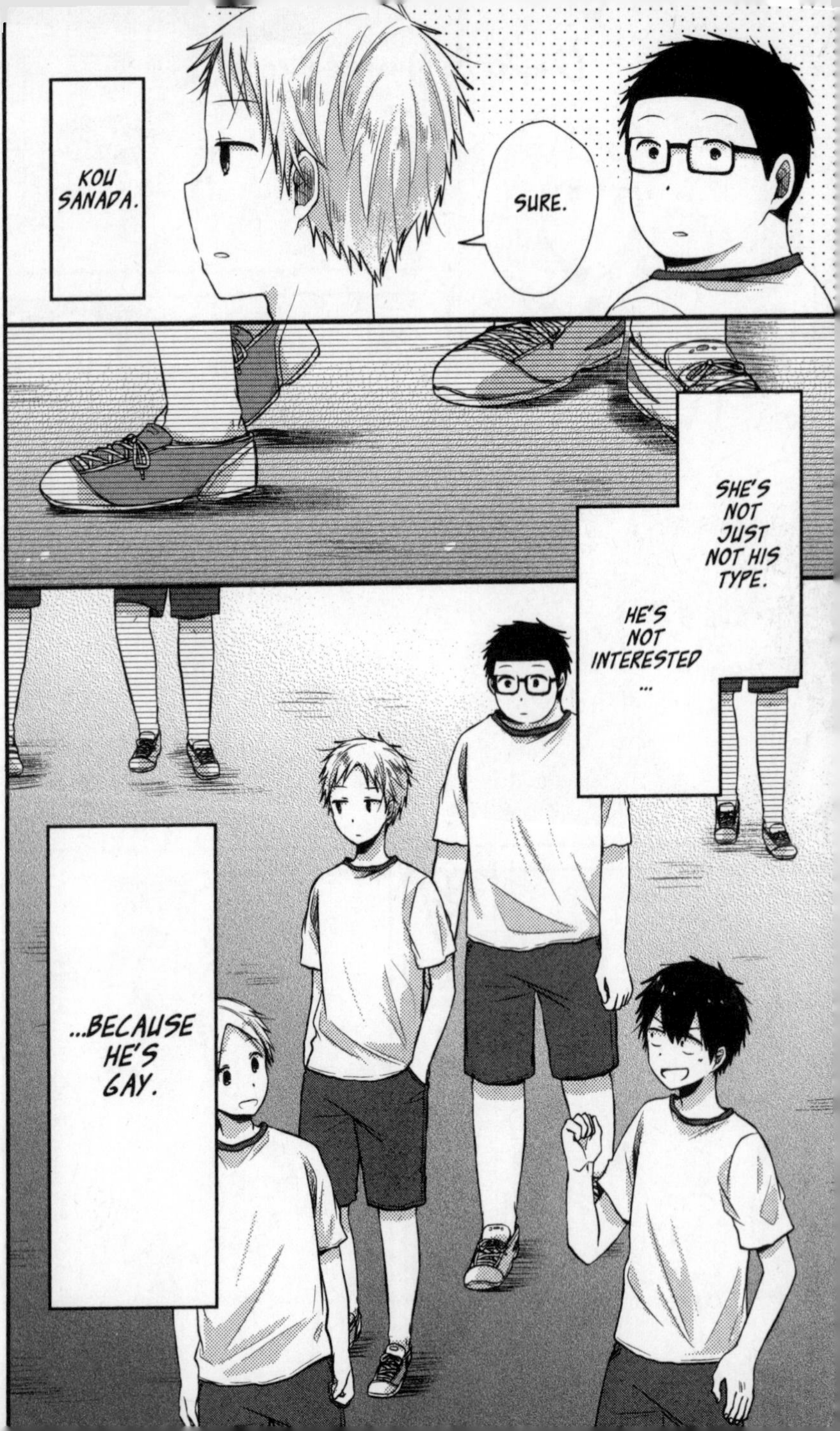
SURE.
KOU SANADA.
SHE'S NOT JUST NOT HIS TYPE.
HE'S NOT INTERESTED...
...BECAUSE HE'S GAY.

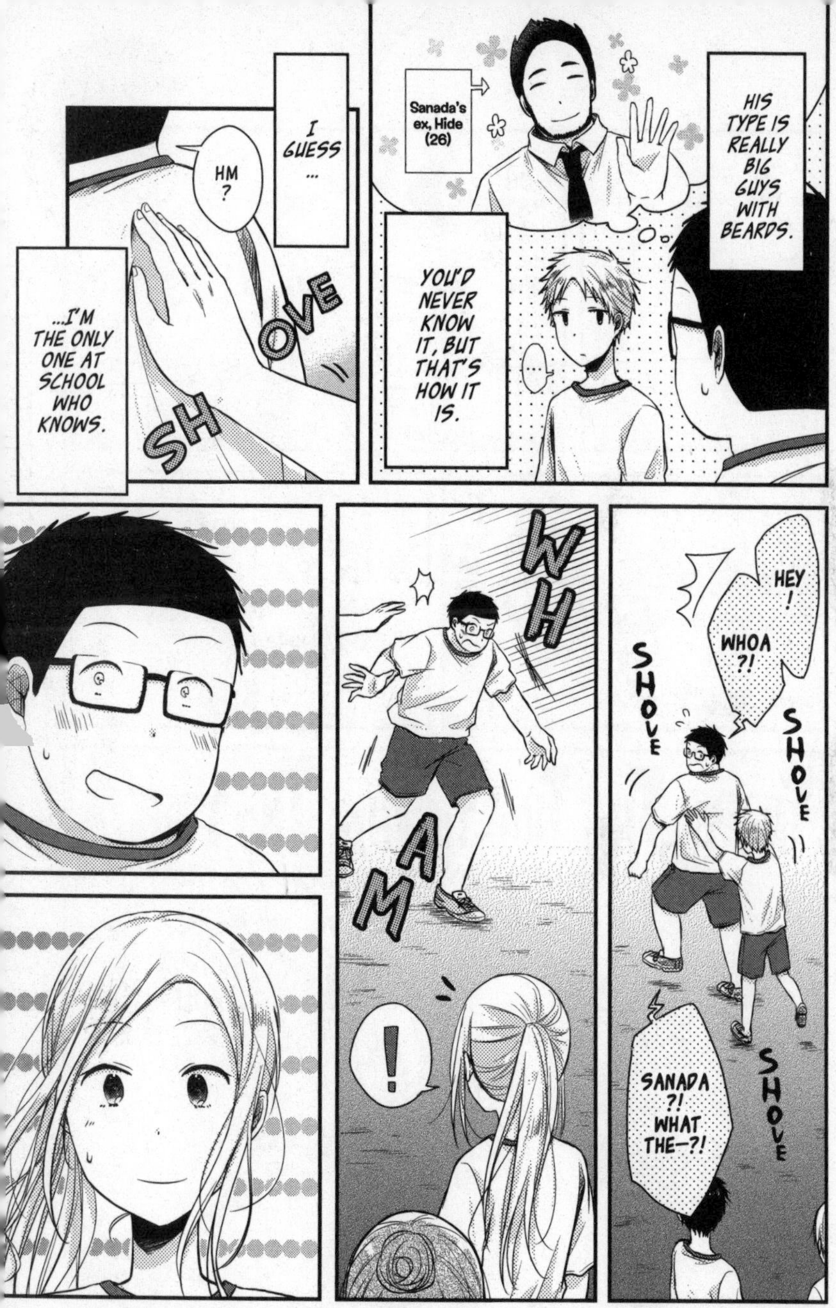
HIS TYPE IS REALLY BIG GUYS WITH BEARDS.
Sanada's ex, Hide (26)
YOU'D NEVER KNOW IT, BUT THAT'S HOW IT IS.
...
I GUESS...
HM?
SHOVE
...I'M THE ONLY ONE AT SCHOOL WHO KNOWS.
HEY!
WHOA?!
SHOVE
SHOVE
SANADA?! WHAT THE—?!
SHOVE
WHAM
!

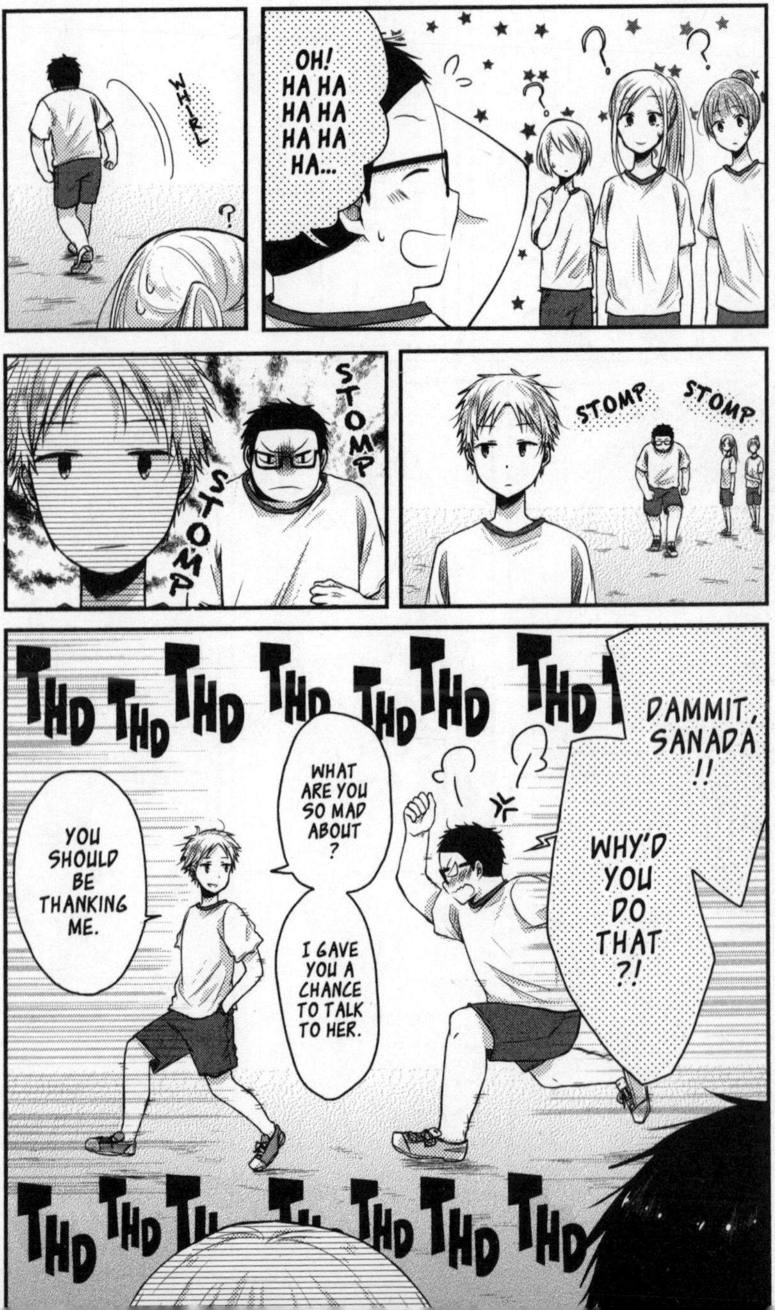
OH! HA HA HA HA HA HA HA...
WHIRL
STOMP STOMP
STOMP STOMP
THD THD THD THD THD THD THD
DAMMIT, SANADA!!
WHY'D YOU DO THAT?!
WHAT ARE YOU SO MAD ABOUT?
I GAVE YOU A CHANCE TO TALK TO HER.
YOU SHOULD BE THANKING ME.
THD THD THD THD THD THD

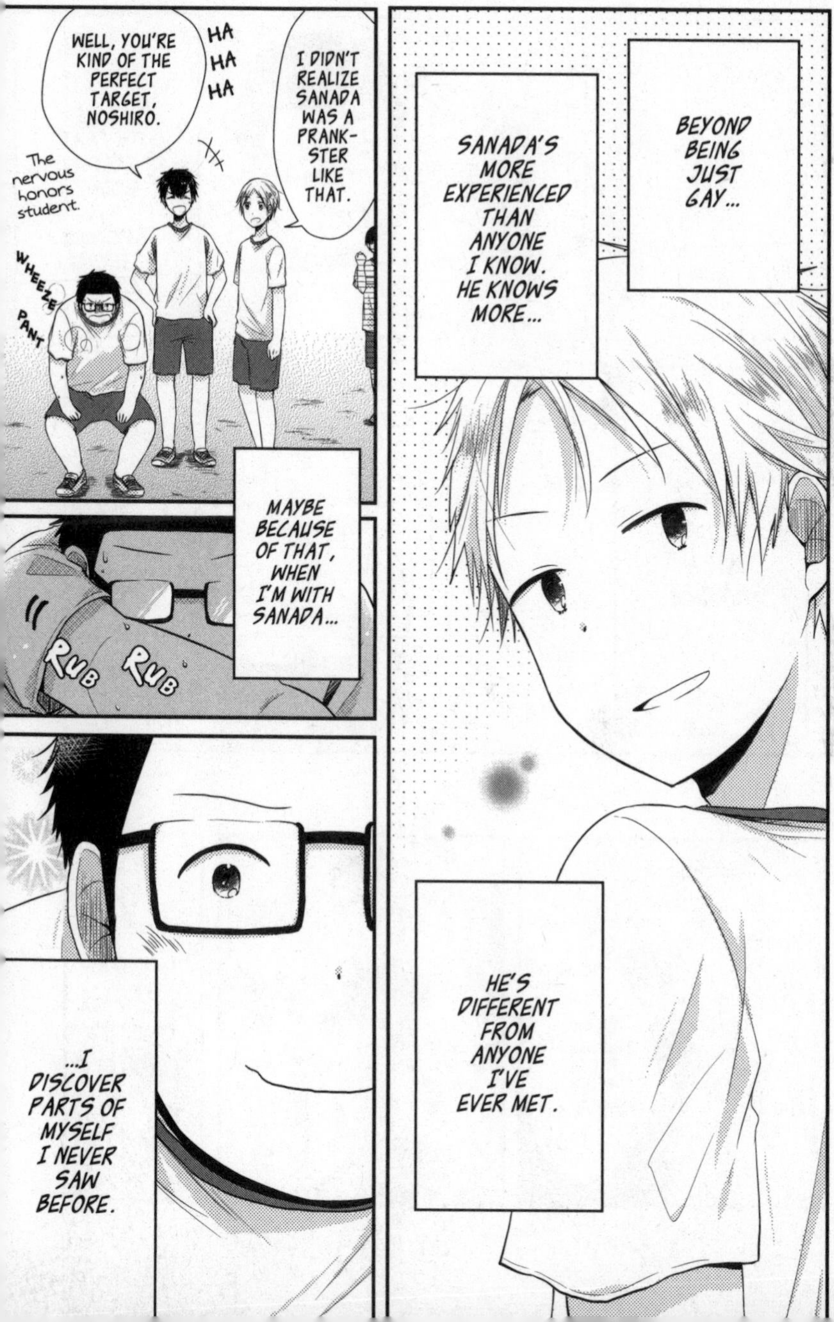
BEYOND BEING JUST GAY...
SANADA'S MORE EXPERIENCED THAN ANYONE I KNOW. HE KNOWS MORE...
HE'S DIFFERENT FROM ANYONE I'VE EVER MET.
I DIDN'T REALIZE SANADA WAS A PRANKSTER LIKE THAT.
HA HA HA
WELL, YOU'RE KIND OF THE PERFECT TARGET, NOSHIRO.
The nervous honors student.
WHEEZE
PANT
MAYBE BECAUSE OF THAT, WHEN I'M WITH SANADA...
RUB RUB
...I DISCOVER PARTS OF MYSELF I NEVER SAW BEFORE.

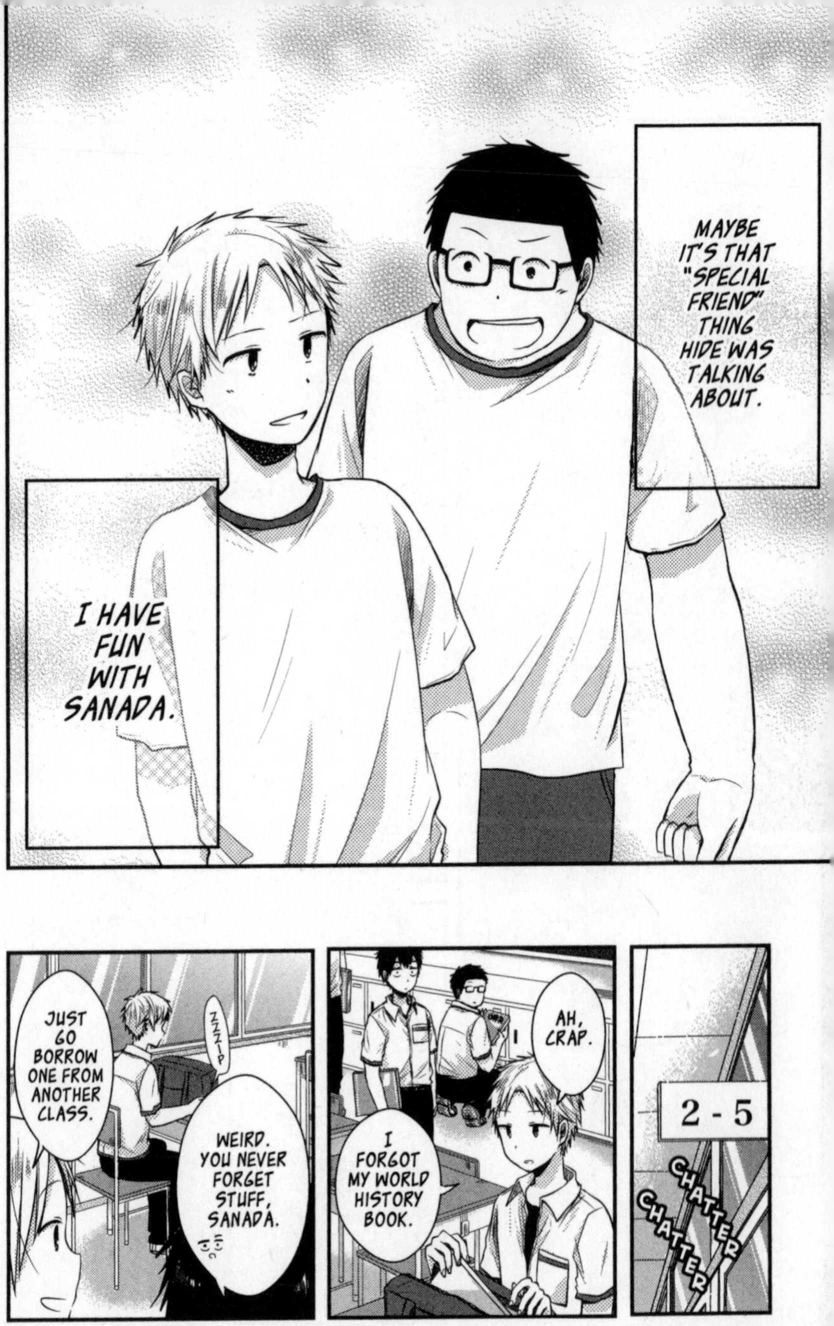

MAYBE IT'S THAT "SPECIAL FRIEND" THING HIDE WAS TALKING ABOUT.
I HAVE FUN WITH SANADA.
2 - 5
CHATTER CHATTER
AH, CRAP.
I FORGOT MY WORLD HISTORY BOOK.
ZZZIP
WEIRD. YOU NEVER FORGET STUFF, SANADA.
JUST GO BORROW ONE FROM ANOTHER CLASS.

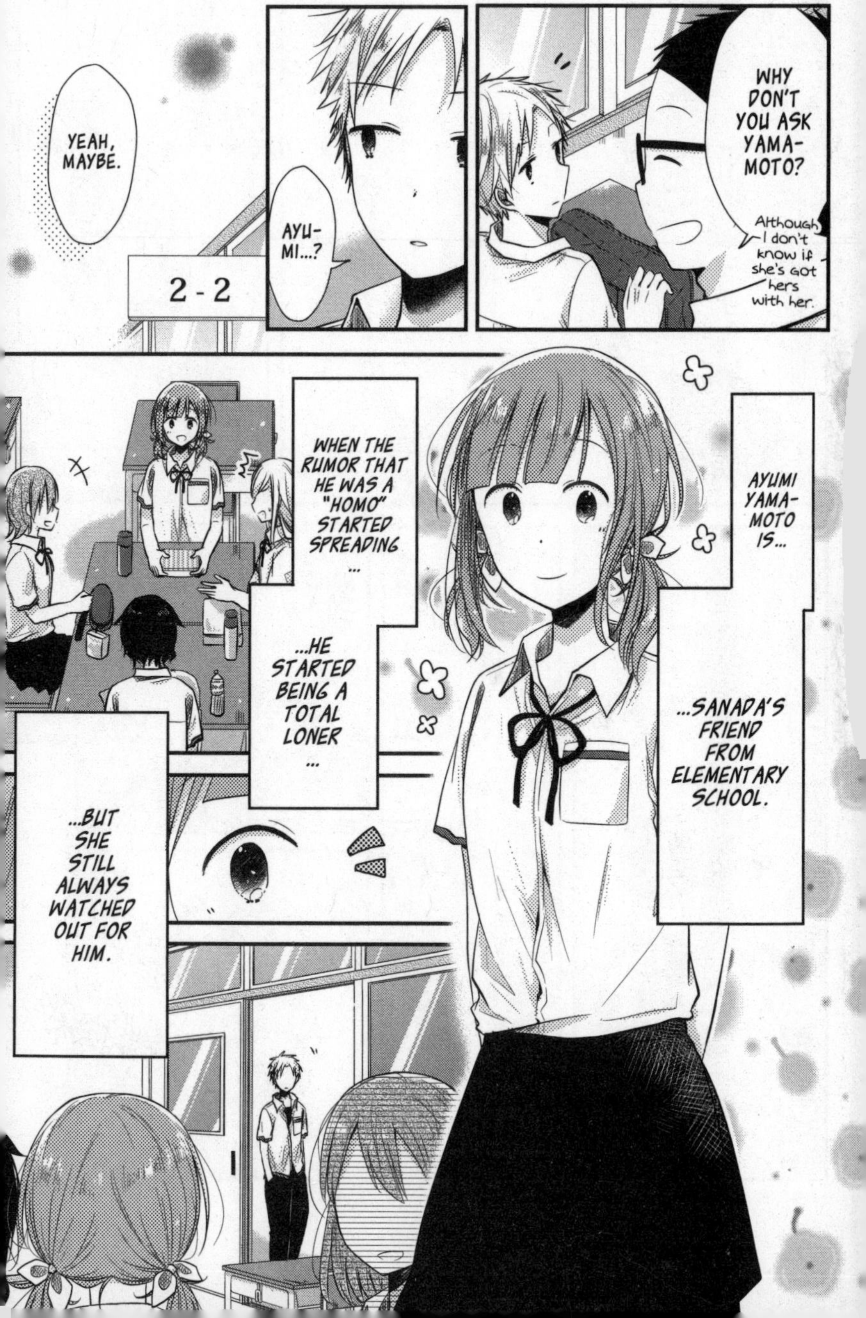

WHY DON'T YOU ASK YAMAMOTO?
Although I don't know if she's got hers with her.
AYUMI...?
YEAH, MAYBE.
2-2
AYUMI YAMAMOTO IS...
...SANADA'S FRIEND FROM ELEMENTARY SCHOOL.
WHEN THE RUMOR THAT HE WAS A "HOMO" STARTED SPREADING...
...HE STARTED BEING A TOTAL LONER...
...BUT SHE STILL ALWAYS WATCHED OUT FOR HIM.

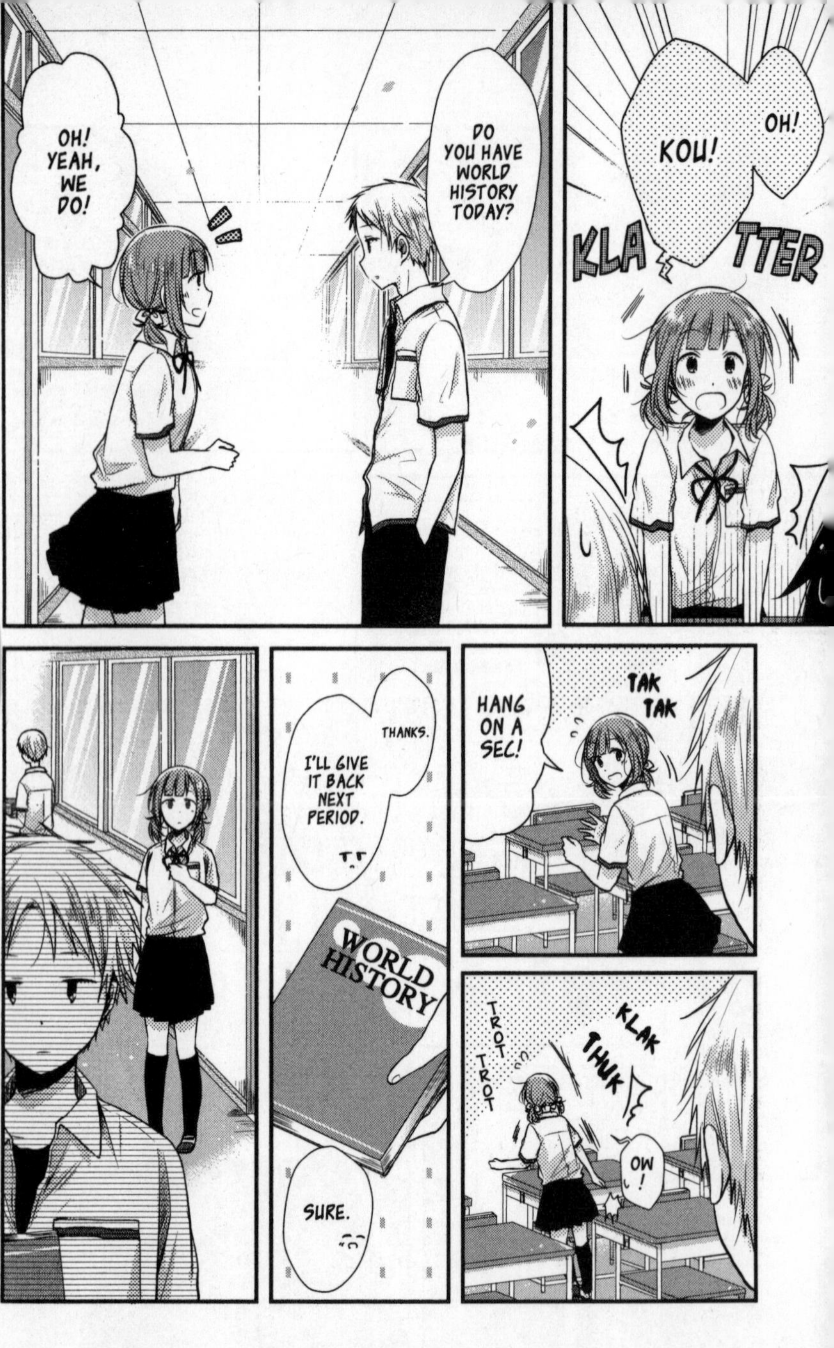

OH!
KOU!
KLATTER
DO YOU HAVE WORLD HISTORY TODAY?
OH! YEAH, WE DO!
TAK TAK
HANG ON A SEC!
KLAK
THUK
TROT TROT
OW!
THANKS.
I'LL GIVE IT BACK NEXT PERIOD.
WORLD HISTORY
SURE.

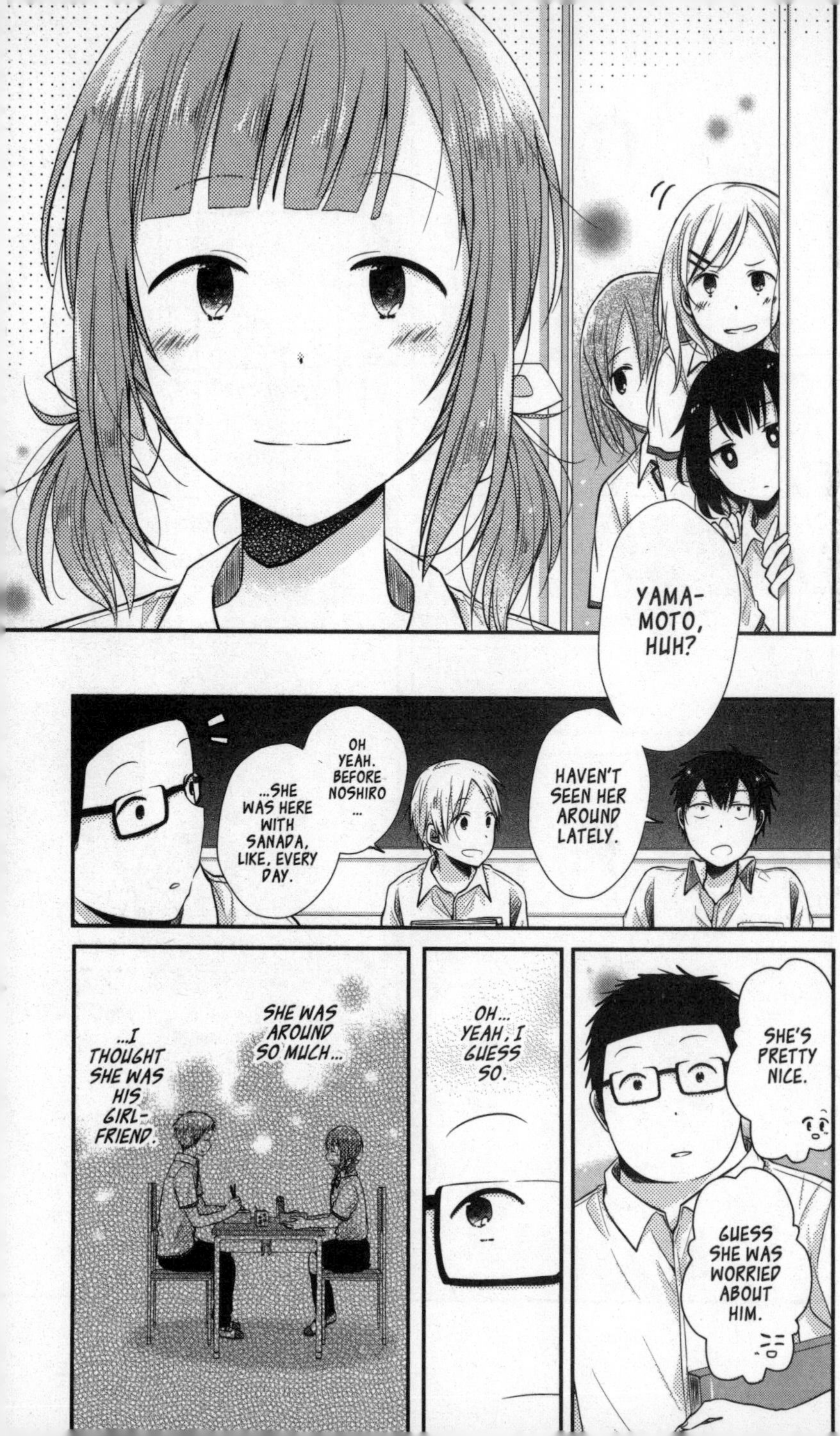
YAMA-MOTO, HUH?
HAVEN'T SEEN HER AROUND LATELY.
OH YEAH. BEFORE NOSHIRO ...
...SHE WAS HERE WITH SANADA, LIKE, EVERY DAY.
SHE'S PRETTY NICE.
GUESS SHE WAS WORRIED ABOUT HIM.
OH... YEAH, I GUESS SO.
SHE WAS AROUND SO MUCH...
...I THOUGHT SHE WAS HIS GIRL-FRIEND.

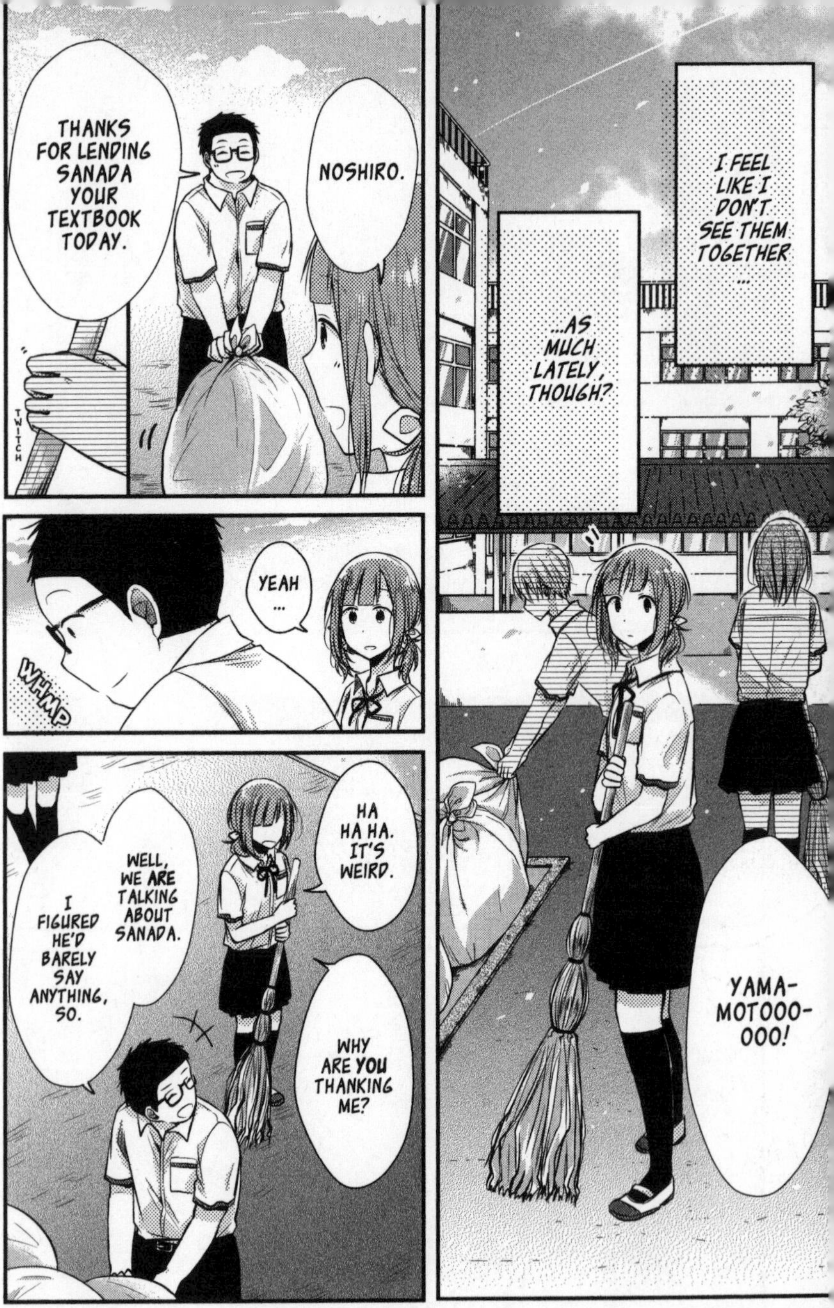
I FEEL LIKE I DON'T SEE THEM TOGETHER...
...AS MUCH LATELY, THOUGH?
YAMA-MOTOOOO-OOO!
NOSHIRO.
THANKS FOR LENDING SANADA YOUR TEXTBOOK TODAY.
TWITCH
YEAH...
WHMP
HA HA HA. IT'S WEIRD.
WHY ARE YOU THANKING ME?
WELL, WE ARE TALKING ABOUT SANADA.
I FIGURED HE'D BARELY SAY ANYTHING, SO.

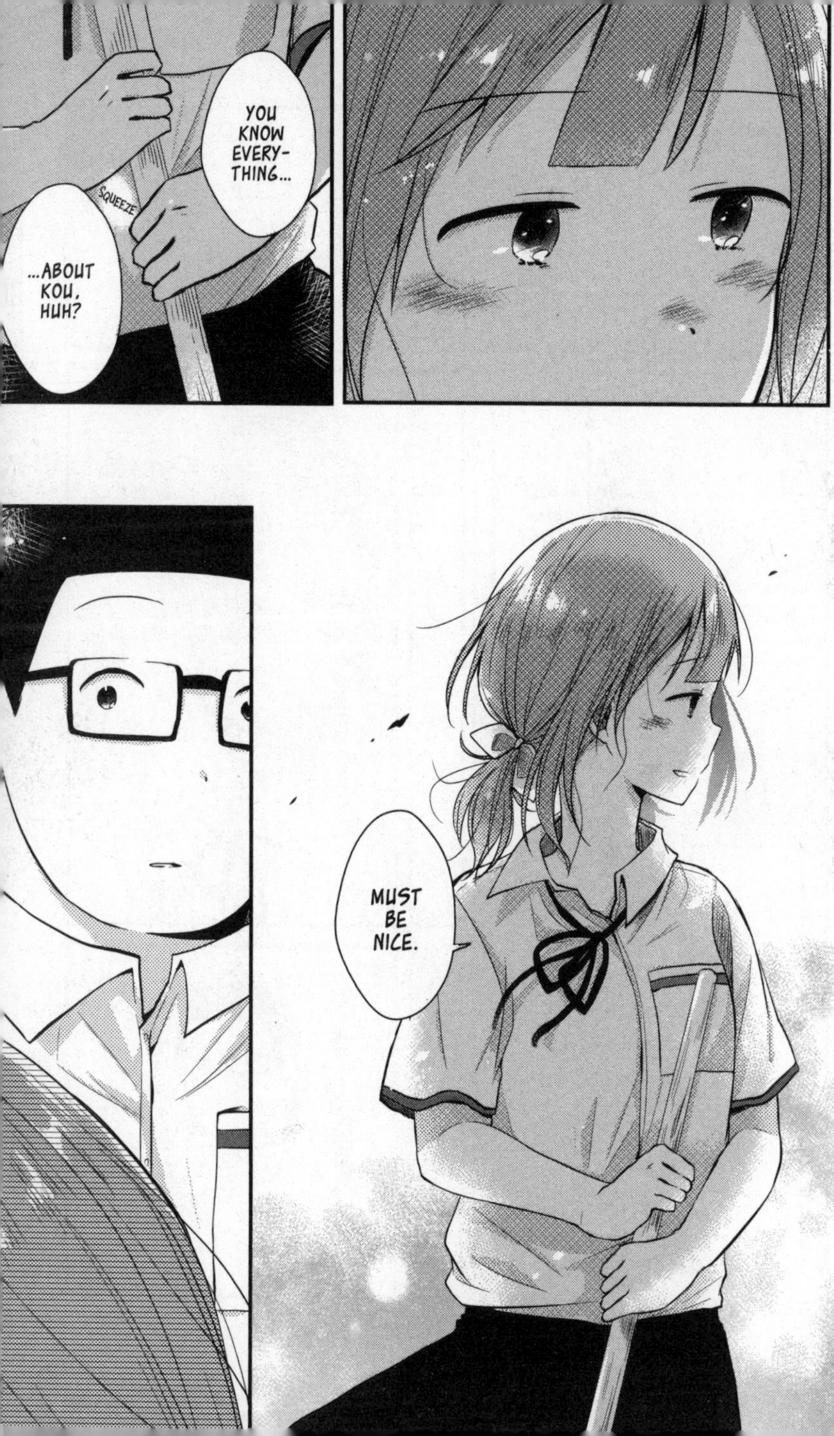
YOU KNOW EVERY-THING...
SQUEEZE
...ABOUT KOU, HUH?
MUST BE NICE.

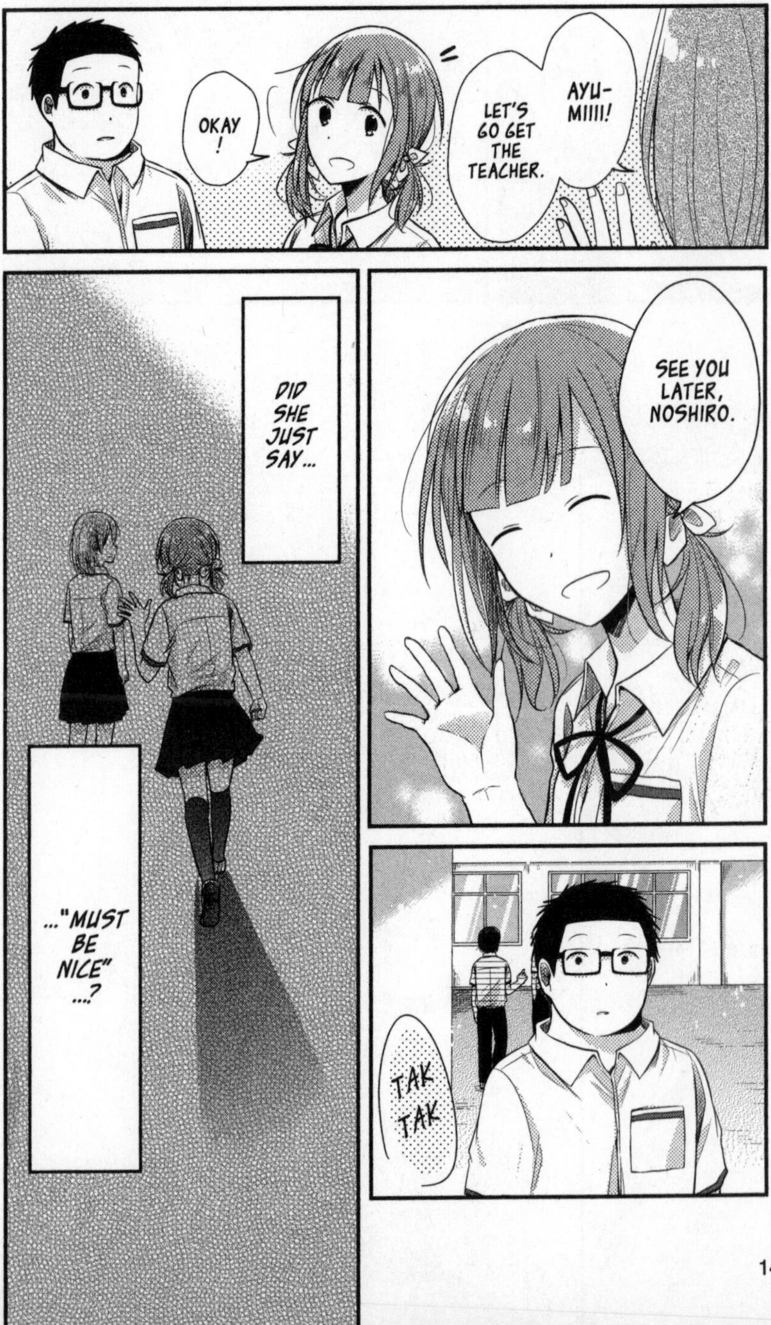
AYU-MIIII!
LET'S GO GET THE TEACHER.
OKAY!
SEE YOU LATER, NOSHIRO.
TAK TAK
DID SHE JUST SAY...
..."MUST BE NICE"...?

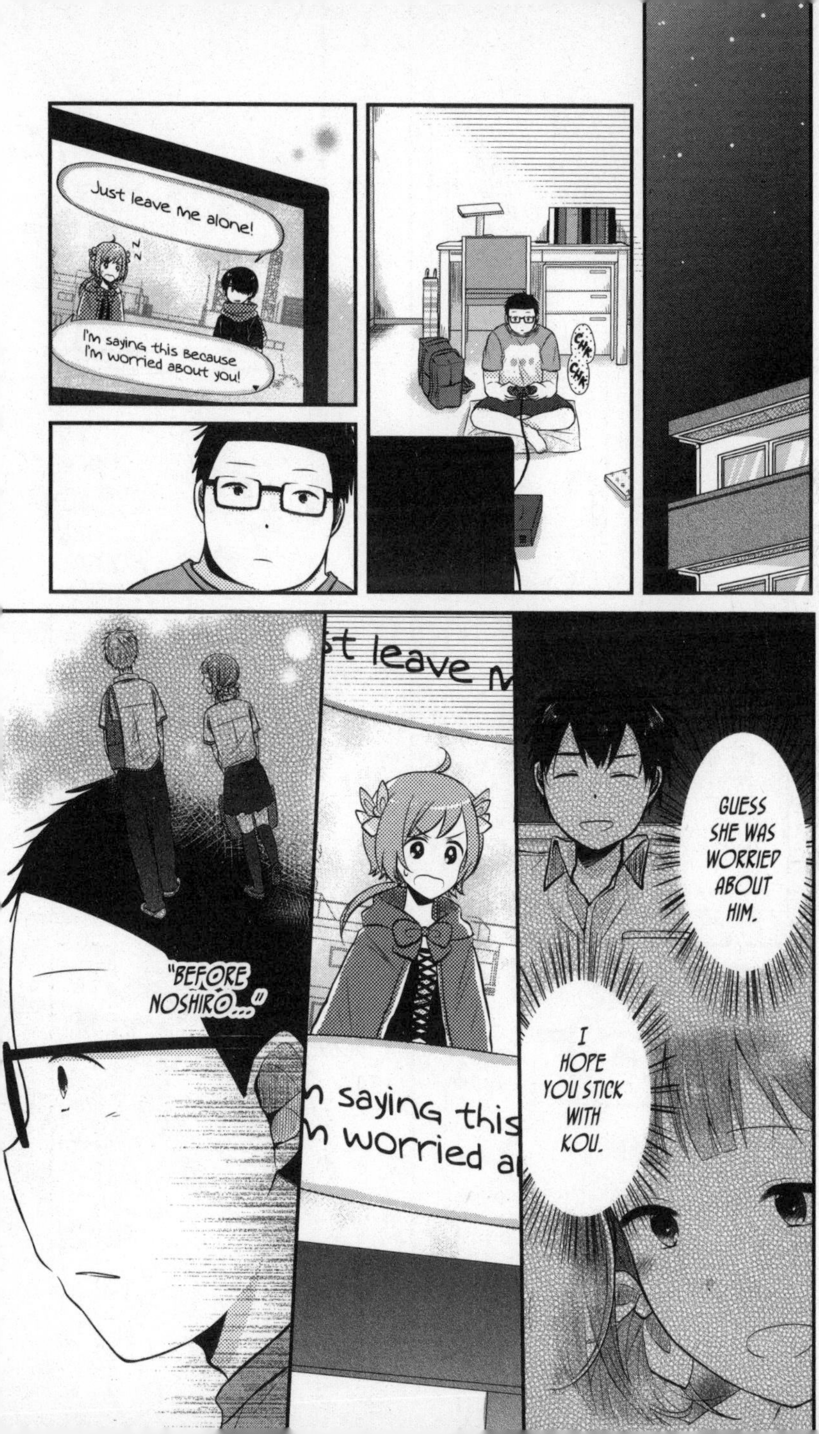
CHK
CHK
Just leave me alone!
I'm saying this because I'm worried about you!
GUESS SHE WAS WORRIED ABOUT HIM.
I HOPE YOU STICK WITH KOU.
st leave M
n saying this
m worried a
"BEFORE NOSHIRO..."

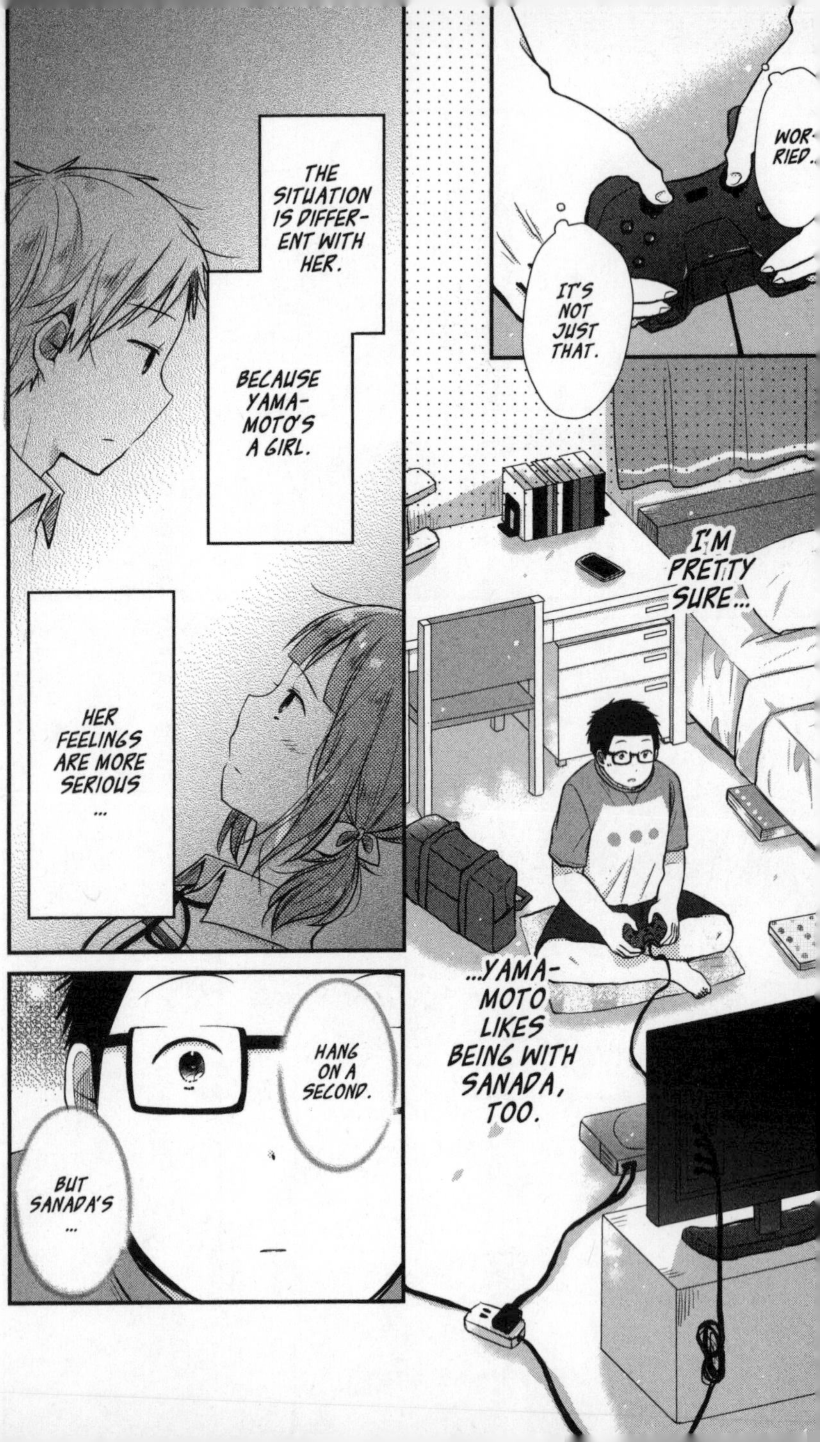
WOR-RIED...
IT'S NOT JUST THAT.
I'M PRETTY SURE...
...YAMA-MOTO LIKES BEING WITH SANADA, TOO.
THE SITUATION IS DIFFER-ENT WITH HER.
BECAUSE YAMA-MOTO'S A GIRL.
HER FEELINGS ARE MORE SERIOUS...
HANG ON A SECOND.
BUT SANADA'S...

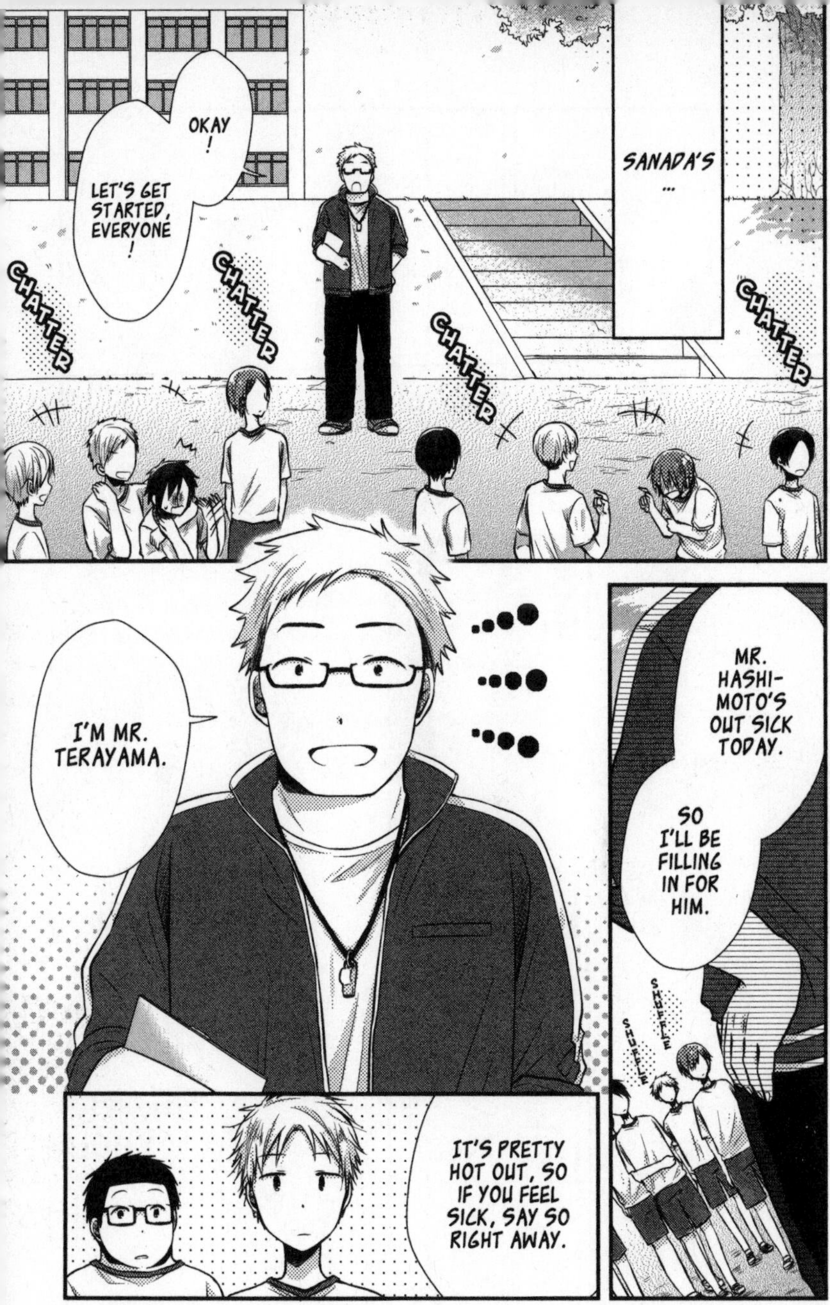
SANADA'S ...
OKAY! LET'S GET STARTED, EVERYONE!
CHATTER
CHATTER
CHATTER
CHATTER
MR. HASHIMOTO'S OUT SICK TODAY.
SO I'LL BE FILLING IN FOR HIM.
SHUFFLE
SHUFFLE
...
...
...
I'M MR. TERAYAMA.
IT'S PRETTY HOT OUT, SO IF YOU FEEL SICK, SAY SO RIGHT AWAY.

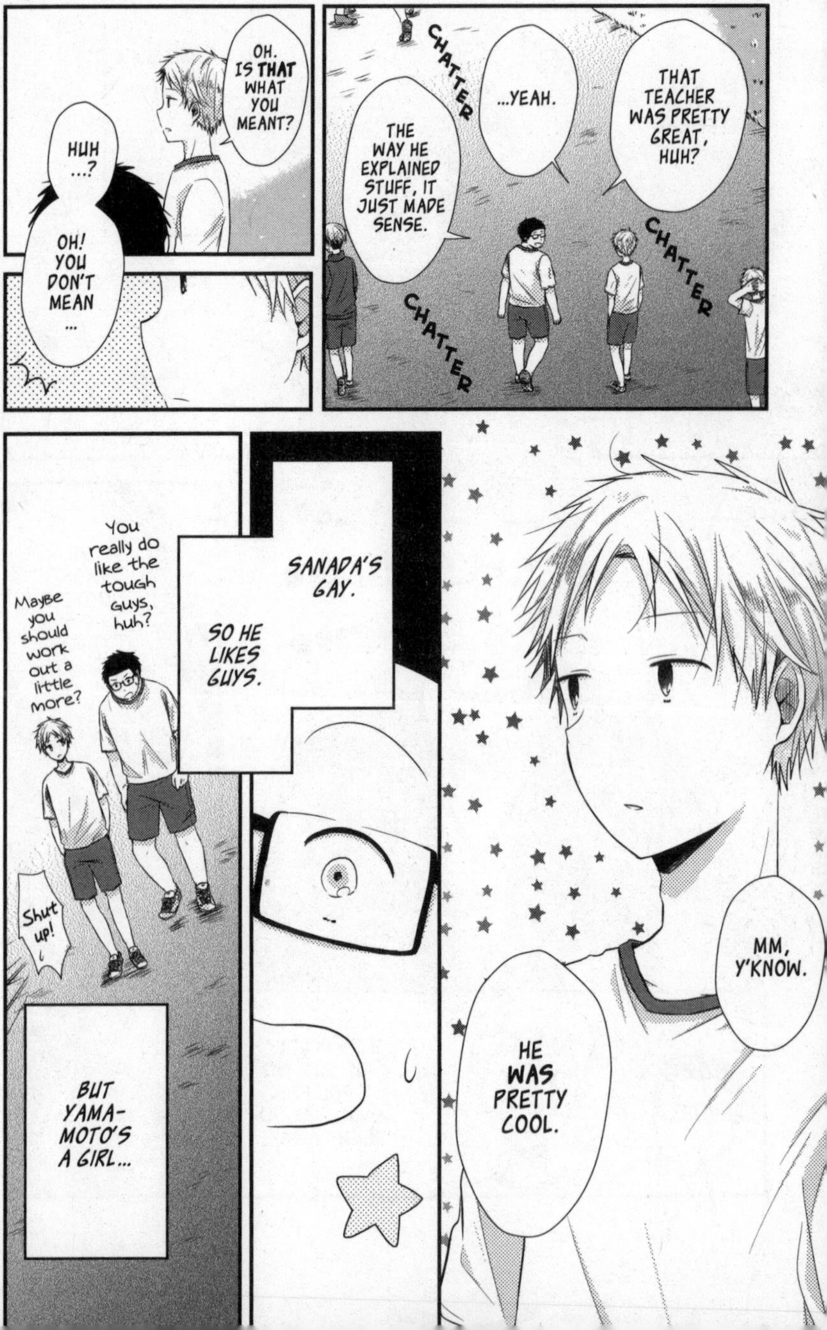
THAT TEACHER WAS PRETTY GREAT, HUH?
...YEAH.
CHATTER
THE WAY HE EXPLAINED STUFF, IT JUST MADE SENSE.
CHATTER
CHATTER
OH. IS THAT WHAT YOU MEANT?
HUH ...?
OH! YOU DON'T MEAN ...
MM, Y'KNOW.
HE WAS PRETTY COOL.
SANADA'S GAY.
SO HE LIKES GUYS.
You really do like the tough guys, huh?
Maybe you should work out a little more?
Shut up!
BUT YAMA-MOTO'S A GIRL...

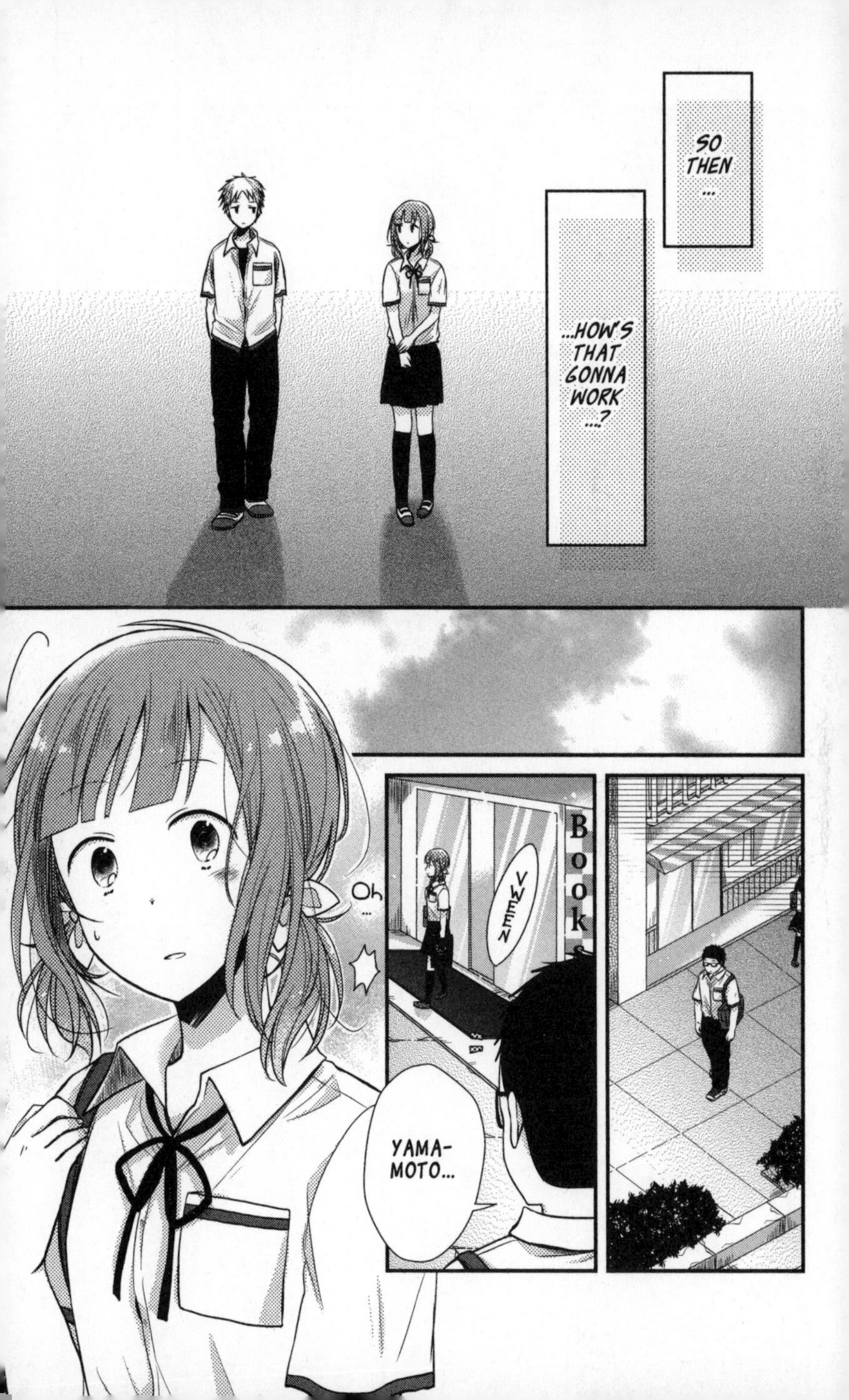
SO THEN ...
...HOW'S THAT GONNA WORK ...?
Books
VWEEN
YAMA-MOTO...
Oh ...

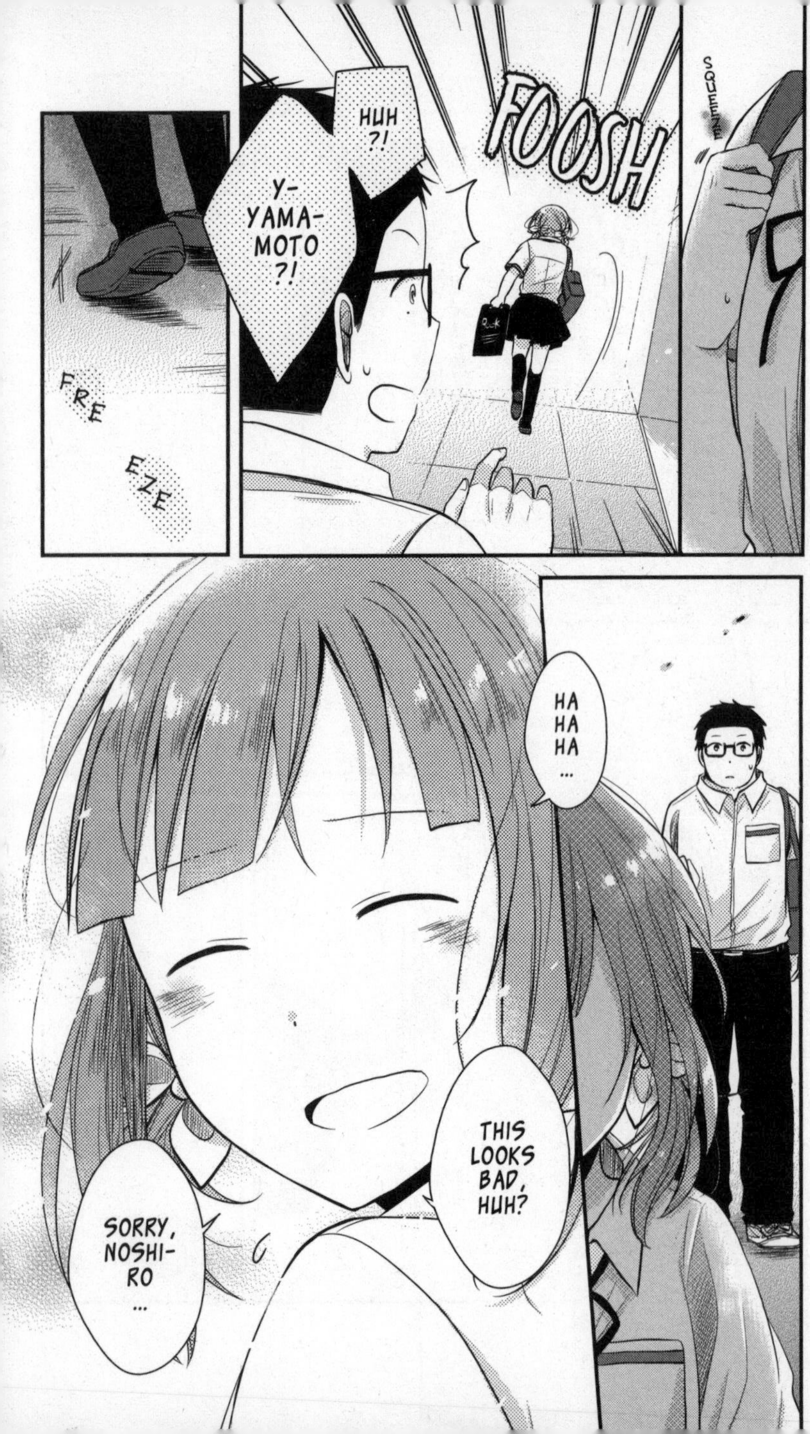
SQUEEZE
FOOSH
HUH?!
Y-YAMAMOTO?!
FREEZE
HA HA HA...
THIS LOOKS BAD, HUH?
SORRY, NOSHIRO...

NOSHIRO.
BEFORE...
...I SAID YOU KNOW EVERYTHING ABOUT SANADA.
TO BE HONEST, I USED TO THINK I DID, TOO.
BUT NOW I DON'T THINK I DID.
WHEN I SEE KOU WITH YOU...
HUH?
IS SANADA DIFFERENT WITH ME?
HE'S DIFFERENT FROM WHEN HE'S WITH HIS JUNIOR HIGH FRIENDS...
...AT LEAST...

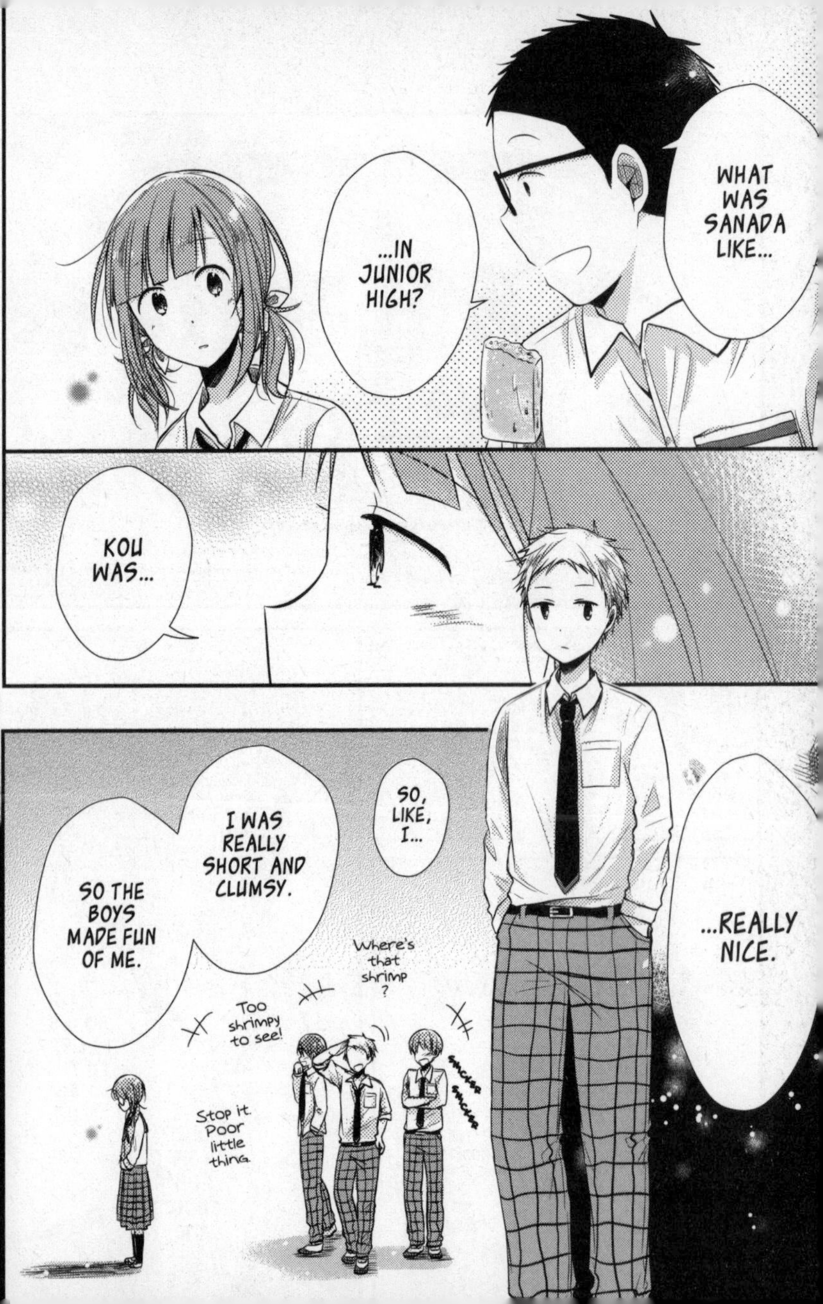
WHAT WAS SANADA LIKE...
...IN JUNIOR HIGH?
KOU WAS...
...REALLY NICE.
SO, LIKE, I...
I WAS REALLY SHORT AND CLUMSY.
SO THE BOYS MADE FUN OF ME.
SNICKER SNICKER
Where's that shrimp?
Too shrimpy to see!
Stop it. Poor little thing.

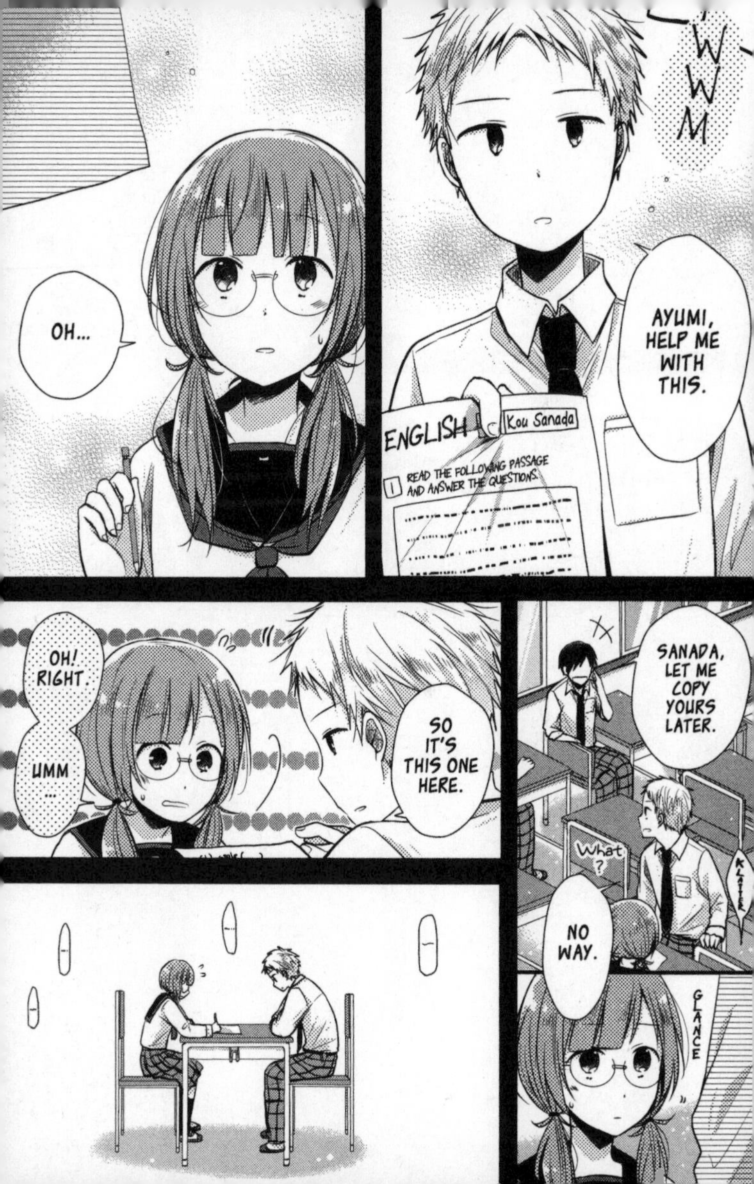
WWM
AYUMI, HELP ME WITH THIS.
ENGLISH
Kou Sanada
1 READ THE FOLLOWING PASSAGE AND ANSWER THE QUESTIONS.
OH...
SANADA, LET ME COPY YOURS LATER.
What?
KLATTER
NO WAY.
GLANCE
SO IT'S THIS ONE HERE.
OH! RIGHT.
UMM ...

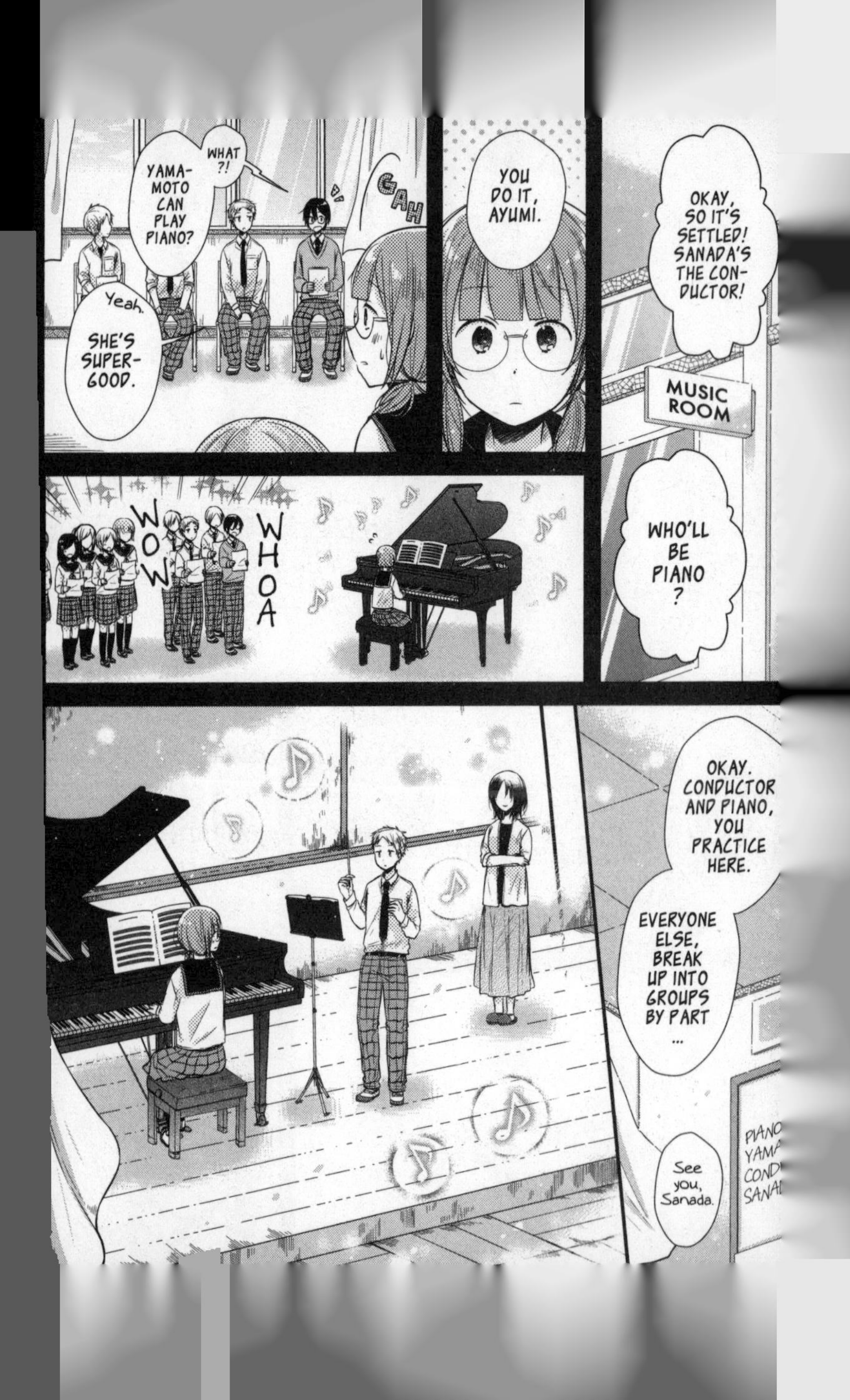
OKAY, SO IT'S SETTLED! SANADA'S THE CONDUCTOR!
MUSIC ROOM
WHO'LL BE PIANO?
YOU DO IT, AYUMI.
GAH
WHAT?!
YAMA-MOTO CAN PLAY PIANO?
Yeah.
SHE'S SUPER-GOOD.
WHOA
WOW
OKAY. CONDUCTOR AND PIANO, YOU PRACTICE HERE.
EVERYONE ELSE, BREAK UP INTO GROUPS BY PART...
See you, Sanada.

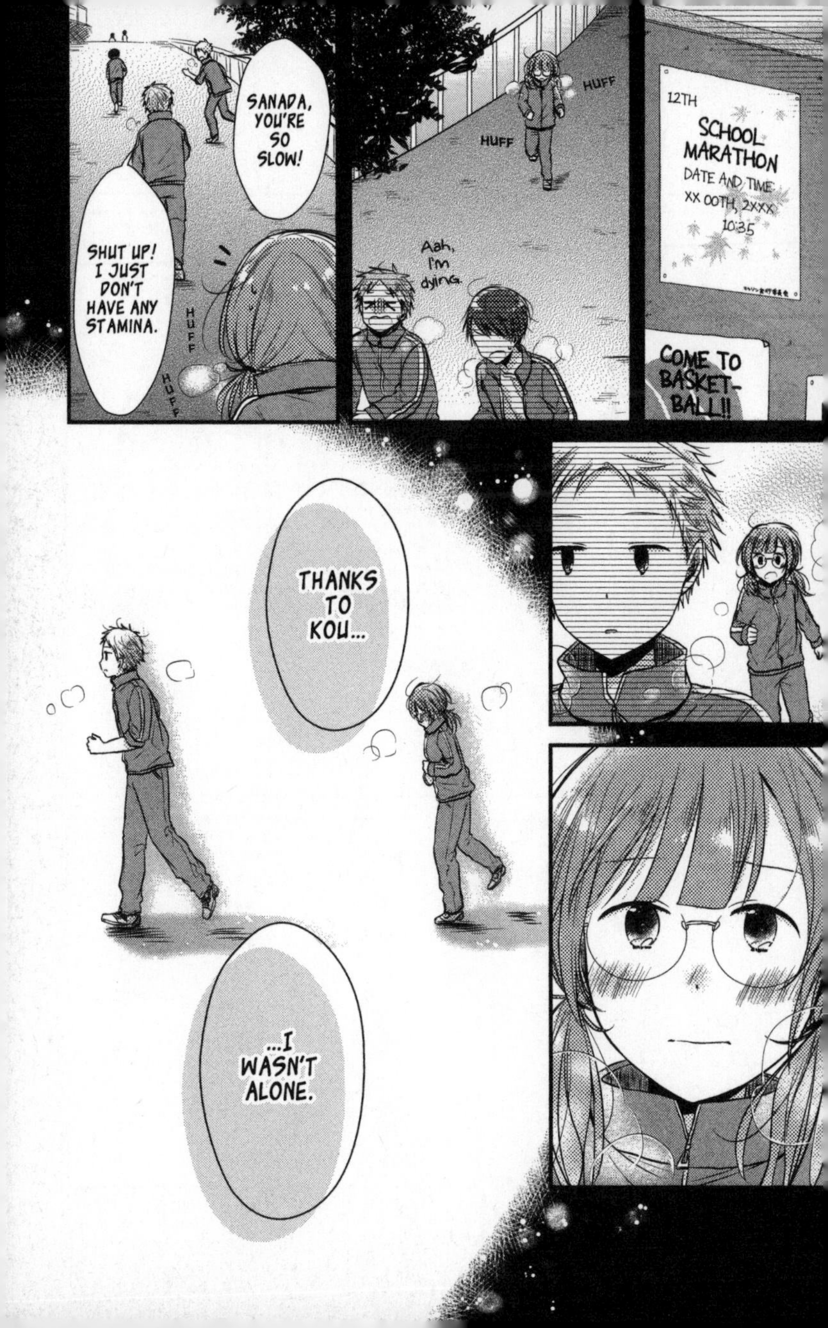
12TH
SCHOOL MARATHON
DATE AND TIME
XX OOTH, 2XXX
10:35
COME TO BASKET-BALL!!
HUFF
HUFF
Aah, I'm dying.
SANADA, YOU'RE SO SLOW!
SHUT UP! I JUST DON'T HAVE ANY STAMINA.
HUFF
HUFF
THANKS TO KOU...
...I WASN'T ALONE.

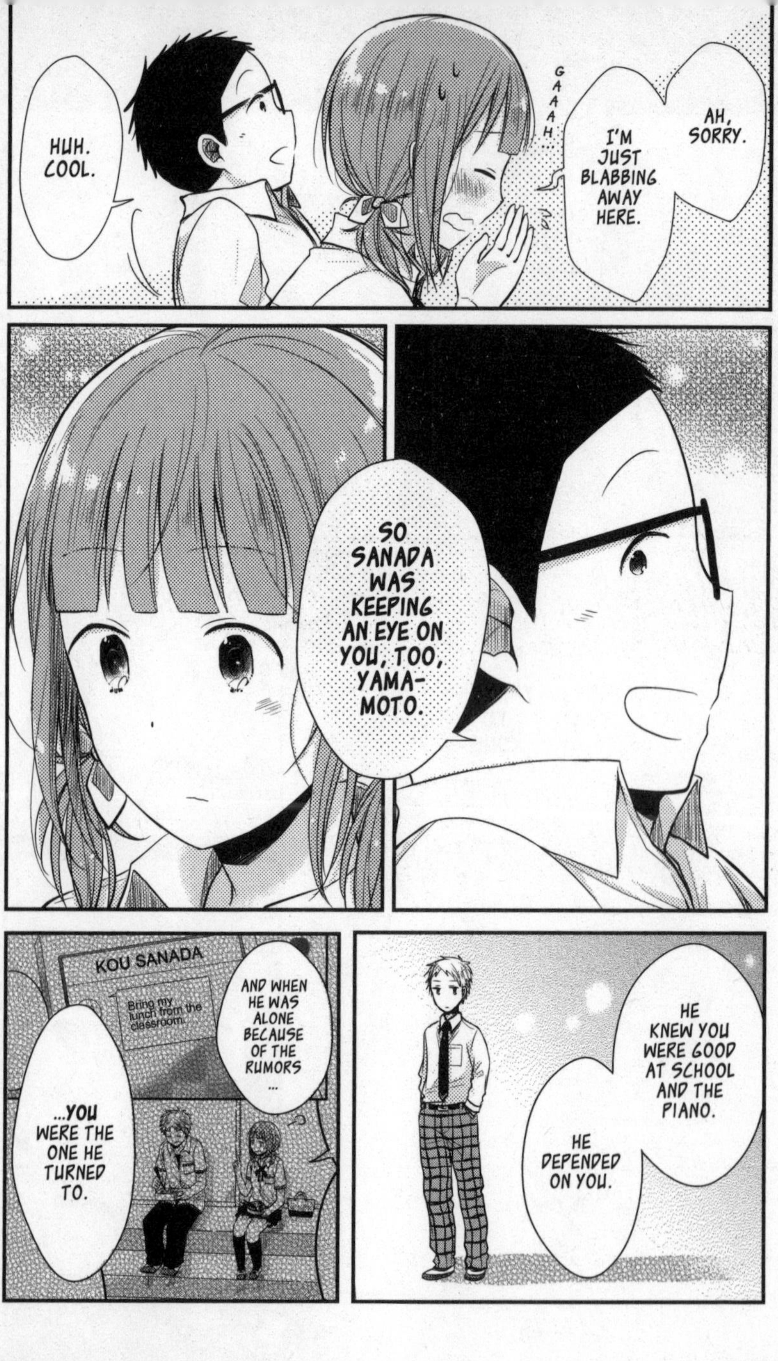
AH, SORRY.
I'M JUST BLABBING AWAY HERE.
GAAAH...
HUH. COOL.
SO SANADA WAS KEEPING AN EYE ON YOU, TOO, YAMAMOTO.
HE KNEW YOU WERE GOOD AT SCHOOL AND THE PIANO.
HE DEPENDED ON YOU.
KOU SANADA
Bring my lunch from the classroom.
AND WHEN HE WAS ALONE BECAUSE OF THE RUMORS...
...YOU WERE THE ONE HE TURNED TO.

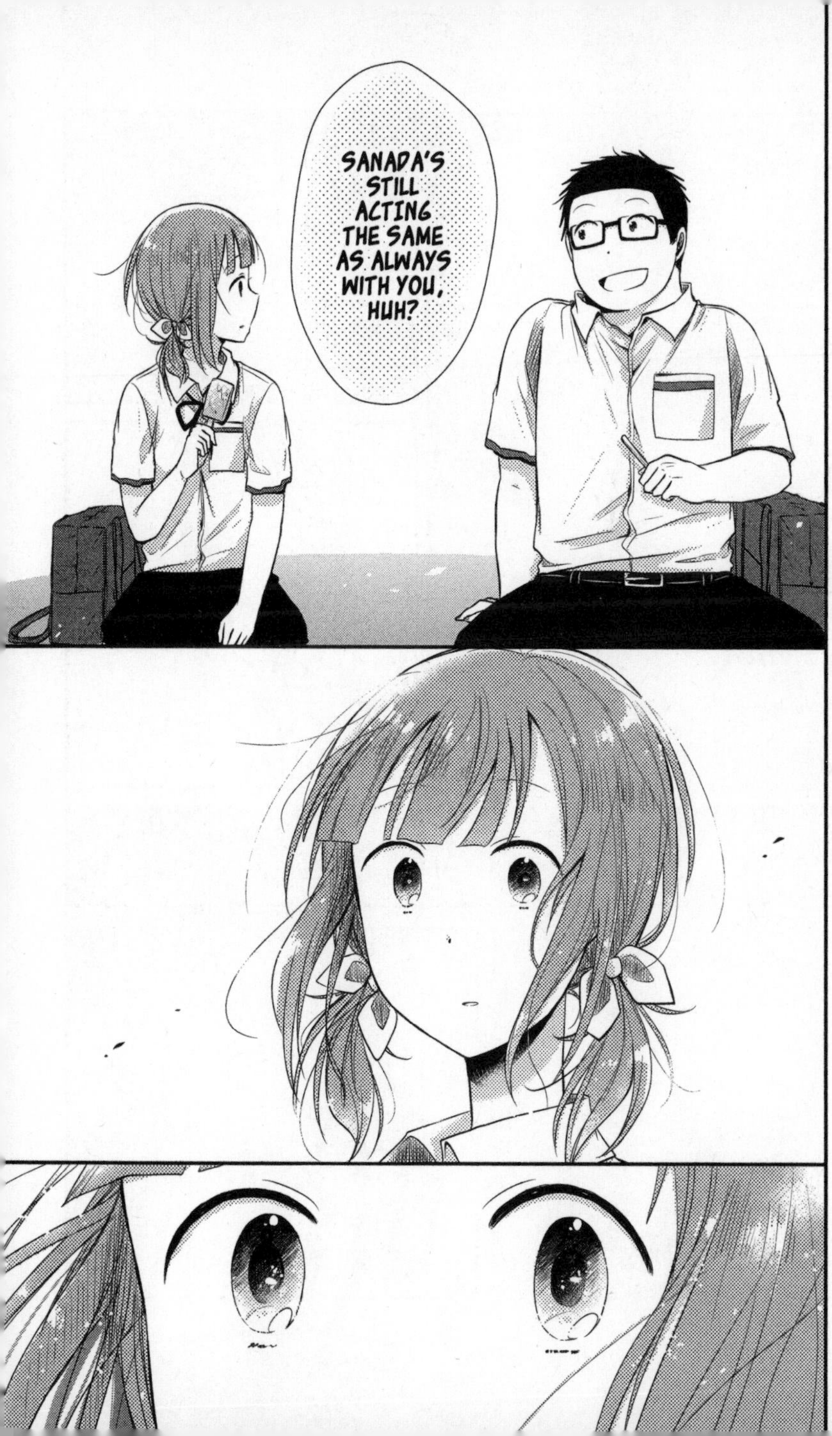
SANADA'S STILL ACTING THE SAME AS ALWAYS WITH YOU, HUH?

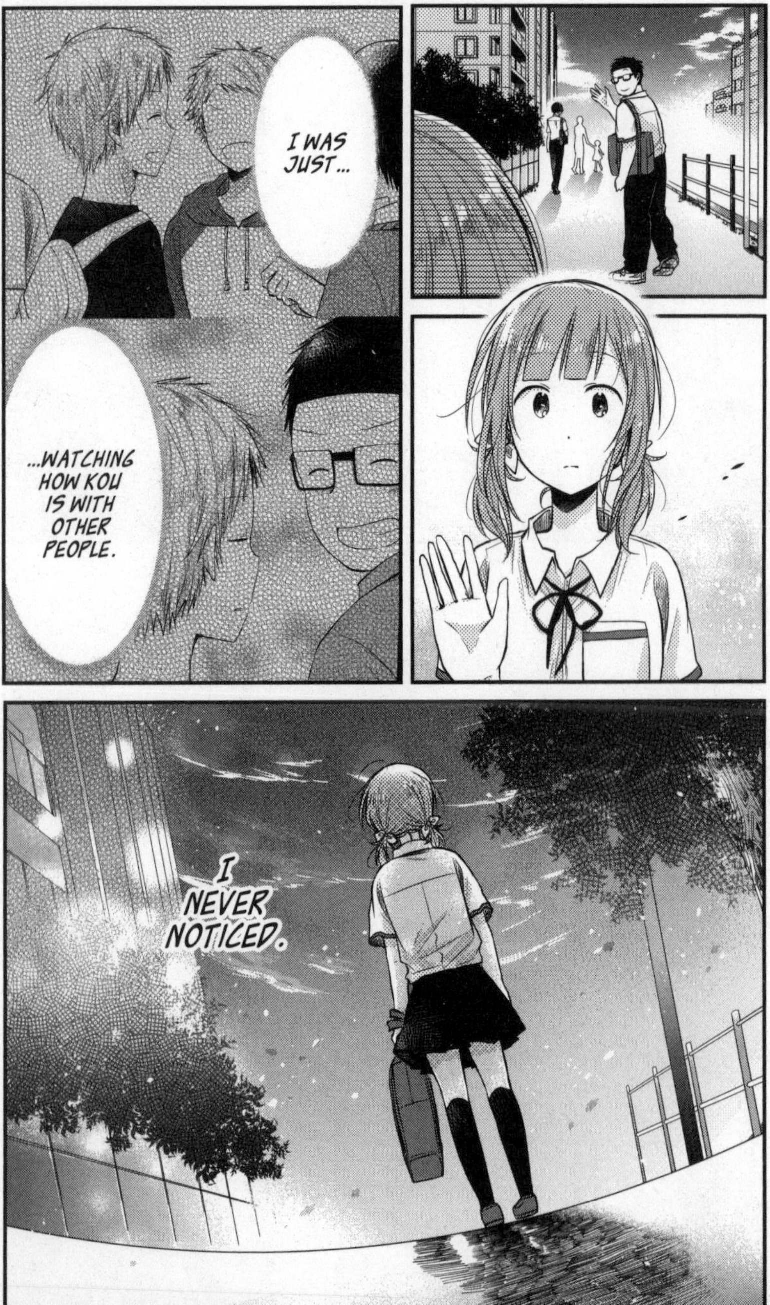
I WAS JUST...
...WATCHING HOW KOU IS WITH OTHER PEOPLE.
I NEVER NOTICED.

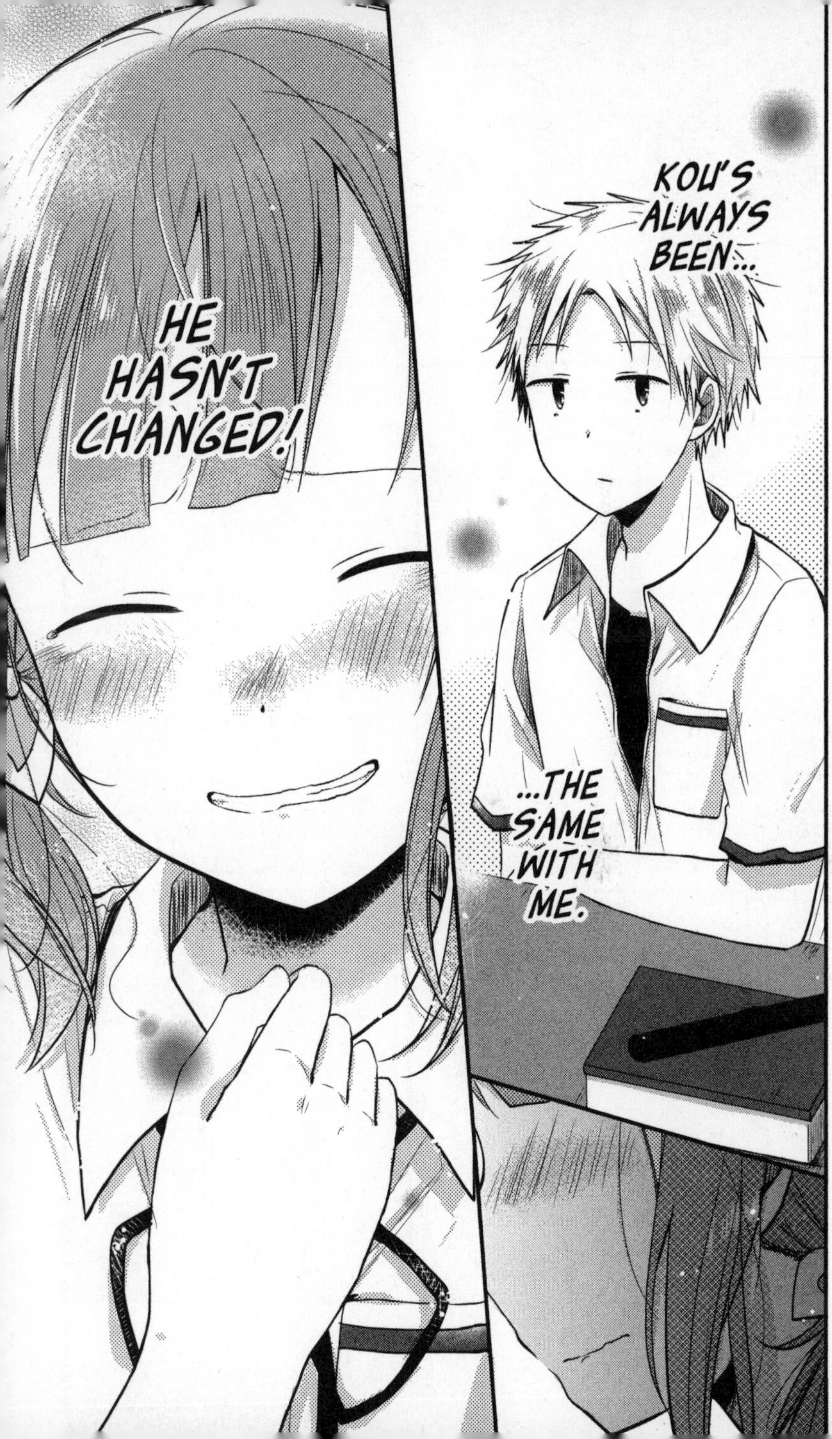
KOU'S ALWAYS BEEN...
...THE SAME WITH ME.
HE HASN'T CHANGED!

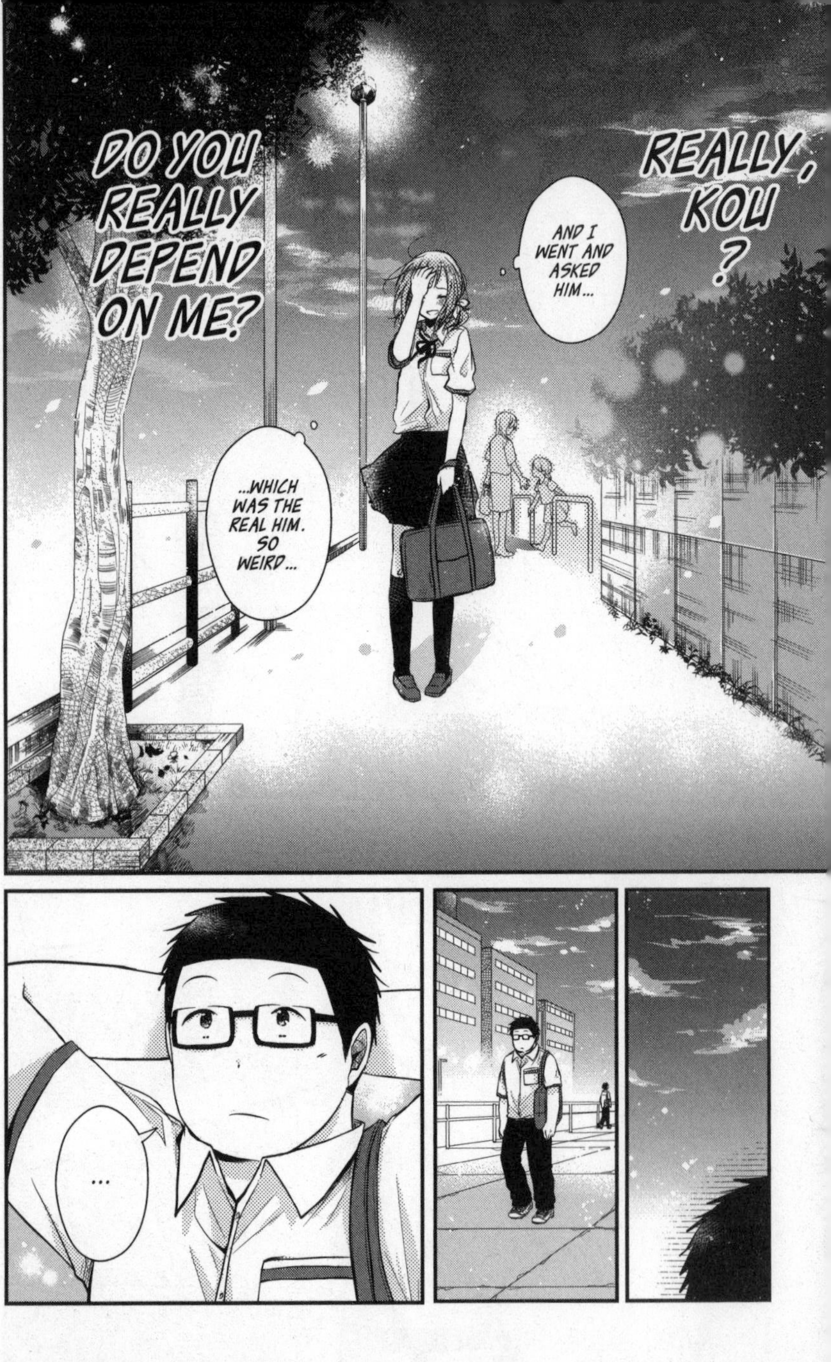
REALLY, KOU?
AND I WENT AND ASKED HIM...
DO YOU REALLY DEPEND ON ME?
...WHICH WAS THE REAL HIM. SO WEIRD...
...

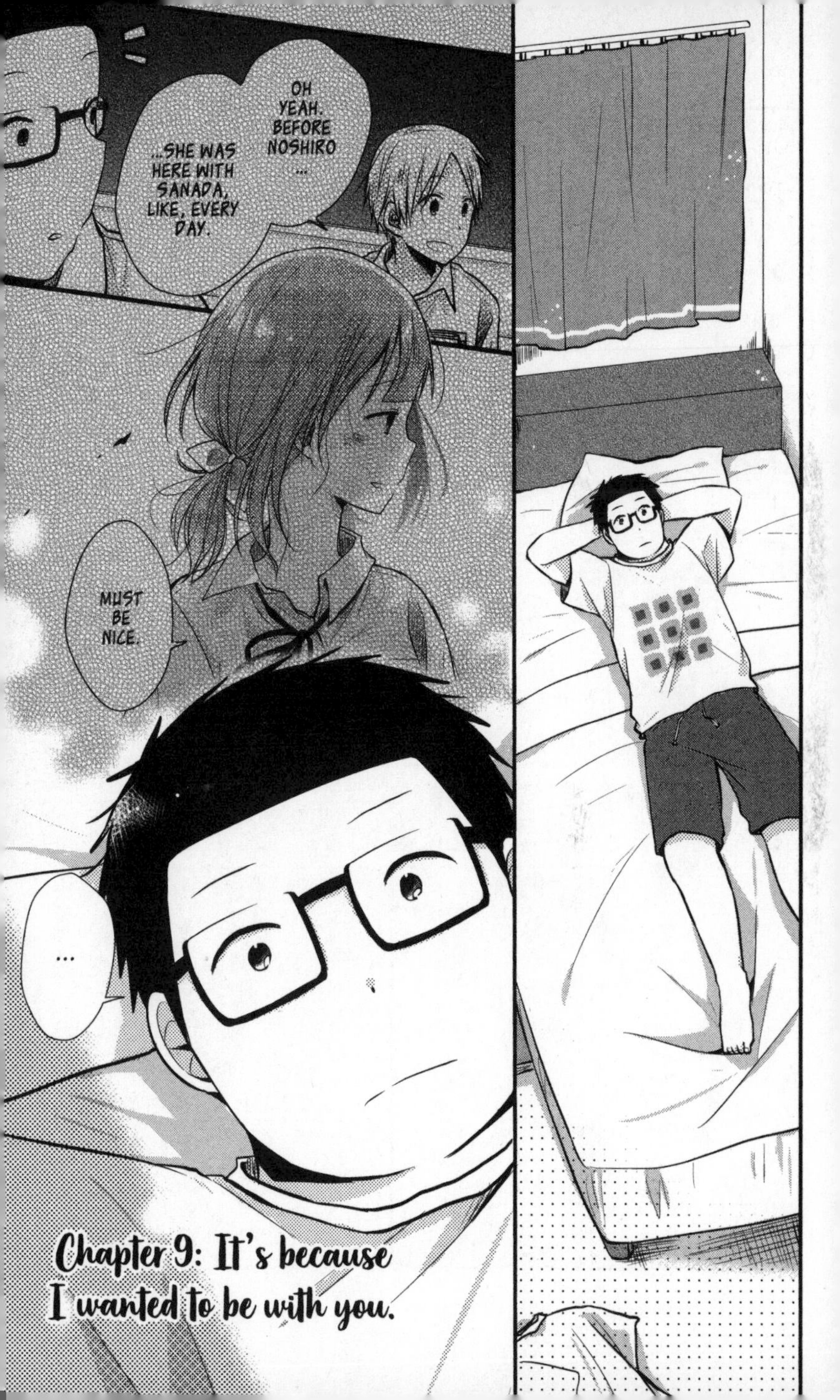
OH YEAH. BEFORE NOSHIRO ...
...SHE WAS HERE WITH SANADA, LIKE, EVERY DAY.
MUST BE NICE.
...
Chapter 9: It's because I wanted to be with you.

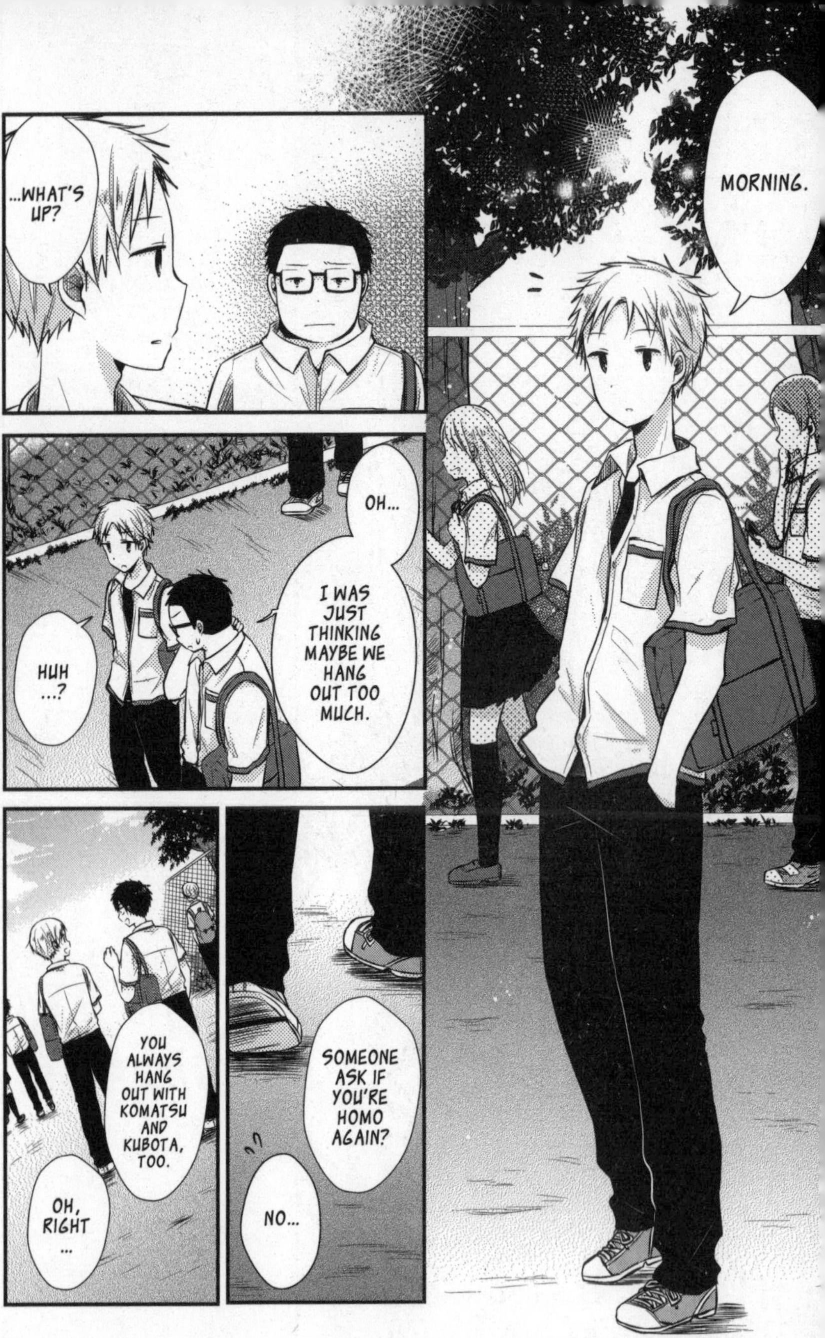
MORNING.
...WHAT'S UP?
OH...
I WAS JUST THINKING MAYBE WE HANG OUT TOO MUCH.
HUH ...?
SOMEONE ASK IF YOU'RE HOMO AGAIN?
NO...
YOU ALWAYS HANG OUT WITH KOMATSU AND KUBOTA, TOO.
OH, RIGHT ...

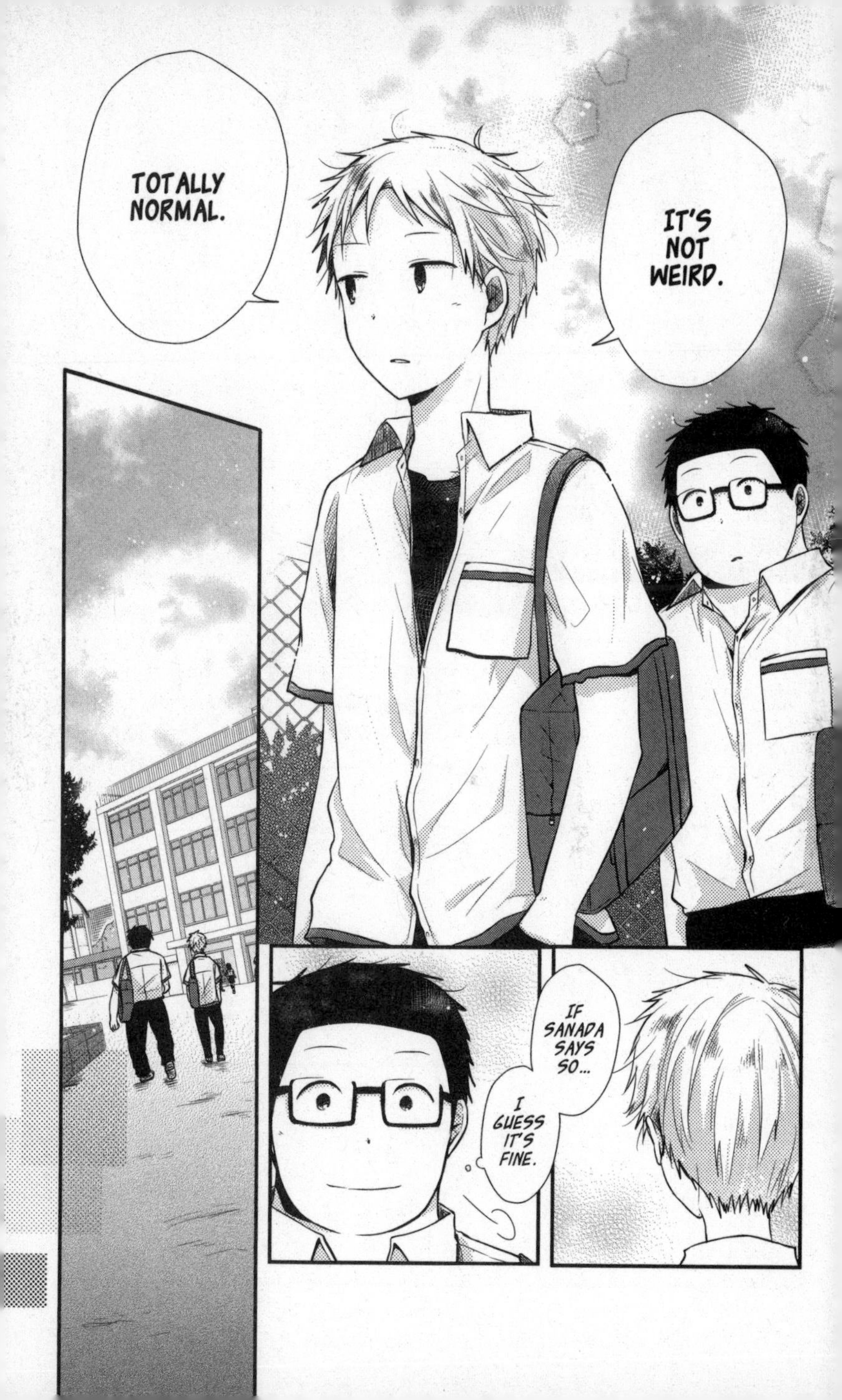
IT'S NOT WEIRD.
TOTALLY NORMAL.
IF SANADA SAYS SO...
I GUESS IT'S FINE.

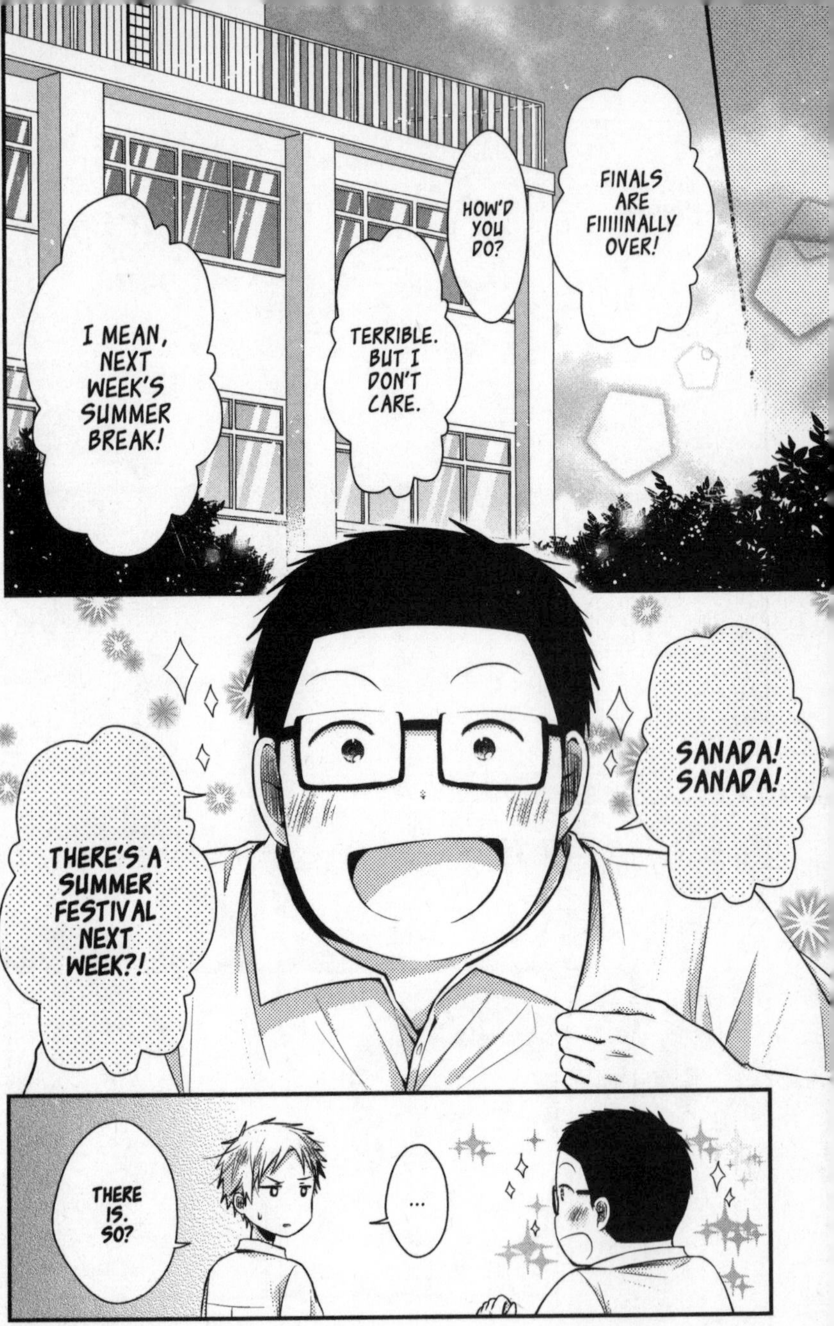
FINALS ARE FIIIIINALLY OVER!
HOW'D YOU DO?
TERRIBLE. BUT I DON'T CARE.
I MEAN, NEXT WEEK'S SUMMER BREAK!
SANADA! SANADA!
THERE'S A SUMMER FESTIVAL NEXT WEEK?!
...
THERE IS. SO?

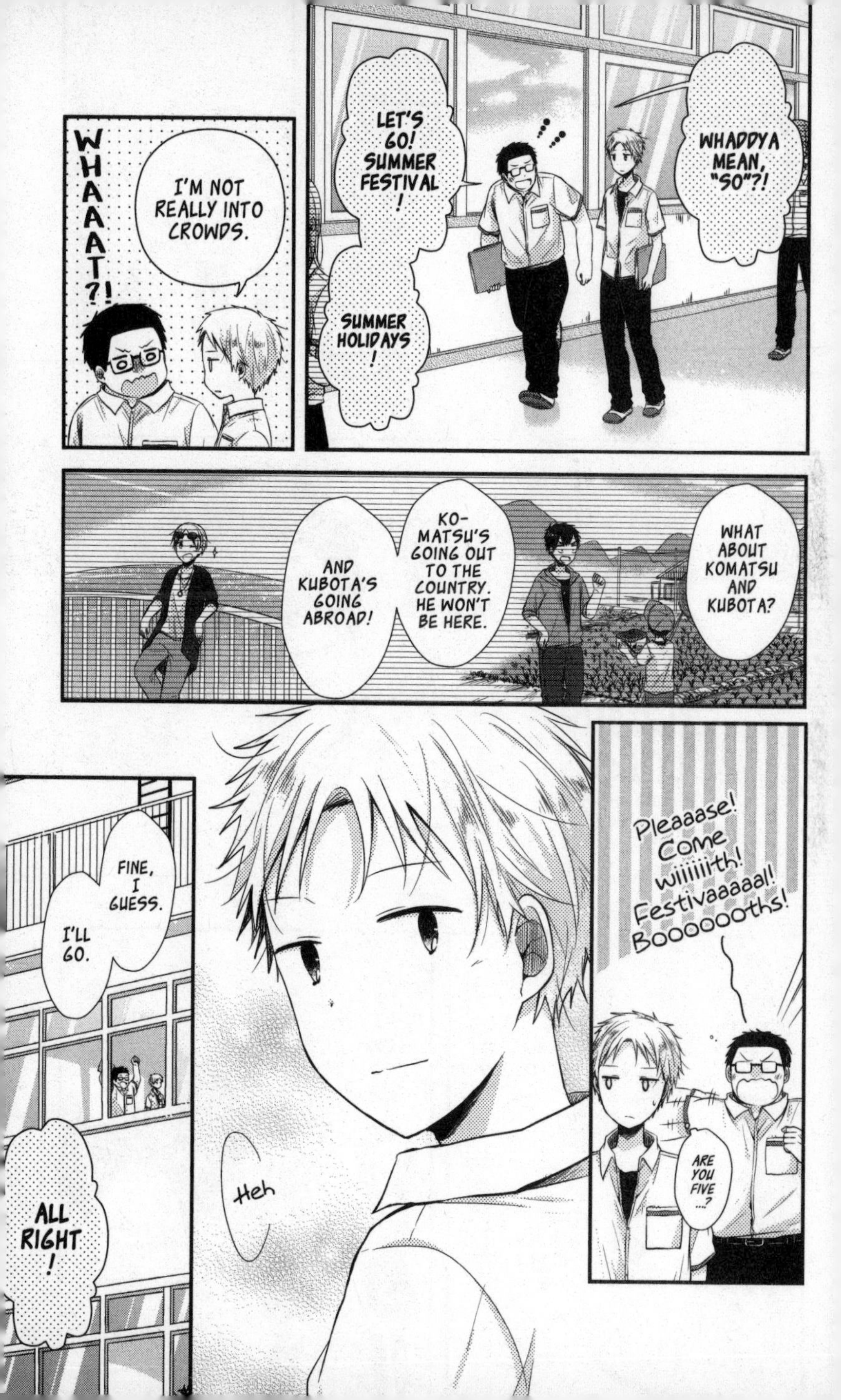

WHADDYA MEAN, "SO"?!
LET'S GO! SUMMER FESTIVAL!
SUMMER HOLIDAYS!
I'M NOT REALLY INTO CROWDS.
WHAAAT?!
WHAT ABOUT KOMATSU AND KUBOTA?
KO-MATSU'S GOING OUT TO THE COUNTRY. HE WON'T BE HERE.
AND KUBOTA'S GOING ABROAD!
Pleaaase! Come wiiiiiith! Festivaaaaal! Booooooths!
ARE YOU FIVE...?
Heh
FINE, I GUESS.
I'LL GO.
ALL RIGHT!

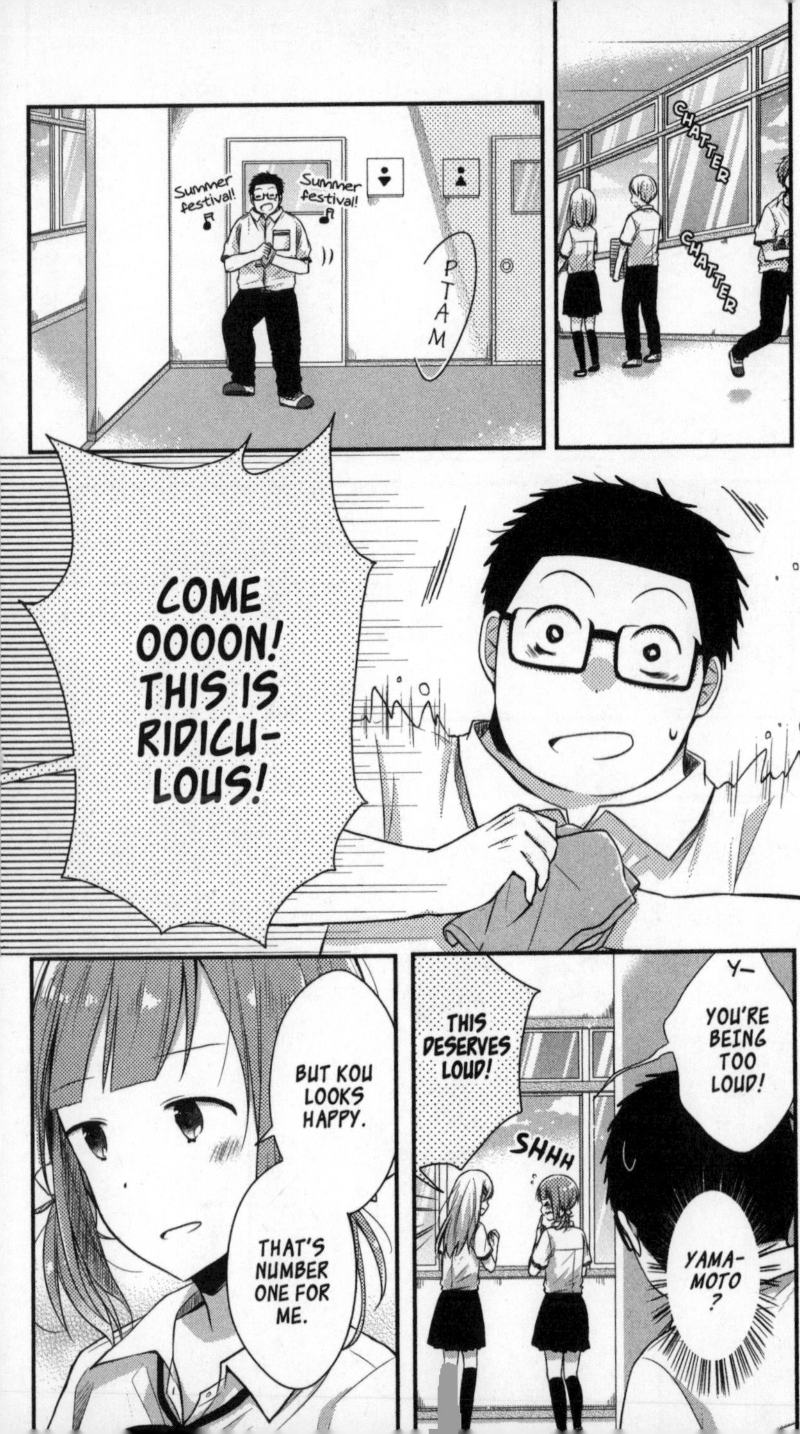
CHATTER
CHATTER
Summer festival!
Summer festival!
PTAM
COME OOOON! THIS IS RIDICU-LOUS!
Y—
YOU'RE BEING TOO LOUD!
THIS DESERVES LOUD!
SHHH
YAMA-MOTO?
BUT KOU LOOKS HAPPY.
THAT'S NUMBER ONE FOR ME.

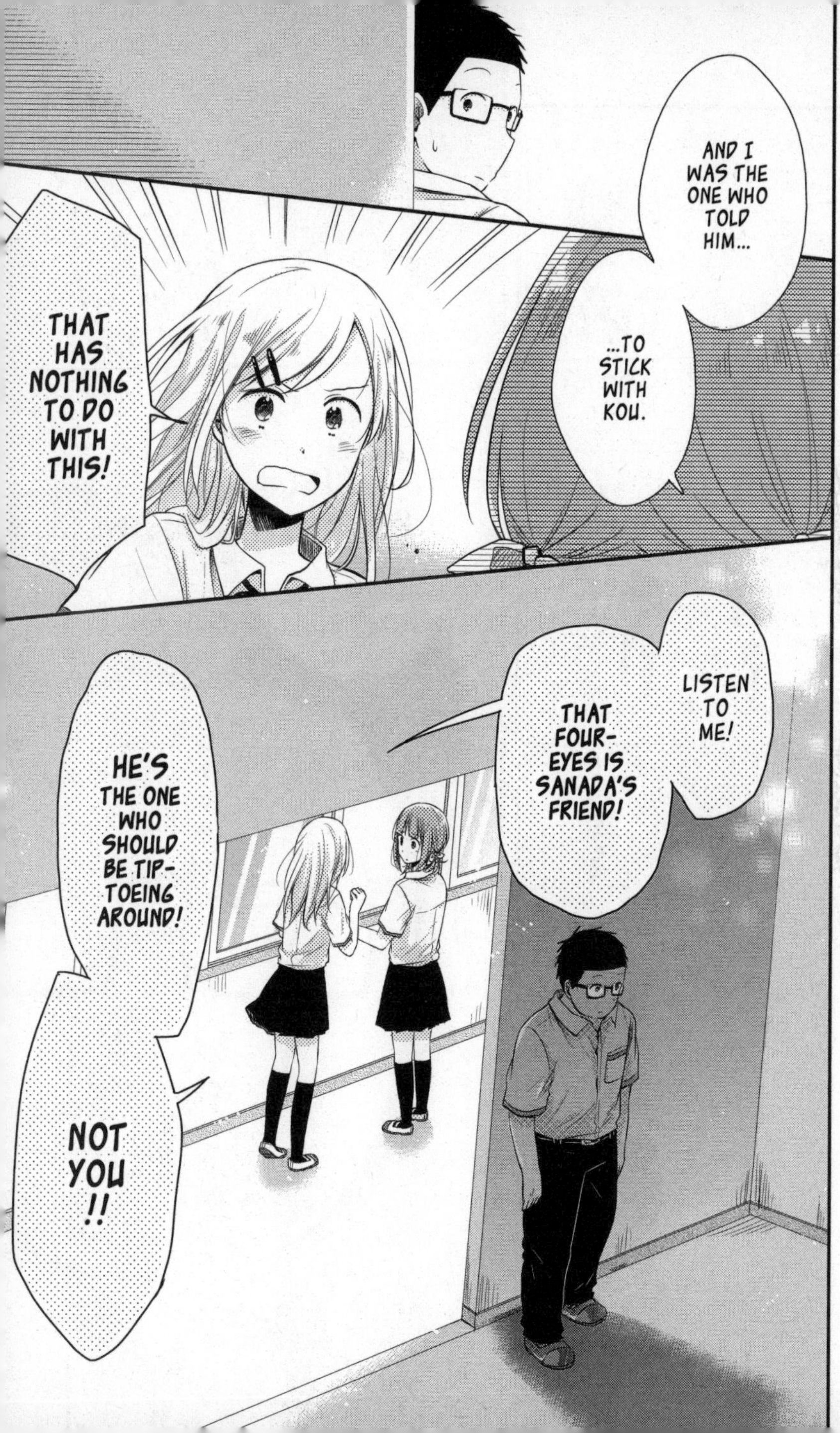
AND I WAS THE ONE WHO TOLD HIM...
...TO STICK WITH KOU.
THAT HAS NOTHING TO DO WITH THIS!
LISTEN TO ME!
THAT FOUR-EYES IS SANADA'S FRIEND!
HE'S THE ONE WHO SHOULD BE TIP-TOEING AROUND!
NOT YOU!!

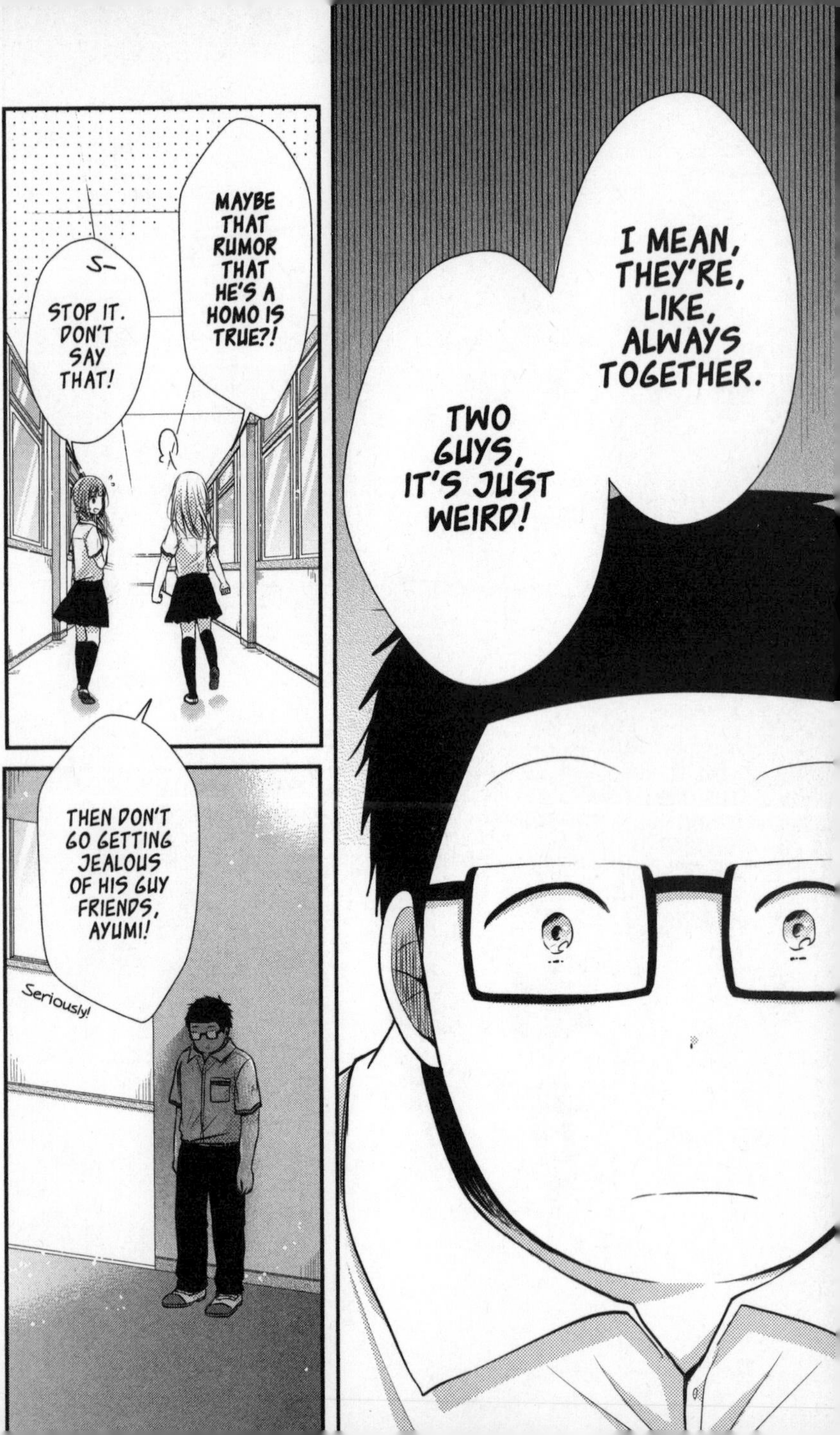
I MEAN, THEY'RE, LIKE, ALWAYS TOGETHER.
TWO GUYS, IT'S JUST WEIRD!
MAYBE THAT RUMOR THAT HE'S A HOMO IS TRUE?!
S–
STOP IT. DON'T SAY THAT!
THEN DON'T GO GETTING JEALOUS OF HIS GUY FRIENDS, AYUMI!
Seriously!

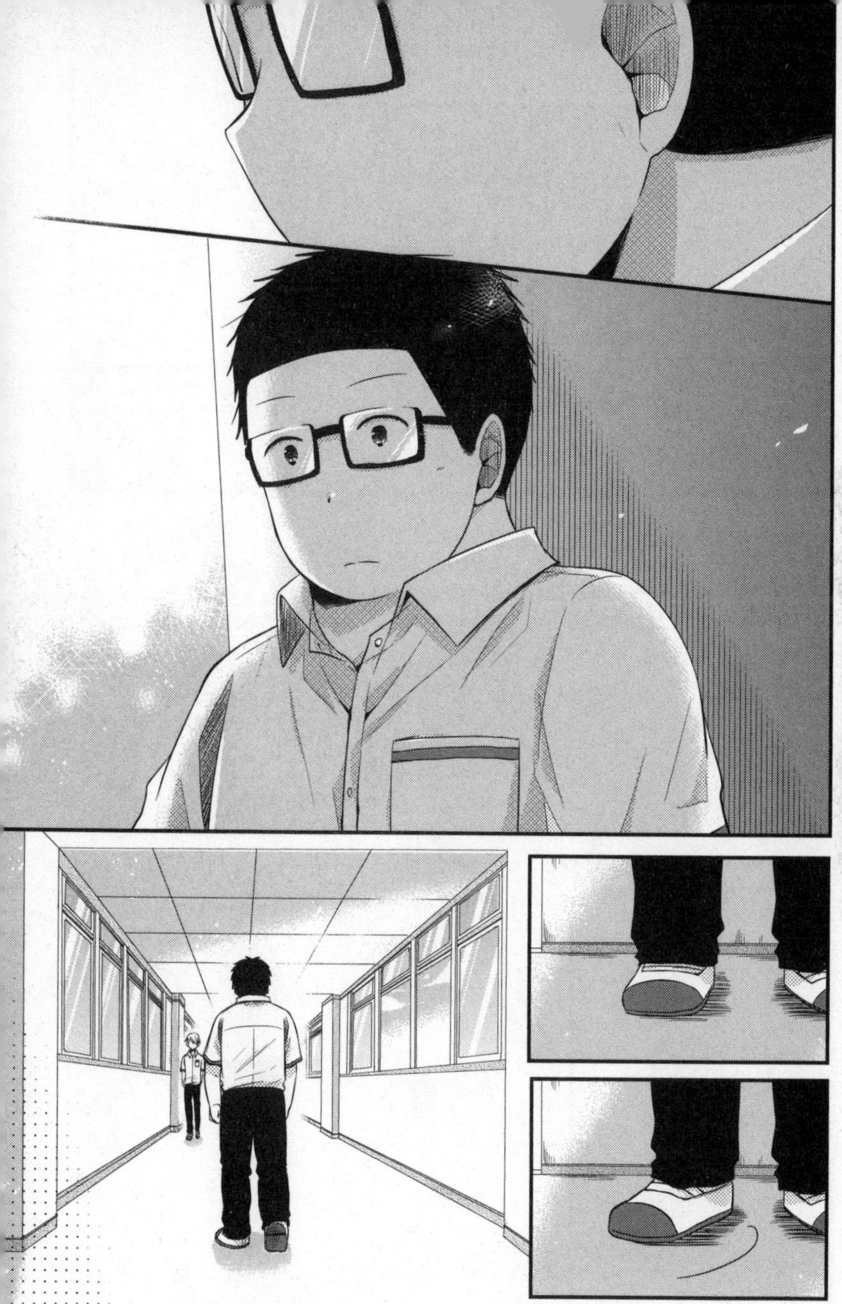

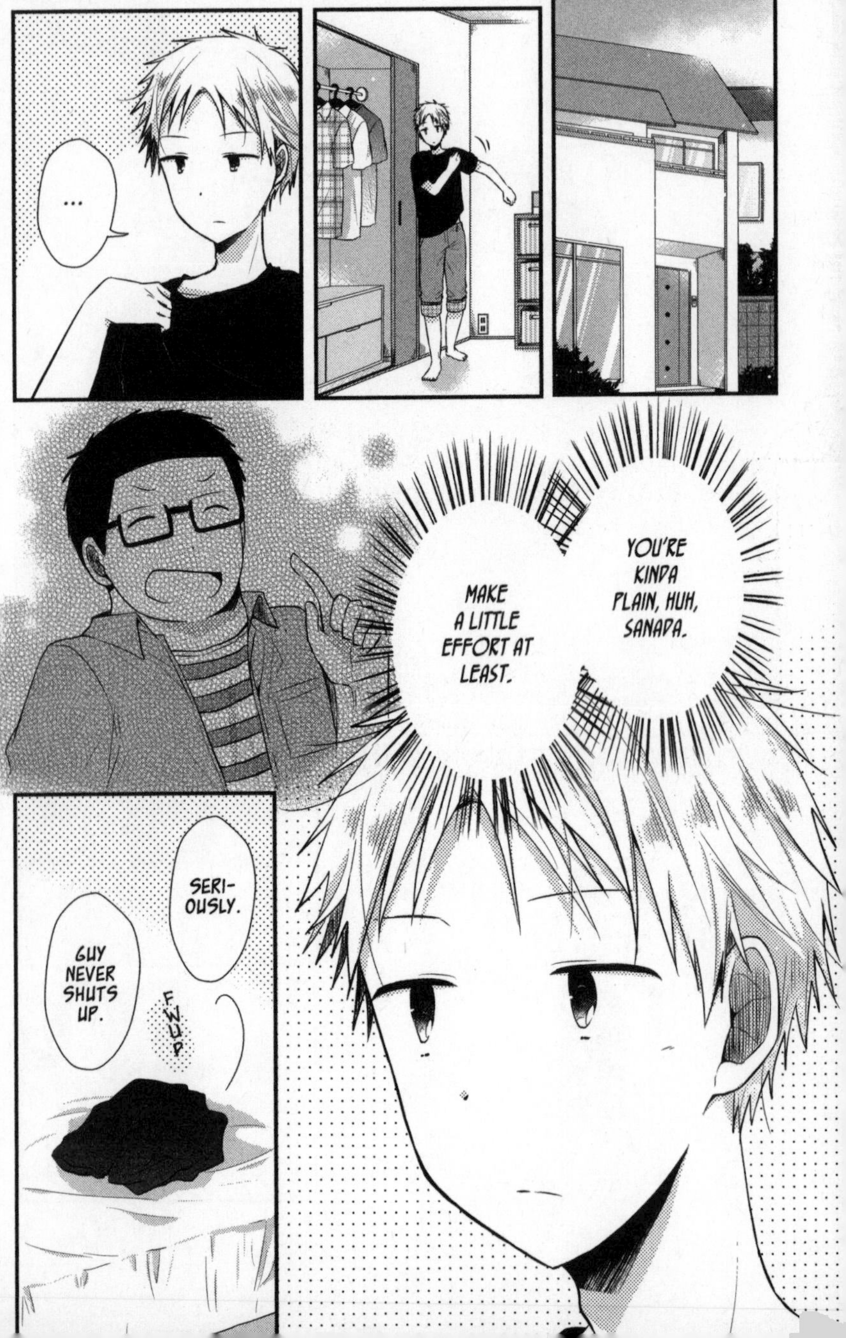
...
YOU'RE KINDA PLAIN, HUH, SANADA.
MAKE A LITTLE EFFORT AT LEAST.
SERI-OUSLY.
GUY NEVER SHUTS UP.
FWUP

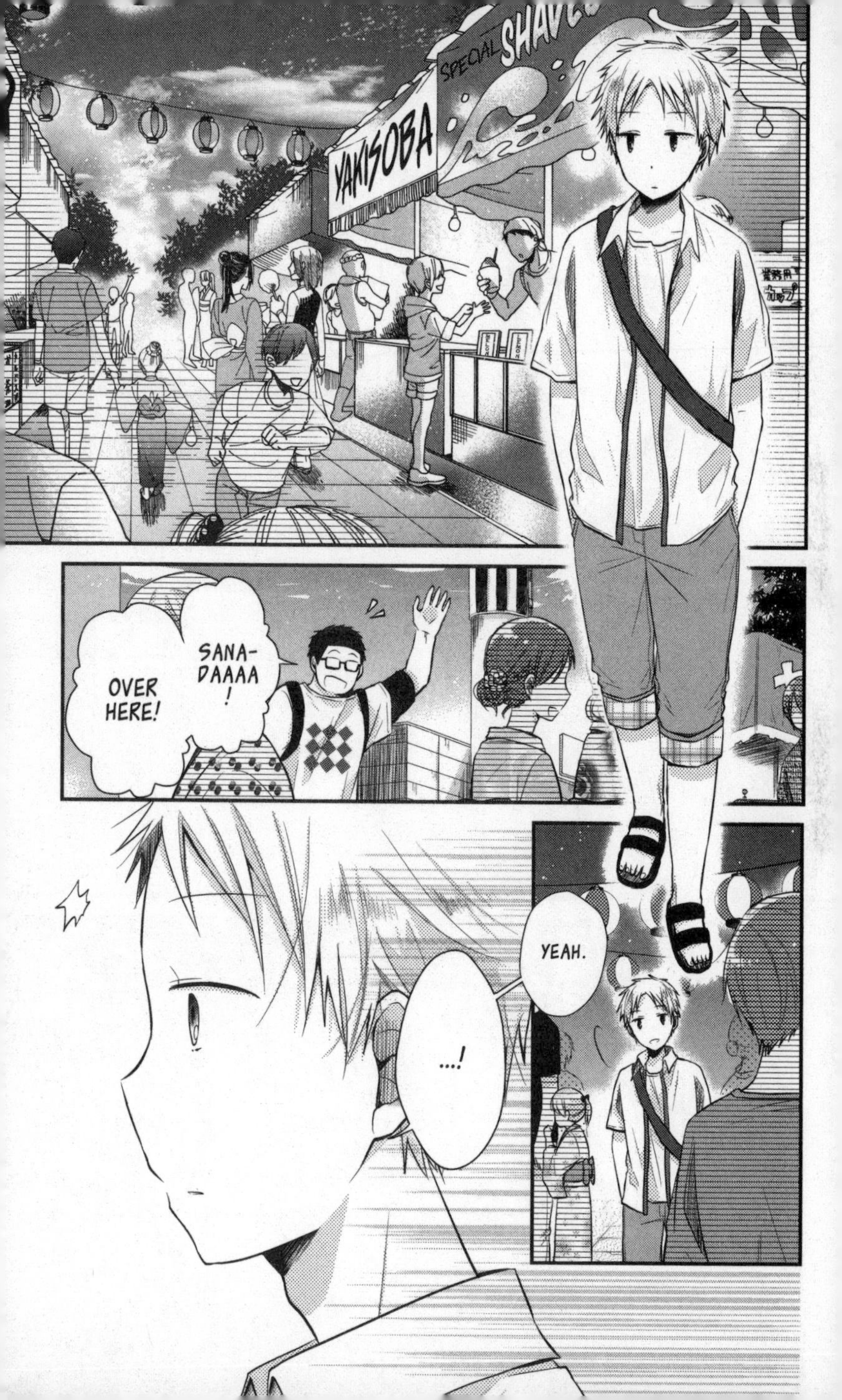
SPECIAL
YAKISOBA
SANA-DAAAA!
OVER HERE!
YEAH.
...!

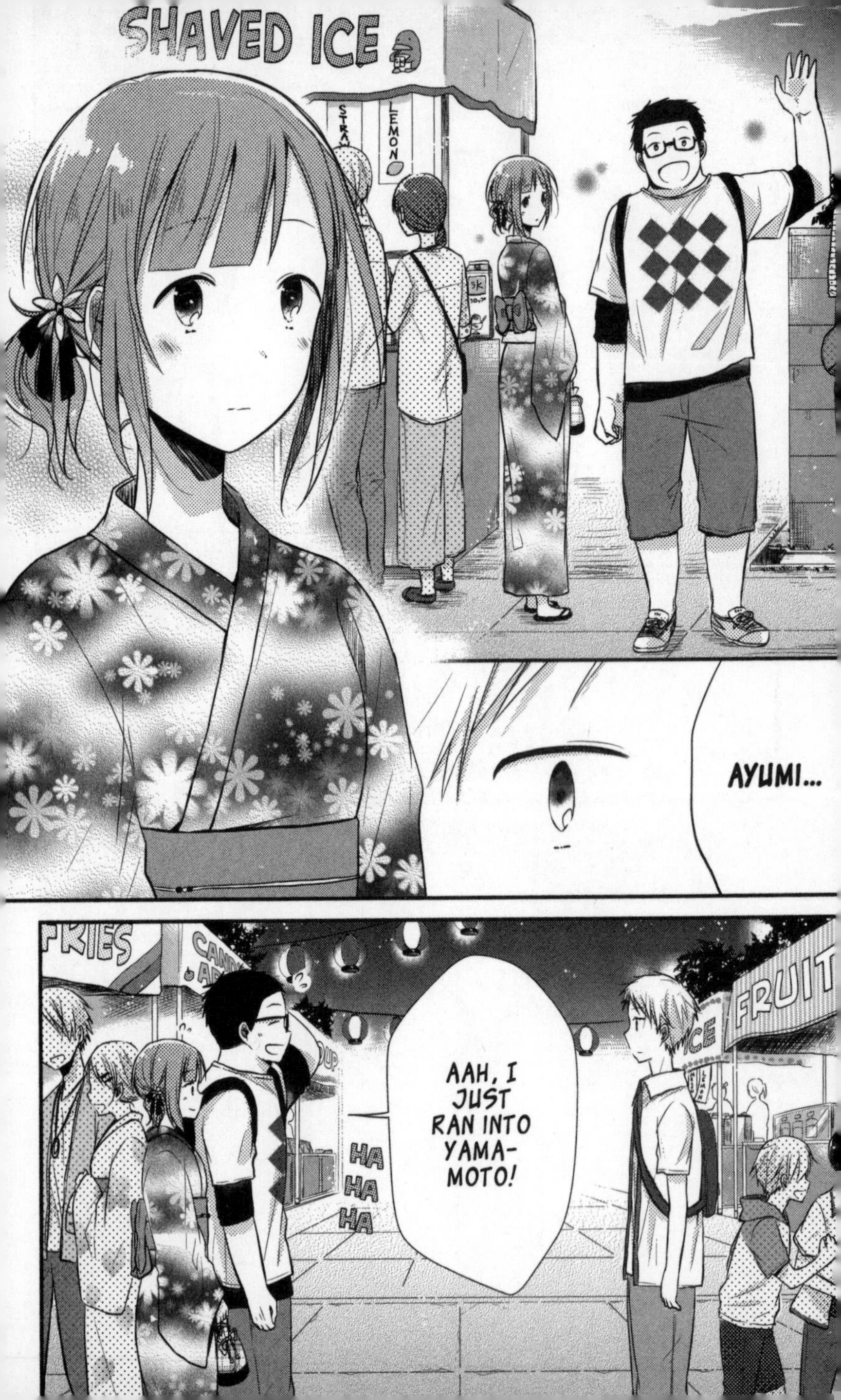
SHAVED ICE
LEMON
AYUMI...
FRUIT
ICE
AAH, I JUST RAN INTO YAMA-MOTO!
HA HA HA HA
FRIES

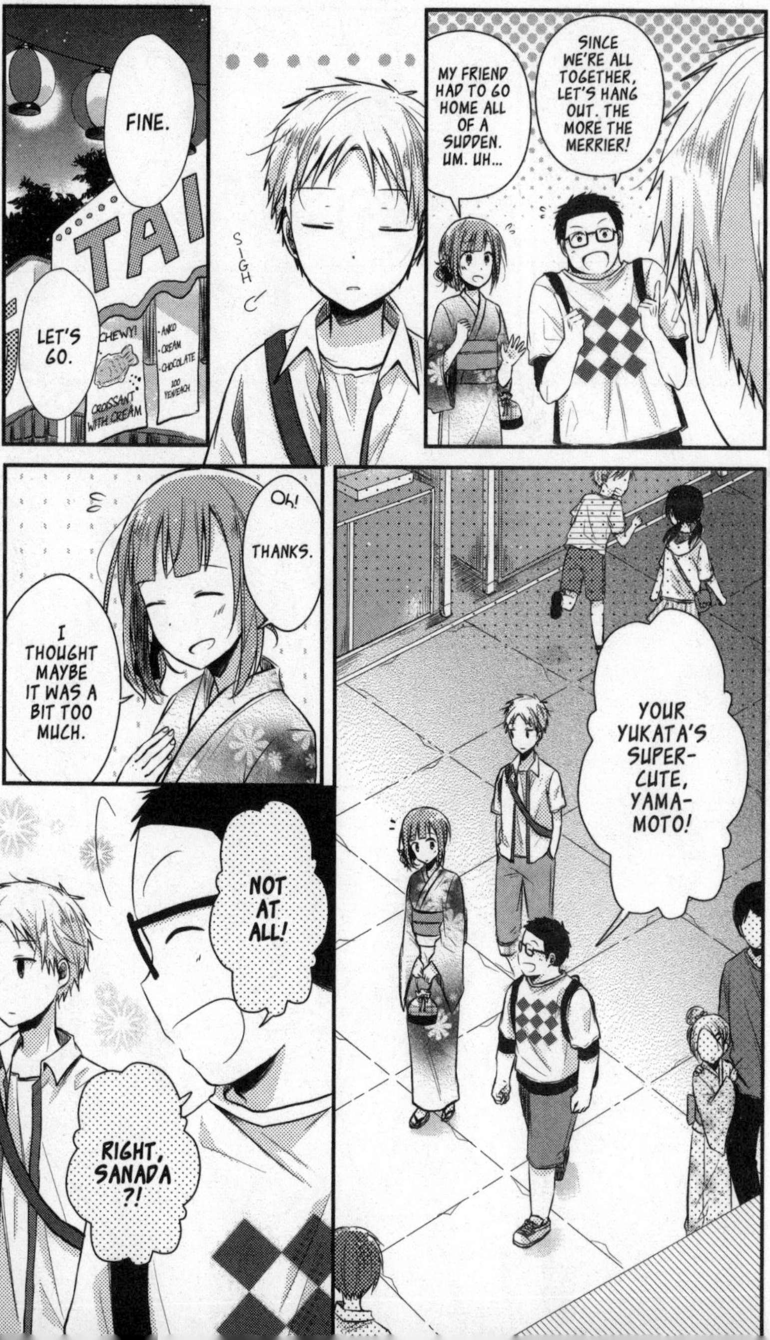

SINCE WE'RE ALL TOGETHER, LET'S HANG OUT. THE MORE THE MERRIER!
MY FRIEND HAD TO GO HOME ALL OF A SUDDEN. UM. UH...
SIGH
FINE.
LET'S GO.
TAI
CHEWY!
CROISSANT WITH CREAM
• ANKO • CREAM • CHOCOLATE 100 YEN/EACH
YOUR YUKATA'S SUPER-CUTE, YAMAMOTO!
Oh!
THANKS.
I THOUGHT MAYBE IT WAS A BIT TOO MUCH.
NOT AT ALL!
RIGHT, SANADA?!

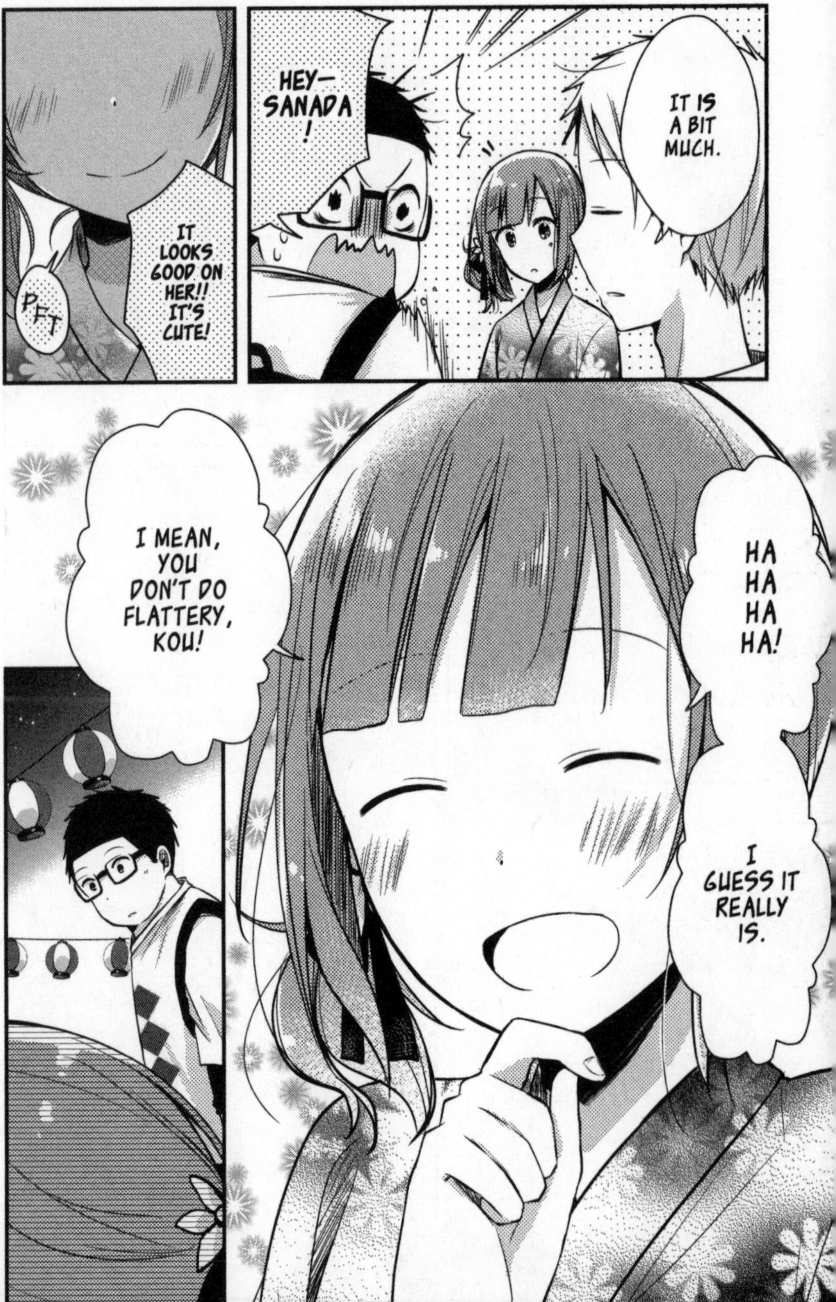
IT IS A BIT MUCH.
HEY— SANADA!
IT LOOKS GOOD ON HER!! IT'S CUTE!
PFT
HA HA HA HA!
I GUESS IT REALLY IS.
I MEAN, YOU DON'T DO FLATTERY, KOU!

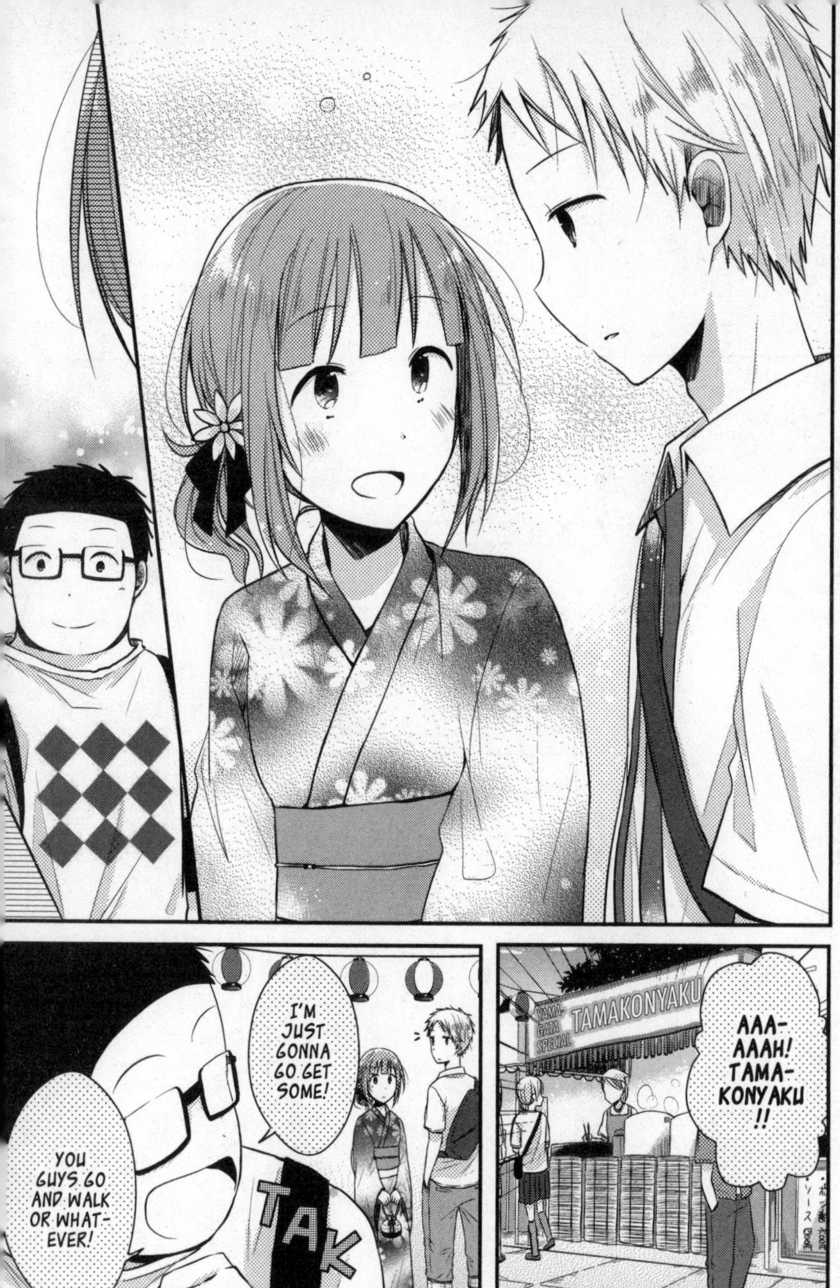
AAA-AAAH! TAMA-KONYAKU!!
YAMA-GATA SPECIAL
TAMAKONYAKU
I'M JUST GONNA GO GET SOME!
YOU GUYS GO AND WALK OR WHAT-EVER!
TAK

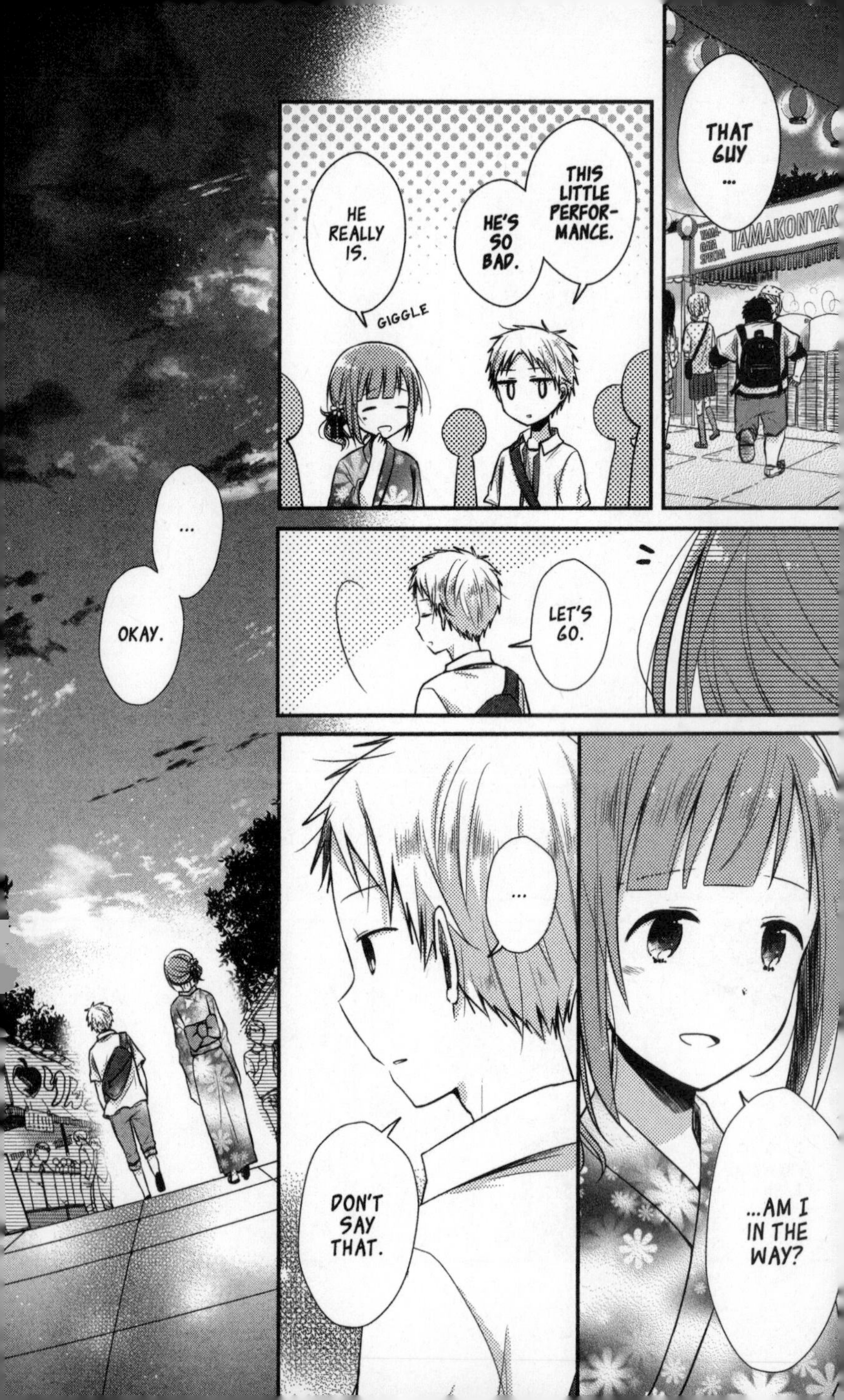
THAT GUY ...
YAMA-GATA SPECIAL
TAMAKONYAK
THIS LITTLE PERFORMANCE.
HE'S SO BAD.
HE REALLY IS.
GIGGLE
LET'S GO.
...AM I IN THE WAY?
...
DON'T SAY THAT.
...
OKAY.

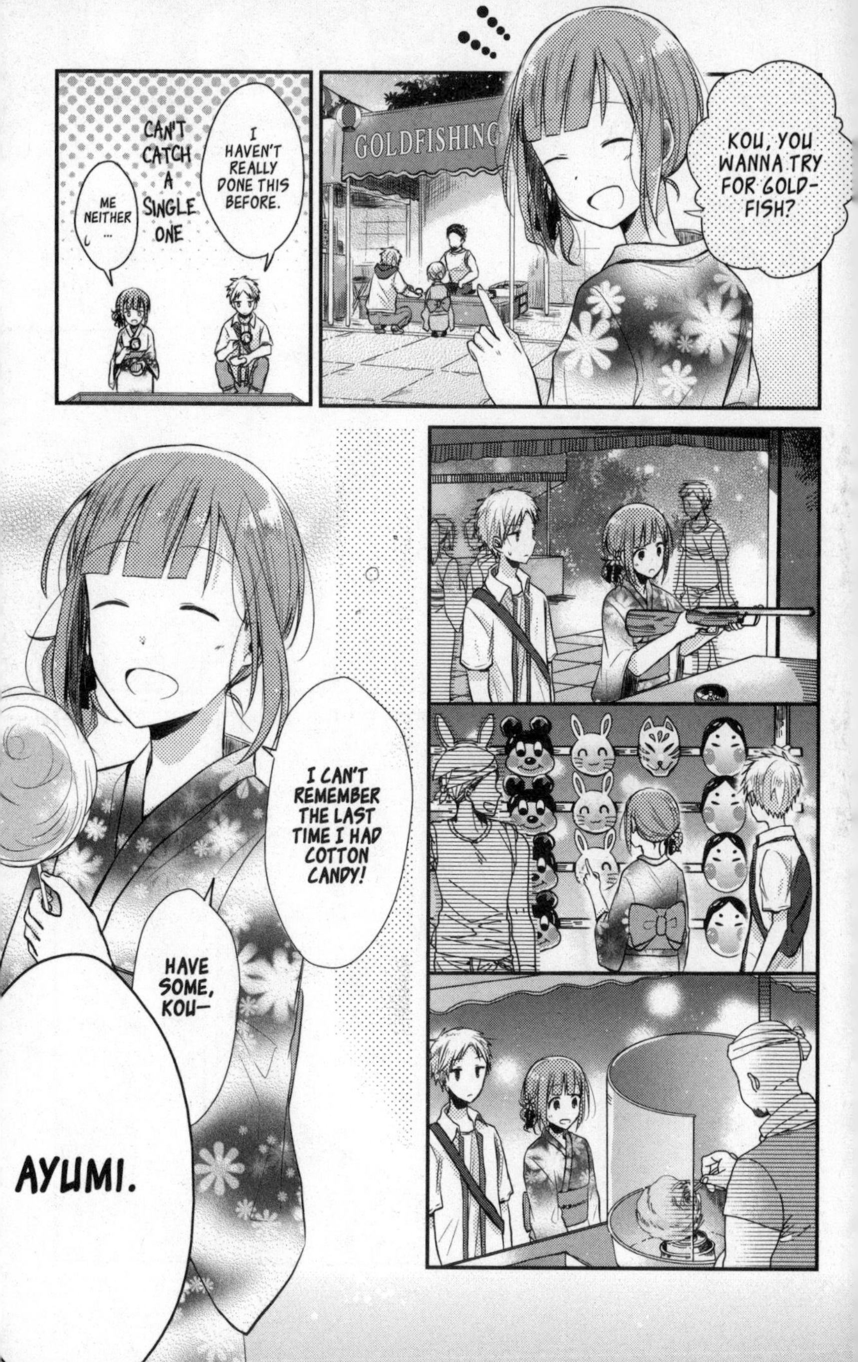

KOU, YOU WANNA TRY FOR GOLD-FISH?
GOLDFISHING
I HAVEN'T REALLY DONE THIS BEFORE.
CAN'T CATCH A SINGLE ONE
ME NEITHER ...
I CAN'T REMEMBER THE LAST TIME I HAD COTTON CANDY!
HAVE SOME, KOU—
AYUMI.

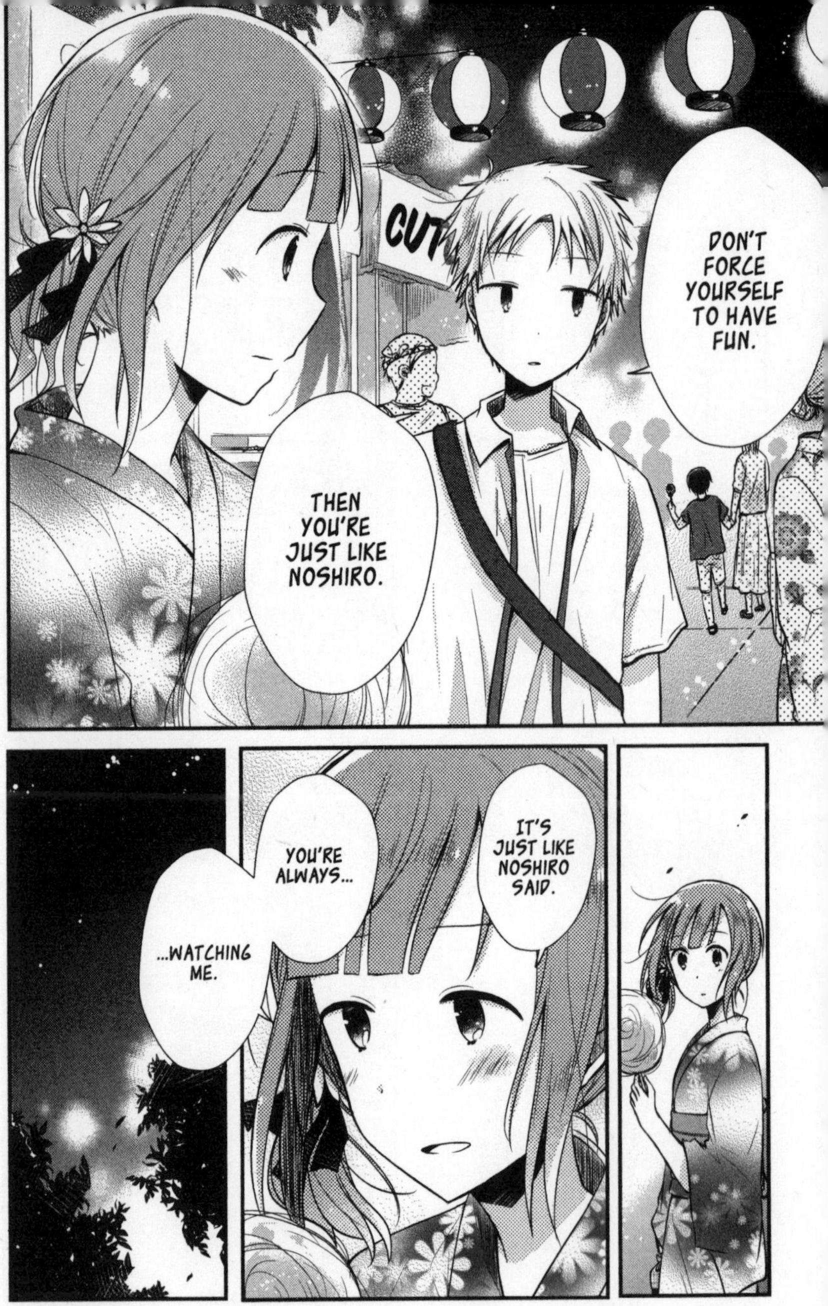
DON'T FORCE YOURSELF TO HAVE FUN.
CUT
THEN YOU'RE JUST LIKE NOSHIRO.
IT'S JUST LIKE NOSHIRO SAID.
YOU'RE ALWAYS...
...WATCHING ME.

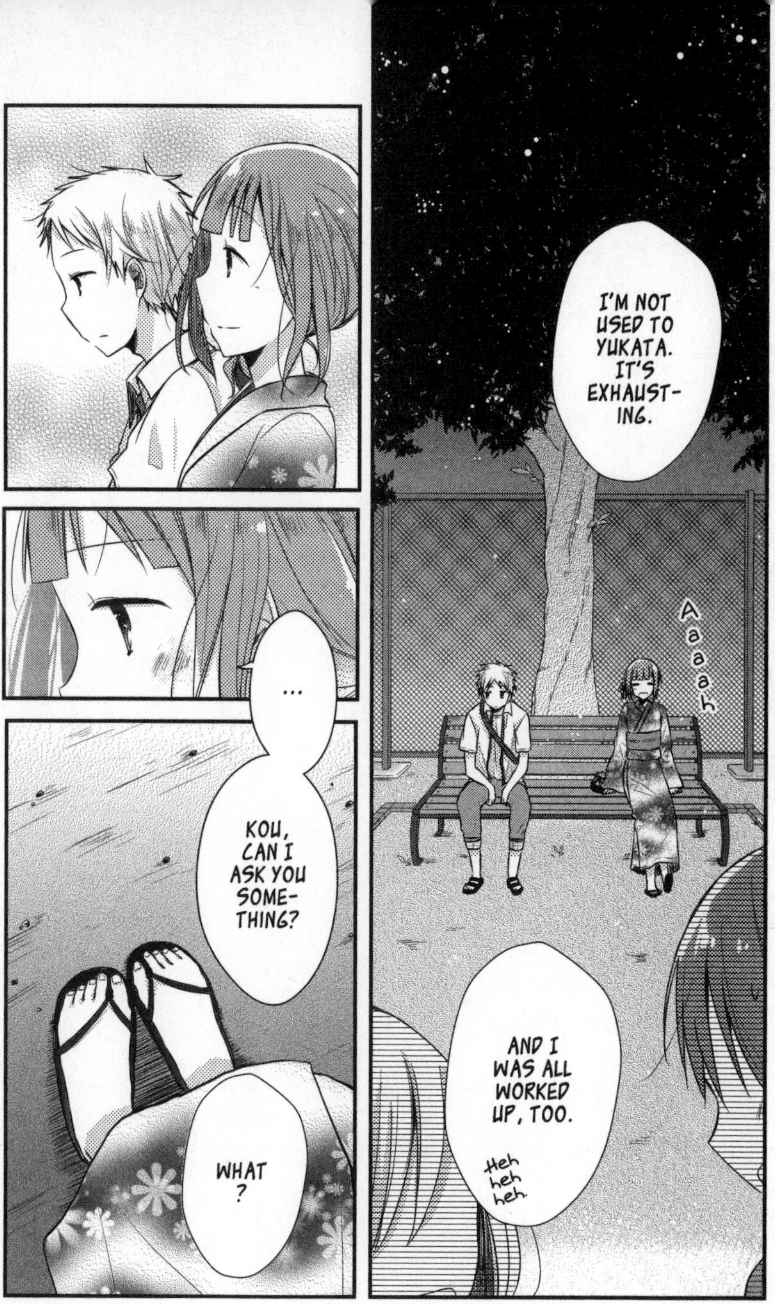
I'M NOT USED TO YUKATA. IT'S EXHAUST-ING.
Aaaah
AND I WAS ALL WORKED UP, TOO.
Heh heh heh.
...
KOU, CAN I ASK YOU SOME-THING?
WHAT?

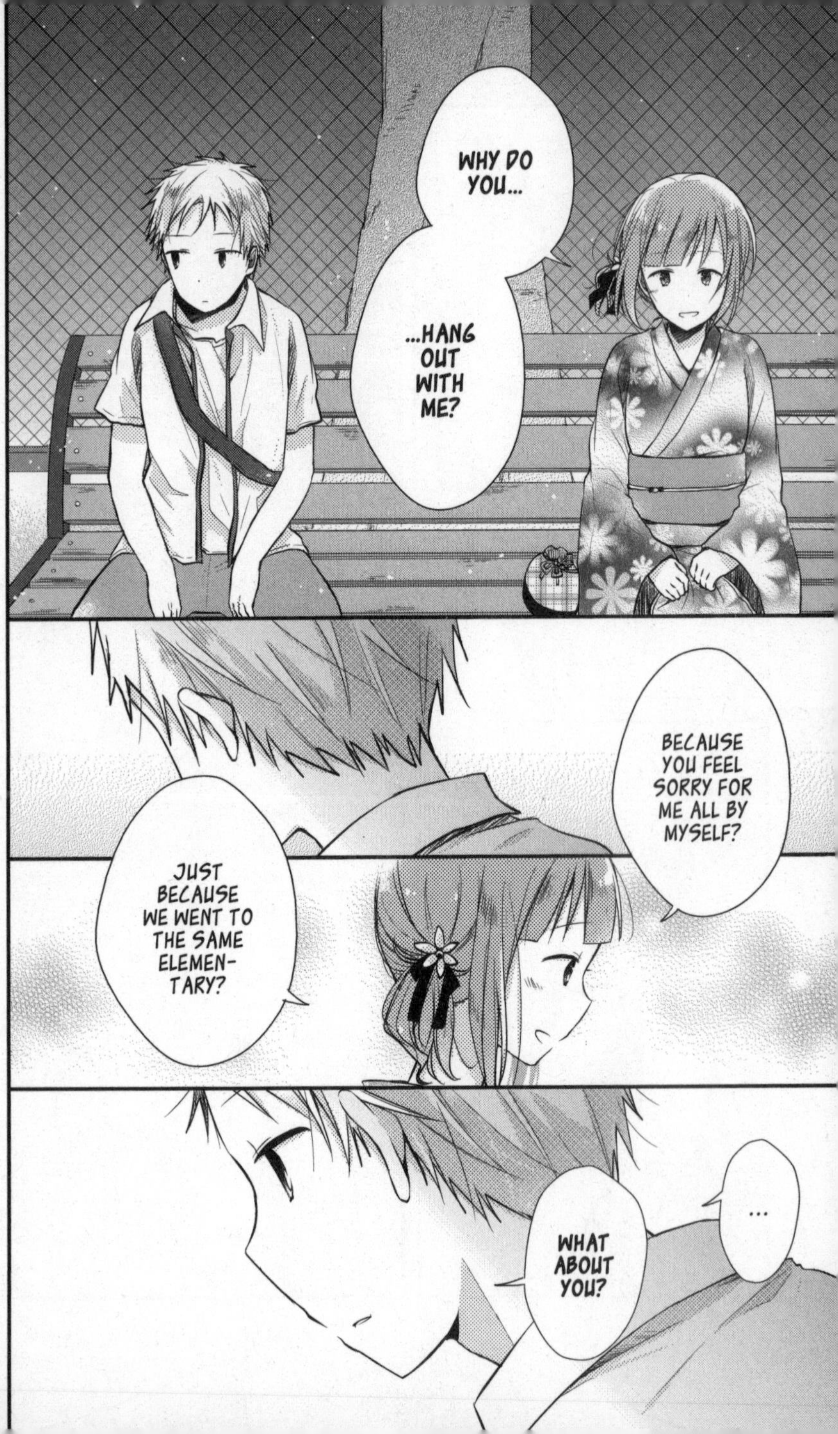
WHY DO YOU...
...HANG OUT WITH ME?
BECAUSE YOU FEEL SORRY FOR ME ALL BY MYSELF?
JUST BECAUSE WE WENT TO THE SAME ELEMENTARY?
...
WHAT ABOUT YOU?

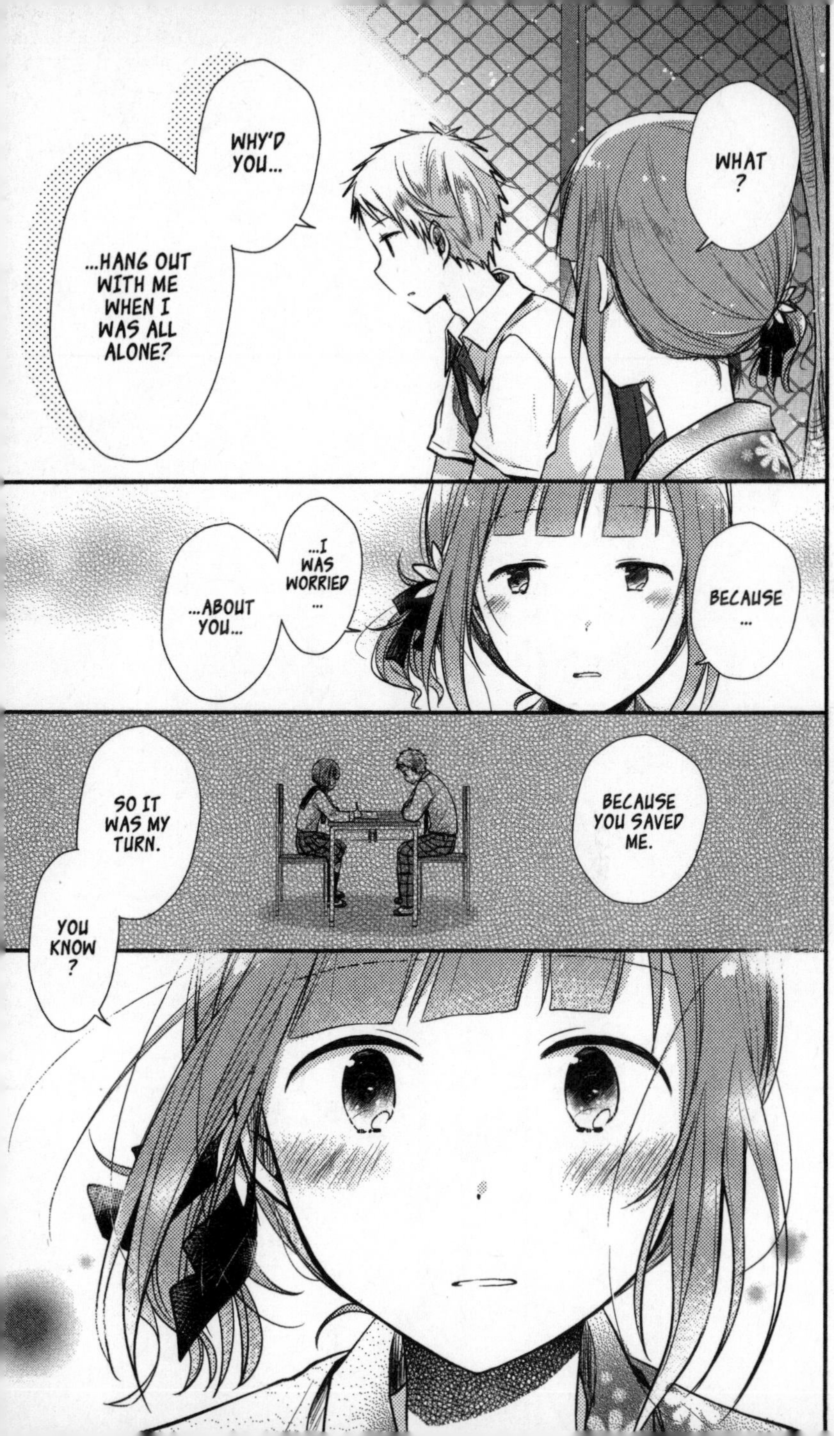
WHAT?
WHY'D YOU...
...HANG OUT WITH ME WHEN I WAS ALL ALONE?
BECAUSE...
...I WAS WORRIED...
...ABOUT YOU...
BECAUSE YOU SAVED ME.
SO IT WAS MY TURN.
YOU KNOW?

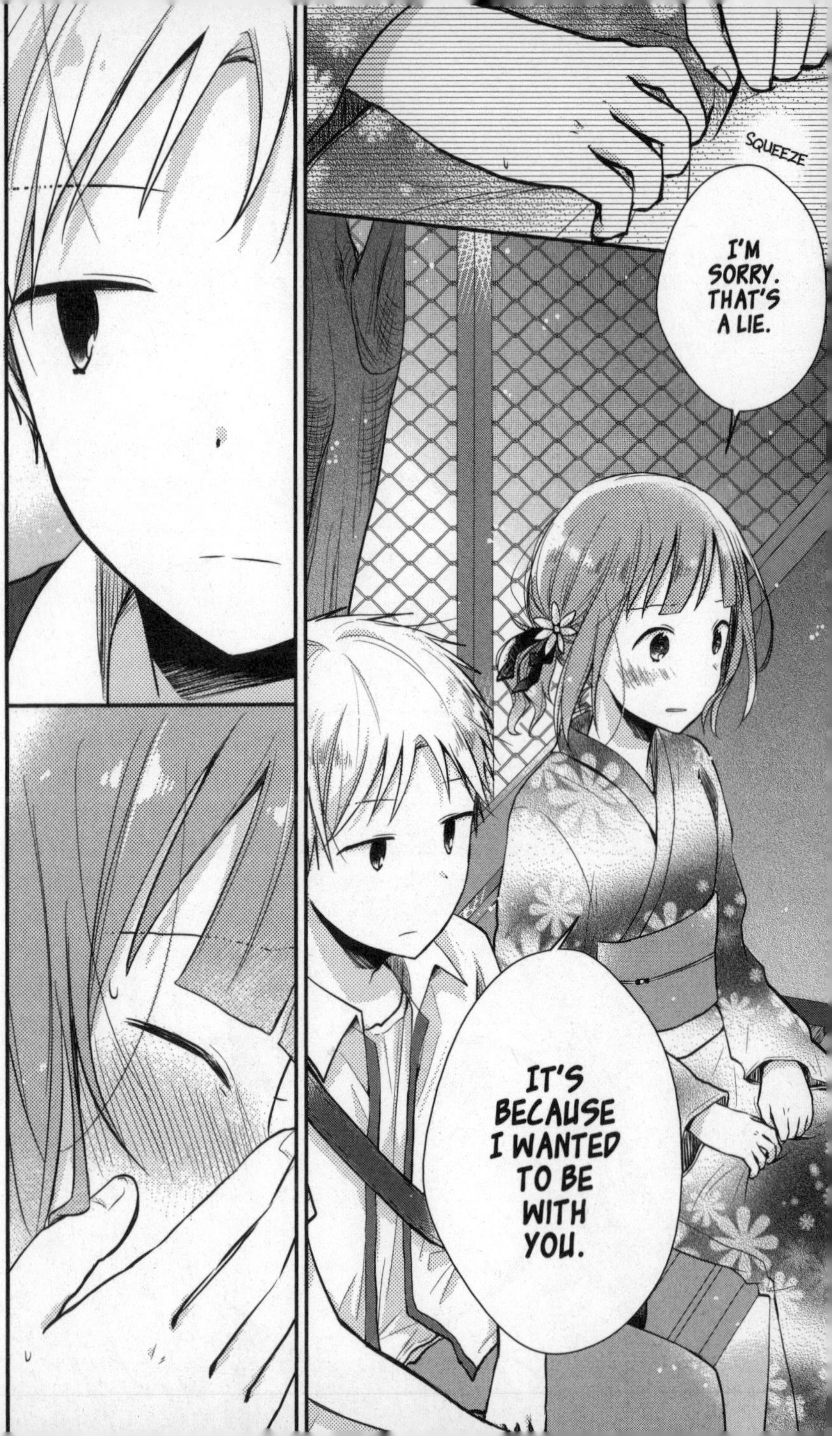
SQUEEZE
I'M SORRY. THAT'S A LIE.
IT'S BECAUSE I WANTED TO BE WITH YOU.

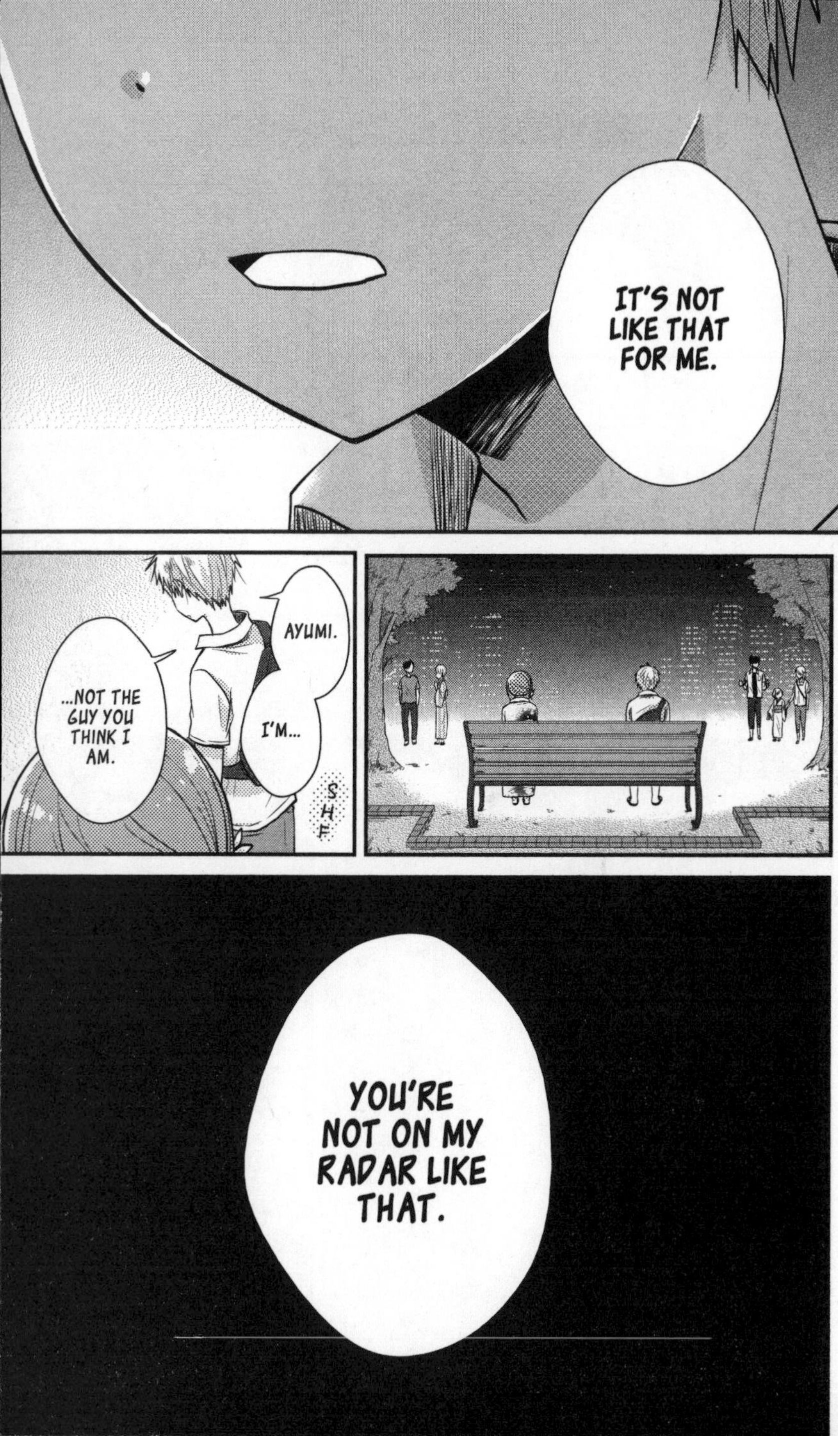
IT'S NOT LIKE THAT FOR ME.
AYUMI.
I'M...
...NOT THE GUY YOU THINK I AM.
SHF
YOU'RE NOT ON MY RADAR LIKE THAT.

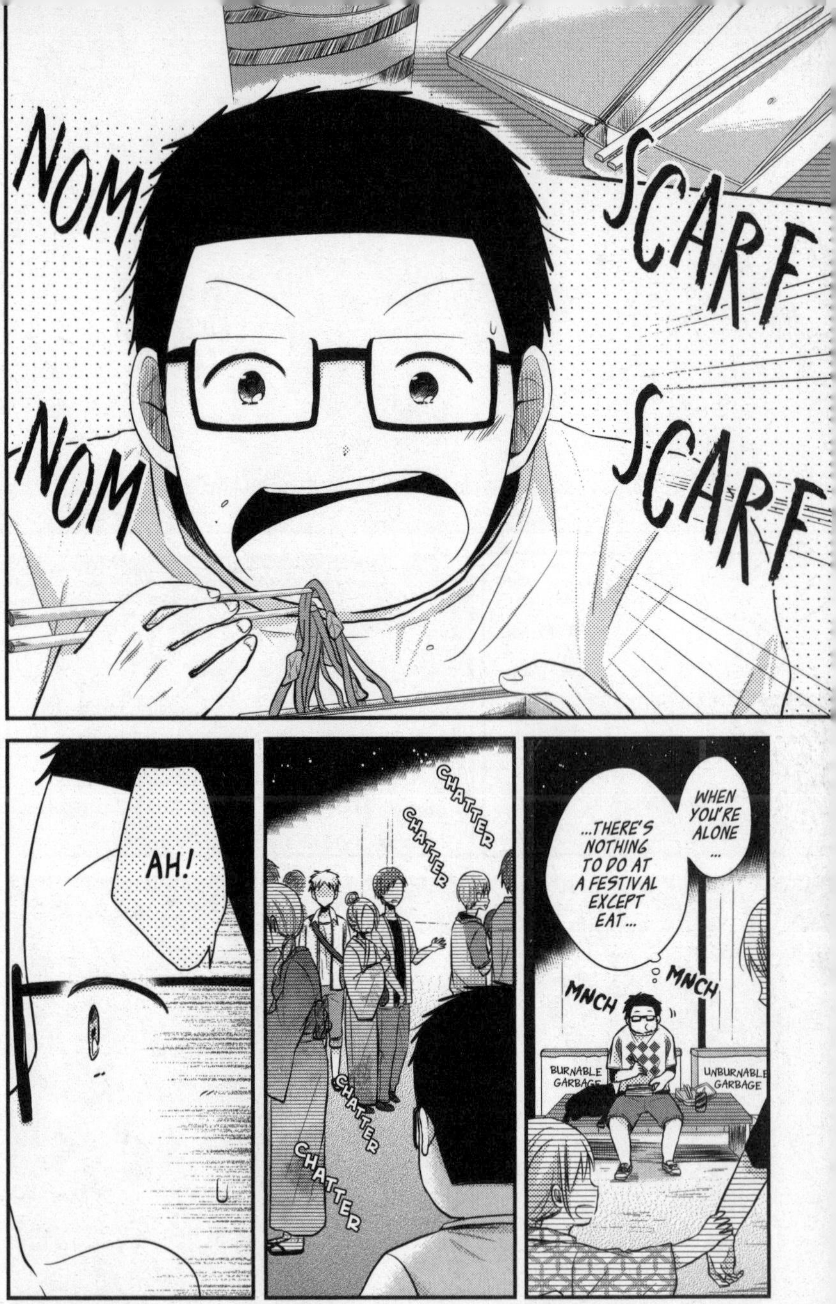
SCARF
SCARF
NOM
NOM
WHEN YOU'RE ALONE ...
...THERE'S NOTHING TO DO AT A FESTIVAL EXCEPT EAT...
MNCH
MNCH
UNBURNABLE GARBAGE
BURNABLE GARBAGE
CHATTER
CHATTER
CHATTER
CHATTER
AH!

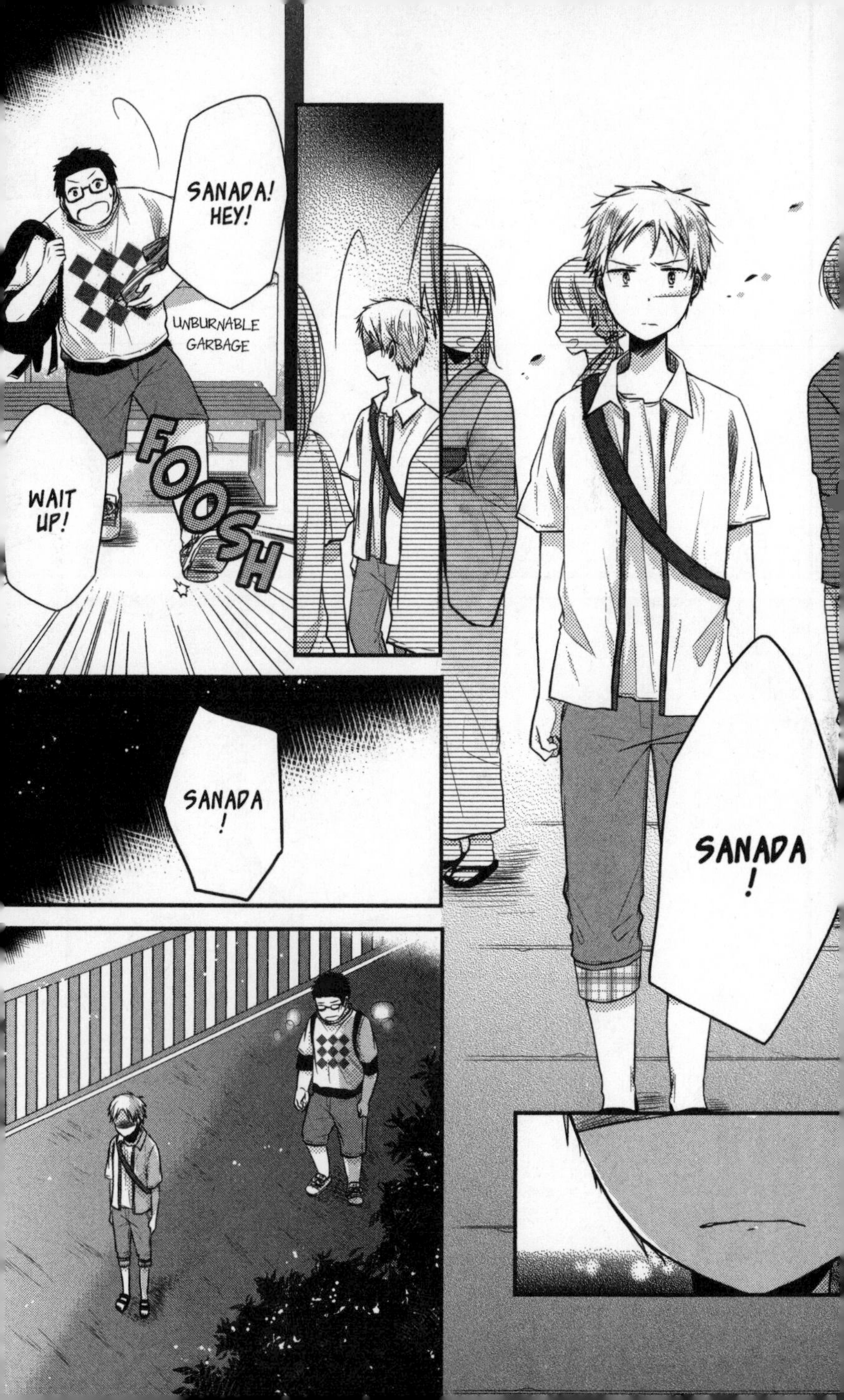
SANADA!
SANADA! HEY!
UNBURNABLE GARBAGE
FOOSH
WAIT UP!
SANADA!

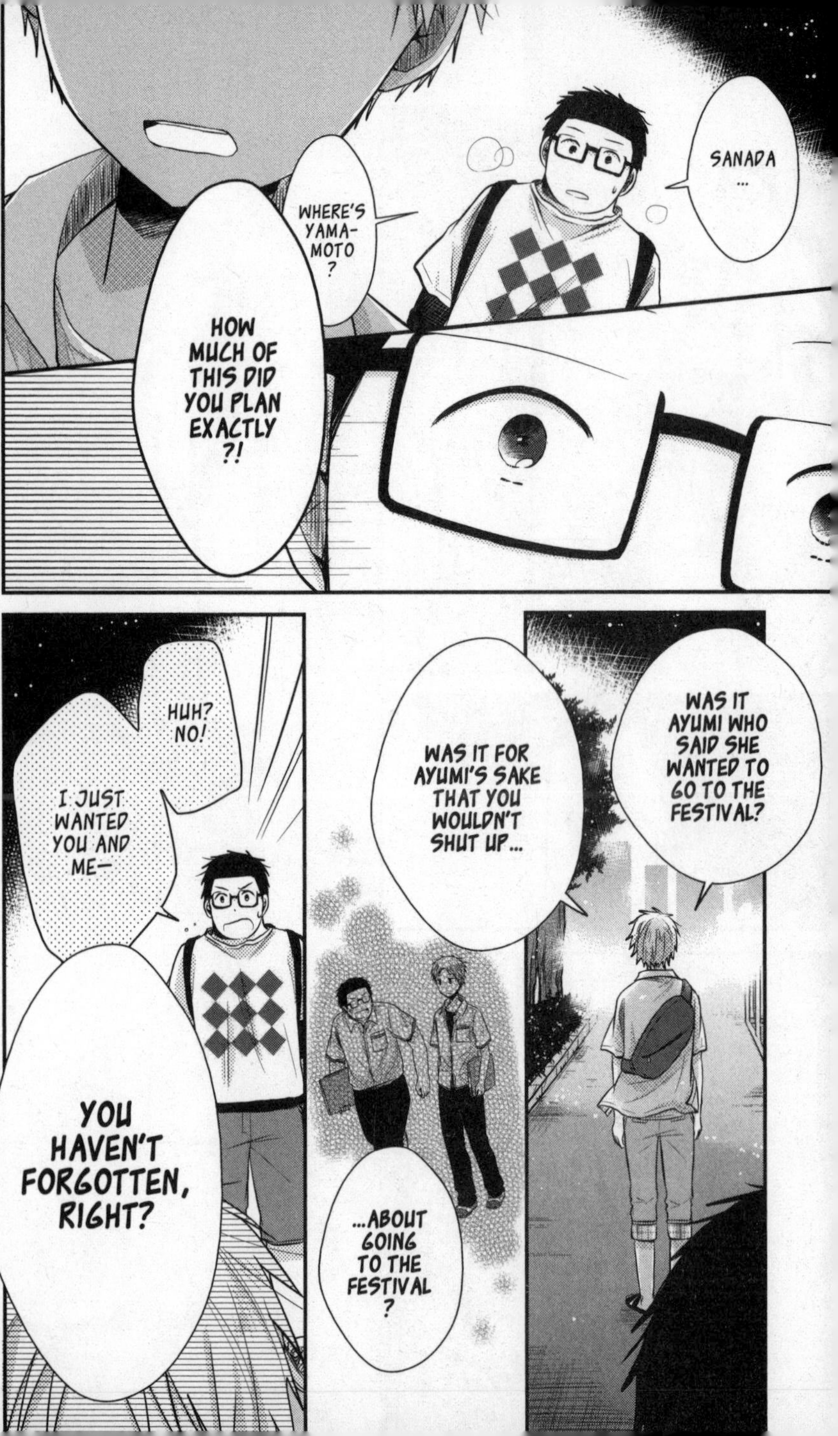
SANADA...
WHERE'S YAMAMOTO?
HOW MUCH OF THIS DID YOU PLAN EXACTLY?!
WAS IT AYUMI WHO SAID SHE WANTED TO GO TO THE FESTIVAL?
WAS IT FOR AYUMI'S SAKE THAT YOU WOULDN'T SHUT UP...
...ABOUT GOING TO THE FESTIVAL?
HUH? NO!
I JUST WANTED YOU AND ME—
YOU HAVEN'T FORGOTTEN, RIGHT?

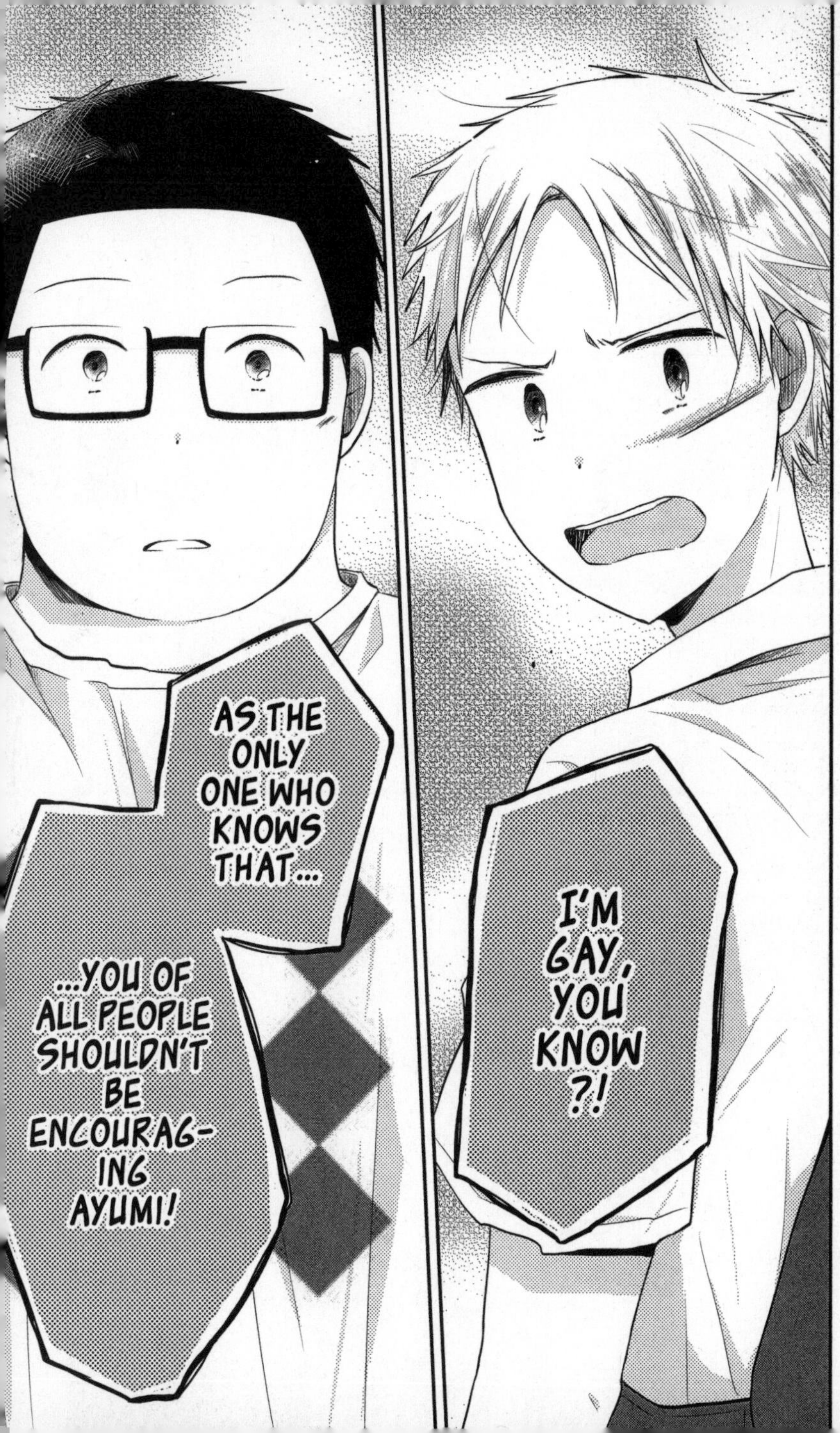
I'M GAY, YOU KNOW?!
AS THE ONLY ONE WHO KNOWS THAT...
...YOU OF ALL PEOPLE SHOULDN'T BE ENCOURAG-ING AYUMI!

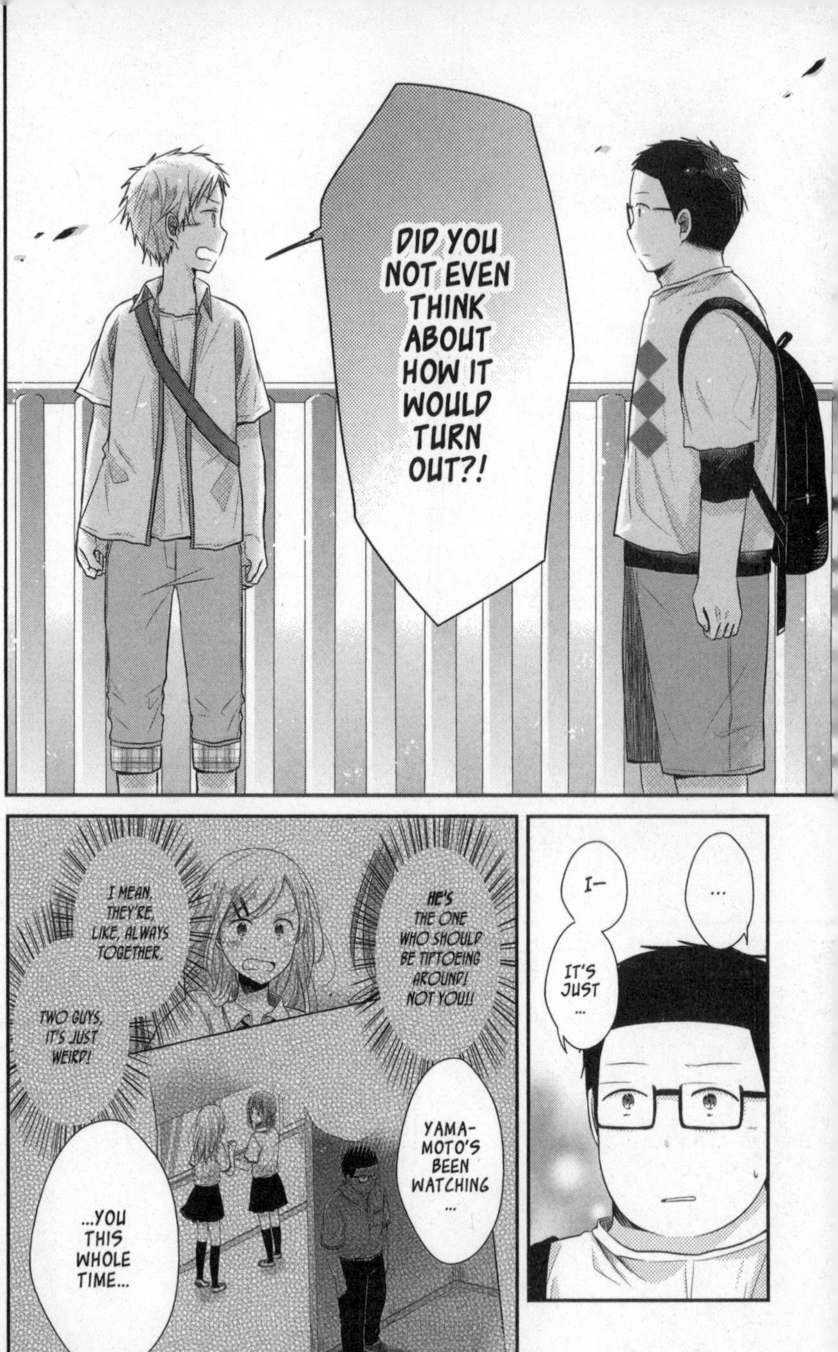
DID YOU NOT EVEN THINK ABOUT HOW IT WOULD TURN OUT?!
...
I—
IT'S JUST ...
HE'S THE ONE WHO SHOULD BE TIPTOEING AROUND! NOT YOU!!
I MEAN, THEY'RE, LIKE, ALWAYS TOGETHER.
TWO GUYS, IT'S JUST WEIRD!
YAMA-MOTO'S BEEN WATCHING ...
...YOU THIS WHOLE TIME...

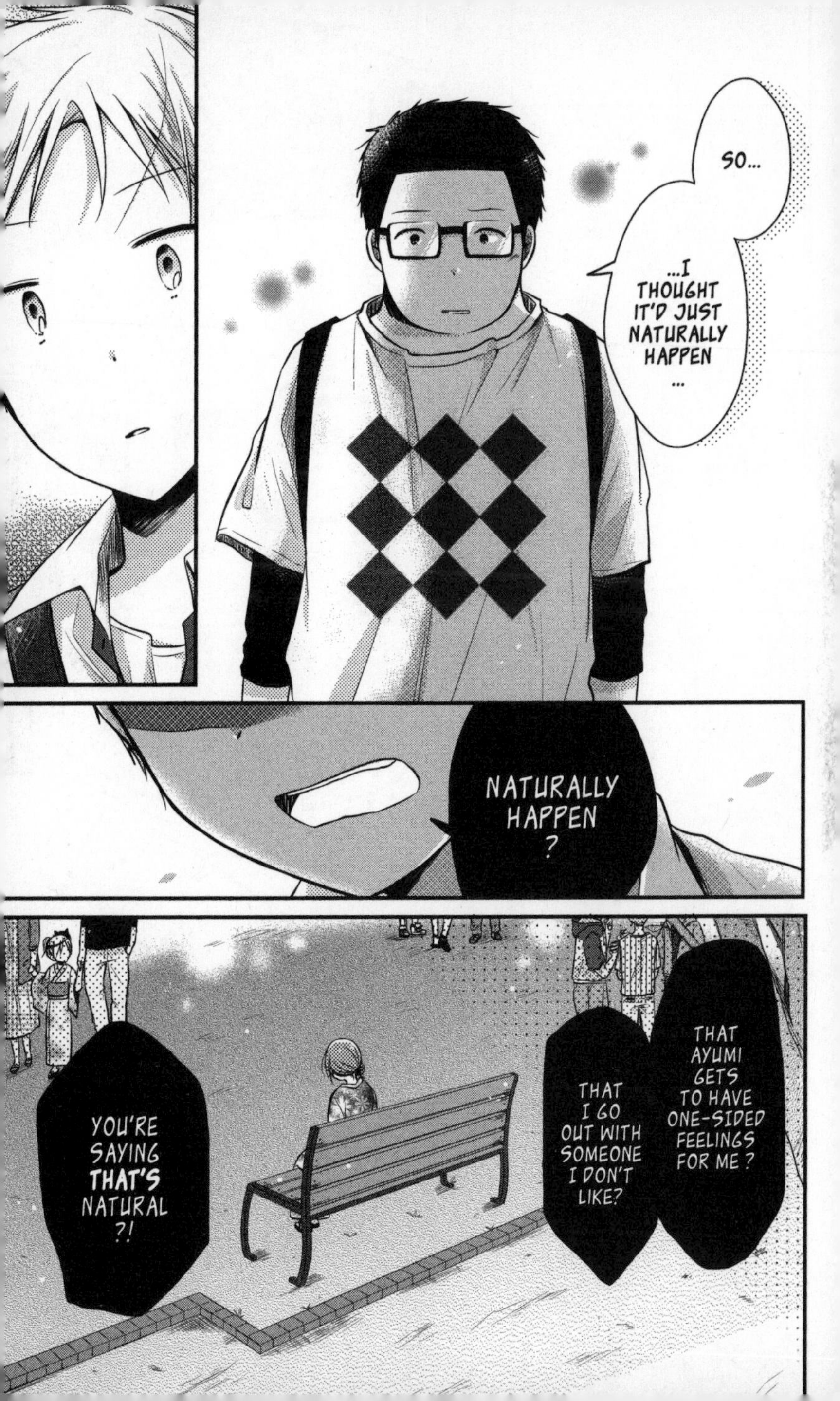
SO...
...I THOUGHT IT'D JUST NATURALLY HAPPEN ...
NATURALLY HAPPEN ?
THAT AYUMI GETS TO HAVE ONE-SIDED FEELINGS FOR ME ?
THAT I GO OUT WITH SOMEONE I DON'T LIKE?
YOU'RE SAYING **THAT'S** NATURAL ?!

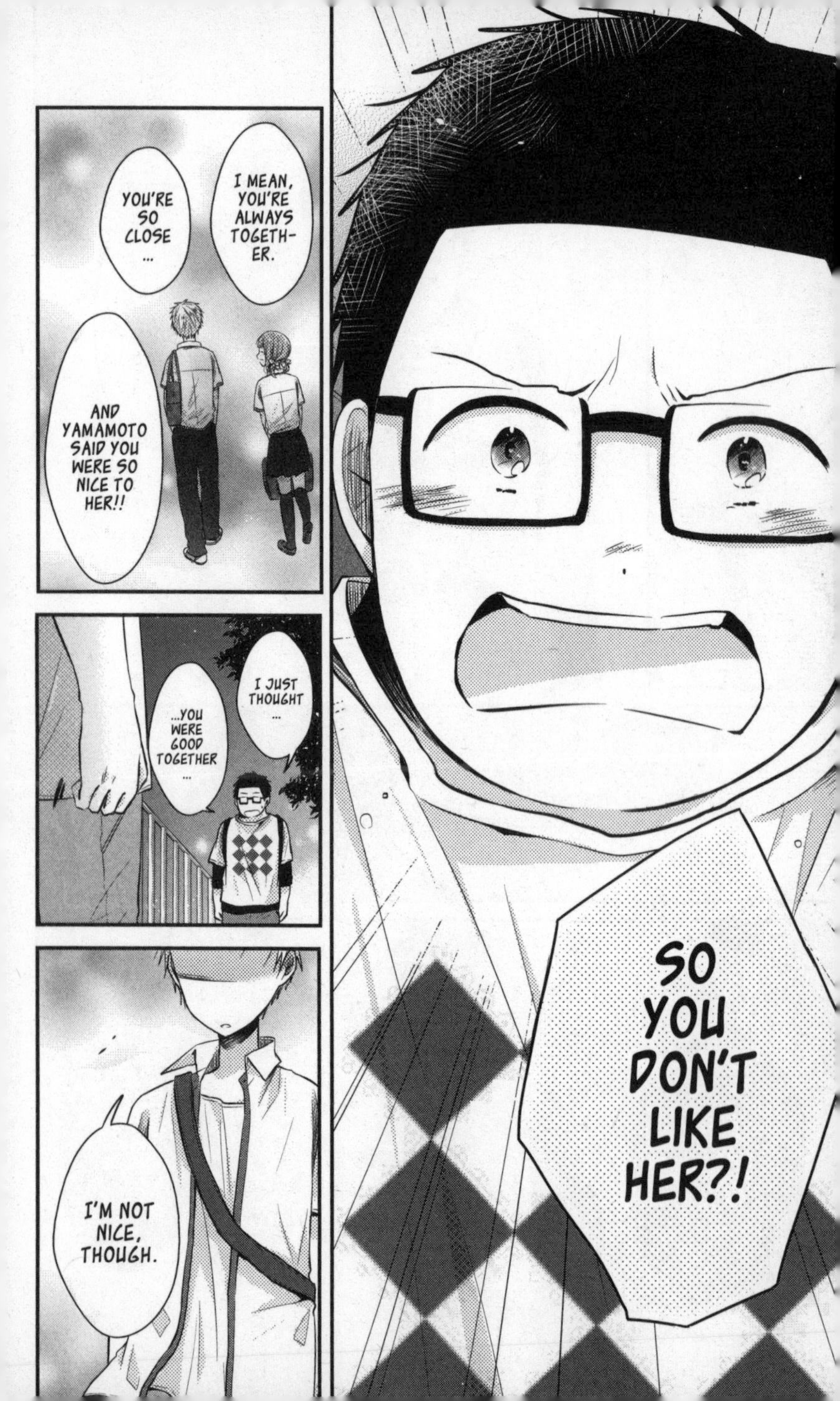
SO YOU DON'T LIKE HER?!
I MEAN, YOU'RE ALWAYS TOGETH-ER.
YOU'RE SO CLOSE ...
AND YAMAMOTO SAID YOU WERE SO NICE TO HER!!
I JUST THOUGHT ...
...YOU WERE GOOD TOGETHER ...
I'M NOT NICE, THOUGH.

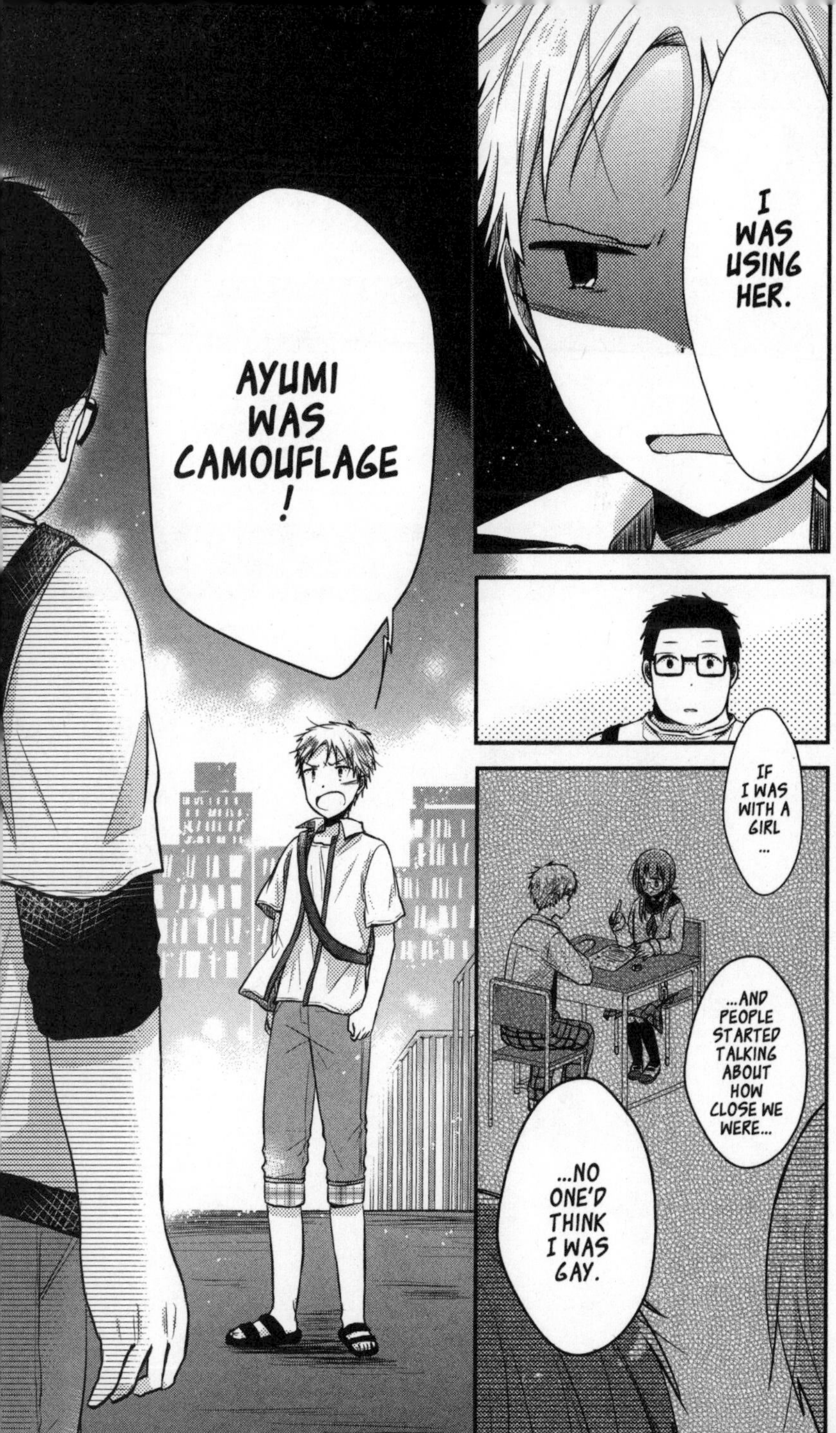
I WAS USING HER.
IF I WAS WITH A GIRL...
...AND PEOPLE STARTED TALKING ABOUT HOW CLOSE WE WERE...
...NO ONE'D THINK I WAS GAY.
AYUMI WAS CAMOUFLAGE!

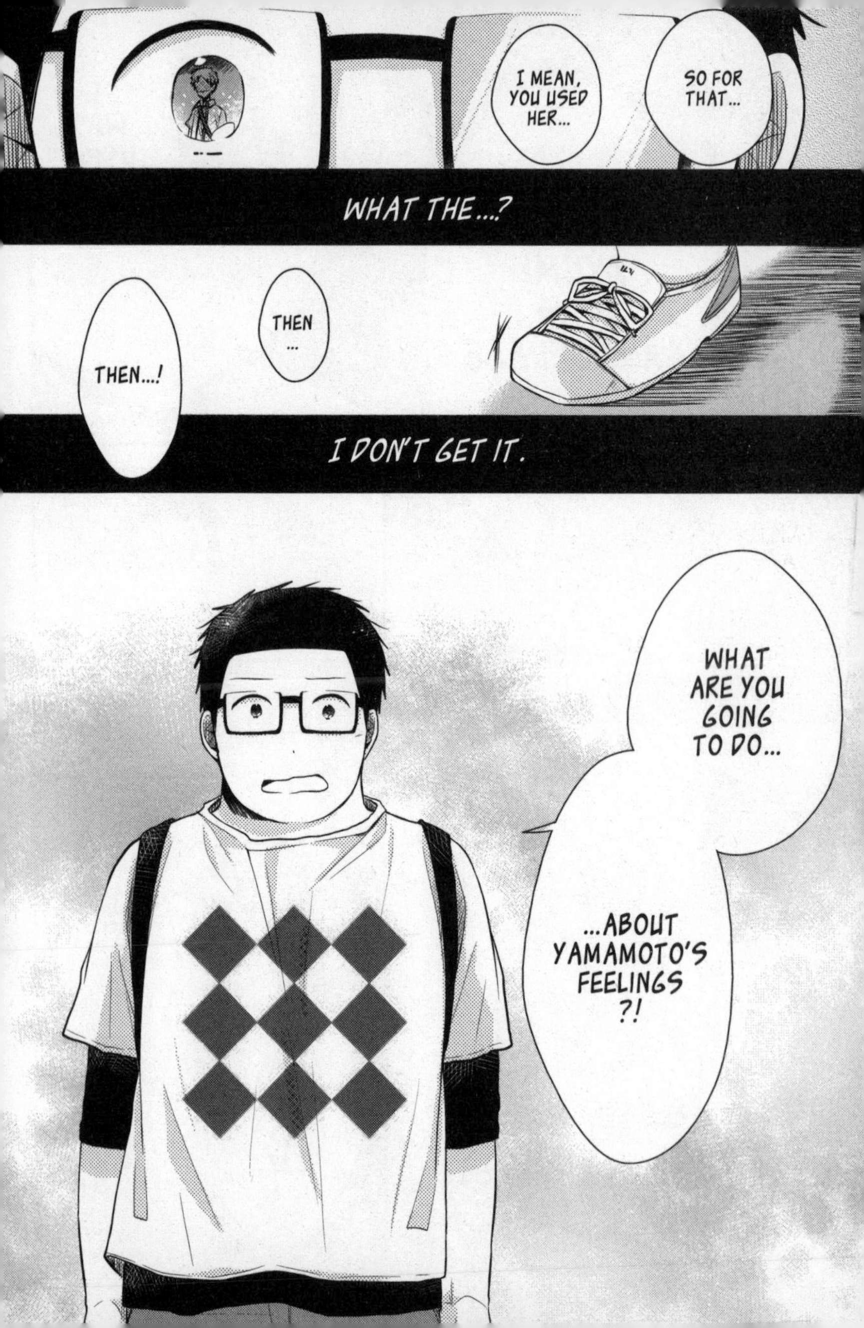
SO FOR THAT...
I MEAN, YOU USED HER...
WHAT THE...?
THEN...
THEN...!
I DON'T GET IT.
WHAT ARE YOU GOING TO DO...
...ABOUT YAMAMOTO'S FEELINGS?!

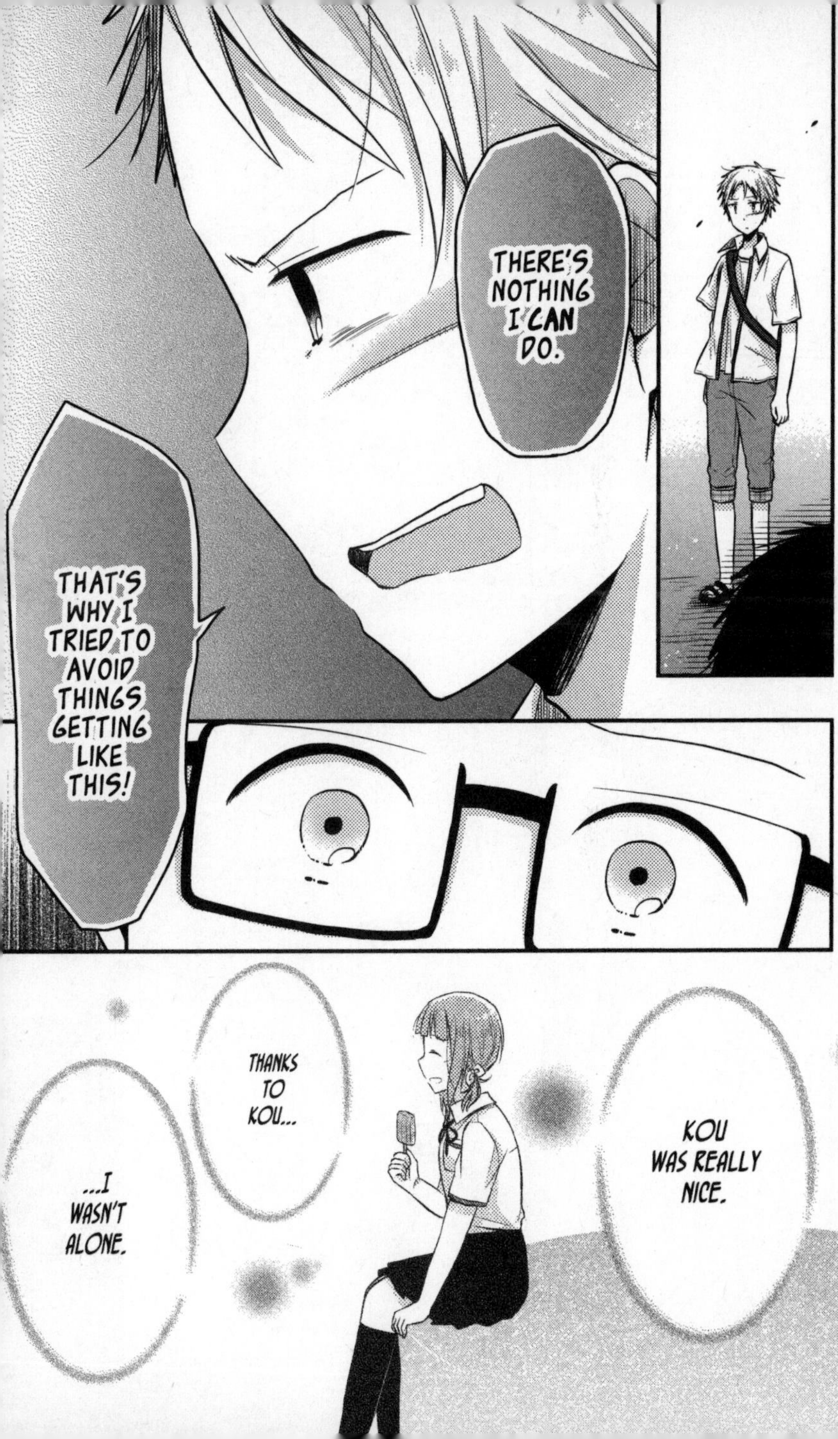
THERE'S NOTHING I CAN DO.
THAT'S WHY I TRIED TO AVOID THINGS GETTING LIKE THIS!
KOU WAS REALLY NICE.
THANKS TO KOU...
...I WASN'T ALONE.

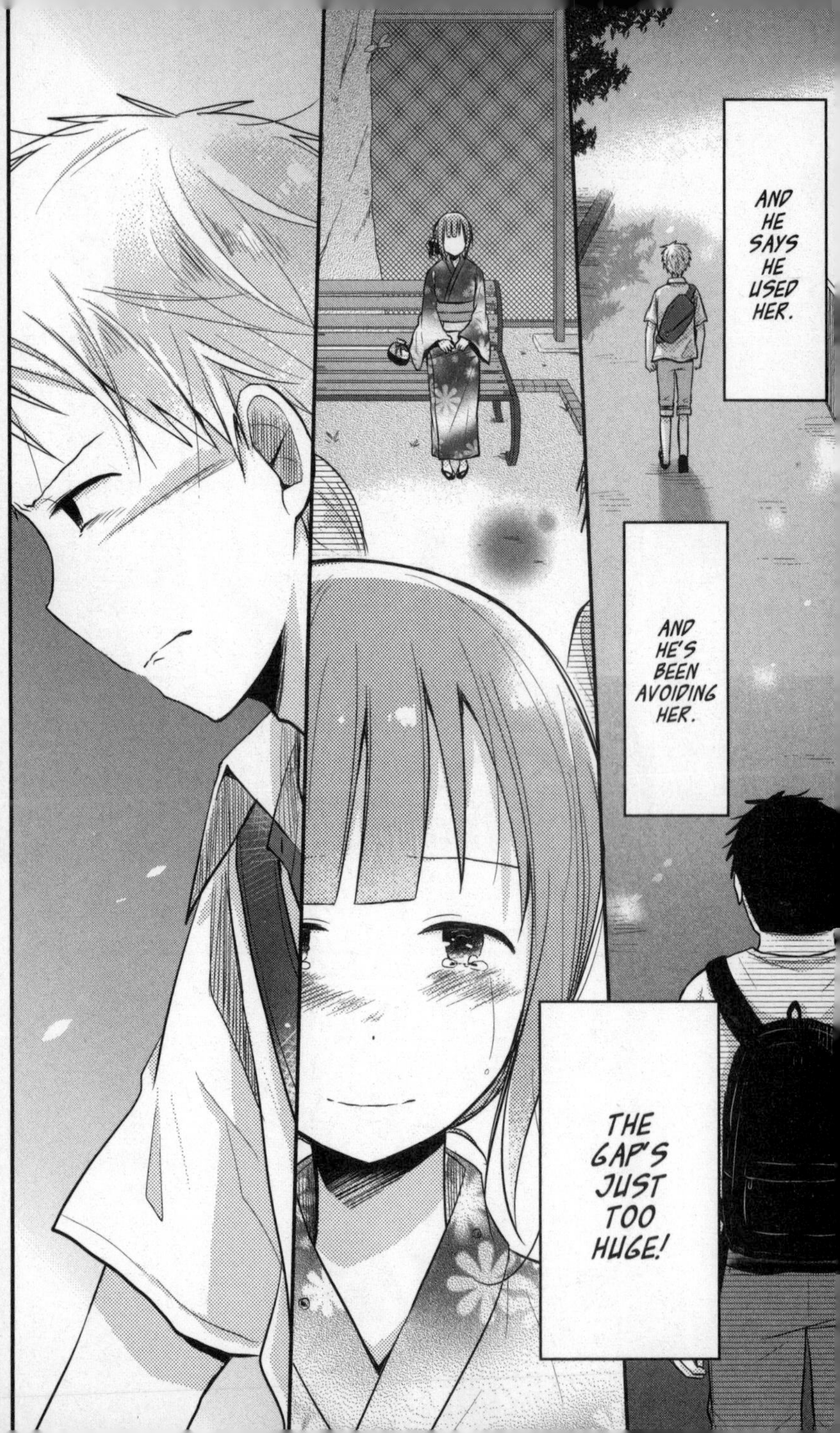
AND HE SAYS HE USED HER.
AND HE'S BEEN AVOIDING HER.
THE GAP'S JUST TOO HUGE!

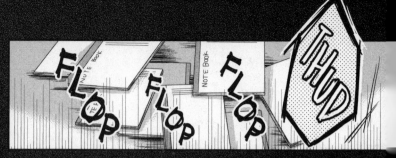

Chapter 10: Sorry.

HA HA

WHOOPSY! SORRY! MY BAD!

HA HA

DIDN'T SEE YOU THERE.

TAK TAK TAK

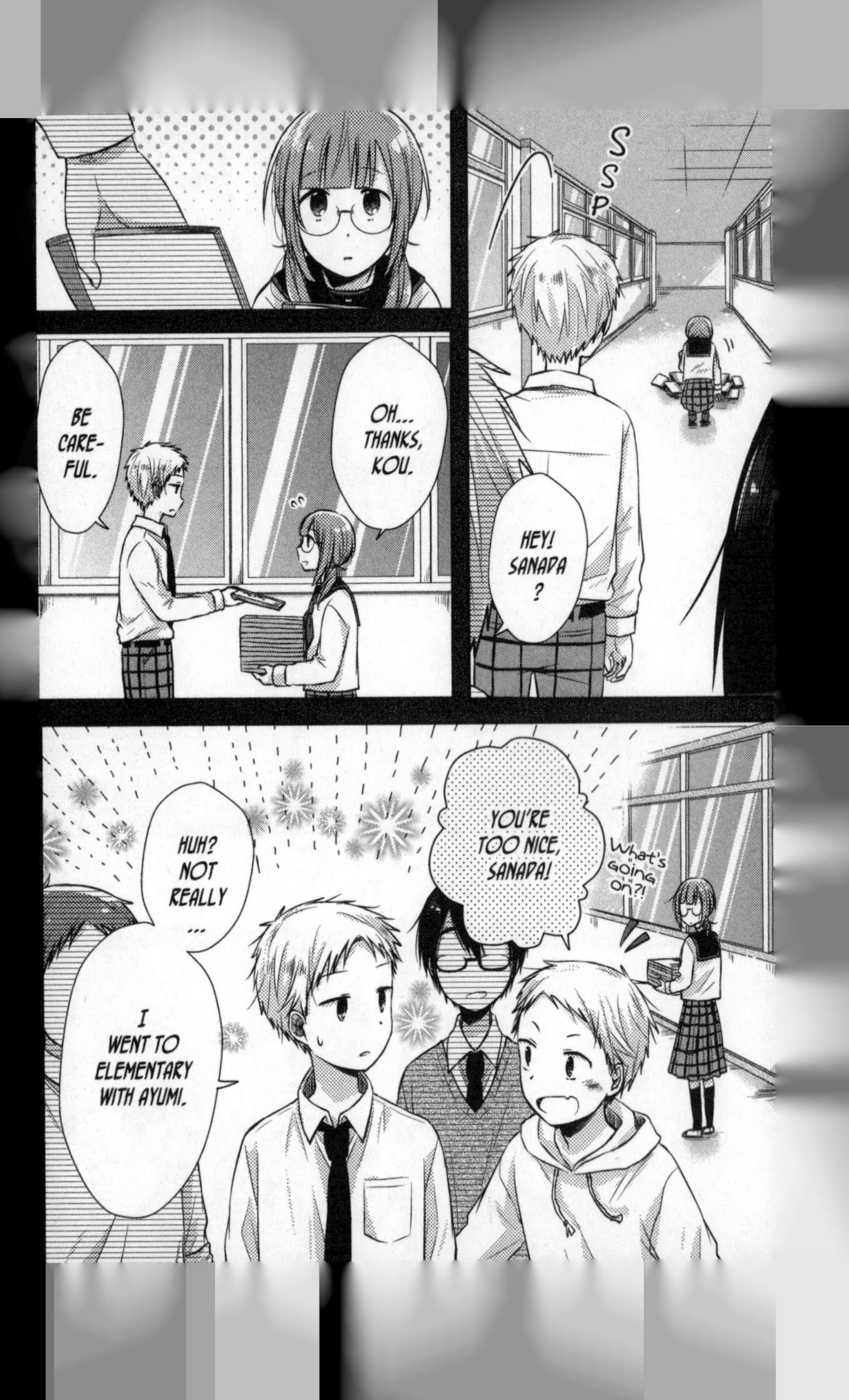
SSP
HEY! SANADA?
OH... THANKS, KOU.
BE CAREFUL.
What's going on?!
YOU'RE TOO NICE, SANADA!
HUH? NOT REALLY...
I WENT TO ELEMENTARY WITH AYUMI.

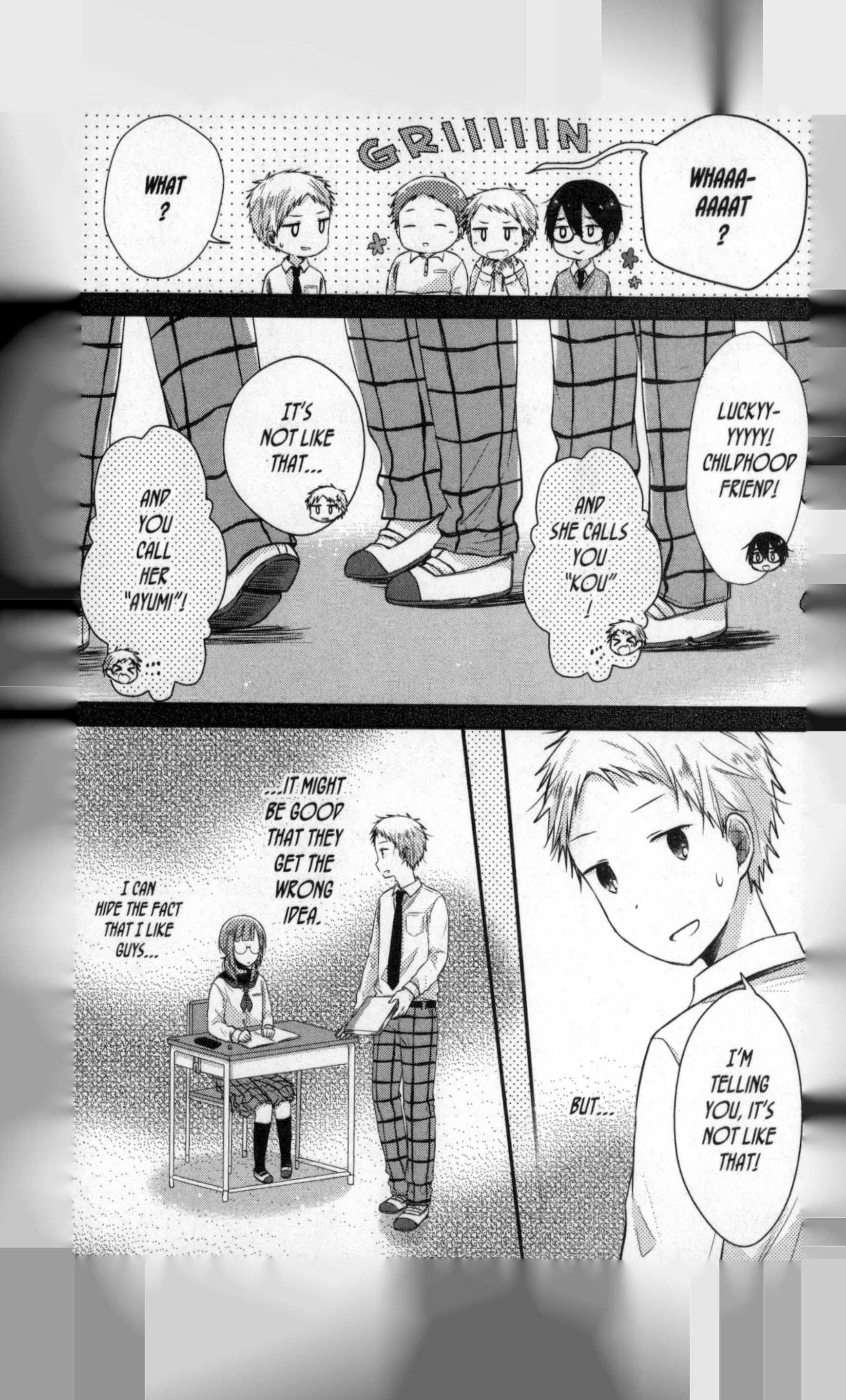
WHAAA-AAAAT?
GRIIIIIN
WHAT?
LUCKYY-YYYYY! CHILDHOOD FRIEND!
AND SHE CALLS YOU "KOU"!
IT'S NOT LIKE THAT...
AND YOU CALL HER "AYUMI"!
I'M TELLING YOU, IT'S NOT LIKE THAT!
BUT...
...IT MIGHT BE GOOD THAT THEY GET THE WRONG IDEA.
I CAN HIDE THE FACT THAT I LIKE GUYS...

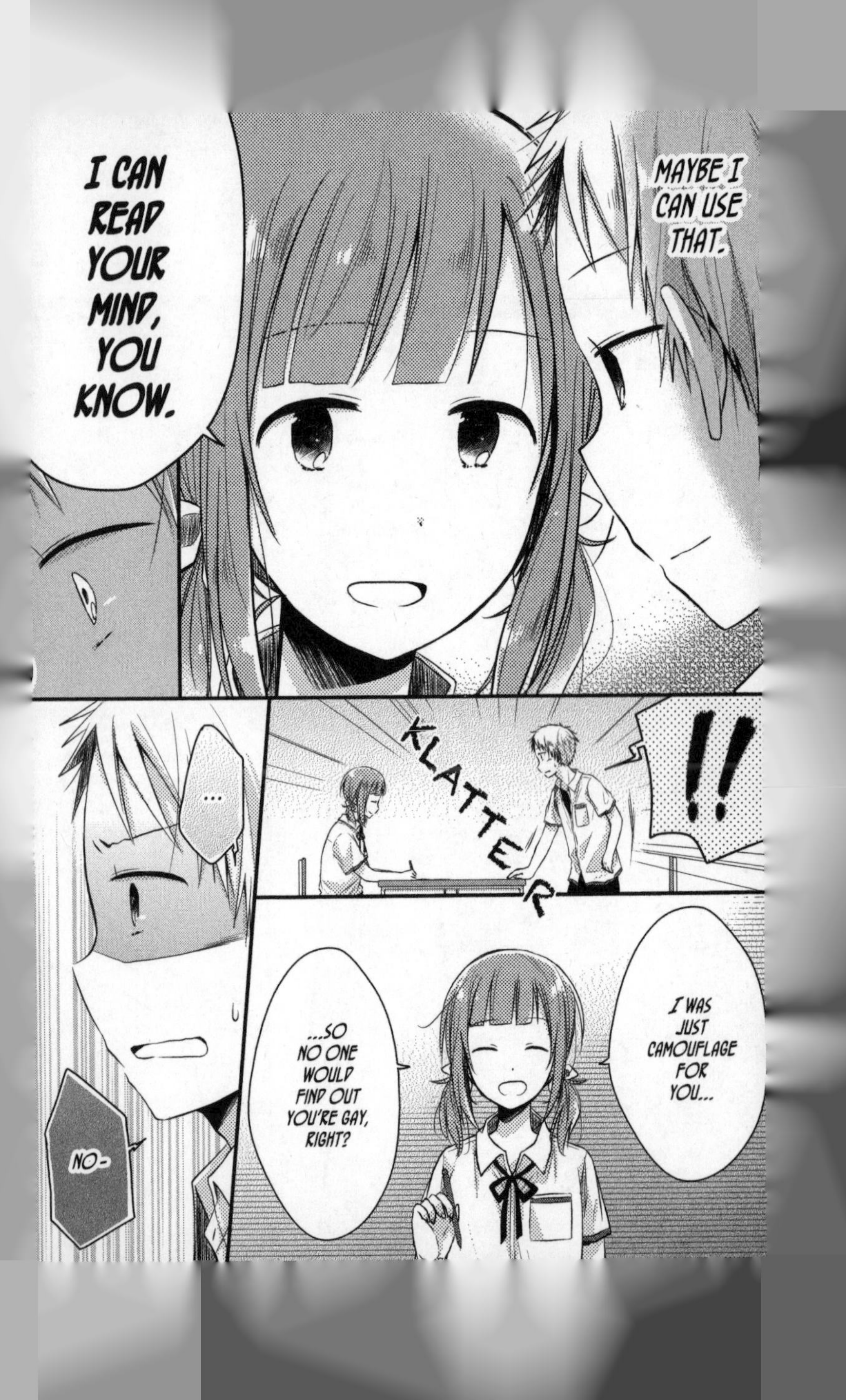
MAYBE I CAN USE THAT.
I CAN READ YOUR MIND, YOU KNOW.
!!
KLATTER
I WAS JUST CAMOUFLAGE FOR YOU...
...SO NO ONE WOULD FIND OUT YOU'RE GAY, RIGHT?
...
NO-

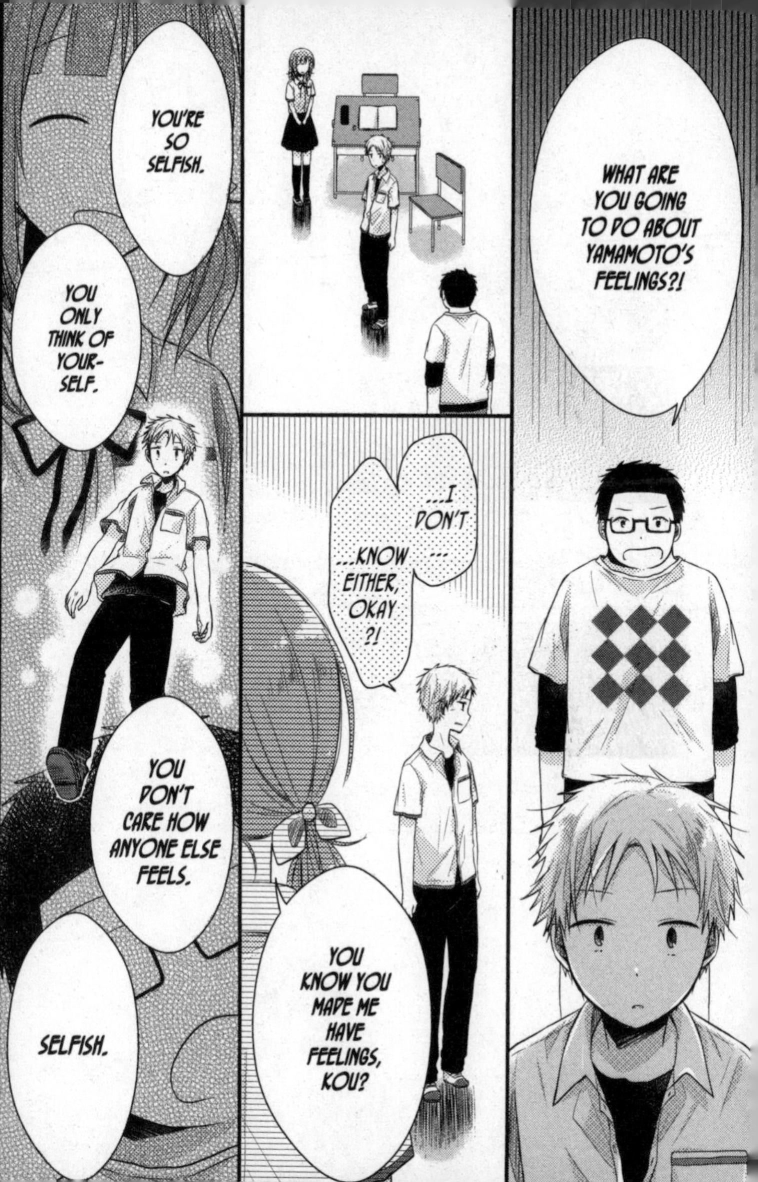
WHAT ARE YOU GOING TO DO ABOUT YAMAMOTO'S FEELINGS?!
...I DON'T ...
...KNOW EITHER, OKAY?!
YOU KNOW YOU MADE ME HAVE FEELINGS, KOU?
YOU'RE SO SELFISH.
YOU ONLY THINK OF YOUR-SELF.
YOU DON'T CARE HOW ANYONE ELSE FEELS.
SELFISH.

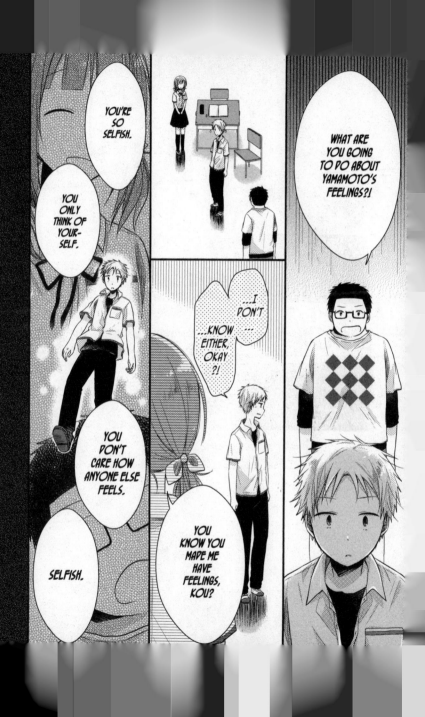

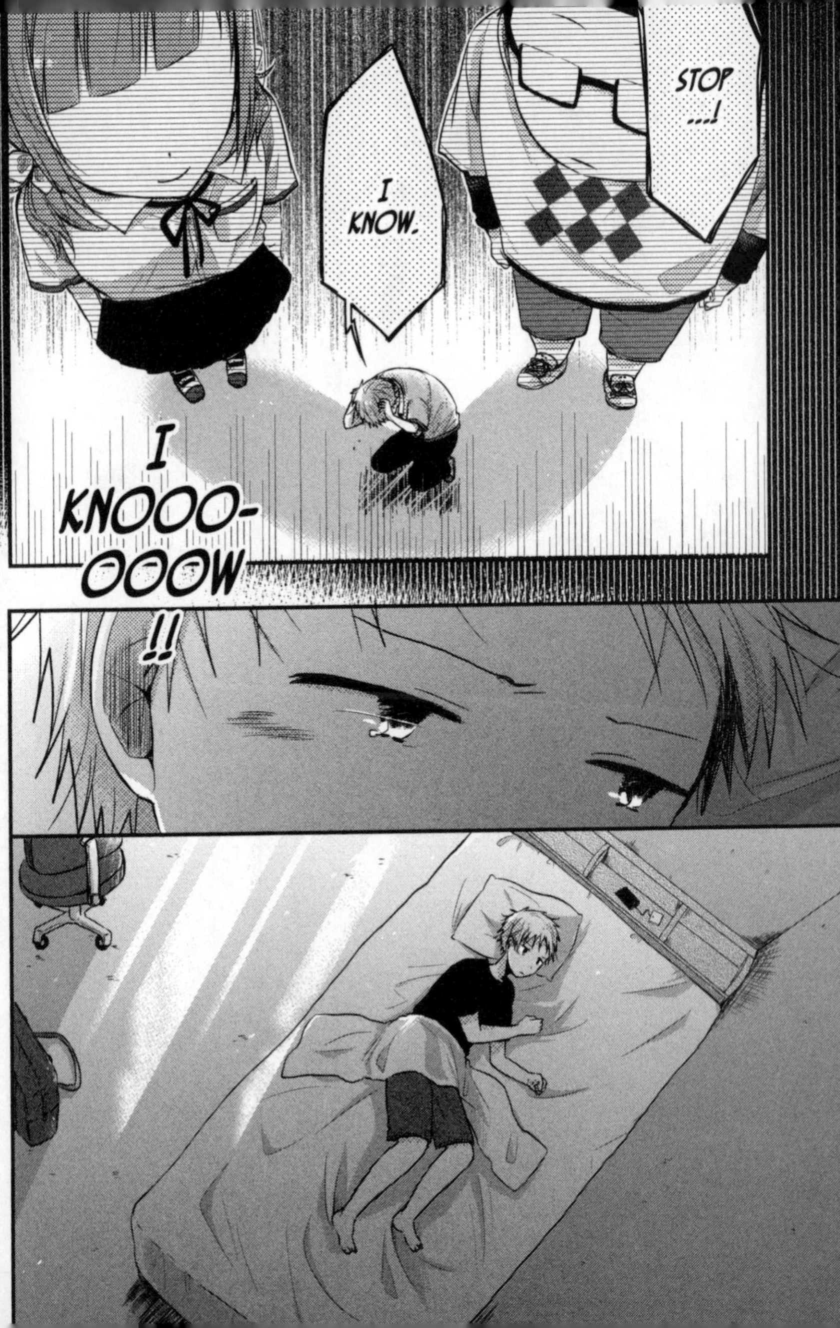
STOP ...!
I KNOW.
I KNOOO-OOOW !!

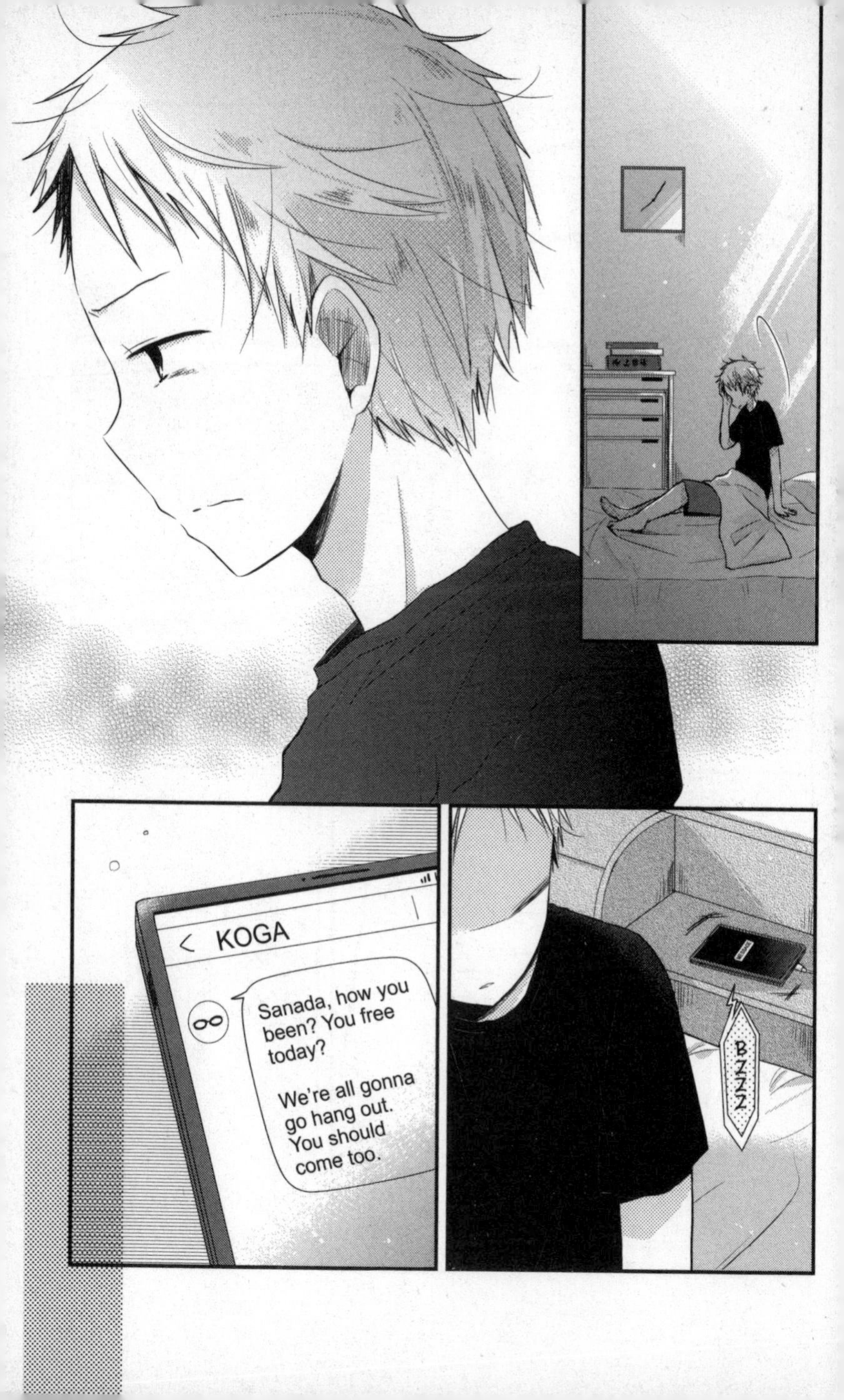
BZZZ
KOGA
Sanada, how you been? You free today?
We're all gonna go hang out. You should come too.

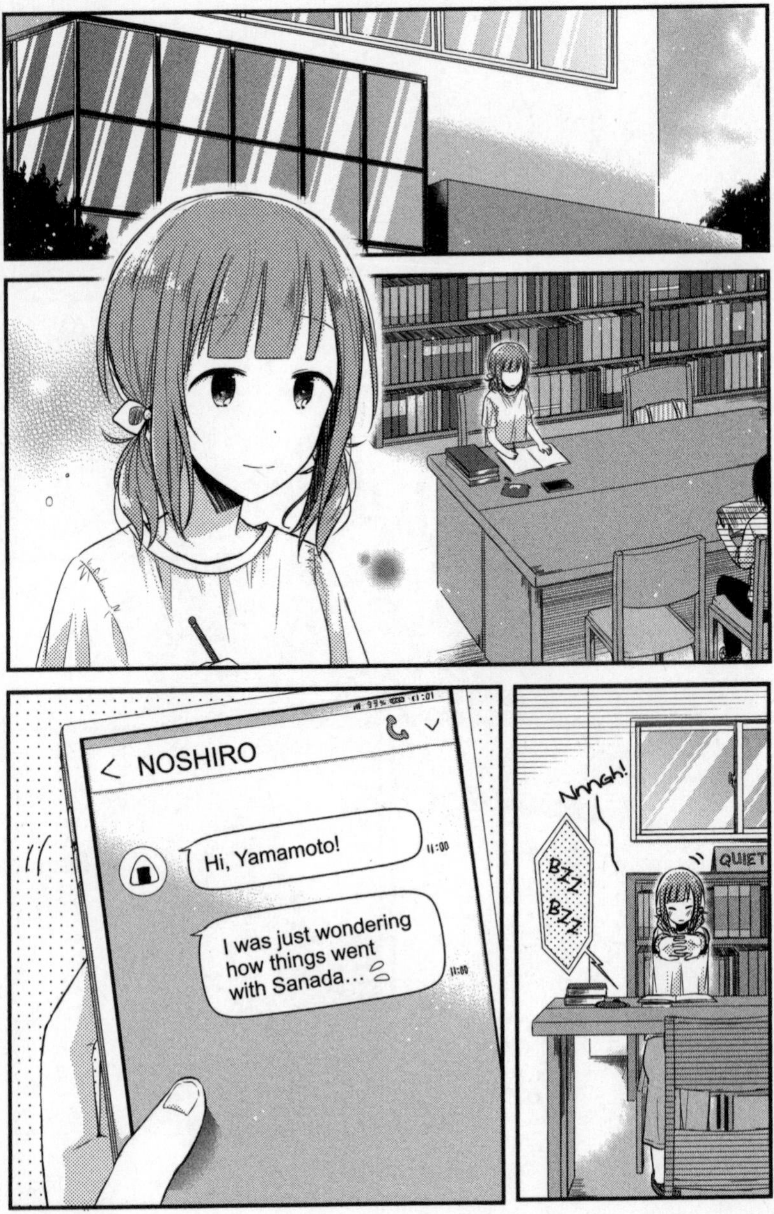
Nnngh!
QUIET
BZZ BZZ
NOSHIRO
Hi, Yamamoto!
I was just wondering how things went with Sanada…

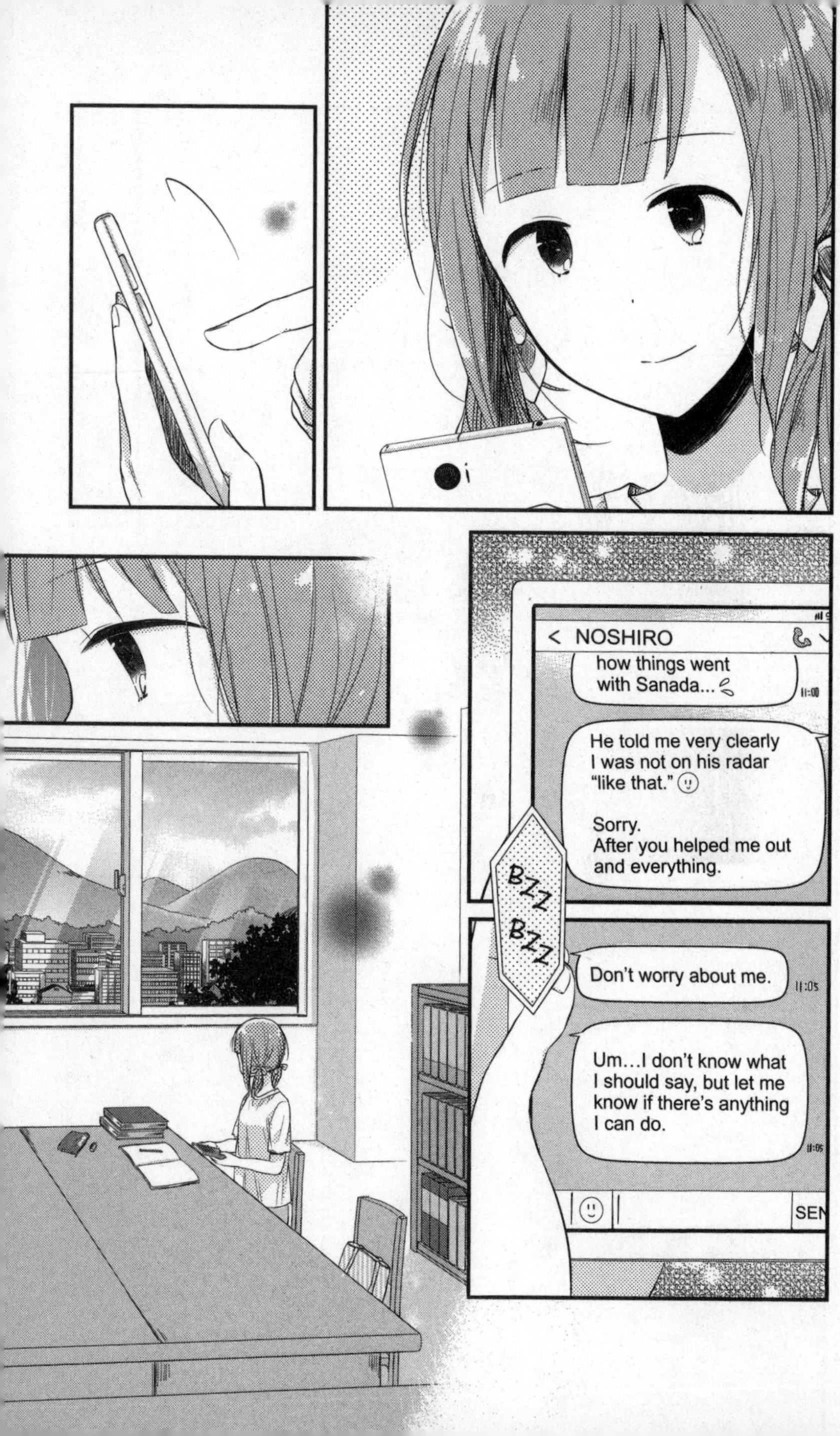

< NOSHIRO
how things went with Sanada...
11:00
He told me very clearly I was not on his radar "like that."
Sorry. After you helped me out and everything.
BZZ BZZ
Don't worry about me.
11:05
Um...I don't know what I should say, but let me know if there's anything I can do.
11:05
SEN

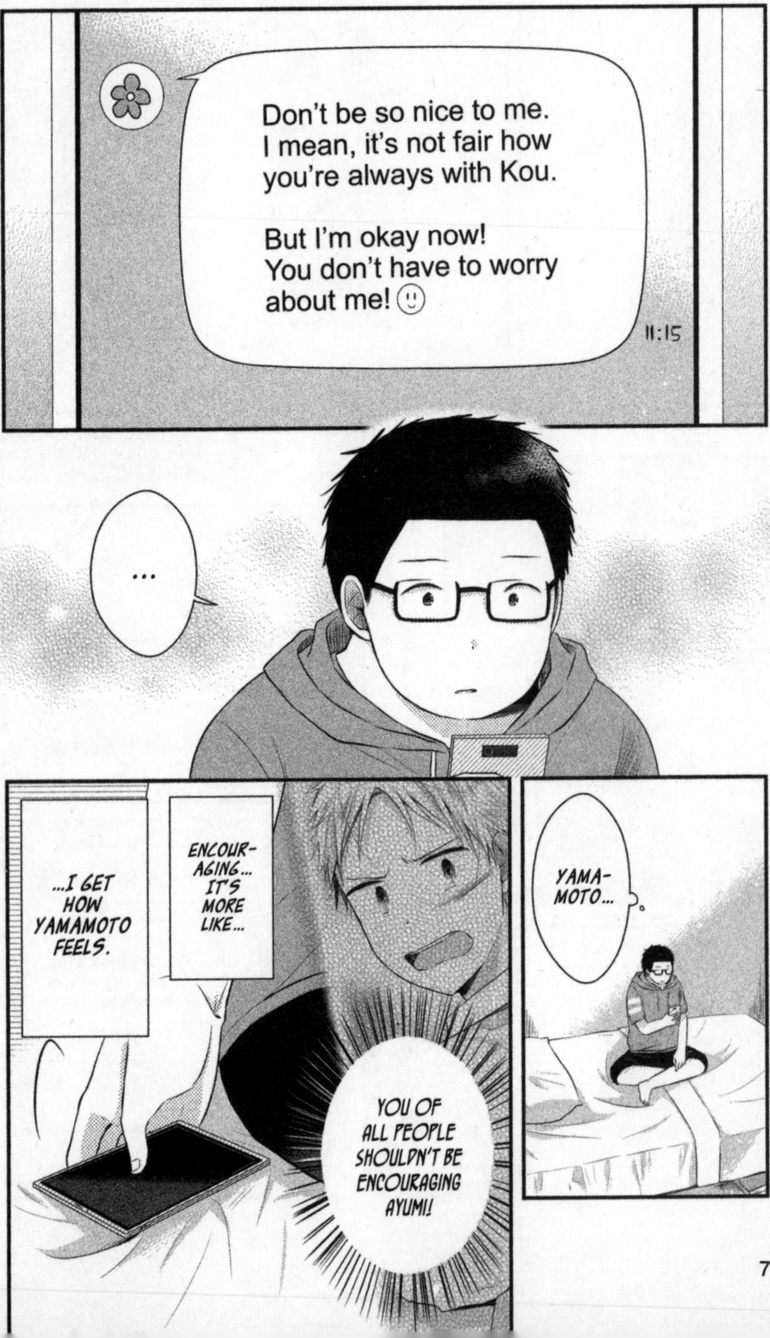
Don't be so nice to me.
I mean, it's not fair how
you're always with Kou.
But I'm okay now!
You don't have to worry
about me! ☺
11:15
...
YAMA-
MOTO...
...I GET HOW YAMAMOTO FEELS.
ENCOUR-
AGING...
IT'S
MORE
LIKE...
YOU OF ALL PEOPLE SHOULDN'T BE ENCOURAGING AYUMI!

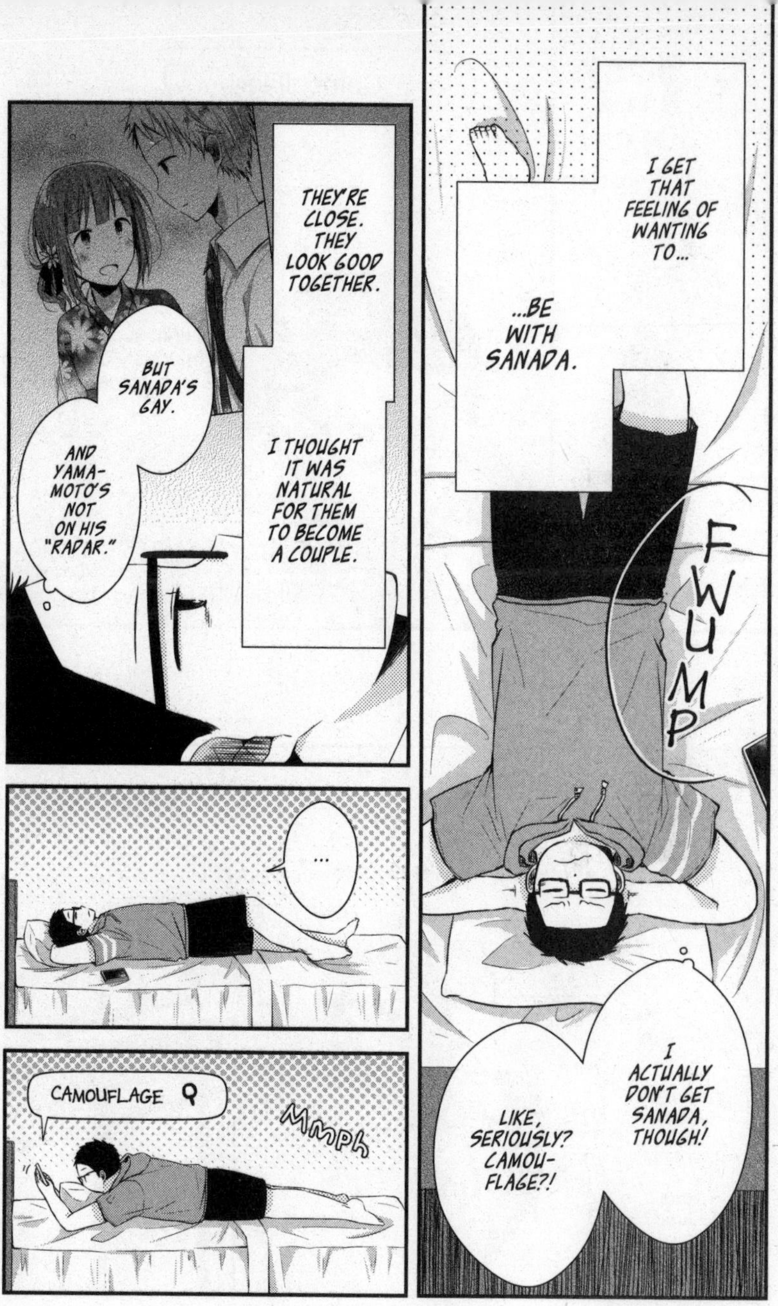
I GET THAT FEELING OF WANTING TO...
...BE WITH SANADA.
FWUMP
I ACTUALLY DON'T GET SANADA, THOUGH!
LIKE, SERIOUSLY? CAMOU-FLAGE?!
THEY'RE CLOSE. THEY LOOK GOOD TOGETHER.
I THOUGHT IT WAS NATURAL FOR THEM TO BECOME A COUPLE.
BUT SANADA'S GAY.
AND YAMA-MOTO'S NOT ON HIS "RADAR."
...
CAMOUFLAGE
Mmph

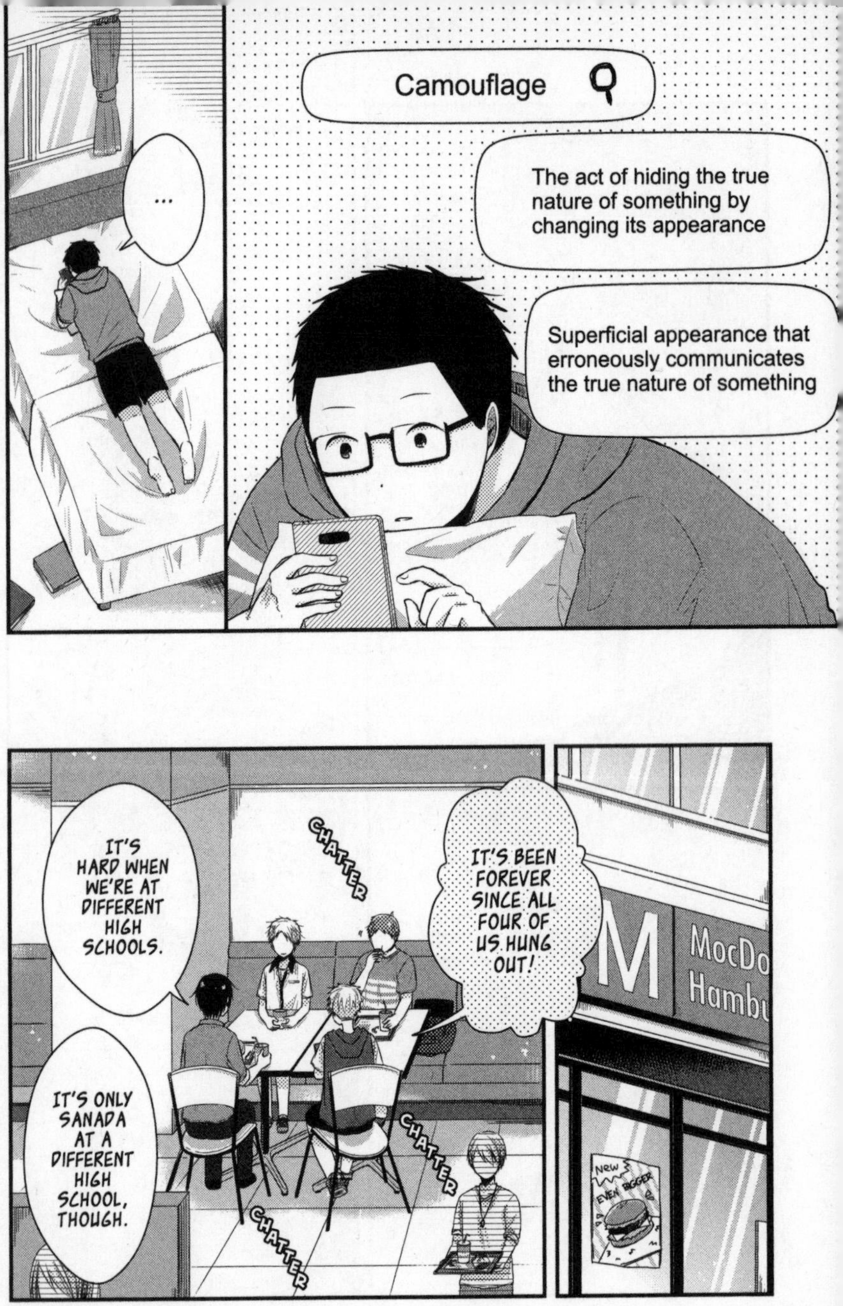
Camouflage
The act of hiding the true nature of something by changing its appearance
Superficial appearance that erroneously communicates the true nature of something
...
M
MocDo
Hambu
New
EVEN BIGGER
IT'S BEEN FOREVER SINCE ALL FOUR OF US HUNG OUT!
CHATTER
IT'S HARD WHEN WE'RE AT DIFFERENT HIGH SCHOOLS.
IT'S ONLY SANADA AT A DIFFERENT HIGH SCHOOL, THOUGH.
CHATTER
CHATTER

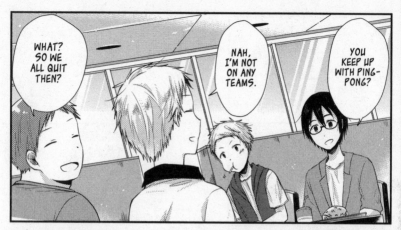

YOU KEEP UP WITH PING-PONG?
NAH, I'M NOT ON ANY TEAMS.
WHAT? SO WE ALL QUIT THEN?
Koga
Kamichi
Nomura
THE THREE GUYS I HUNG OUT WITH IN JUNIOR HIGH.
THE THREE OF THEM WERE ALREADY FRIENDS.
AND THEY LET ME JOIN THEM.
JUST BECAUSE I SAT NEXT TO KOGA.

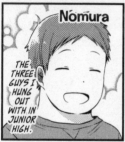

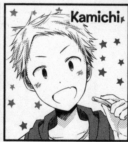

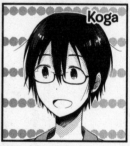

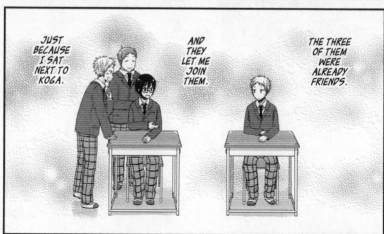

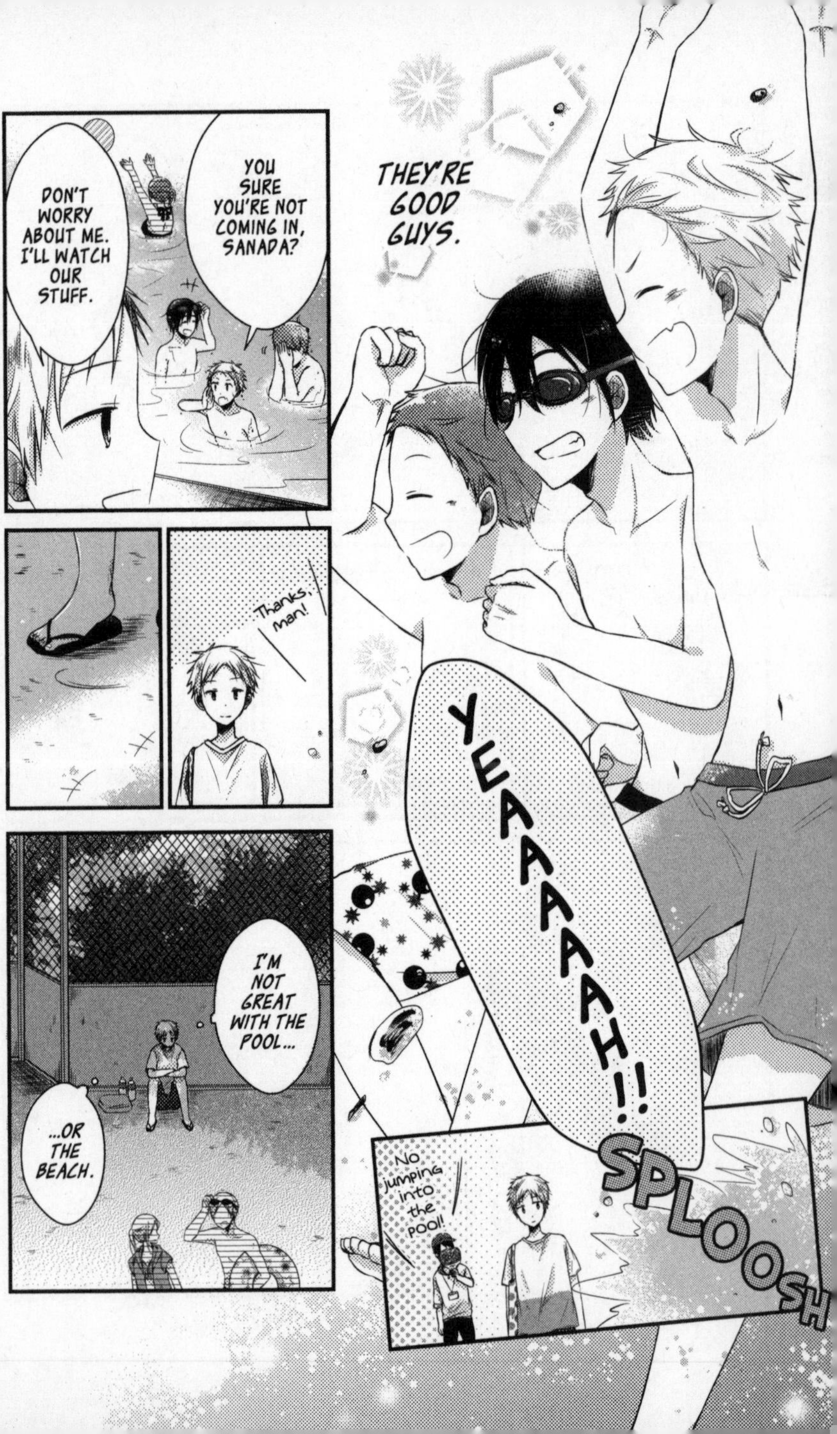
THEY'RE GOOD GUYS.
YEAAAAAH!!
SPLOOSH
No jumping into the pool!
YOU SURE YOU'RE NOT COMING IN, SANADA?
DON'T WORRY ABOUT ME. I'LL WATCH OUR STUFF.
Thanks, man!
I'M NOT GREAT WITH THE POOL...
...OR THE BEACH.

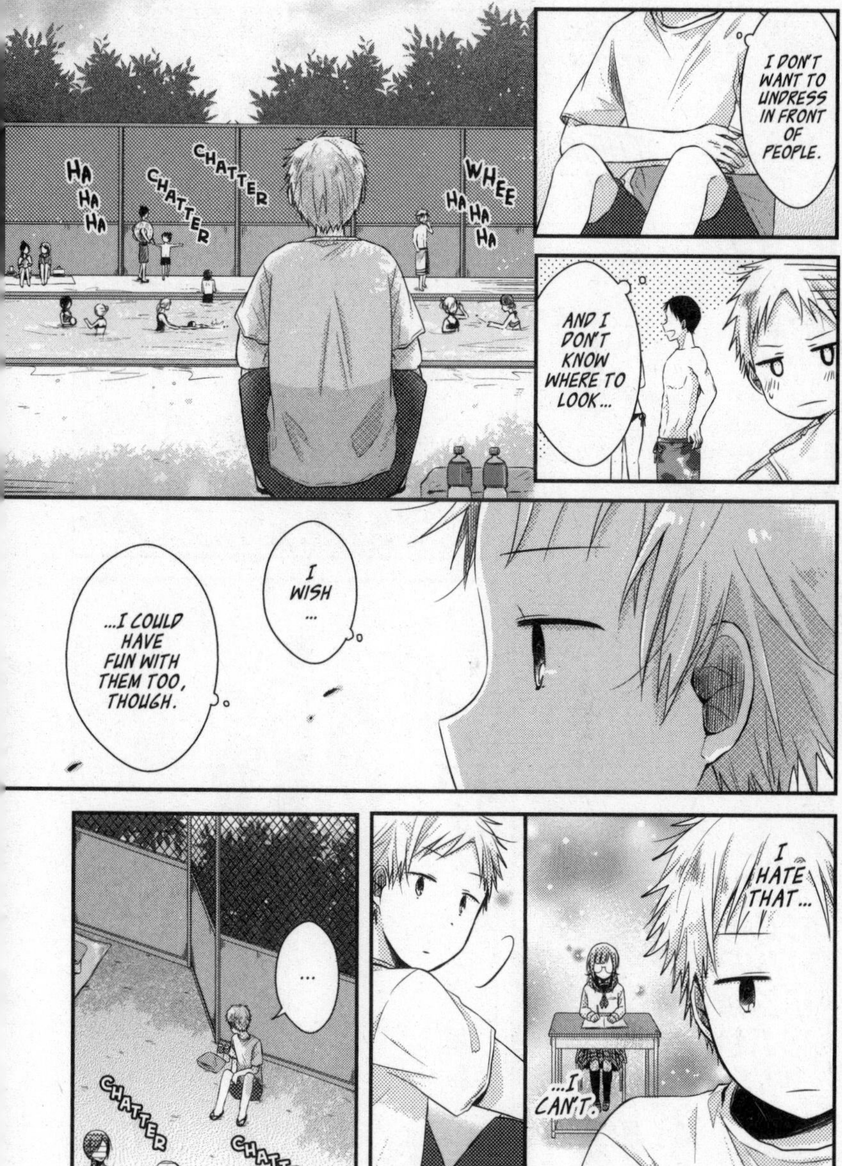
I DON'T WANT TO UNDRESS IN FRONT OF PEOPLE.
AND I DON'T KNOW WHERE TO LOOK...
WHEE
HA HA HA
CHATTER
CHATTER
HA HA HA
I WISH...
...I COULD HAVE FUN WITH THEM TOO, THOUGH.
I HATE THAT...
...I CAN'T.
...
CHATTER
CHATTER

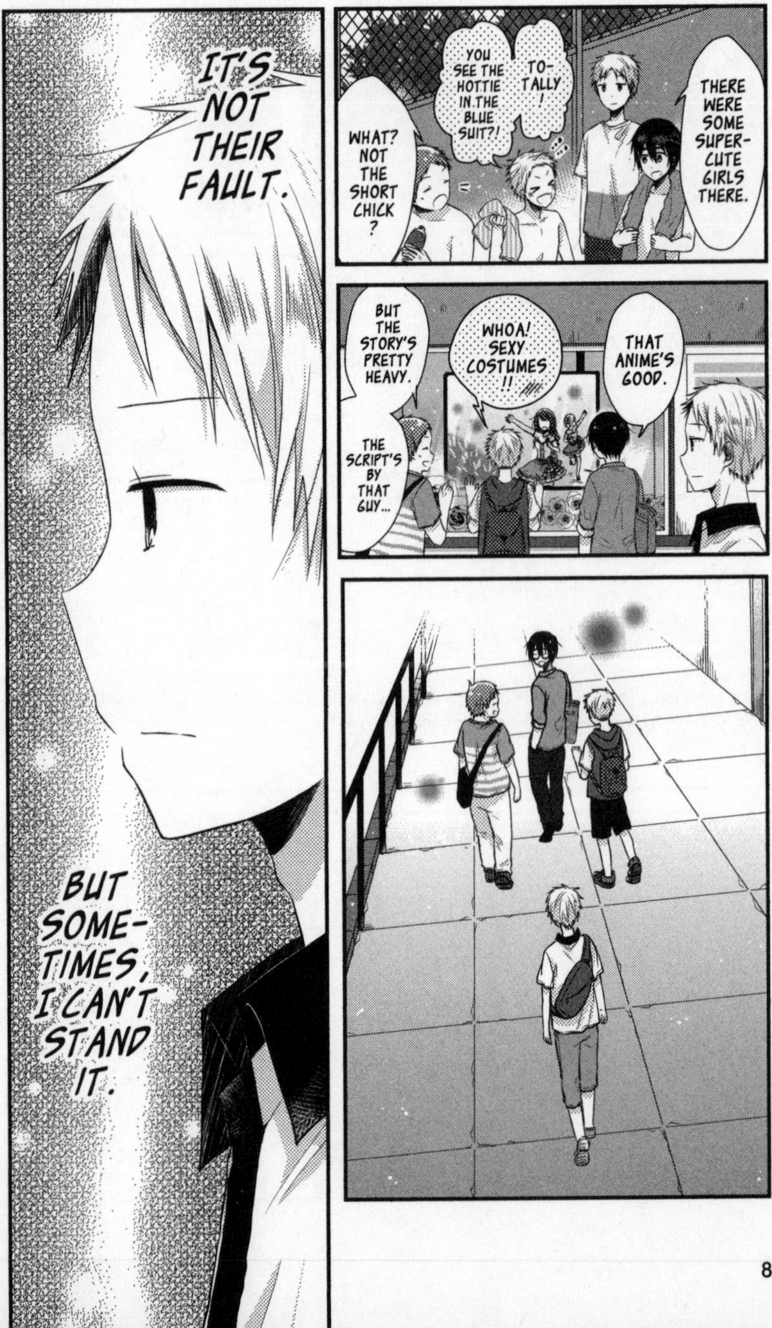
THERE WERE SOME SUPER-CUTE GIRLS THERE.
YOU SEE THE HOTTIE IN THE BLUE SUIT?!
TO-TALLY!
WHAT? NOT THE SHORT CHICK?
THAT ANIME'S GOOD.
WHOA! SEXY COSTUMES!!
BUT THE STORY'S PRETTY HEAVY.
THE SCRIPT'S BY THAT GUY...
IT'S NOT THEIR FAULT.
BUT SOMETIMES, I CAN'T STAND IT.

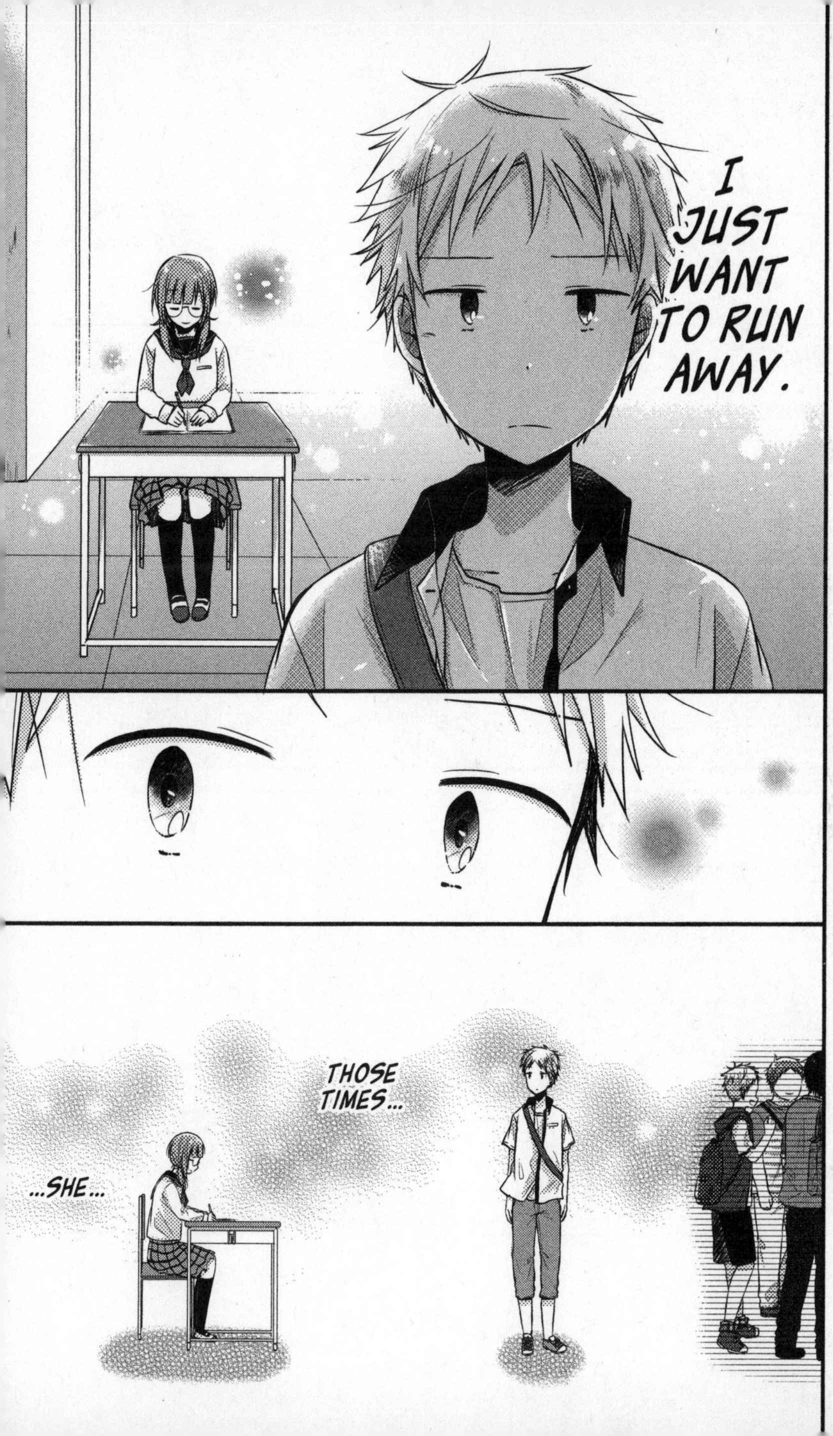
I JUST WANT TO RUN AWAY.
THOSE TIMES...
...SHE...

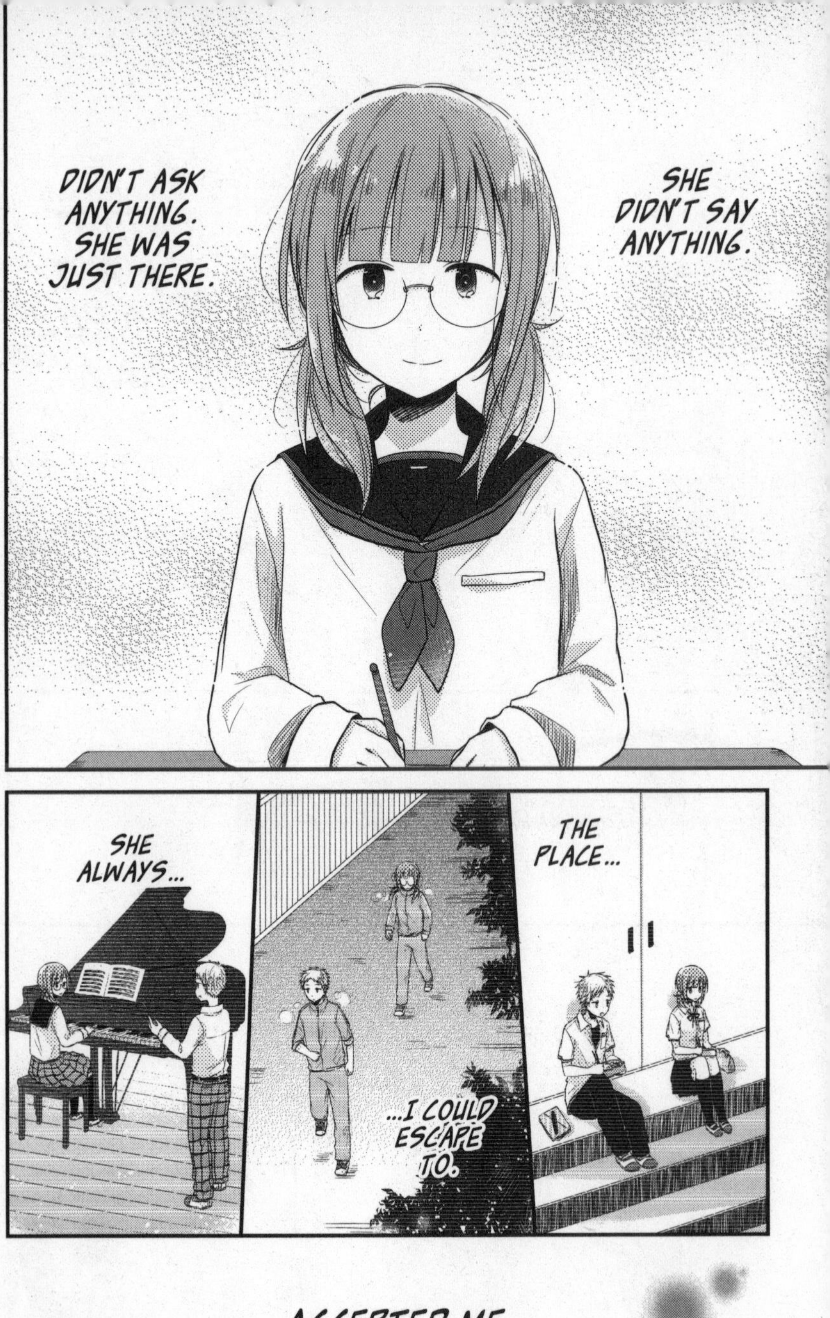
SHE DIDN'T SAY ANYTHING.
DIDN'T ASK ANYTHING. SHE WAS JUST THERE.
THE PLACE...
...I COULD ESCAPE TO.
SHE ALWAYS...
...ACCEPTED ME.

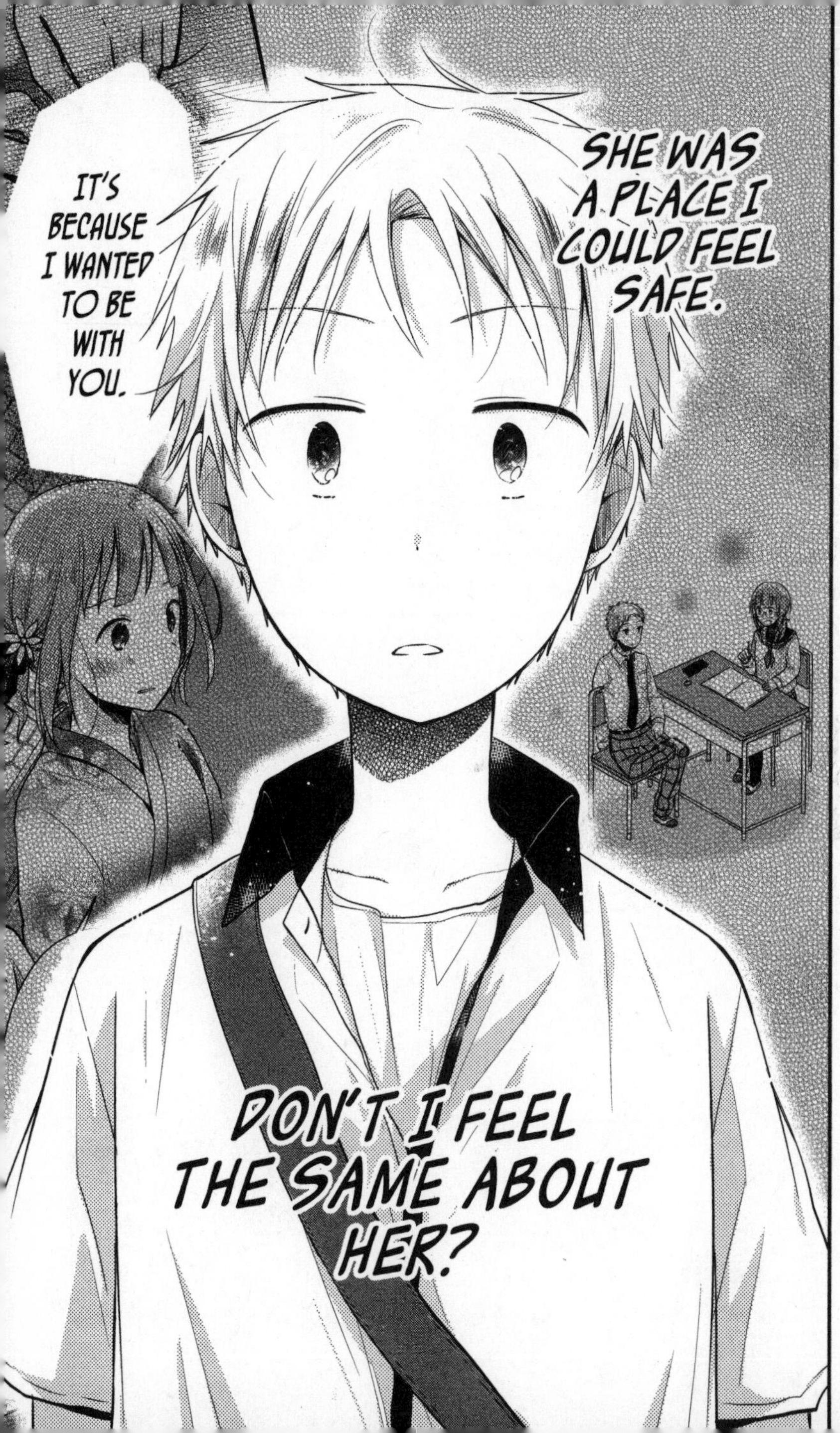
SHE WAS A PLACE I COULD FEEL SAFE.
IT'S BECAUSE I WANTED TO BE WITH YOU.
DON'T I FEEL THE SAME ABOUT HER?

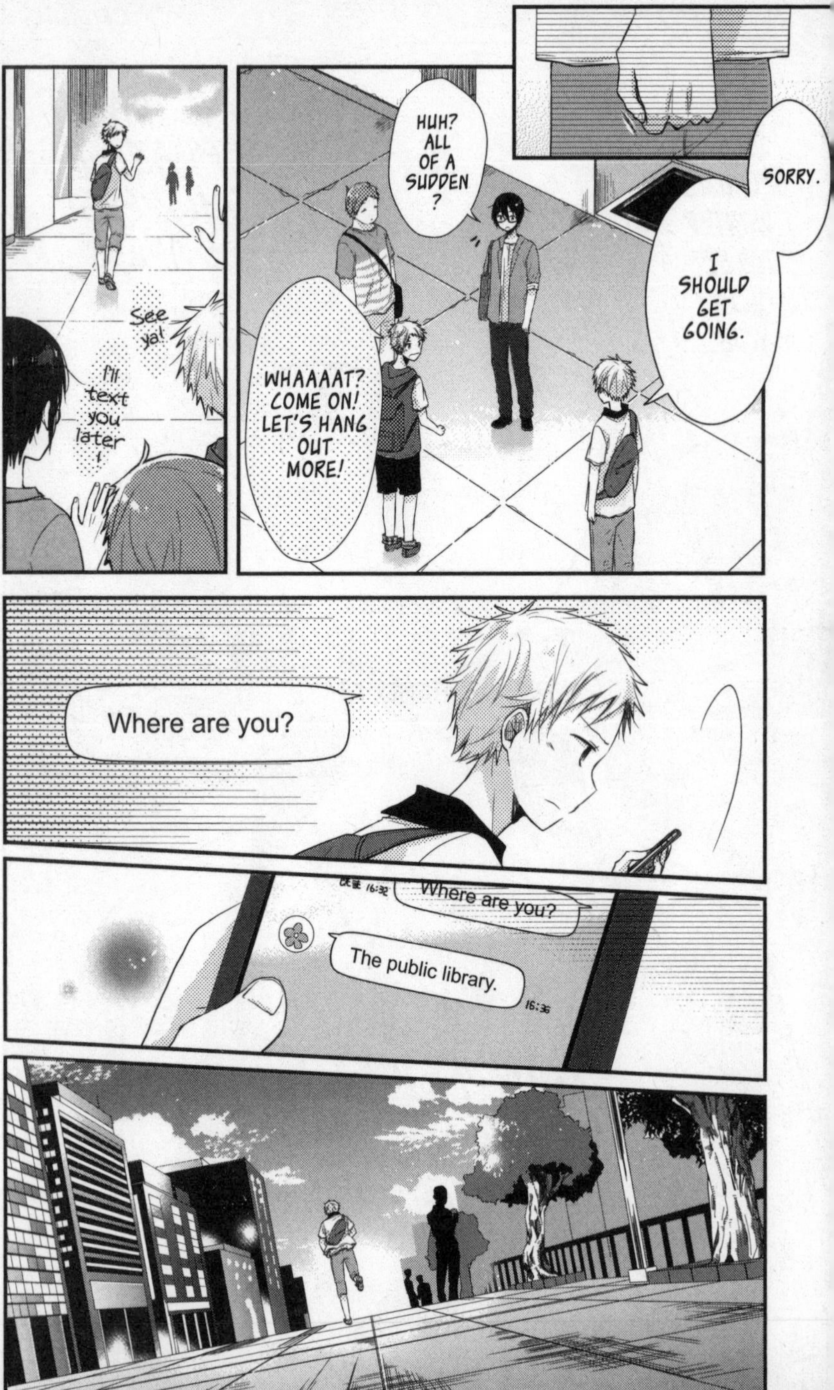
SORRY.
I SHOULD GET GOING.
HUH? ALL OF A SUDDEN?
WHAAAAT? COME ON! LET'S HANG OUT MORE!
See ya!
I'll text you later!
Where are you?
16:32
Where are you?
The public library.
16:36

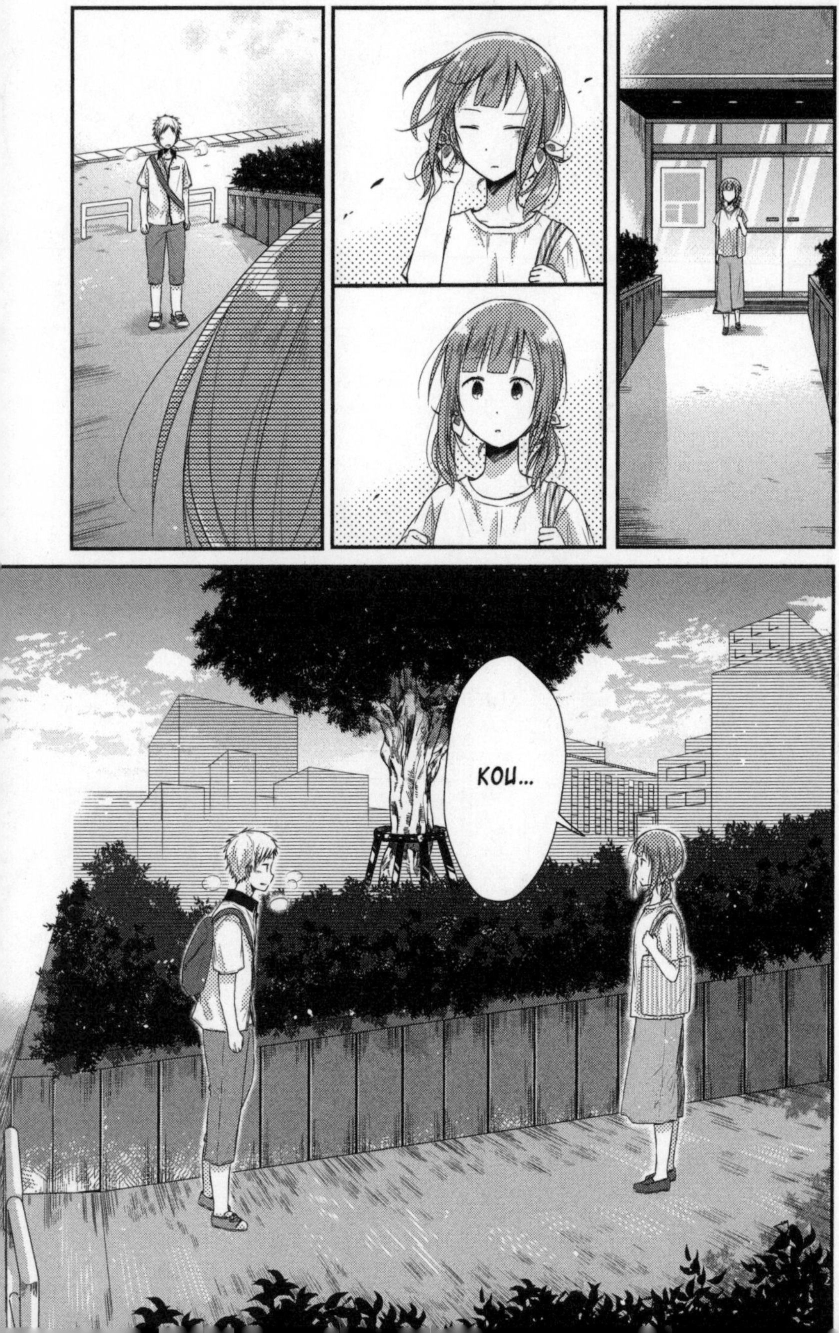
KOU...

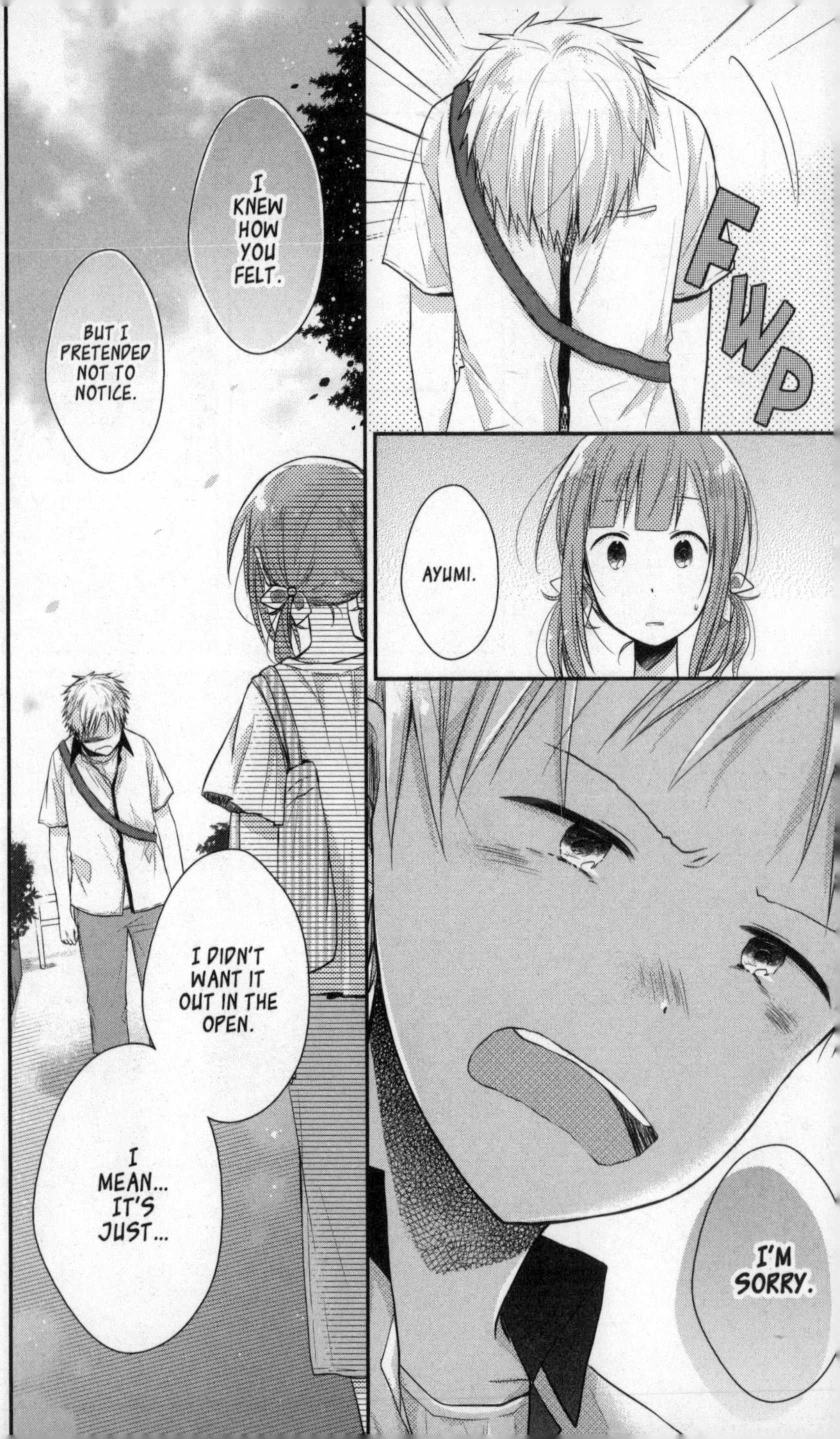
FWP
AYUMI.
I'M SORRY.
I KNEW HOW YOU FELT.
BUT I PRETENDED NOT TO NOTICE.
I DIDN'T WANT IT OUT IN THE OPEN.
I MEAN... IT'S JUST...

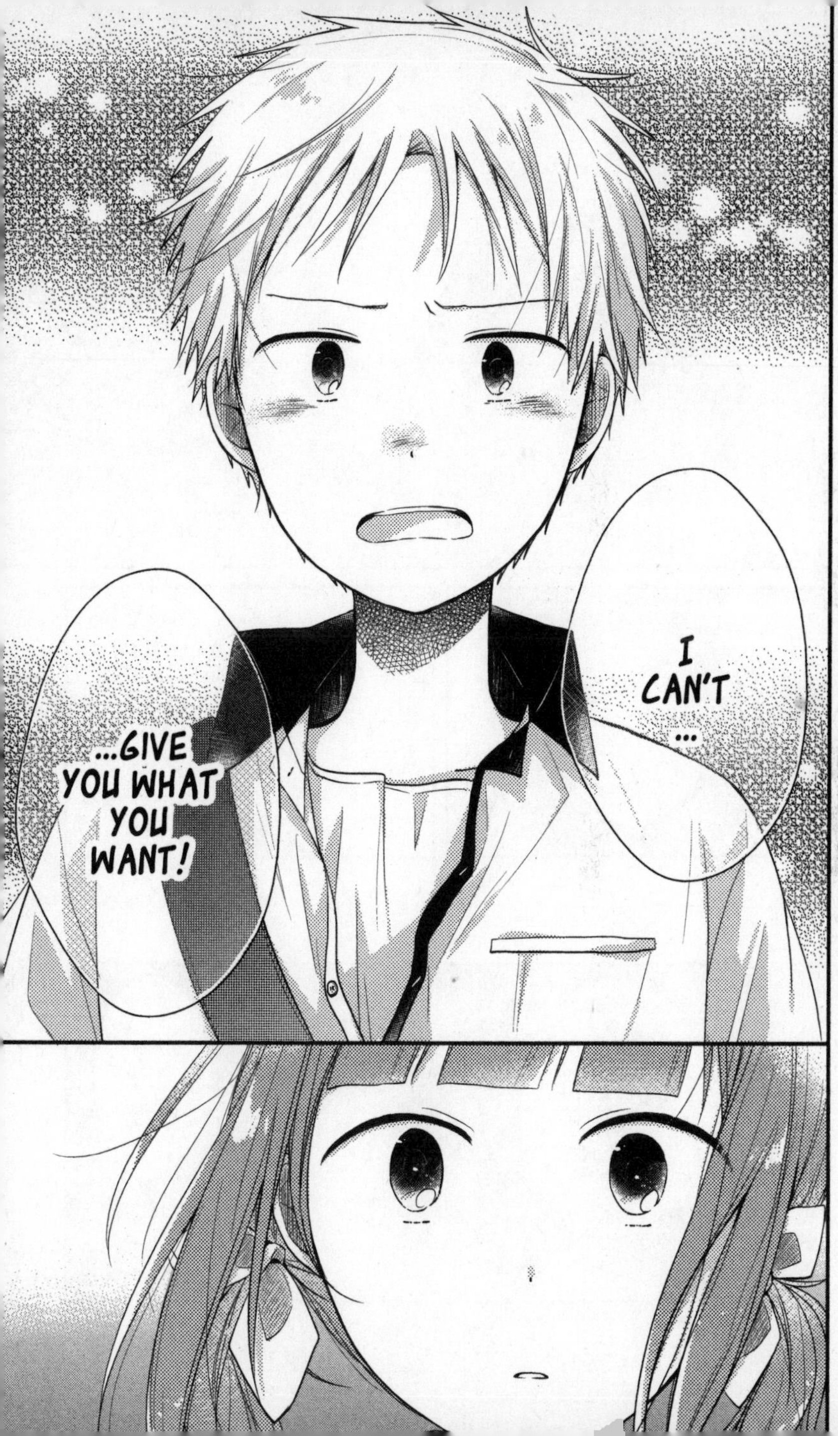
I CAN'T ...
...GIVE YOU WHAT YOU WANT!

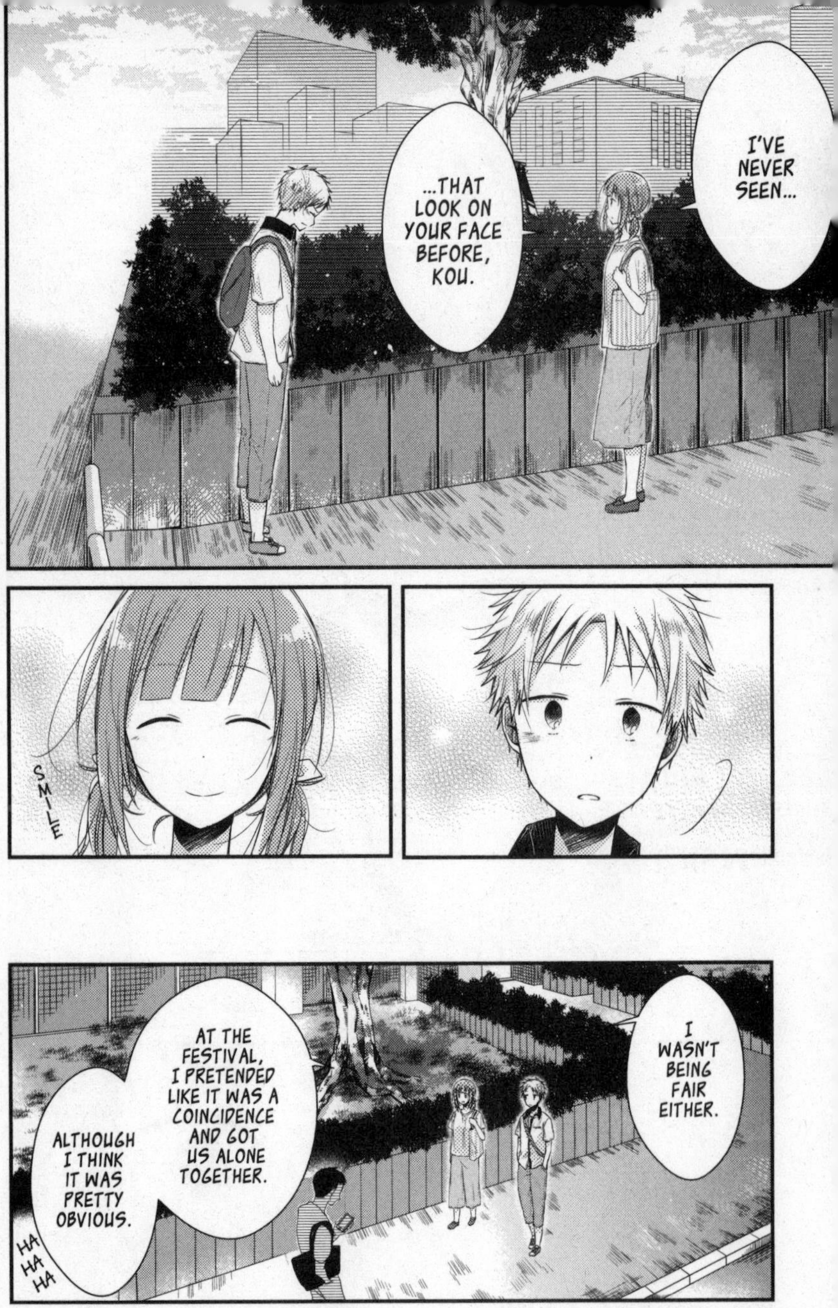
I'VE NEVER SEEN...
...THAT LOOK ON YOUR FACE BEFORE, KOU.
SMILE
I WASN'T BEING FAIR EITHER.
AT THE FESTIVAL, I PRETENDED LIKE IT WAS A COINCIDENCE AND GOT US ALONE TOGETHER.
ALTHOUGH I THINK IT WAS PRETTY OBVIOUS.
HA HA HA

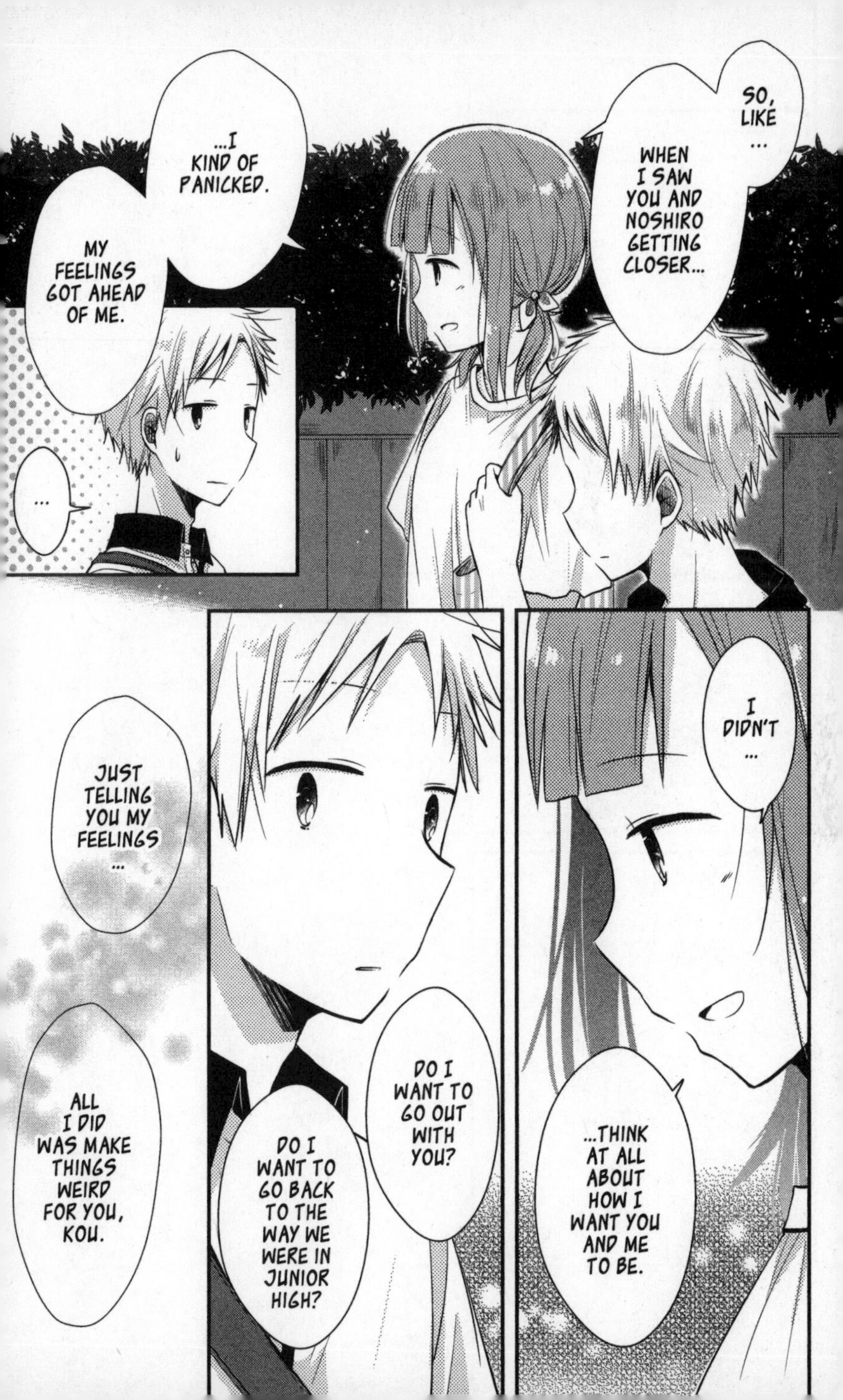
SO, LIKE ...
WHEN I SAW YOU AND NOSHIRO GETTING CLOSER...
...I KIND OF PANICKED.
MY FEELINGS GOT AHEAD OF ME.
...
I DIDN'T ...
...THINK AT ALL ABOUT HOW I WANT YOU AND ME TO BE.
DO I WANT TO GO OUT WITH YOU?
DO I WANT TO GO BACK TO THE WAY WE WERE IN JUNIOR HIGH?
JUST TELLING YOU MY FEELINGS ...
ALL I DID WAS MAKE THINGS WEIRD FOR YOU, KOU.

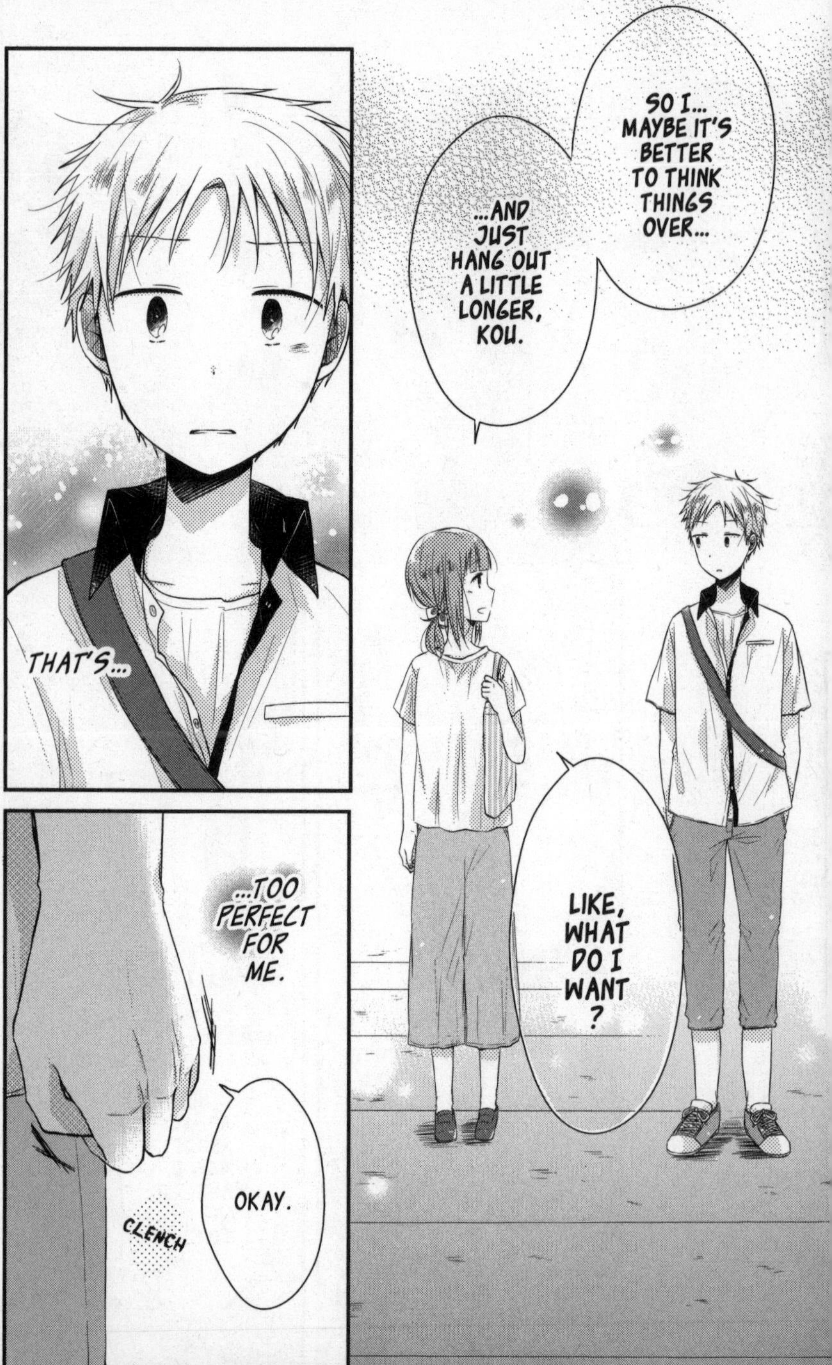
SO I... MAYBE IT'S BETTER TO THINK THINGS OVER...
...AND JUST HANG OUT A LITTLE LONGER, KOU.
LIKE, WHAT DO I WANT?
THAT'S...
...TOO PERFECT FOR ME.
OKAY.
CLENCH

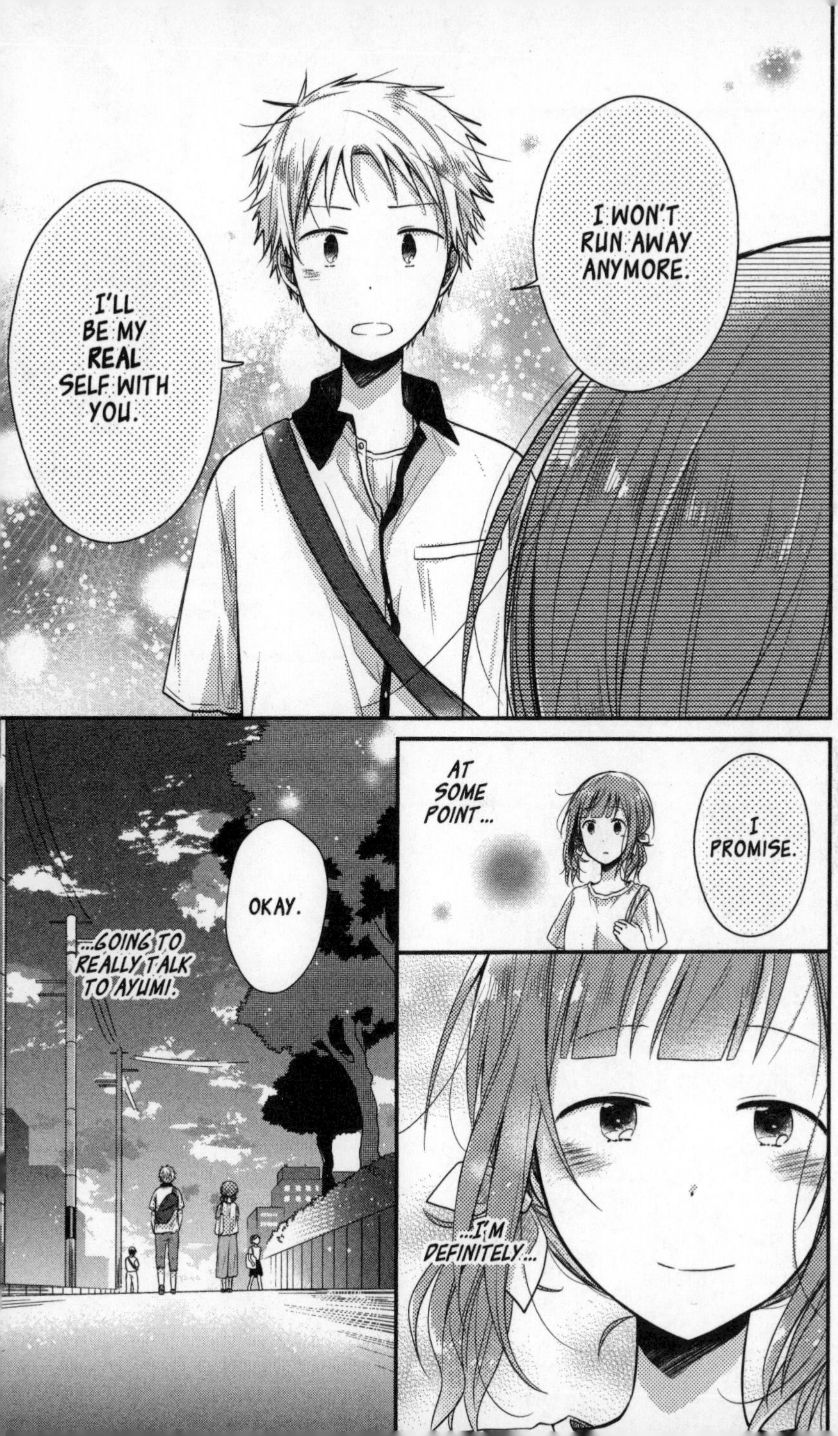
I WON'T RUN AWAY ANYMORE.
I'LL BE MY REAL SELF WITH YOU.
I PROMISE.
AT SOME POINT...
...I'M DEFINITELY...
OKAY.
...GOING TO REALLY TALK TO AYUMI.

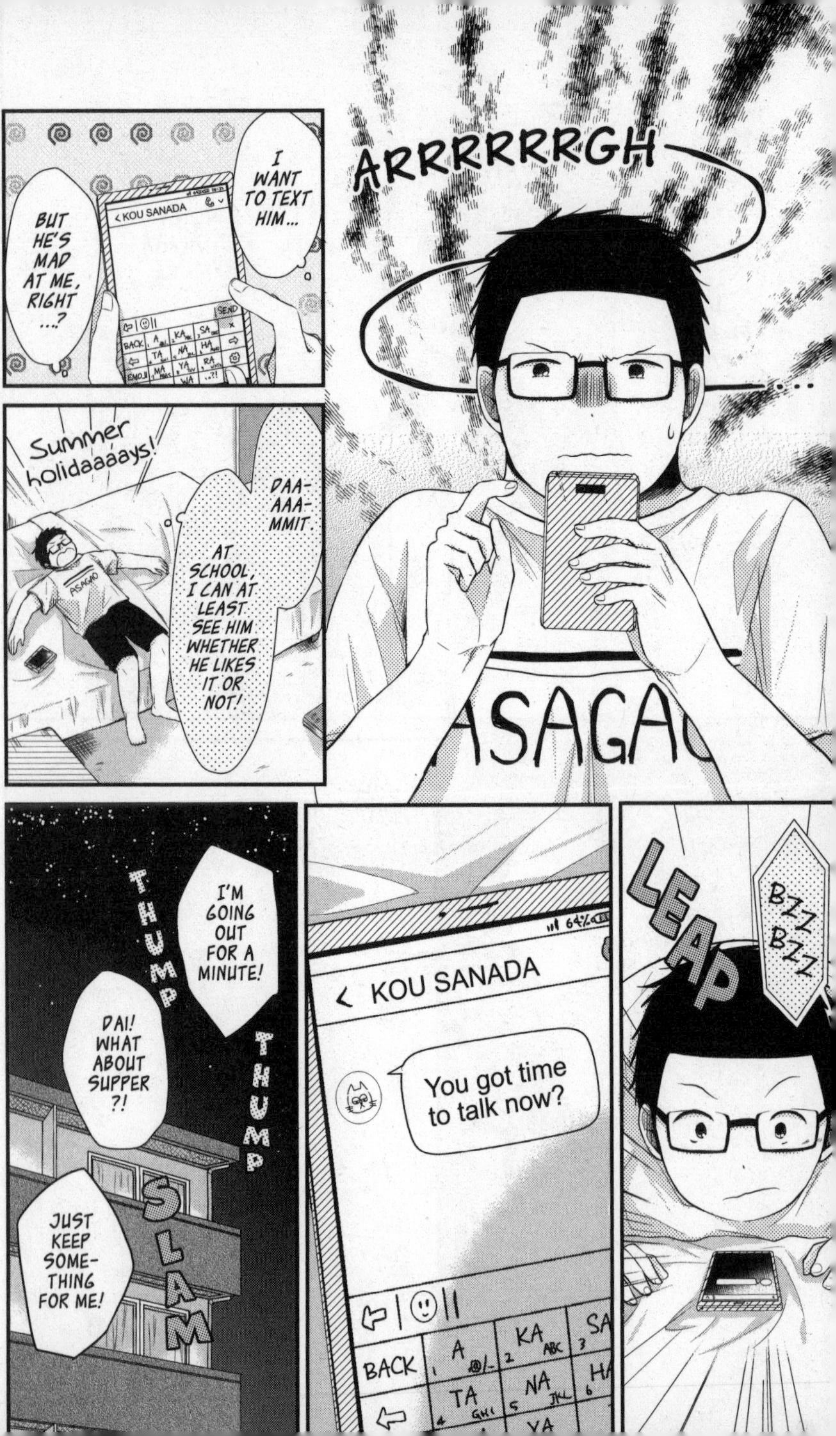
ARRRRRRGH
...
I WANT TO TEXT HIM...
BUT HE'S MAD AT ME, RIGHT ...?
KOU SANADA
SEND
BACK
A
KA
SA
TA
NA
HA
EMOJI
MA
YA
RA
WA
Summer holidaaaays!
DAA-AAAM-MMIT.
AT SCHOOL, I CAN AT LEAST SEE HIM WHETHER HE LIKES IT OR NOT!
ASAGAO
ASAGAO
BZZ BZZ
LEAP
KOU SANADA
You got time to talk now?
BACK
A
KA
SA
TA
NA
YA
I'M GOING OUT FOR A MINUTE!
THUMP
THUMP
DAI! WHAT ABOUT SUPPER?!
JUST KEEP SOME-THING FOR ME!
SLAM

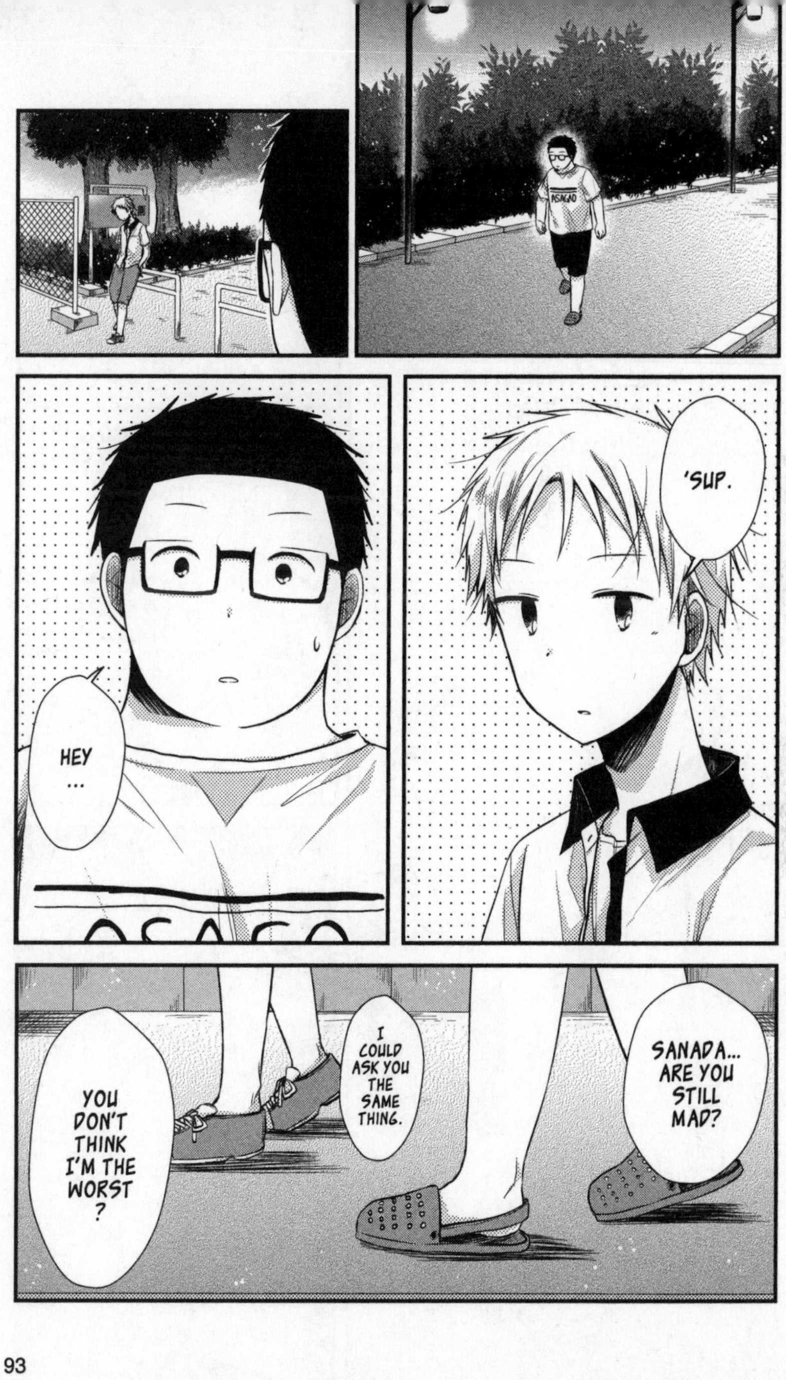
'SUP.
HEY ...
SANADA... ARE YOU STILL MAD?
I COULD ASK YOU THE SAME THING.
YOU DON'T THINK I'M THE WORST?

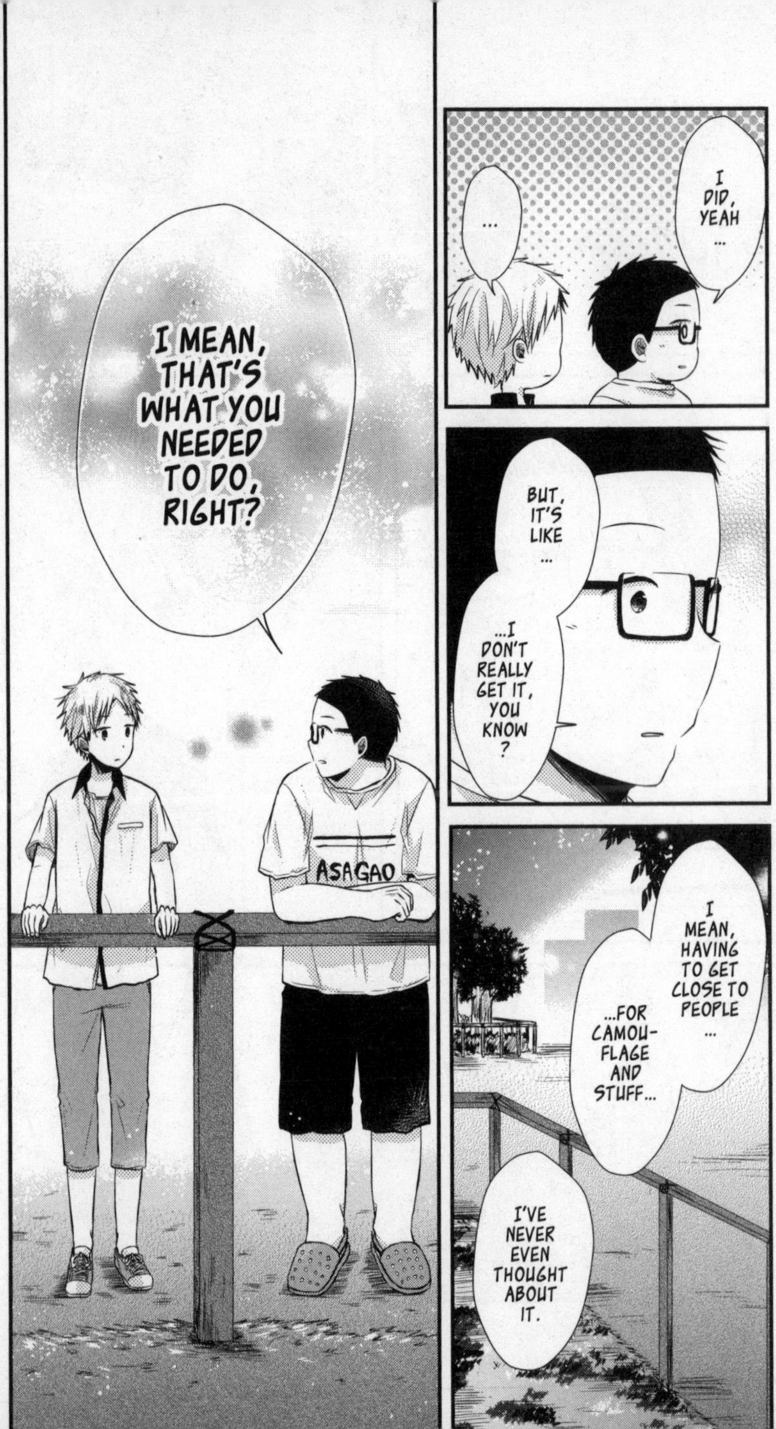
I DID, YEAH ...
...
BUT, IT'S LIKE ...
...I DON'T REALLY GET IT, YOU KNOW?
I MEAN, HAVING TO GET CLOSE TO PEOPLE ...
...FOR CAMOU-FLAGE AND STUFF...
I'VE NEVER EVEN THOUGHT ABOUT IT.
I MEAN, THAT'S WHAT YOU NEEDED TO DO, RIGHT?
ASAGAO

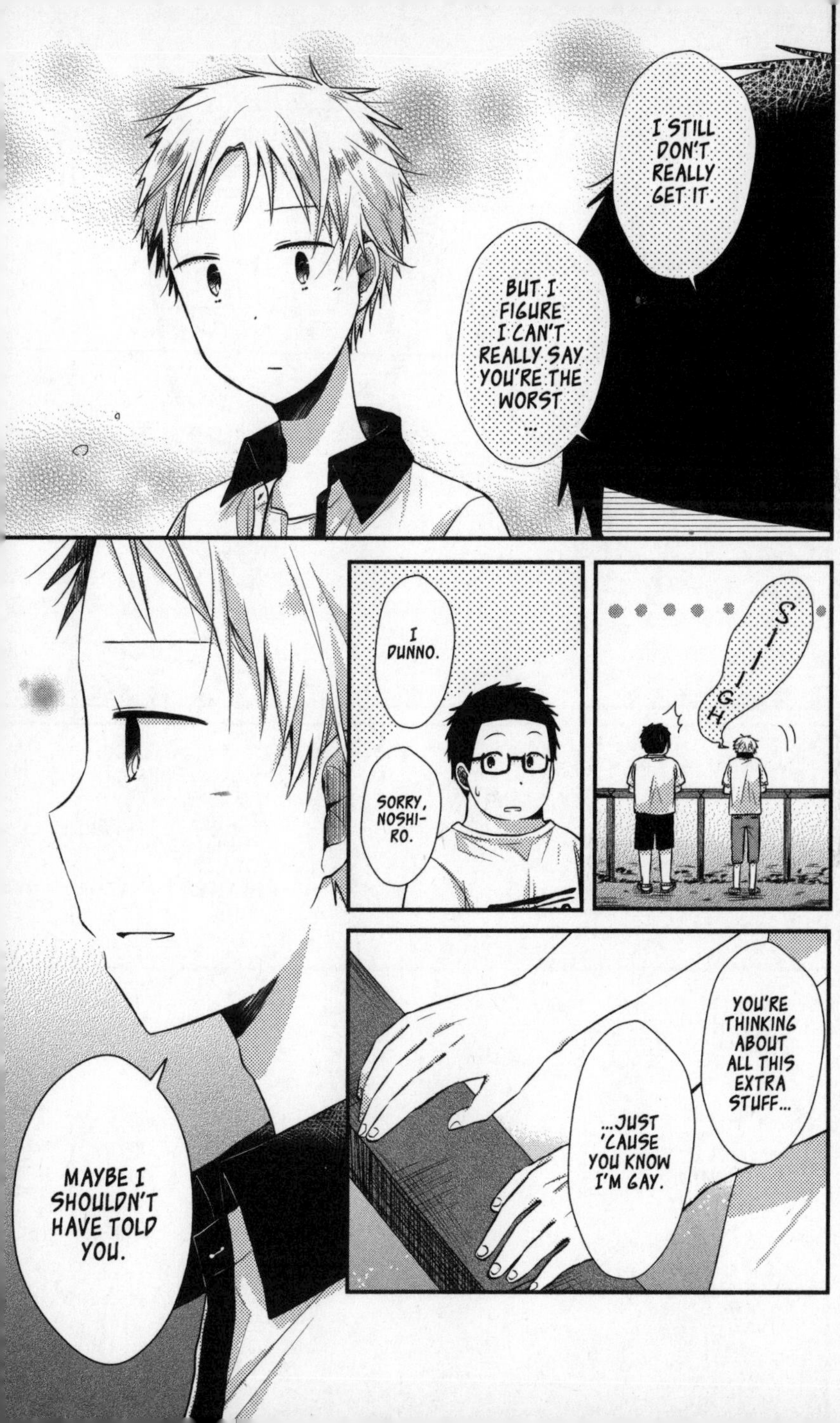
I STILL DON'T REALLY GET IT.
BUT I FIGURE I CAN'T REALLY SAY YOU'RE THE WORST ...
S-I-I-I-I-GH
I DUNNO.
SORRY, NOSHIRO.
YOU'RE THINKING ABOUT ALL THIS EXTRA STUFF...
...JUST 'CAUSE YOU KNOW I'M GAY.
MAYBE I SHOULDN'T HAVE TOLD YOU.

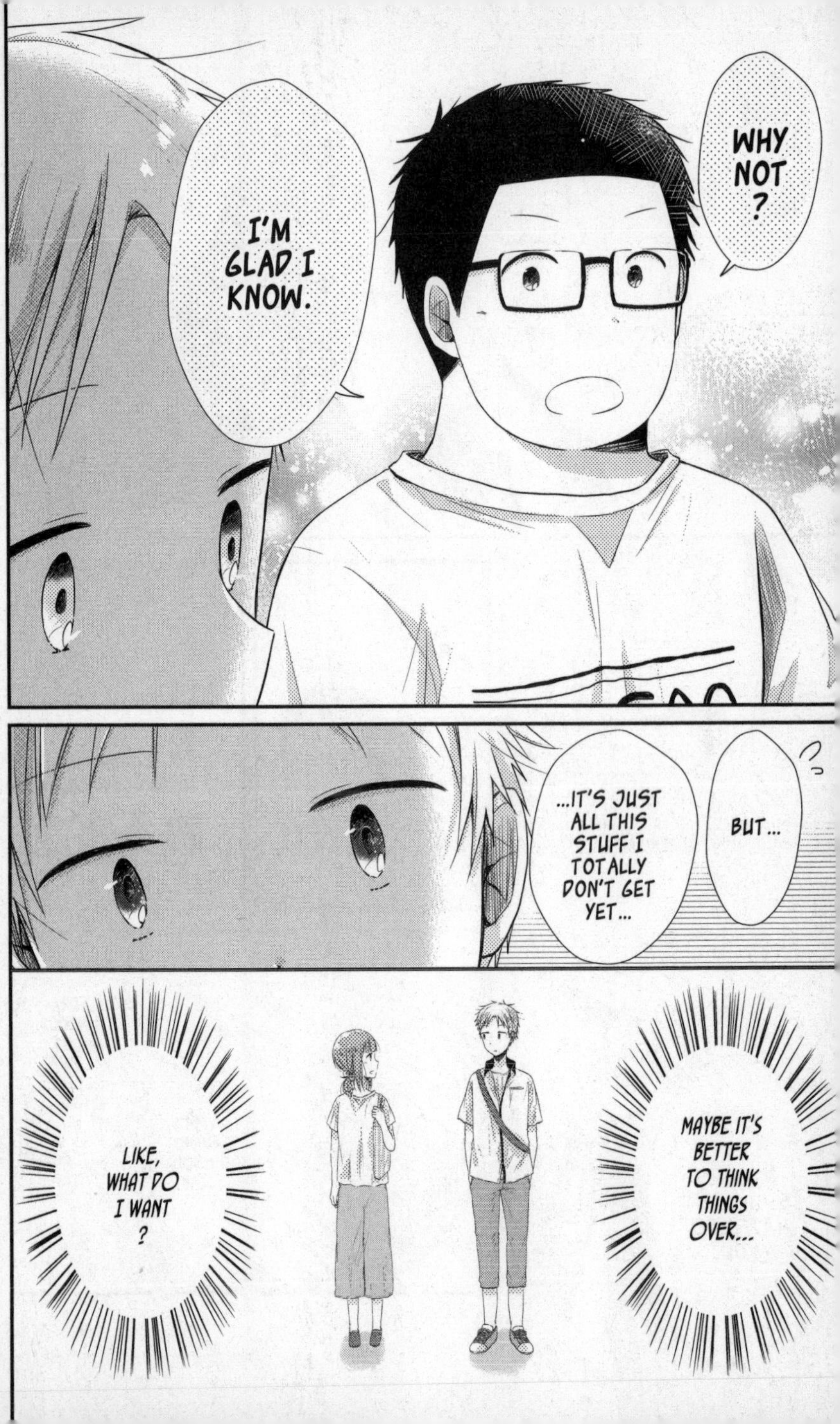
WHY NOT?
I'M GLAD I KNOW.
BUT...
...IT'S JUST ALL THIS STUFF I TOTALLY DON'T GET YET...
MAYBE IT'S BETTER TO THINK THINGS OVER...
LIKE, WHAT DO I WANT?

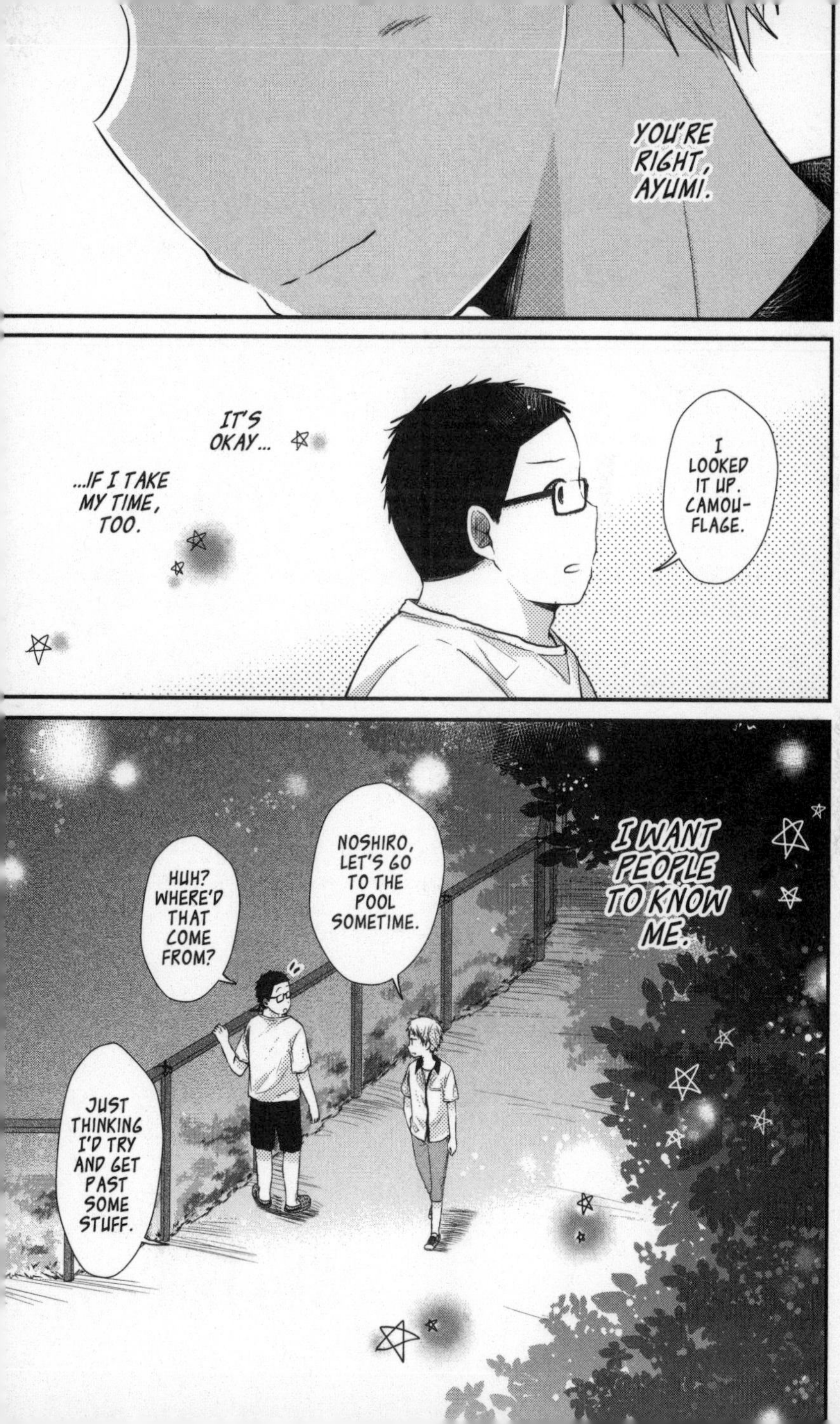
YOU'RE RIGHT, AYUMI.
I LOOKED IT UP. CAMOU-FLAGE.
IT'S OKAY...
...IF I TAKE MY TIME, TOO.
I WANT PEOPLE TO KNOW ME.
NOSHIRO, LET'S GO TO THE POOL SOMETIME.
HUH? WHERE'D THAT COME FROM?
JUST THINKING I'D TRY AND GET PAST SOME STUFF.

That Blue
Sky Feeling

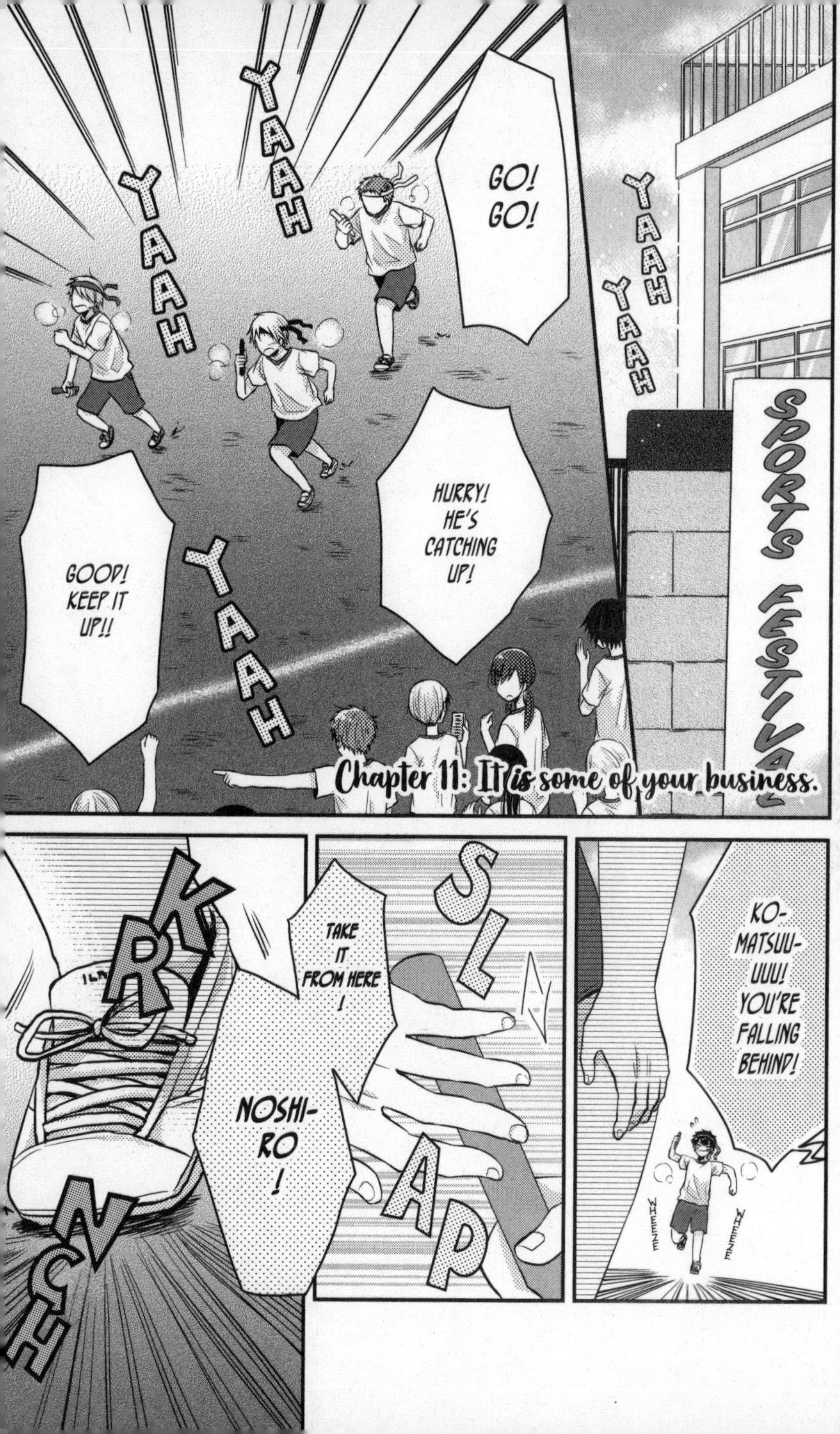
YAAH YAAH
SPORTS FESTIVAL
GO! GO!
YAAH
YAAH
HURRY! HE'S CATCHING UP!
YAAH
GOOD! KEEP IT UP!!
Chapter 11: It is some of your business.
KO-MATSUU-UUU! YOU'RE FALLING BEHIND!
WHEEZE
WHEEZE
SLAP
TAKE IT FROM HERE!
NOSHI-RO!
KRNCH

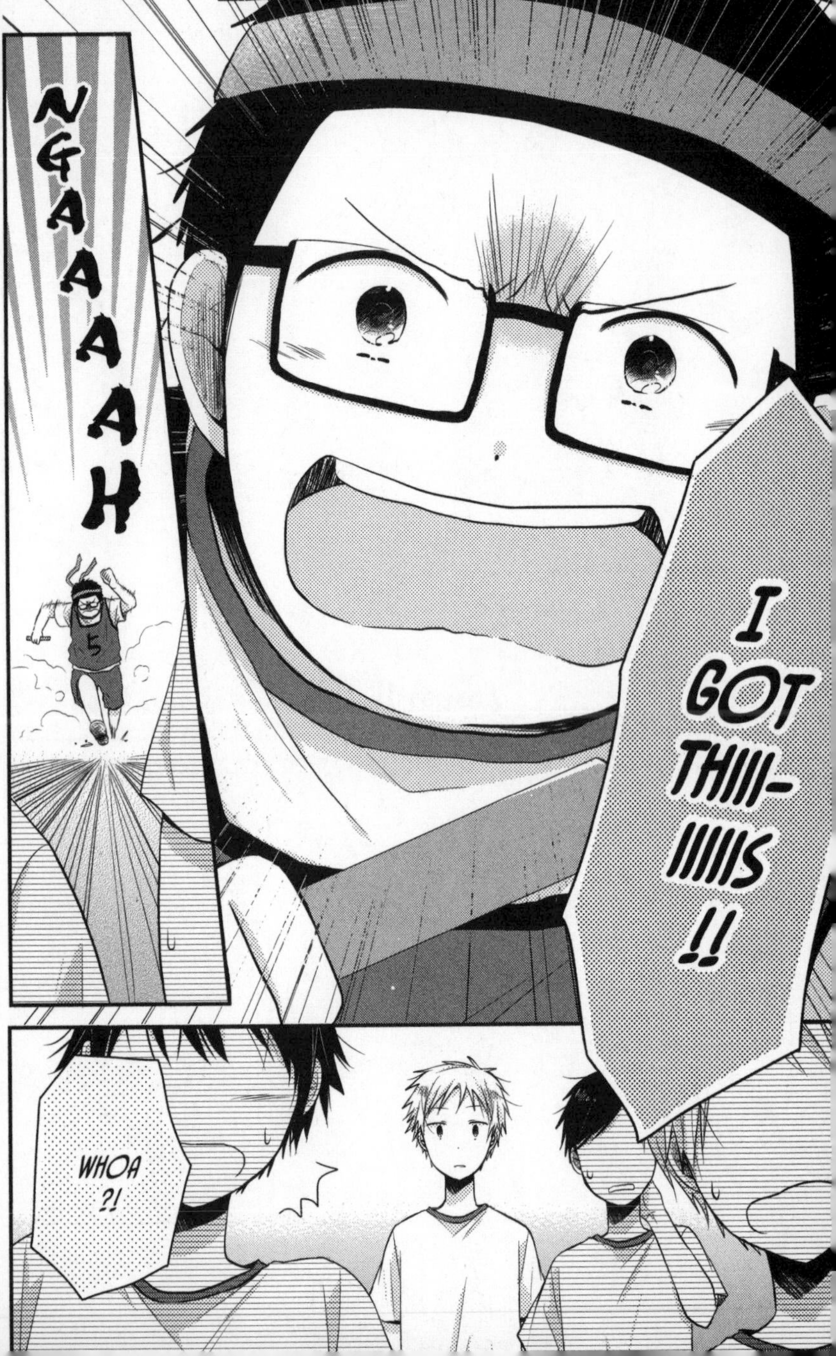
I GOT THIII-IIIIS!!
NGAAAH
WHOA?!

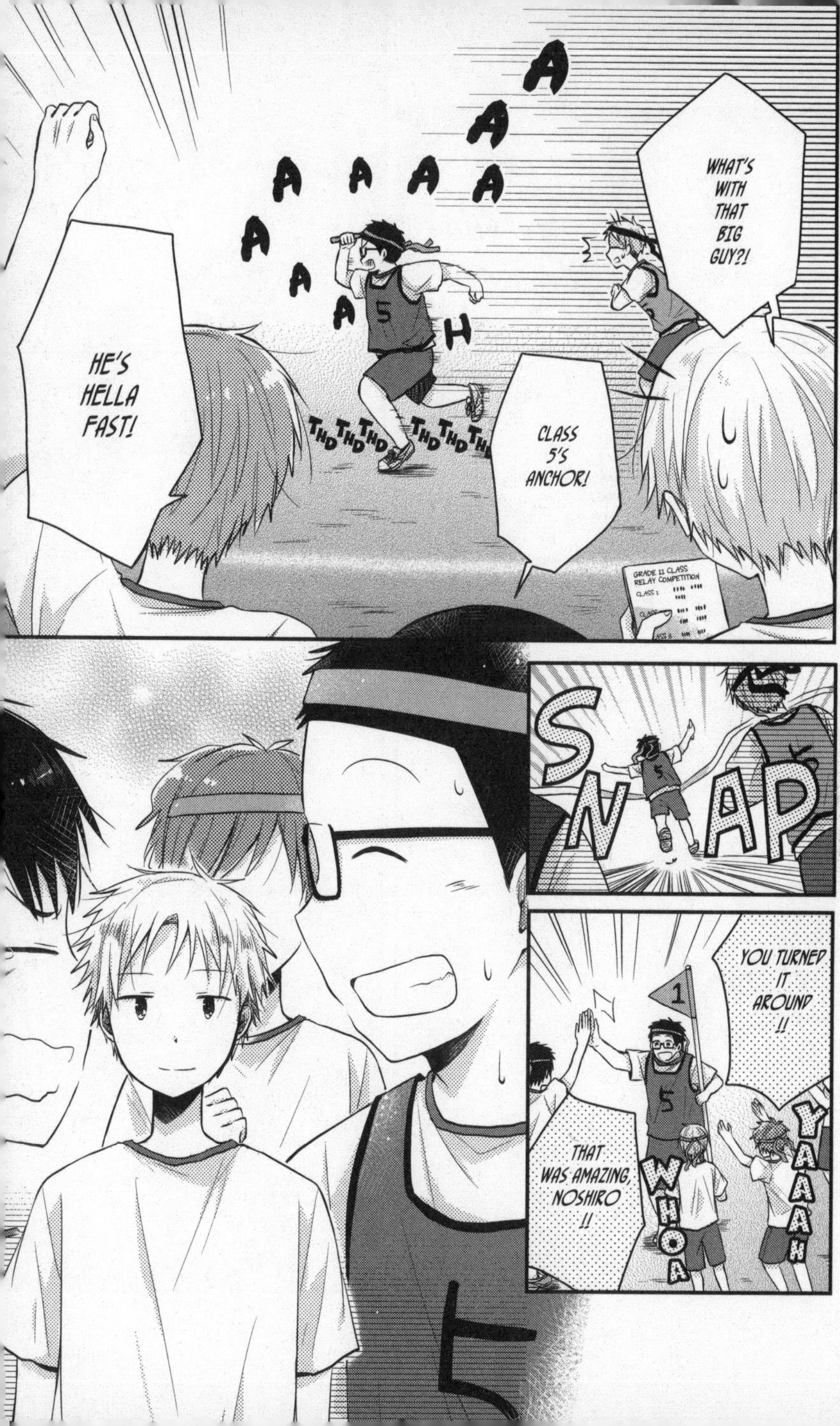
WHAT'S WITH THAT BIG GUY?!
AAAAAAAAAH
CLASS 5'S ANCHOR!
HE'S HELLA FAST!
THD THD THD THD THD THD
GRADE 11 CLASS RELAY COMPETITION
CLASS 1
SNAP
YOU TURNED IT AROUND!!
YAAAAH
THAT WAS AMAZING, NOSHIRO!!
WHOA

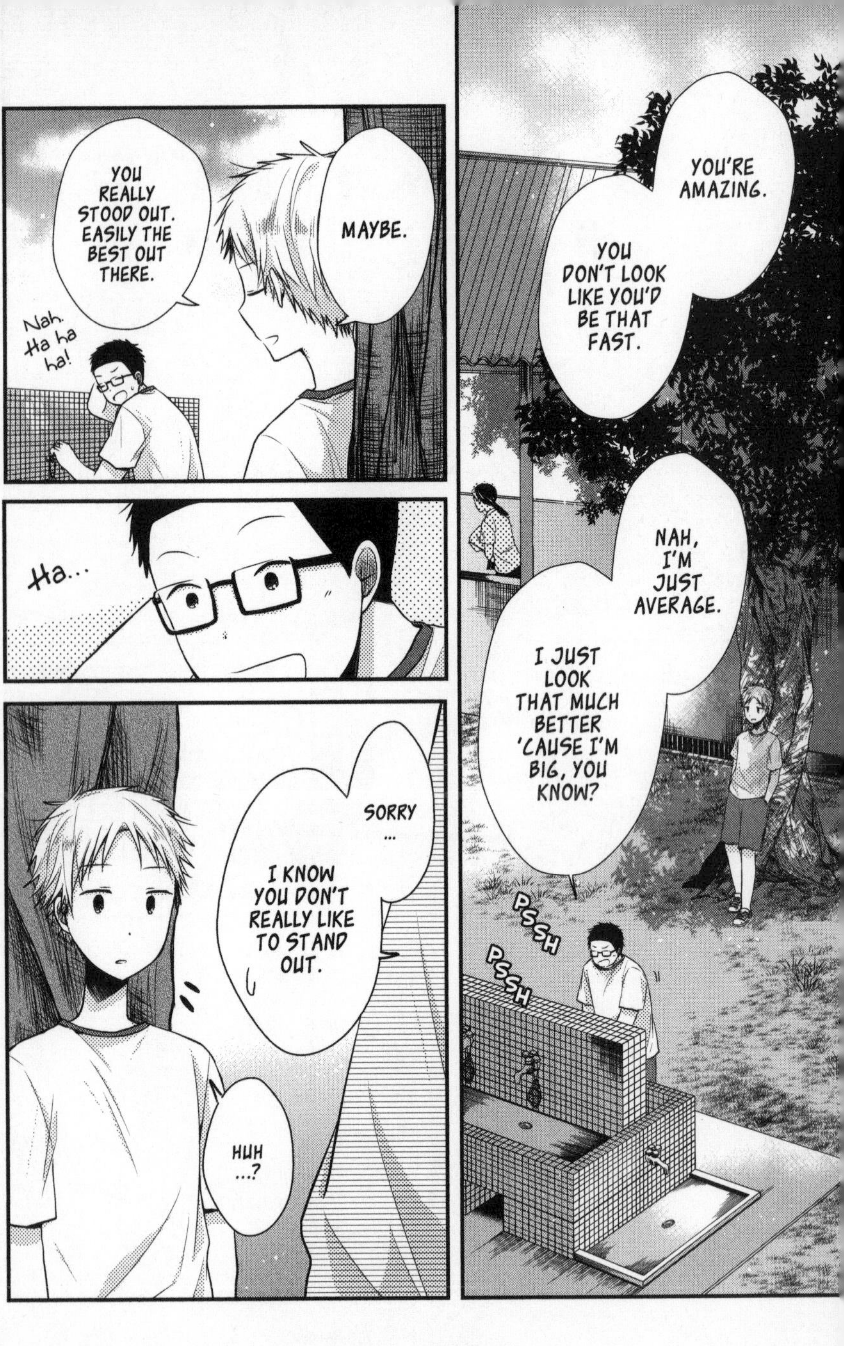
YOU'RE AMAZING.
YOU DON'T LOOK LIKE YOU'D BE THAT FAST.
NAH, I'M JUST AVERAGE.
I JUST LOOK THAT MUCH BETTER 'CAUSE I'M BIG, YOU KNOW?
PSSH
PSSH
YOU REALLY STOOD OUT. EASILY THE BEST OUT THERE.
MAYBE.
Nah. Ha ha ha!
Ha...
SORRY...
I KNOW YOU DON'T REALLY LIKE TO STAND OUT.
HUH...?

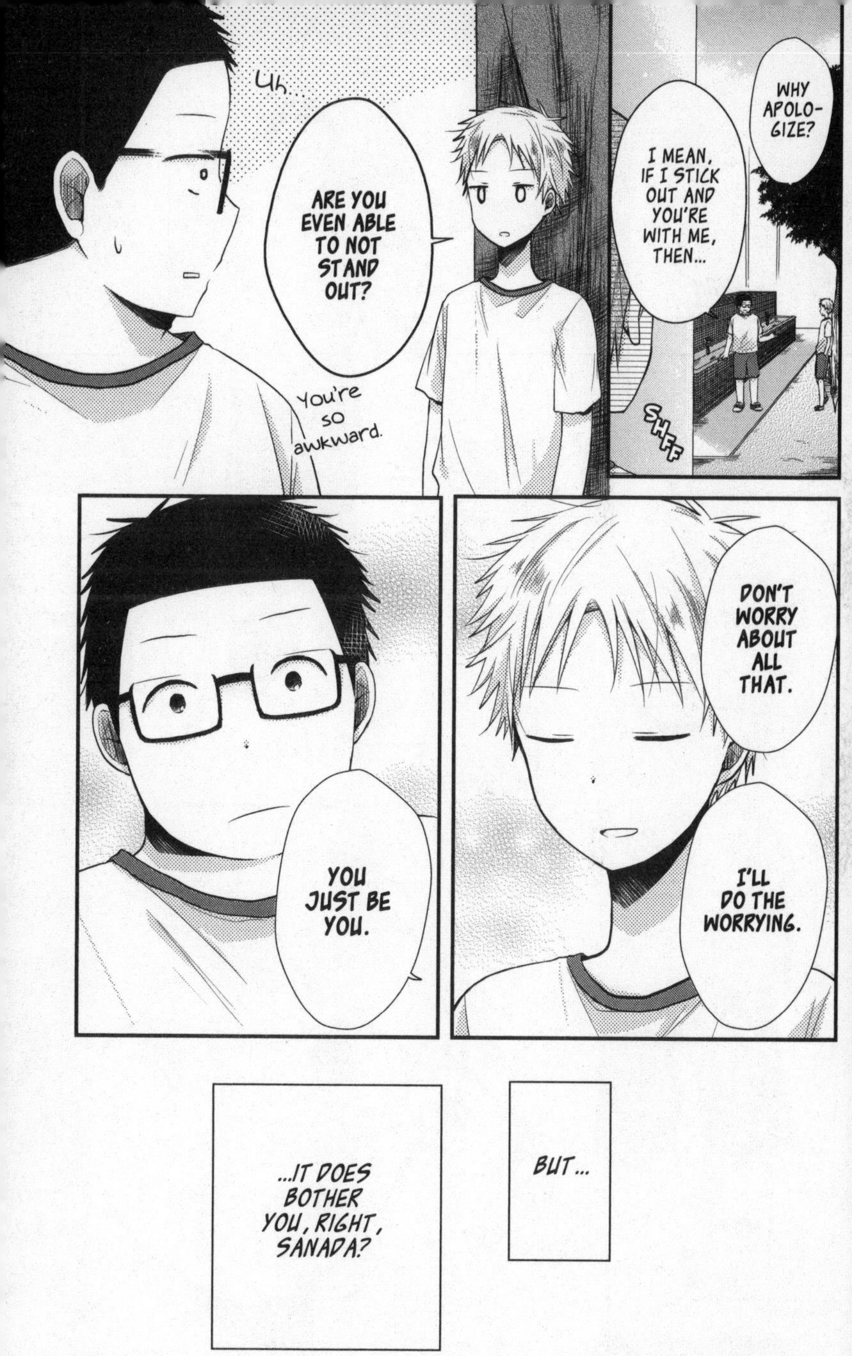
WHY APOLOGIZE?
I MEAN, IF I STICK OUT AND YOU'RE WITH ME, THEN...
SHFF
ARE YOU EVEN ABLE TO NOT STAND OUT?
You're so awkward.
Uh...
DON'T WORRY ABOUT ALL THAT.
I'LL DO THE WORRYING.
YOU JUST BE YOU.
BUT...
...IT DOES BOTHER YOU, RIGHT, SANADA?

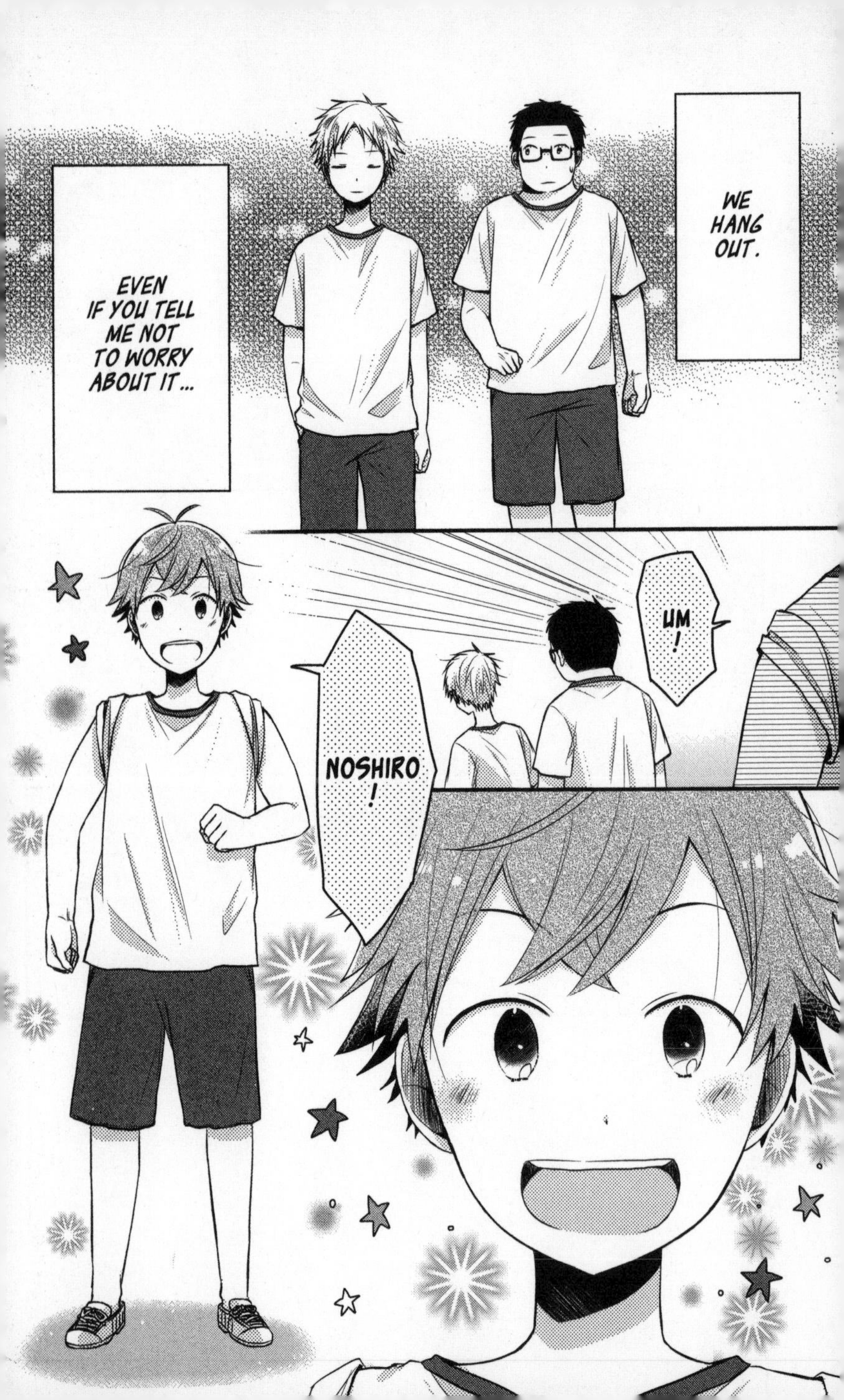
WE HANG OUT.
EVEN IF YOU TELL ME NOT TO WORRY ABOUT IT...
UM!
NOSHIRO!

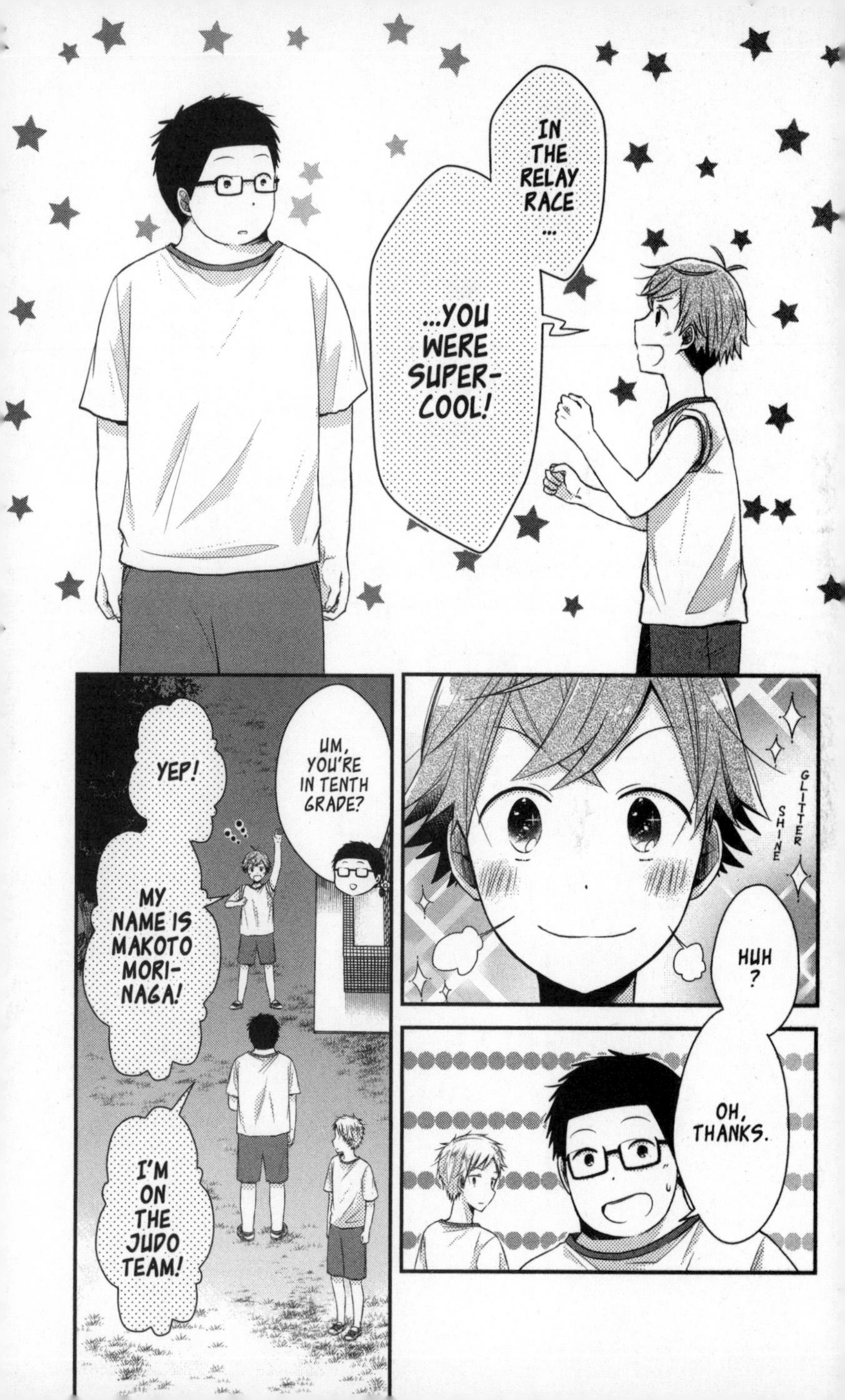
IN THE RELAY RACE ...
...YOU WERE SUPER-COOL!
GLITTER
SHINE
HUH?
OH, THANKS.
UM, YOU'RE IN TENTH GRADE?
YEP!
MY NAME IS MAKOTO MORI-NAGA!
I'M ON THE JUDO TEAM!

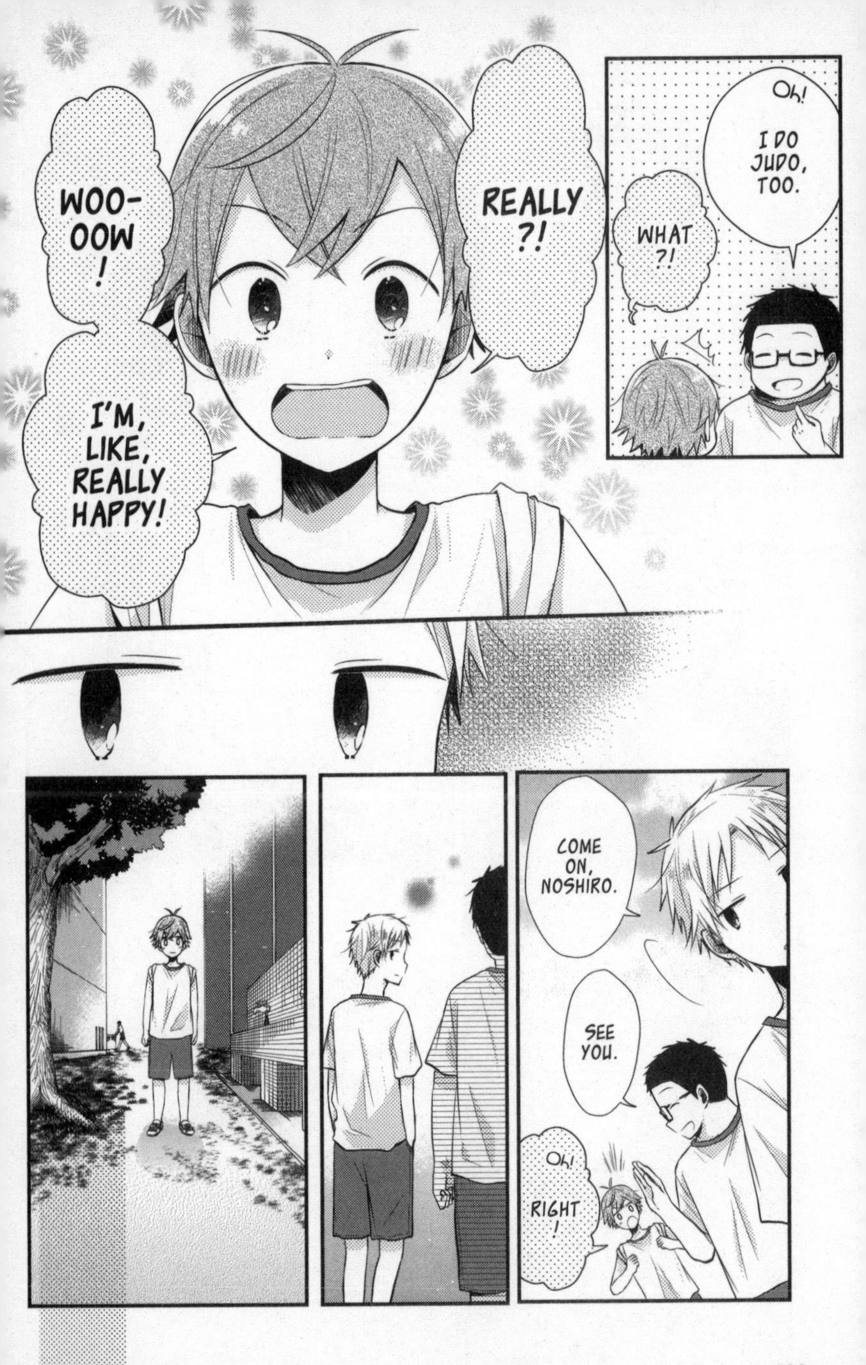
Oh!
I DO JUDO, TOO.
WHAT?!
REALLY?!
WOOO-OOW!
I'M, LIKE, REALLY HAPPY!
COME ON, NOSHIRO.
SEE YOU.
Oh!
RIGHT!

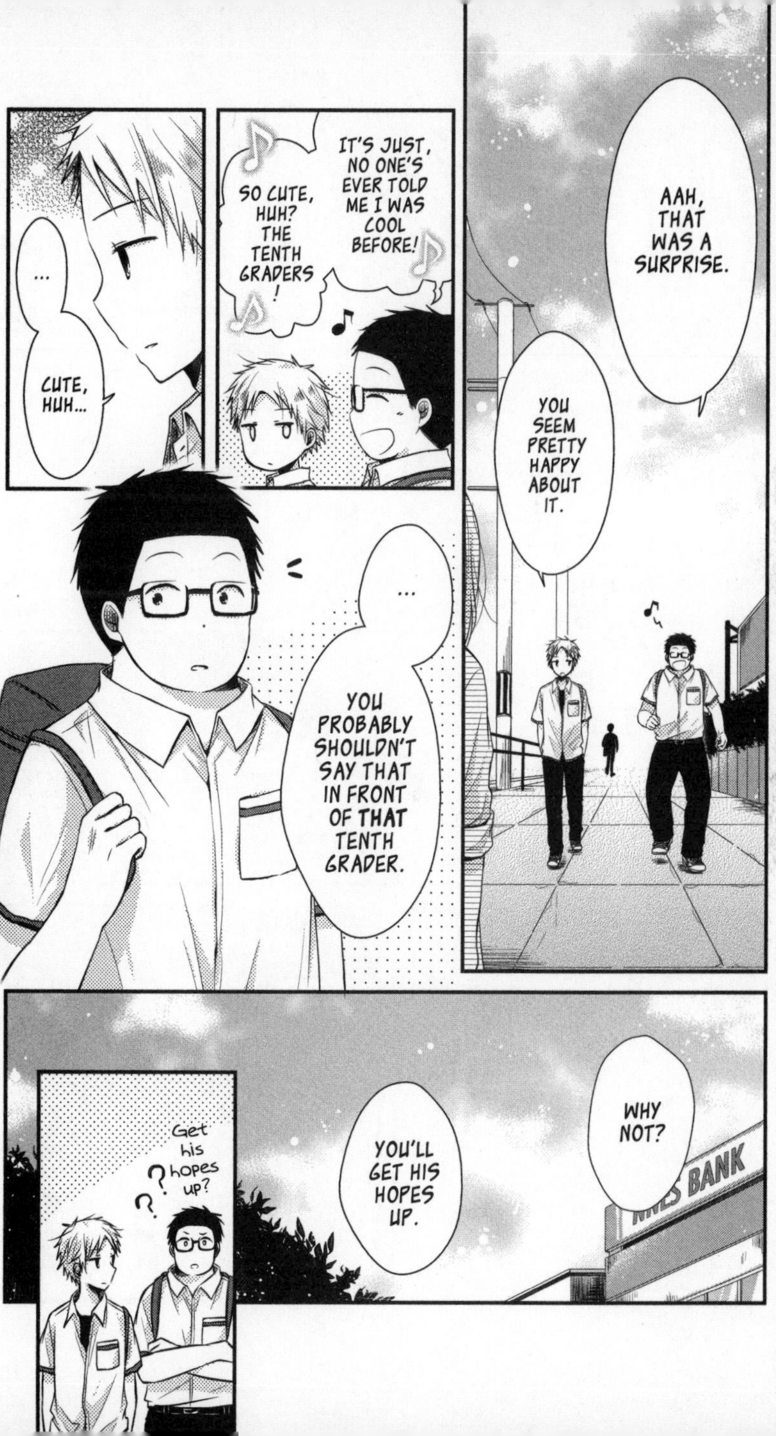
AAH, THAT WAS A SURPRISE.
YOU SEEM PRETTY HAPPY ABOUT IT.
IT'S JUST, NO ONE'S EVER TOLD ME I WAS COOL BEFORE!
SO CUTE, HUH? THE TENTH GRADERS!
...
CUTE, HUH...
...
YOU PROBABLY SHOULDN'T SAY THAT IN FRONT OF THAT TENTH GRADER.
WHY NOT?
YOU'LL GET HIS HOPES UP.
Get his hopes up?

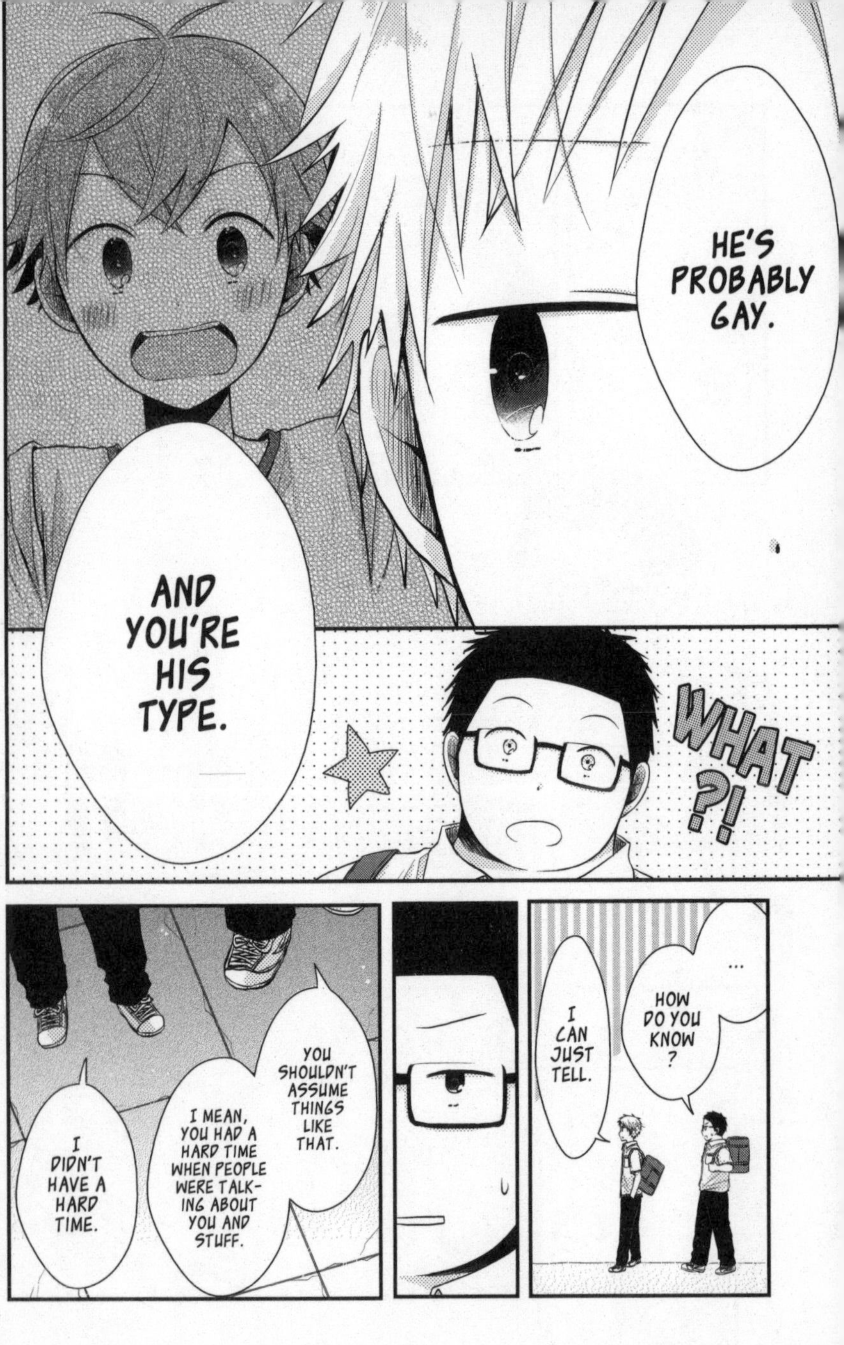
HE'S PROBABLY GAY.
AND YOU'RE HIS TYPE.
WHAT?!
...
HOW DO YOU KNOW?
I CAN JUST TELL.
YOU SHOULDN'T ASSUME THINGS LIKE THAT.
I MEAN, YOU HAD A HARD TIME WHEN PEOPLE WERE TALK-ING ABOUT YOU AND STUFF.
I DIDN'T HAVE A HARD TIME.

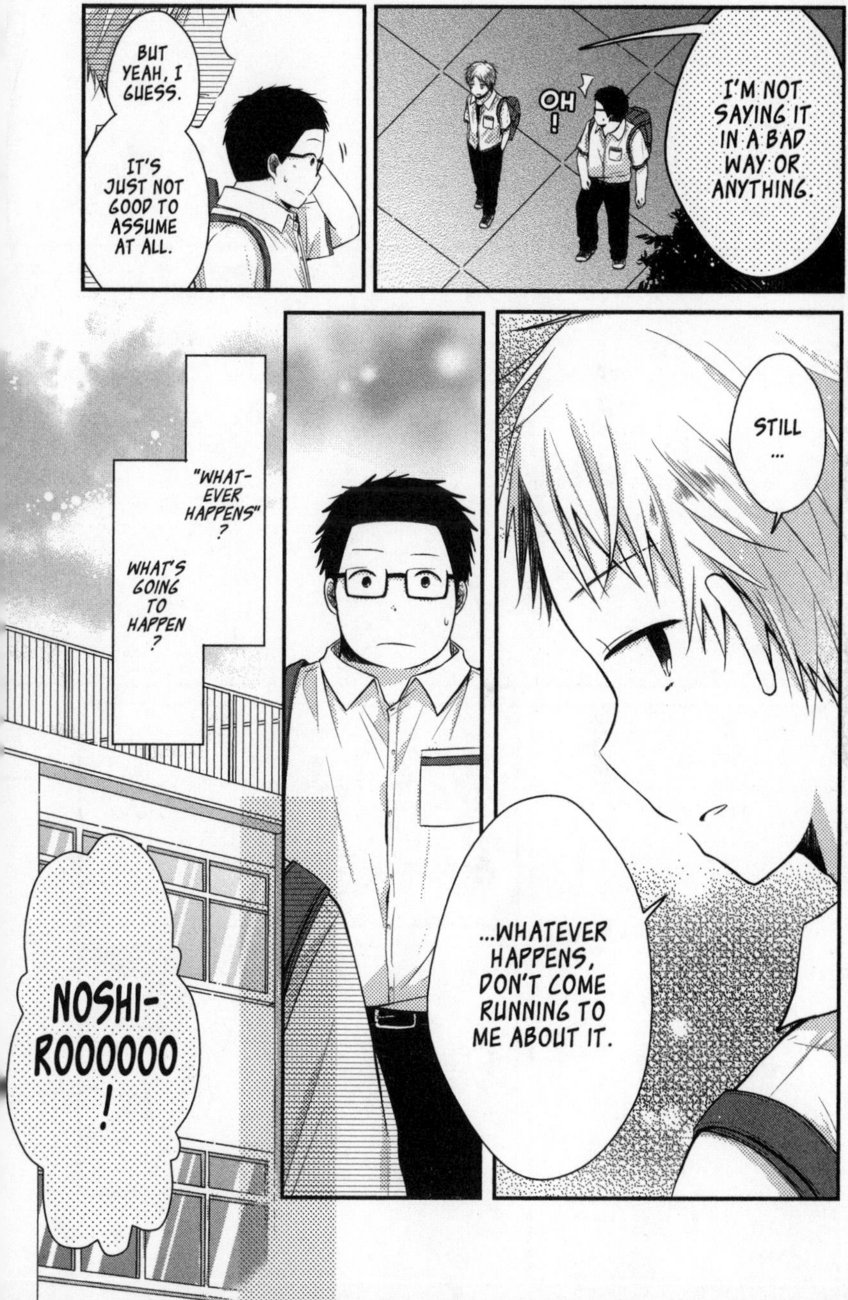
I'M NOT SAYING IT IN A BAD WAY OR ANYTHING.
OH!
BUT YEAH, I GUESS.
IT'S JUST NOT GOOD TO ASSUME AT ALL.
STILL...
...WHATEVER HAPPENS, DON'T COME RUNNING TO ME ABOUT IT.
"WHATEVER HAPPENS"?
WHAT'S GOING TO HAPPEN?
NOSHI-ROOOOOO!

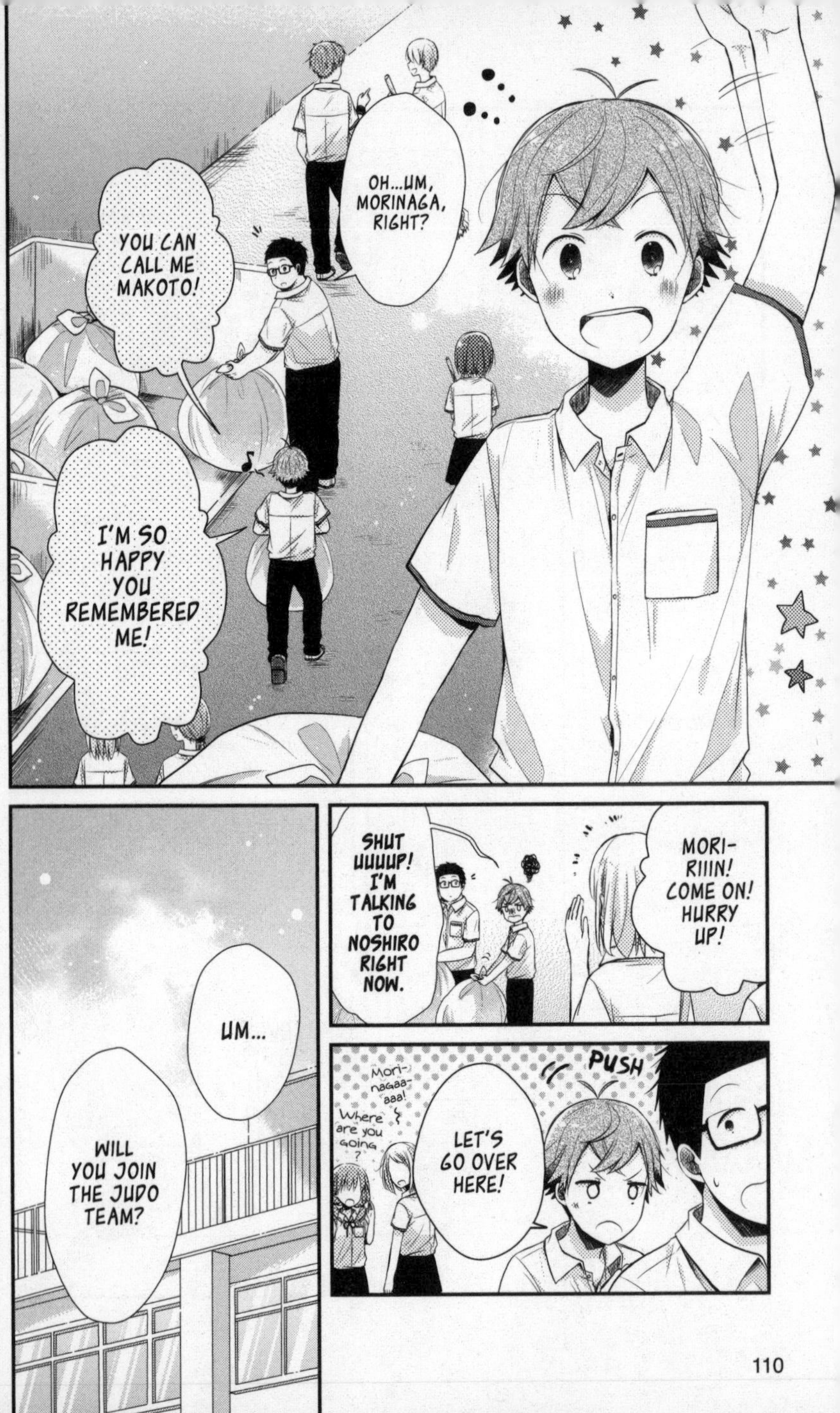
OH...UM, MORINAGA, RIGHT?
YOU CAN CALL ME MAKOTO!
I'M SO HAPPY YOU REMEMBERED ME!
MORI-RIIIN! COME ON! HURRY UP!
SHUT UUUUP! I'M TALKING TO NOSHIRO RIGHT NOW.
PUSH
LET'S GO OVER HERE!
Mori-nagaa-aaa!
Where are you going?
UM...
WILL YOU JOIN THE JUDO TEAM?

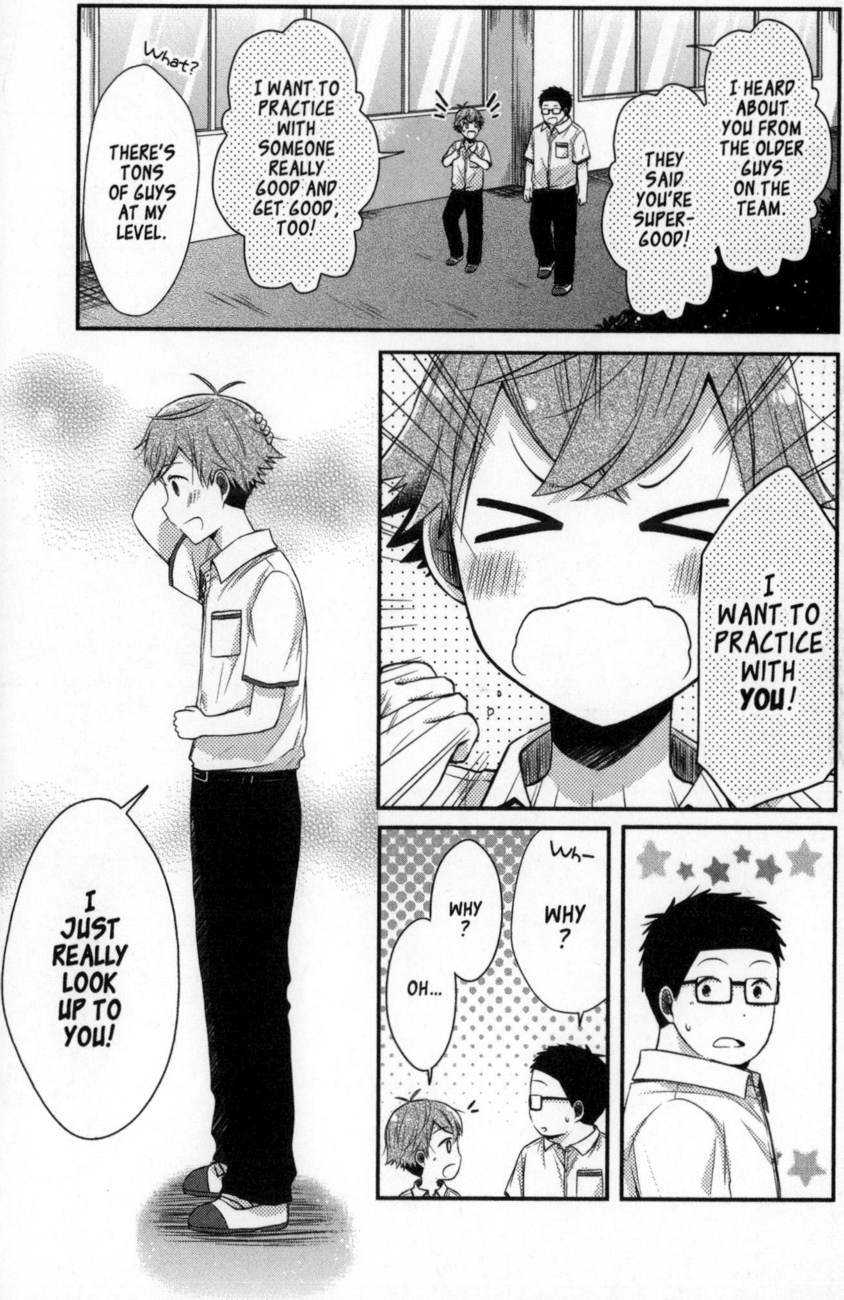
I HEARD ABOUT YOU FROM THE OLDER GUYS ON THE TEAM.
THEY SAID YOU'RE SUPER-GOOD!
I WANT TO PRACTICE WITH SOMEONE REALLY GOOD AND GET GOOD, TOO!
What?
THERE'S TONS OF GUYS AT MY LEVEL.
I WANT TO PRACTICE WITH YOU!
Wh-
WHY?
WHY?
OH...
I JUST REALLY LOOK UP TO YOU!

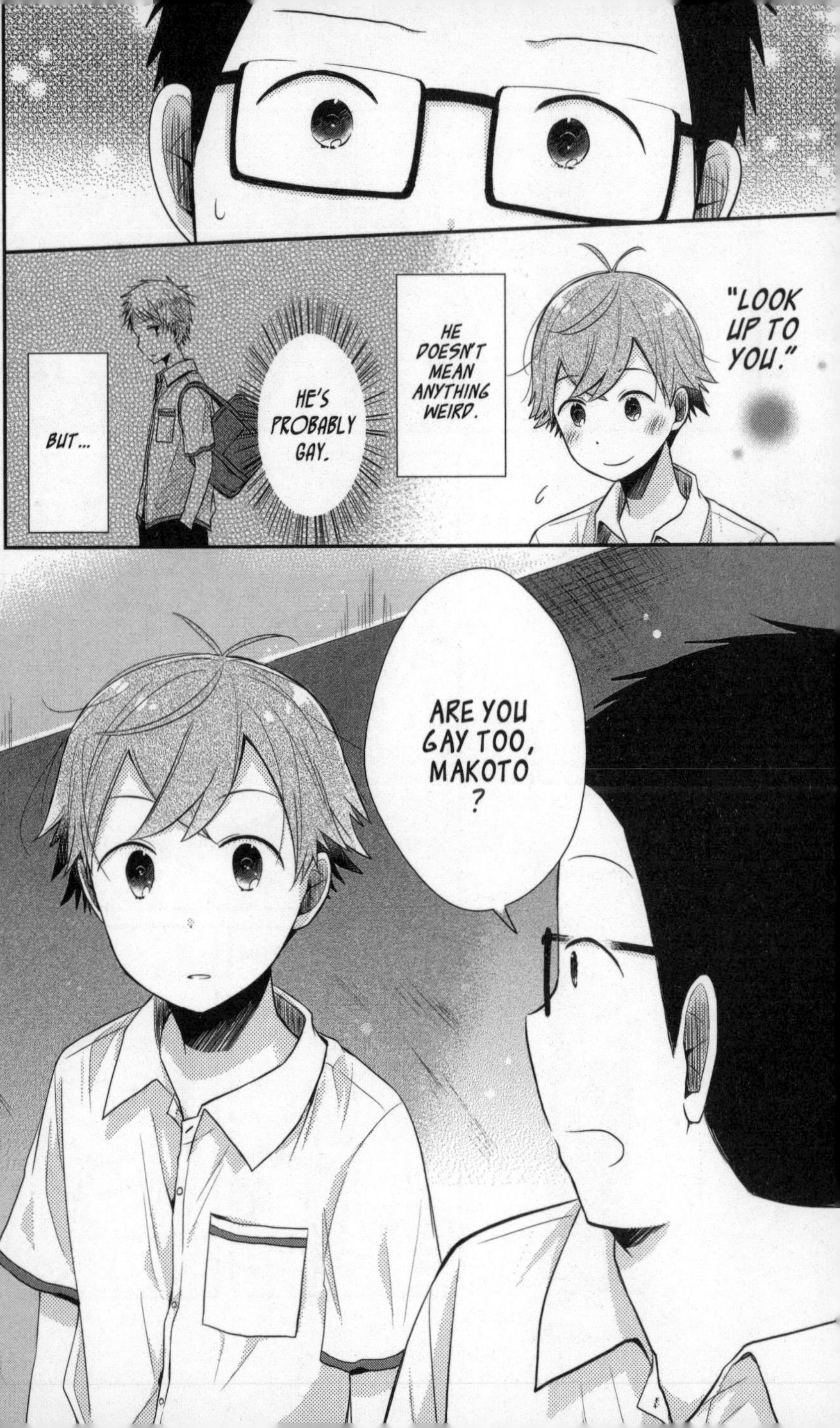
"LOOK UP TO YOU."
HE DOESN'T MEAN ANYTHING WEIRD.
HE'S PROBABLY GAY.
BUT...
ARE YOU GAY TOO, MAKOTO?

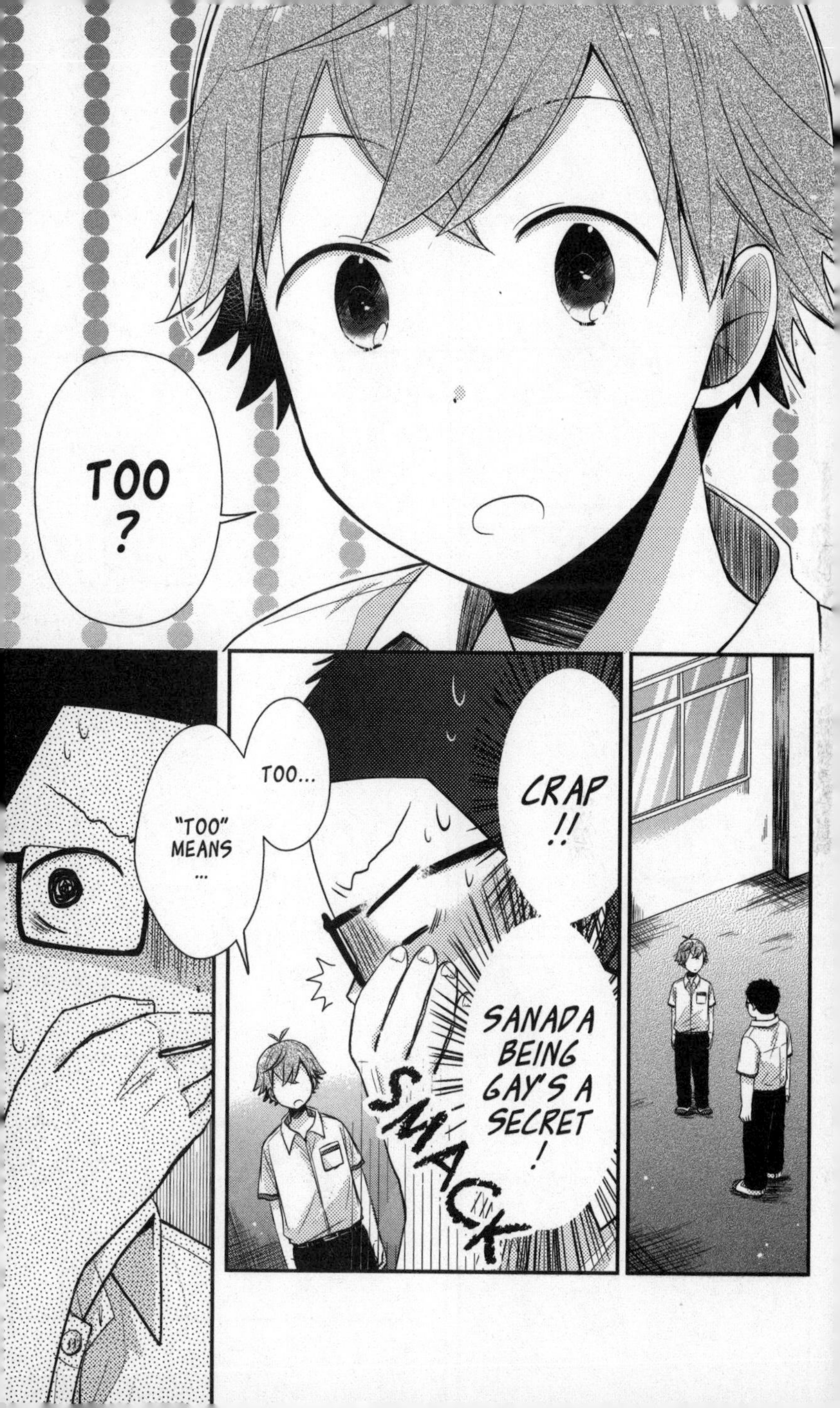

TOO ?
CRAP !!
TOO...
"TOO" MEANS ...
SANADA BEING GAY'S A SECRET !
SMACK

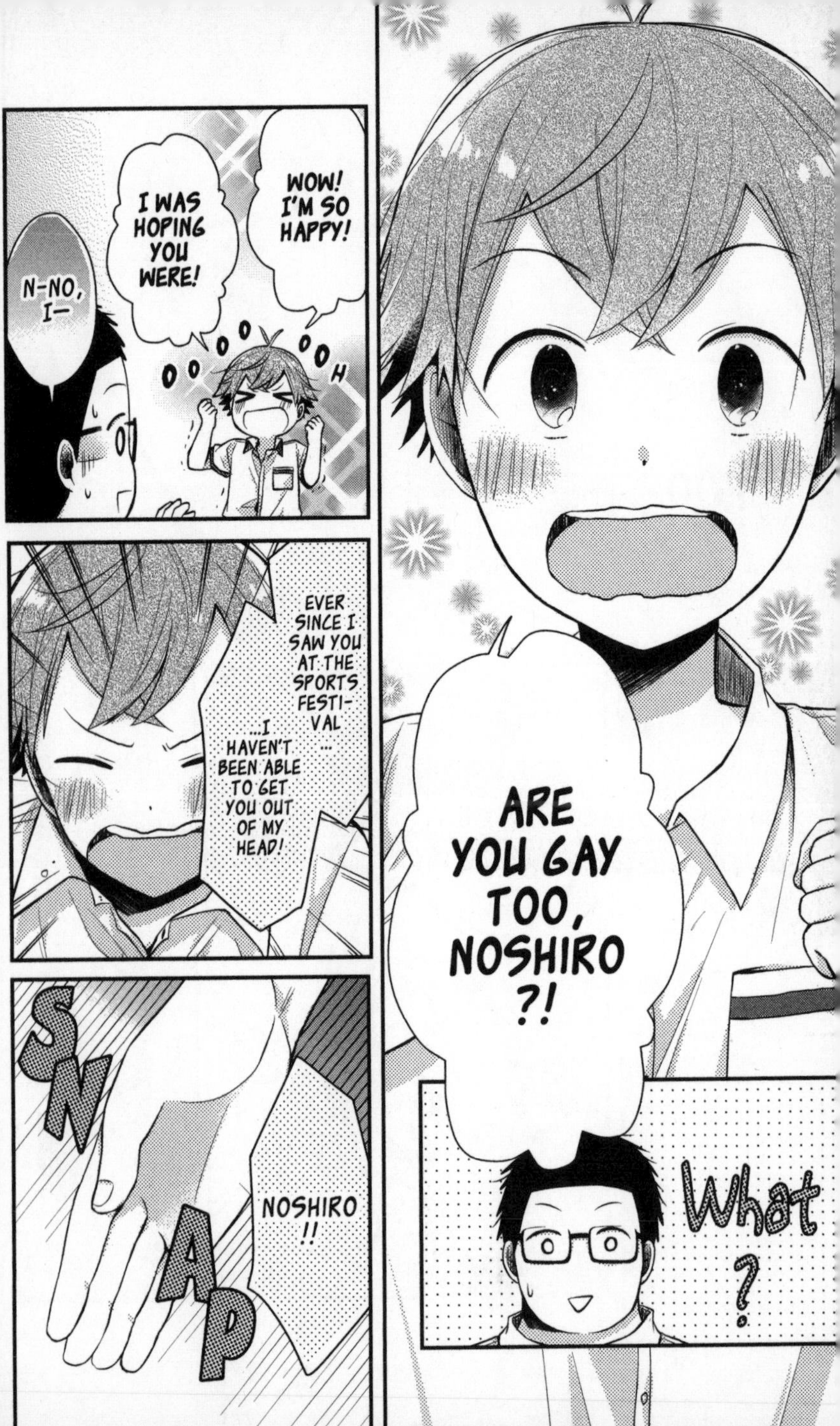
ARE YOU GAY TOO, NOSHIRO?!
What?
WOW! I'M SO HAPPY!
I WAS HOPING YOU WERE!
OOOOOOOH
N-NO, I—
EVER SINCE I SAW YOU AT THE SPORTS FESTIVAL...
...I HAVEN'T BEEN ABLE TO GET YOU OUT OF MY HEAD!
NOSHIRO!!
SNAP

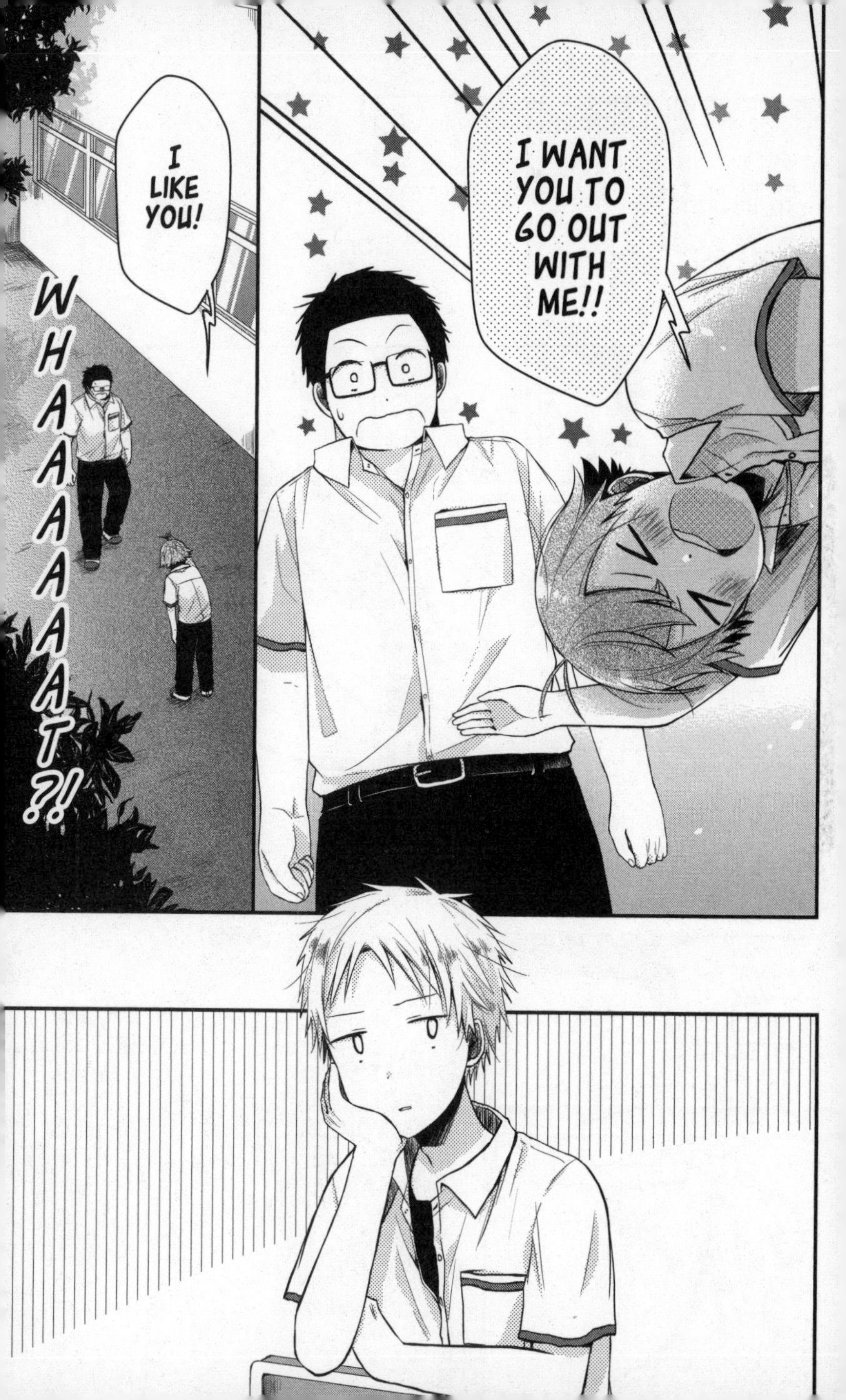
I WANT YOU TO GO OUT WITH ME!!
I LIKE YOU!
WHAAAAAAAAT?!

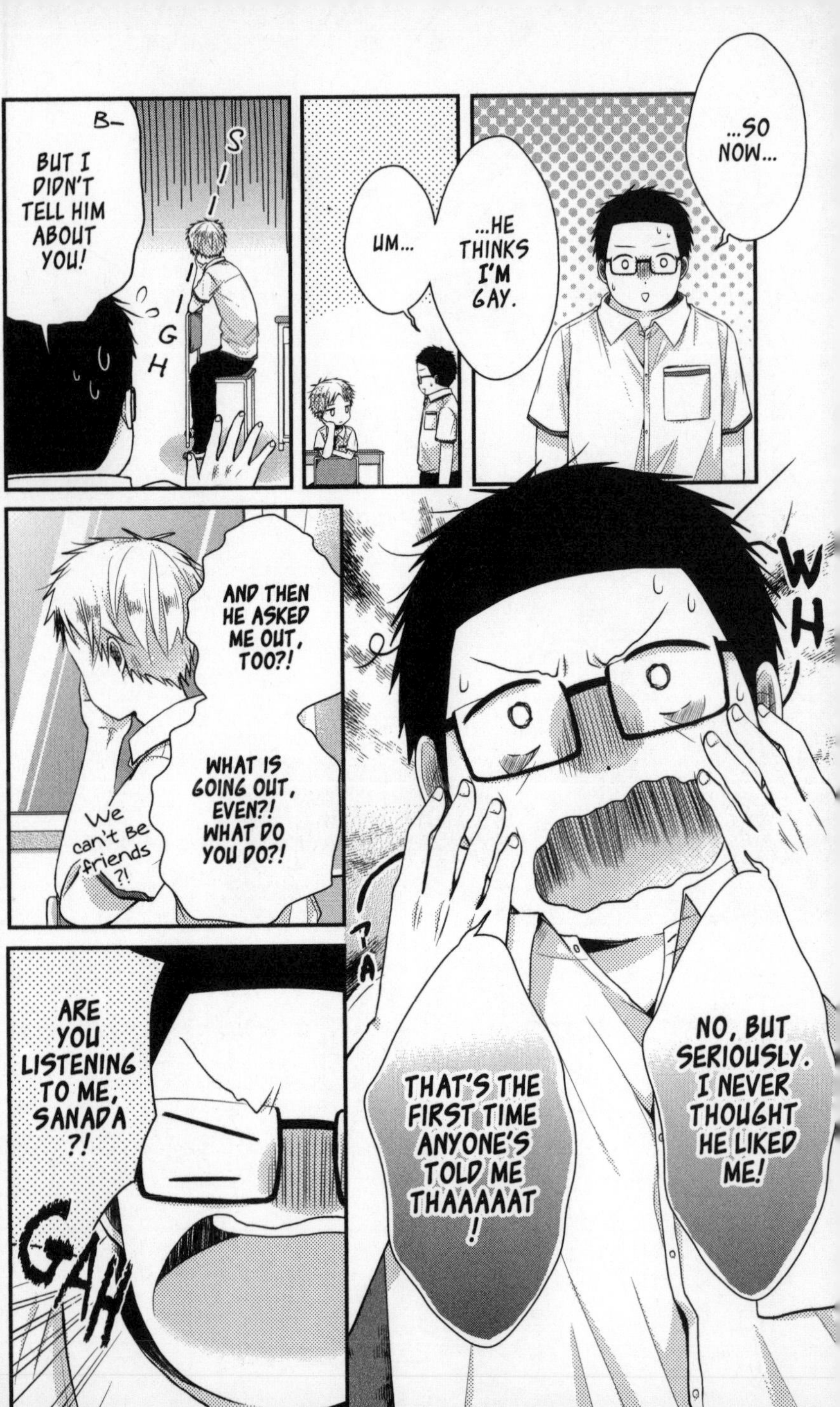
...SO NOW...
...HE THINKS I'M GAY.
UM...
B—
BUT I DIDN'T TELL HIM ABOUT YOU!
SIIIIGH
WHH
NO, BUT SERIOUSLY. I NEVER THOUGHT HE LIKED ME!
THAT'S THE FIRST TIME ANYONE'S TOLD ME THAAAAAT!
AND THEN HE ASKED ME OUT, TOO?!
WHAT IS GOING OUT, EVEN?! WHAT DO YOU DO?!
We can't be friends?!
ARE YOU LISTENING TO ME, SANADA?!
GAH

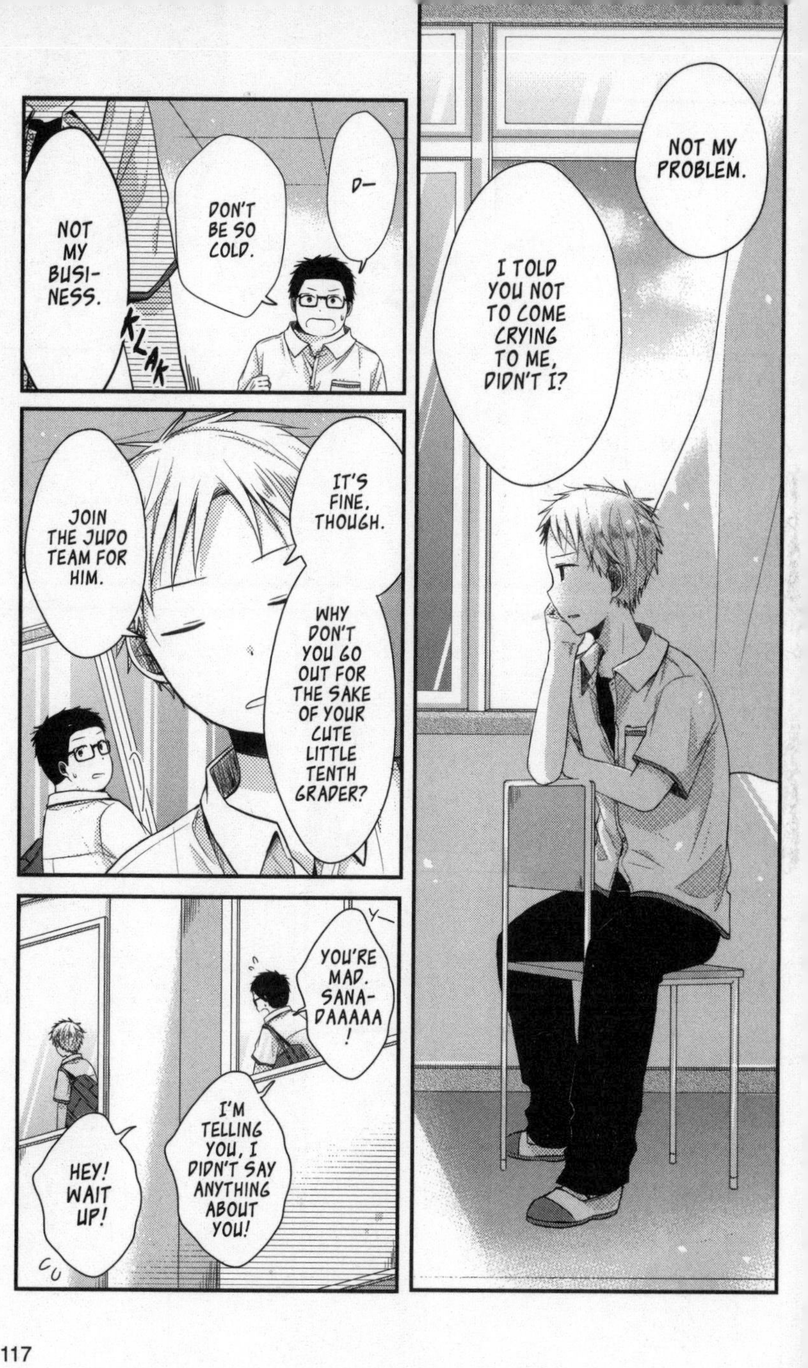
NOT MY PROBLEM.
I TOLD YOU NOT TO COME CRYING TO ME, DIDN'T I?
D—
DON'T BE SO COLD.
NOT MY BUSINESS.
KLAK
IT'S FINE, THOUGH.
WHY DON'T YOU GO OUT FOR THE SAKE OF YOUR CUTE LITTLE TENTH GRADER?
JOIN THE JUDO TEAM FOR HIM.
Y—
YOU'RE MAD. SANA-DAAAAAA!
I'M TELLING YOU, I DIDN'T SAY ANYTHING ABOUT YOU!
HEY! WAIT UP!

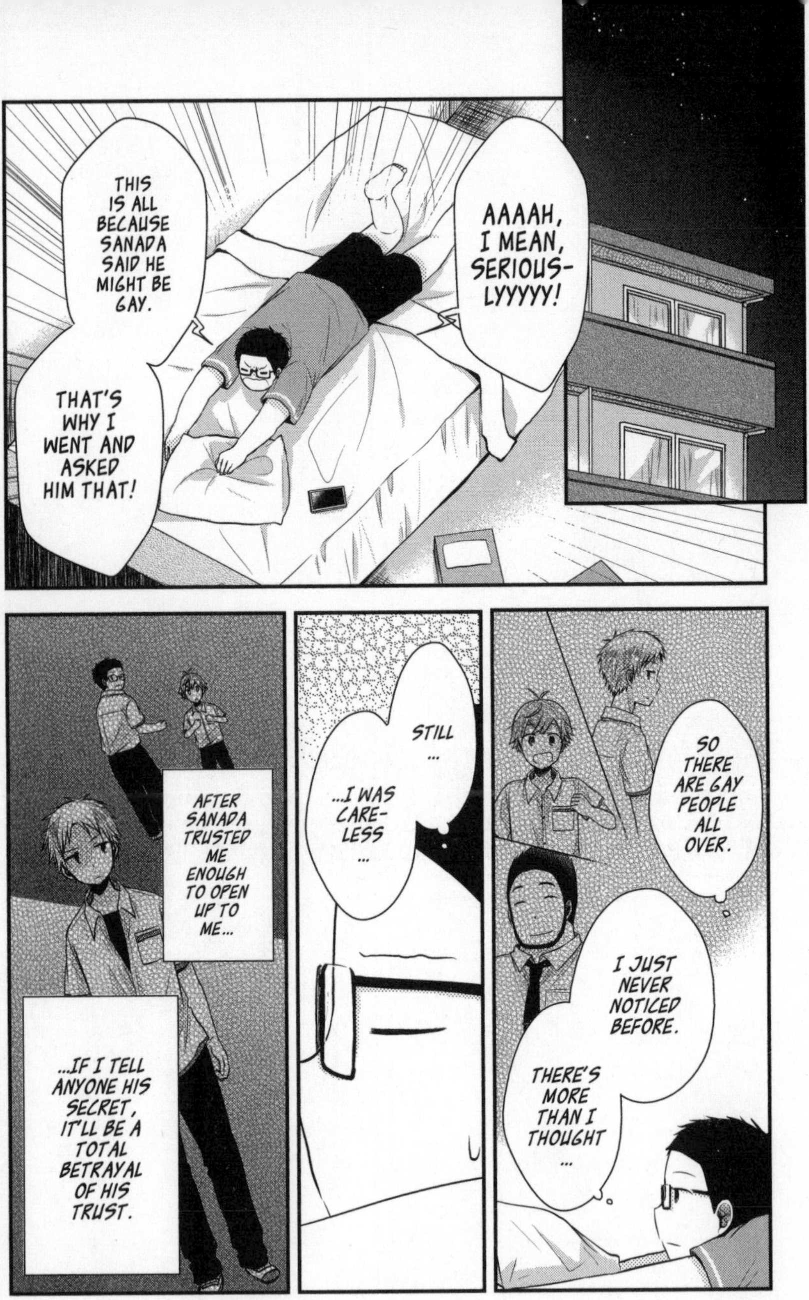
AAAAH, I MEAN, SERIOUS-LYYYYY!
THIS IS ALL BECAUSE SANADA SAID HE MIGHT BE GAY.
THAT'S WHY I WENT AND ASKED HIM THAT!
SO THERE ARE GAY PEOPLE ALL OVER.
I JUST NEVER NOTICED BEFORE.
THERE'S MORE THAN I THOUGHT...
STILL...
...I WAS CARELESS...
AFTER SANADA TRUSTED ME ENOUGH TO OPEN UP TO ME...
...IF I TELL ANYONE HIS SECRET, IT'LL BE A TOTAL BETRAYAL OF HIS TRUST.

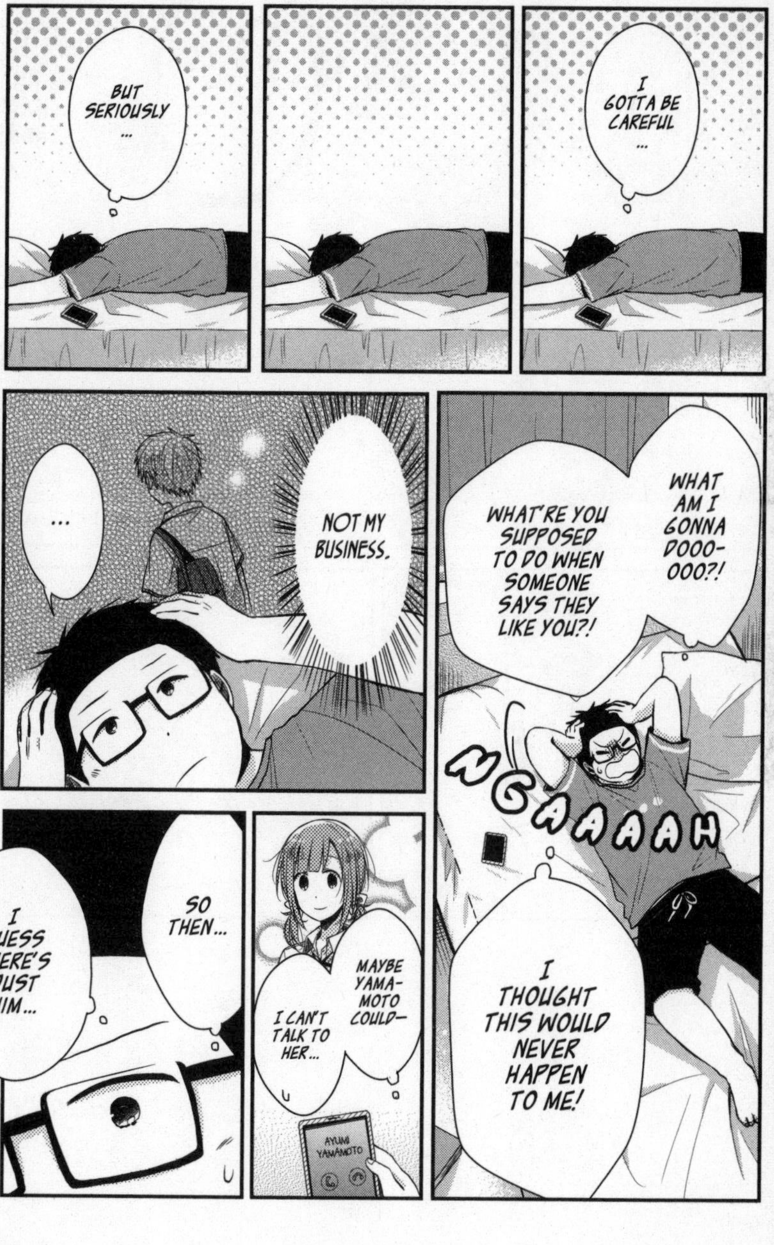
I GOTTA BE CAREFUL...
BUT SERIOUSLY...
WHAT AM I GONNA DOOOO-OOO?!
WHAT'RE YOU SUPPOSED TO DO WHEN SOMEONE SAYS THEY LIKE YOU?!
NGAAAAAH
I THOUGHT THIS WOULD NEVER HAPPEN TO ME!
NOT MY BUSINESS.
...
MAYBE YAMAMOTO COULD—
I CAN'T TALK TO HER...
AYUMI YAMAMOTO
SO THEN...
I GUESS THERE'S JUST HIM...

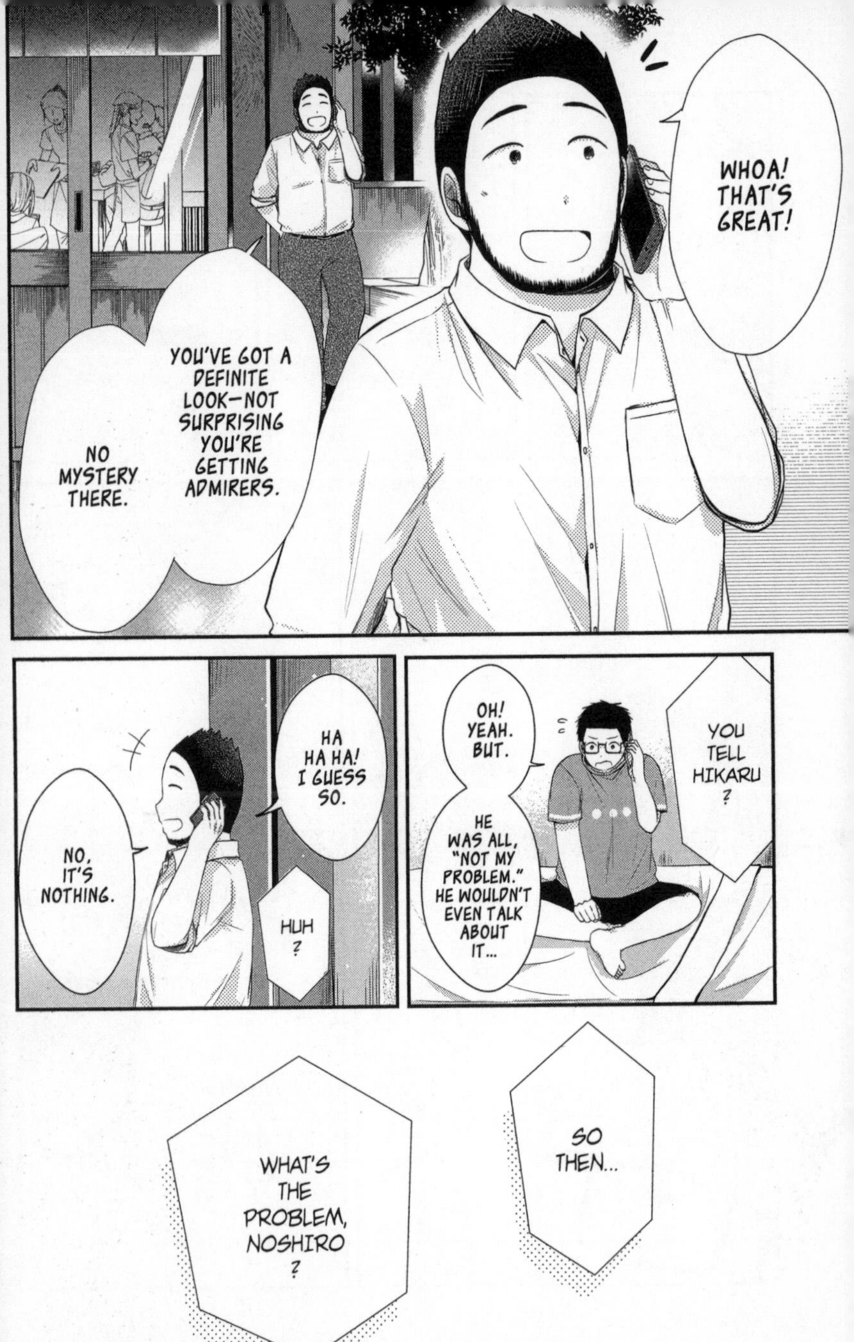
WHOA! THAT'S GREAT!
YOU'VE GOT A DEFINITE LOOK—NOT SURPRISING YOU'RE GETTING ADMIRERS.
NO MYSTERY THERE.
YOU TELL HIKARU?
OH! YEAH. BUT.
HE WAS ALL, "NOT MY PROBLEM." HE WOULDN'T EVEN TALK ABOUT IT...
HA HA HA! I GUESS SO.
HUH?
NO, IT'S NOTHING.
SO THEN...
WHAT'S THE PROBLEM, NOSHIRO?

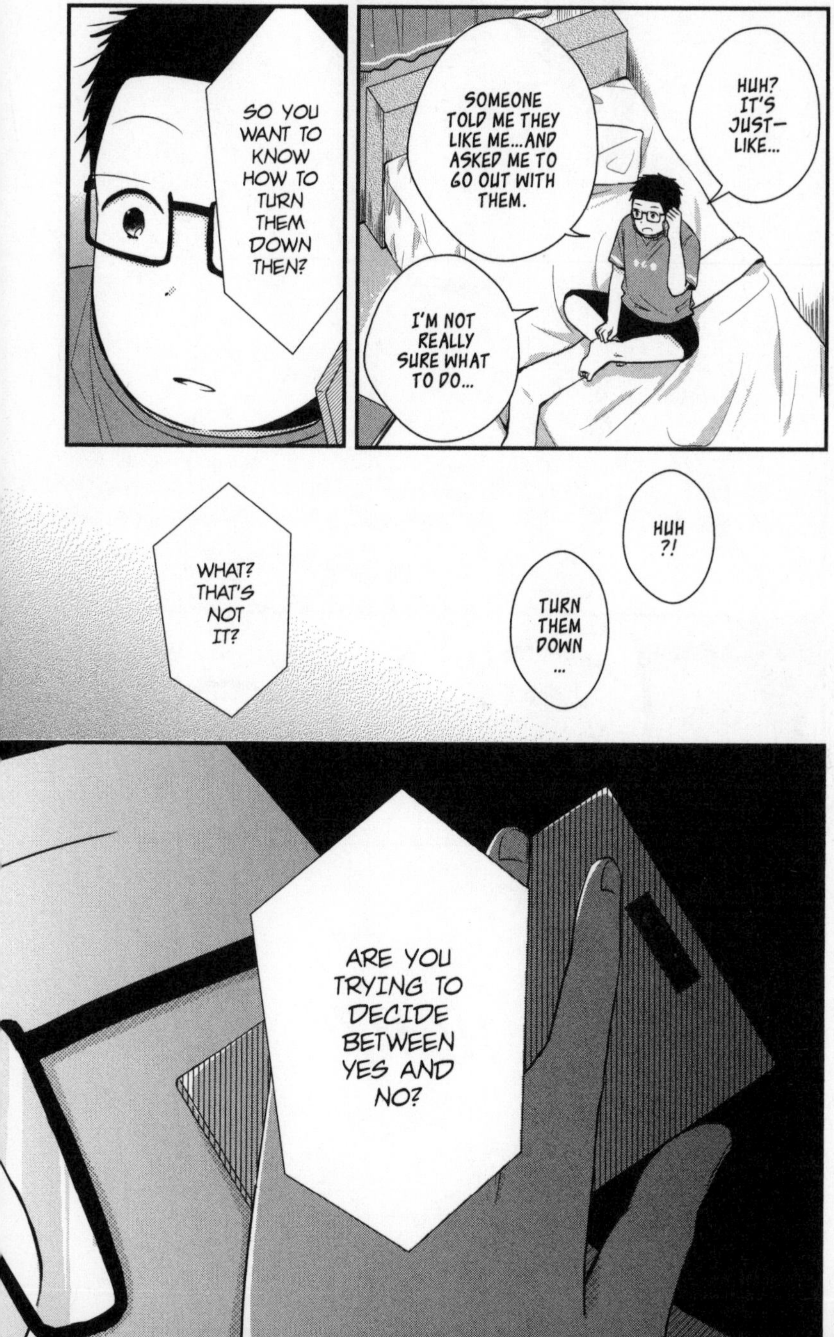
HUH? IT'S JUST— LIKE...
SOMEONE TOLD ME THEY LIKE ME...AND ASKED ME TO GO OUT WITH THEM.
I'M NOT REALLY SURE WHAT TO DO...
SO YOU WANT TO KNOW HOW TO TURN THEM DOWN THEN?
HUH ?!
TURN THEM DOWN ...
WHAT? THAT'S NOT IT?
ARE YOU TRYING TO DECIDE BETWEEN YES AND NO?

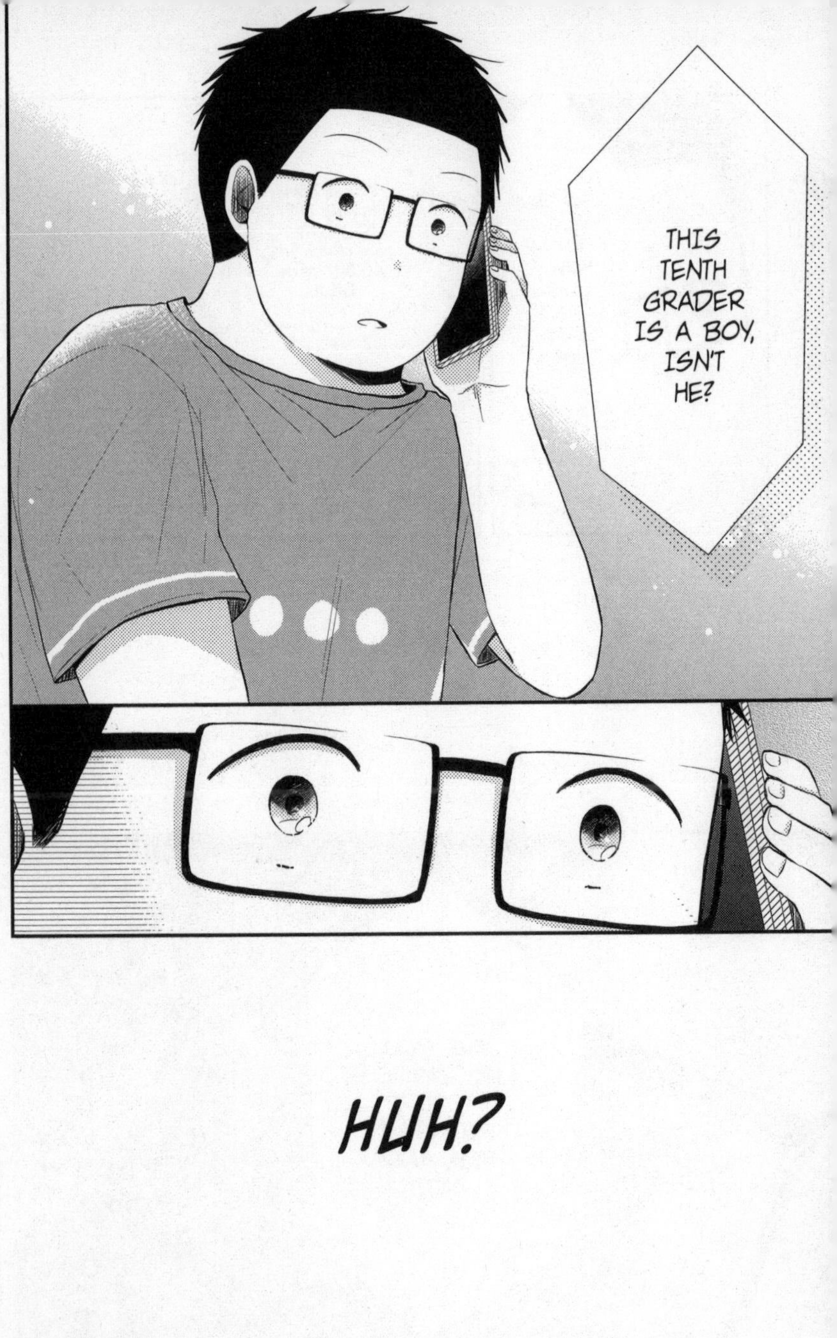
THIS TENTH GRADER IS A BOY, ISN'T HE?
HUH?

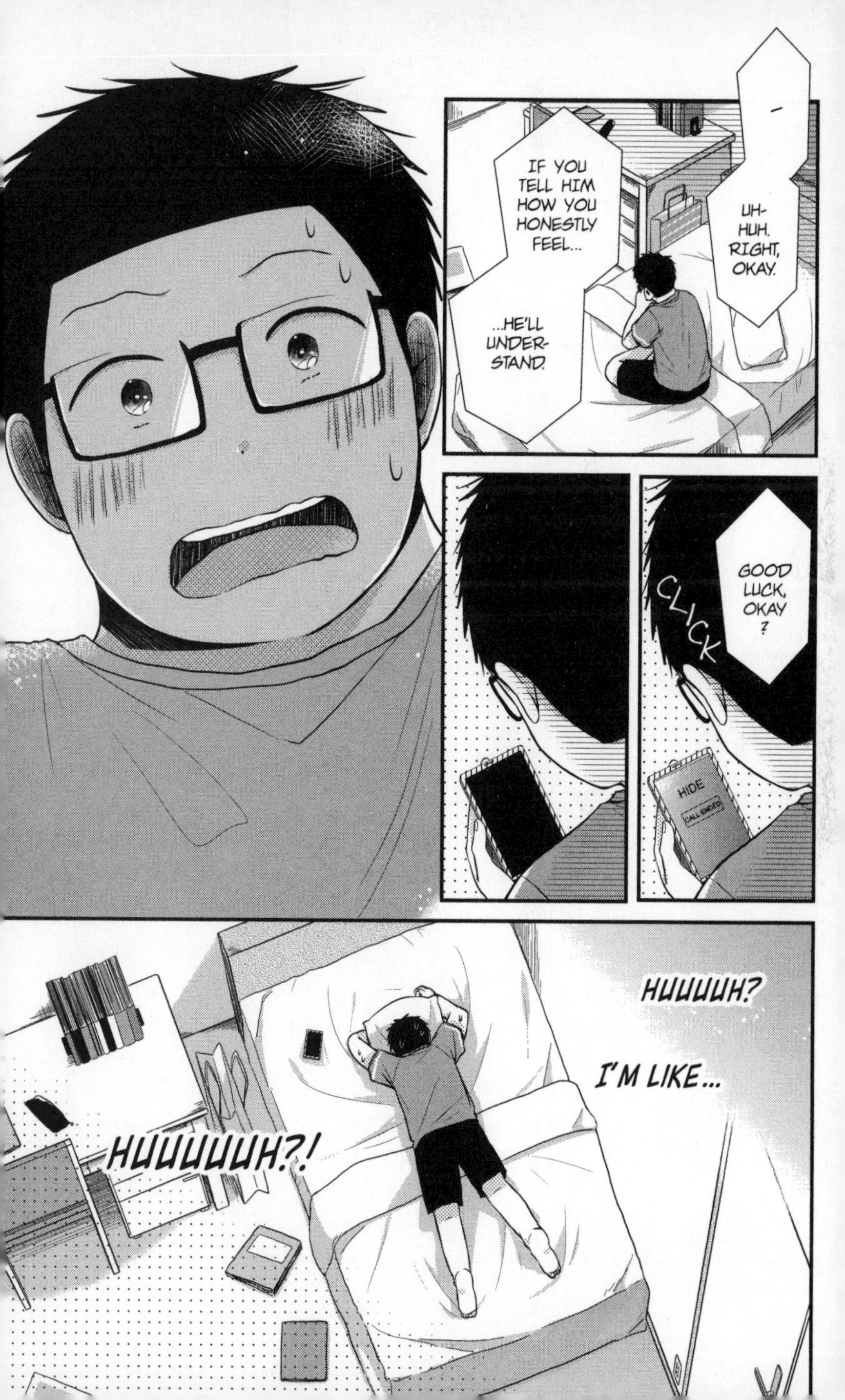
—
UH-HUH. RIGHT, OKAY.
IF YOU TELL HIM HOW YOU HONESTLY FEEL...
...HE'LL UNDERSTAND.
GOOD LUCK, OKAY?
CLICK
HIDE
CALL ENDED
HUUUUH?
I'M LIKE...
HUUUUUUH?!

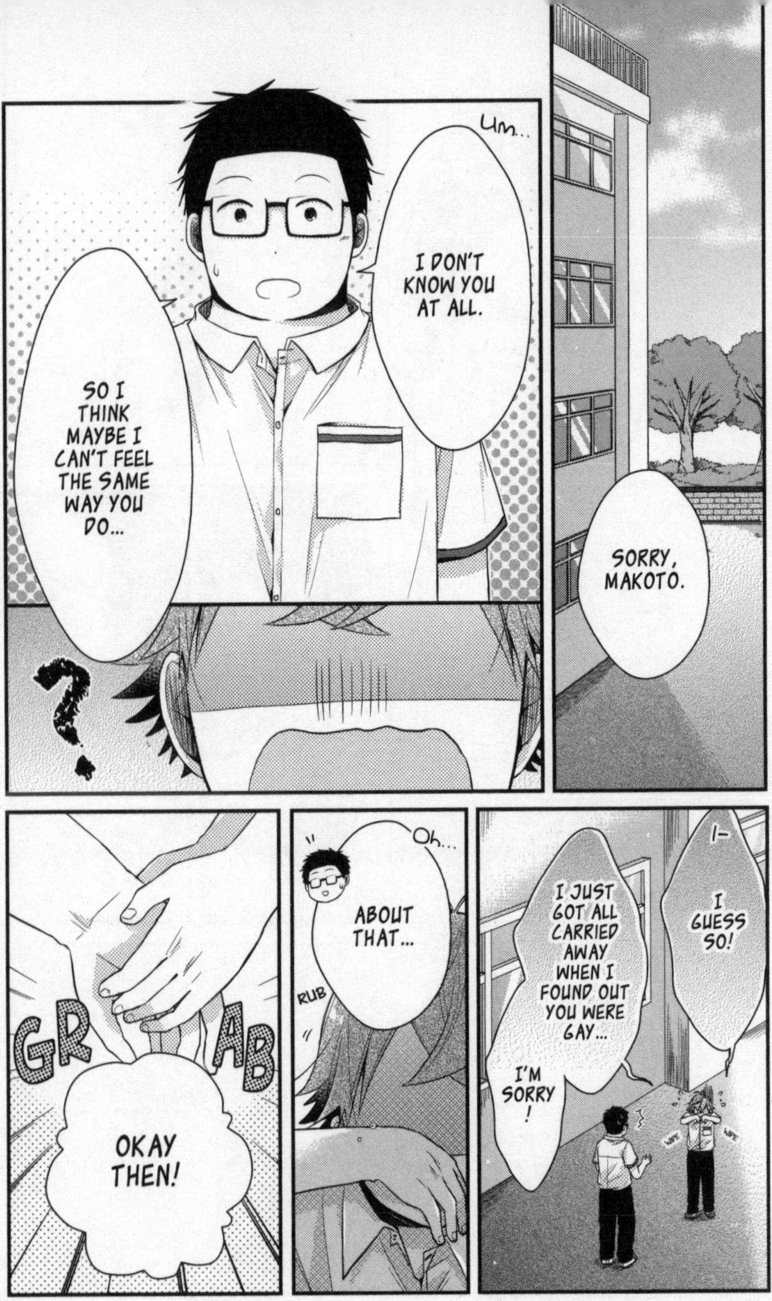
SORRY, MAKOTO.
Um...
I DON'T KNOW YOU AT ALL.
SO I THINK MAYBE I CAN'T FEEL THE SAME WAY YOU DO...
?
I-
I GUESS SO!
I JUST GOT ALL CARRIED AWAY WHEN I FOUND OUT YOU WERE GAY...
I'M SORRY!
WIPE
WIPE
Oh...
ABOUT THAT...
RUB
GRAB
OKAY THEN!

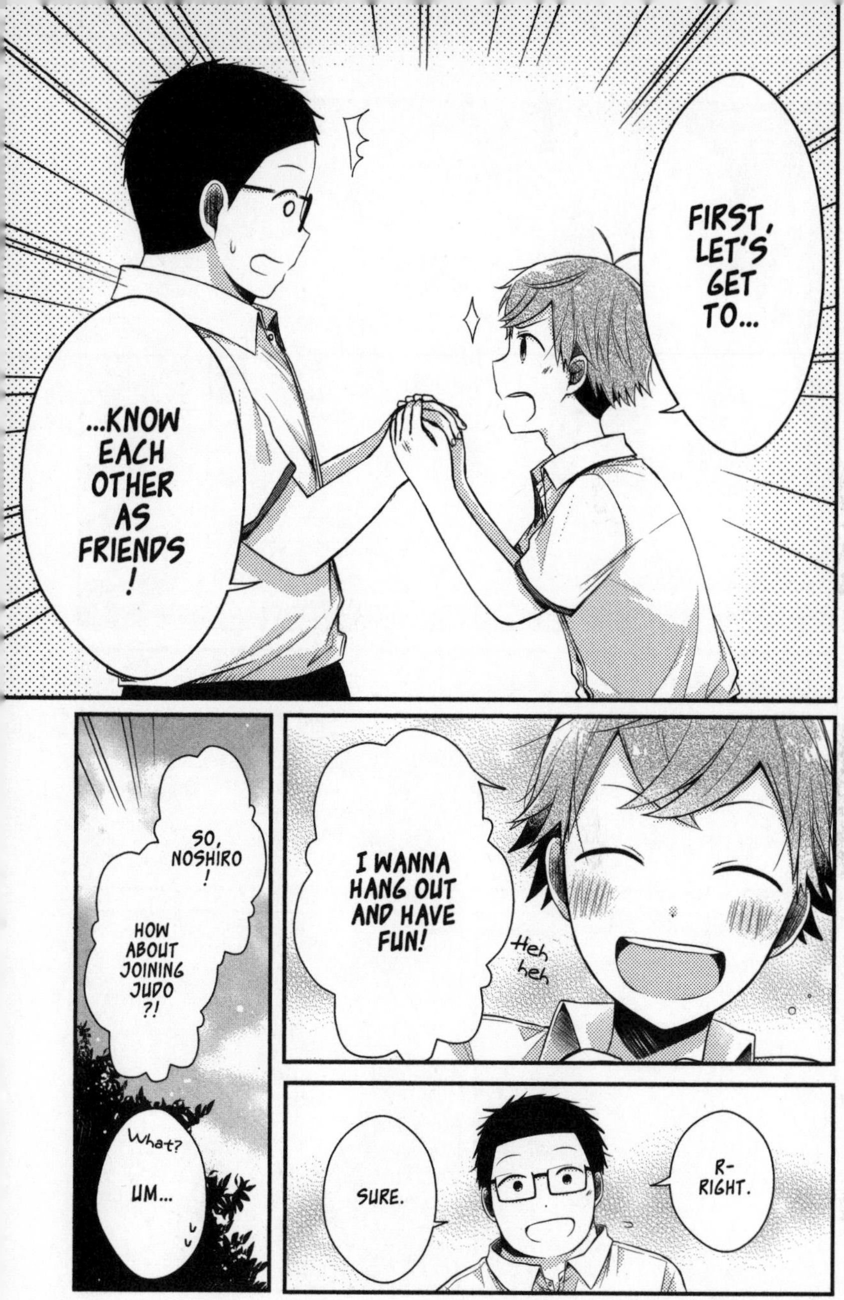
FIRST, LET'S GET TO...
...KNOW EACH OTHER AS FRIENDS!
I WANNA HANG OUT AND HAVE FUN!
Heh heh
R-RIGHT.
SURE.
SO, NOSHIRO!
HOW ABOUT JOINING JUDO?!
What?
UM...

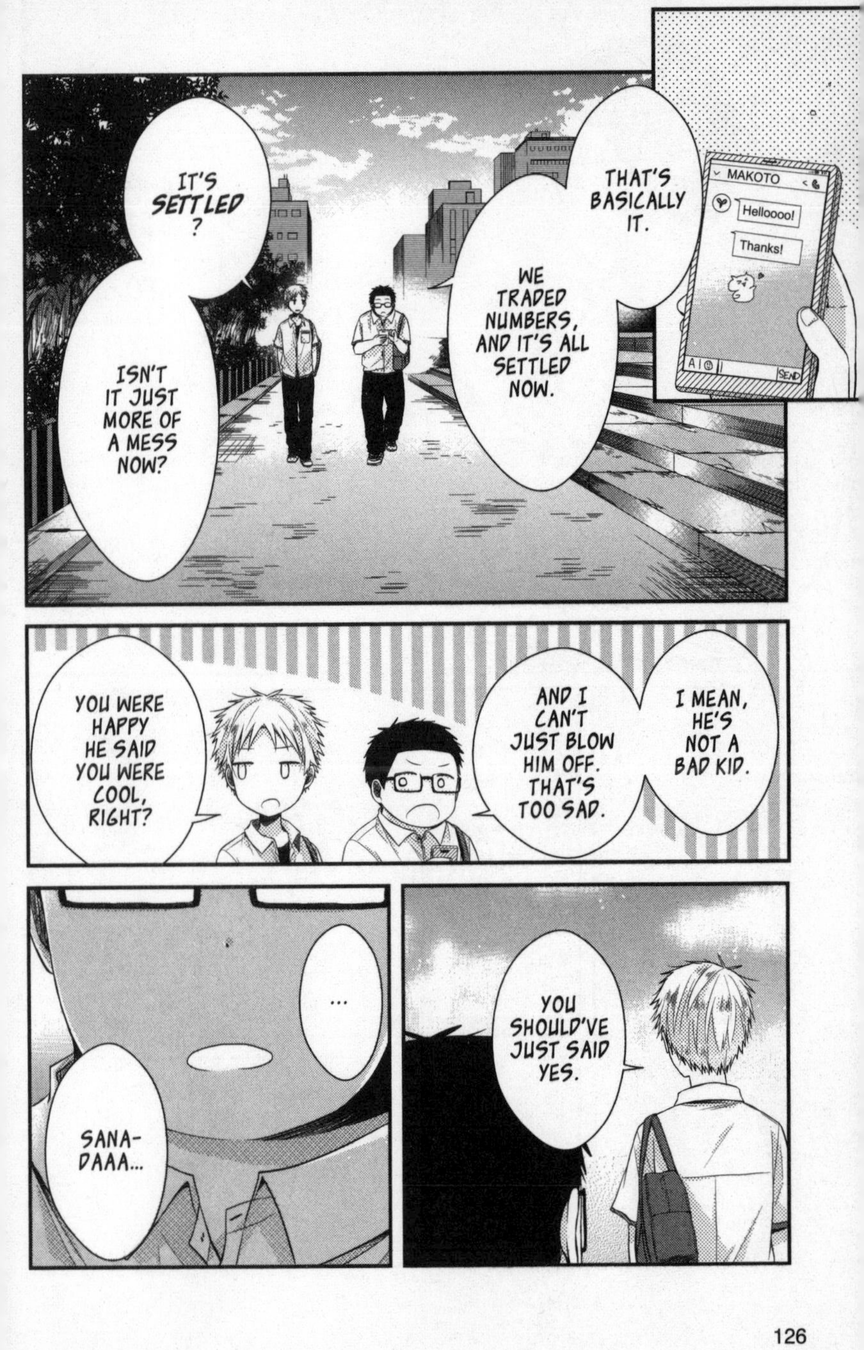
MAKOTO
Helloooo!
Thanks!
SEND
THAT'S BASICALLY IT.
WE TRADED NUMBERS, AND IT'S ALL SETTLED NOW.
IT'S SETTLED?
ISN'T IT JUST MORE OF A MESS NOW?
I MEAN, HE'S NOT A BAD KID.
AND I CAN'T JUST BLOW HIM OFF. THAT'S TOO SAD.
YOU WERE HAPPY HE SAID YOU WERE COOL, RIGHT?
YOU SHOULD'VE JUST SAID YES.
...
SANA-DAAA...

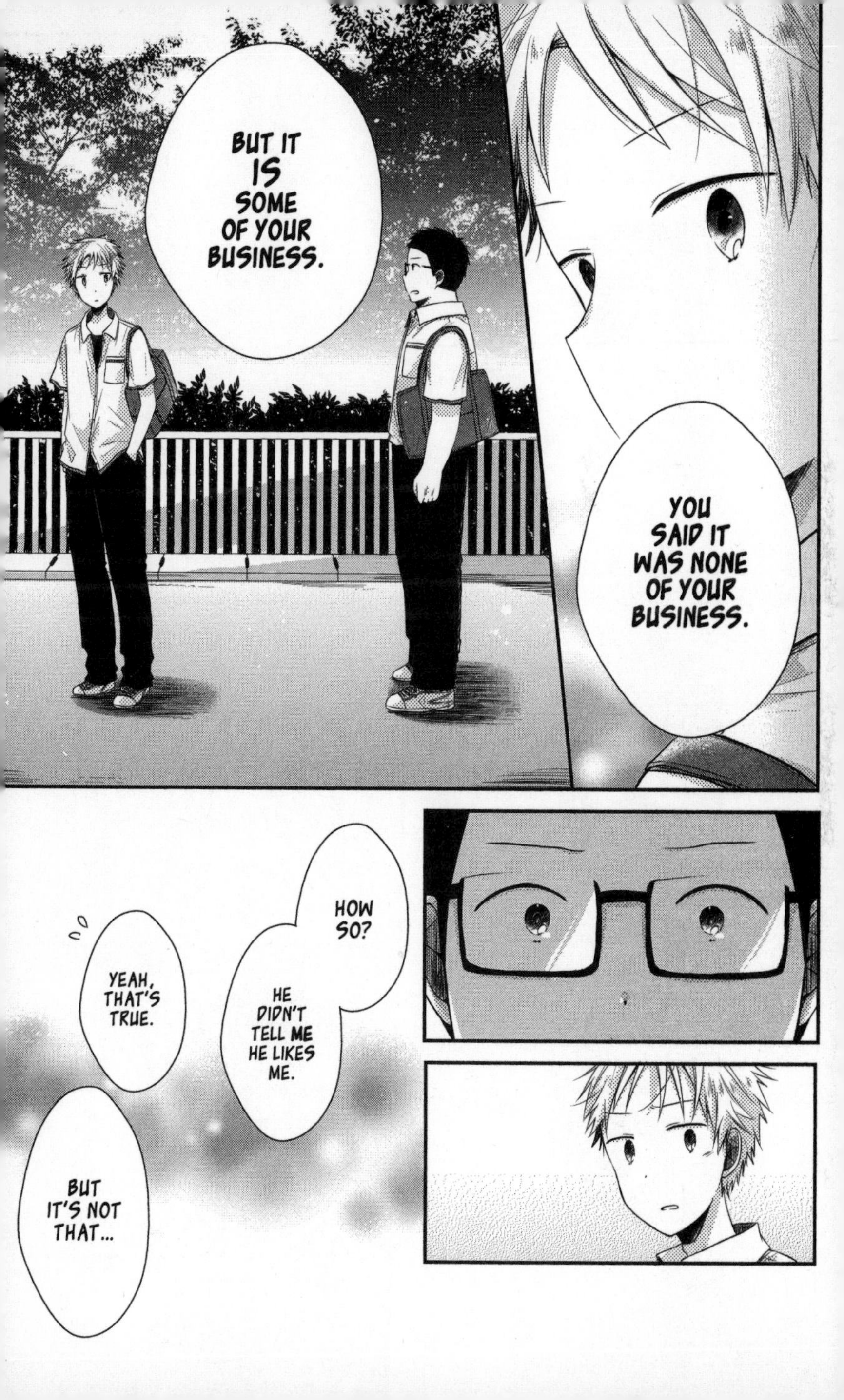
YOU SAID IT WAS NONE OF YOUR BUSINESS.
BUT IT IS SOME OF YOUR BUSINESS.
HOW SO?
HE DIDN'T TELL ME HE LIKES ME.
YEAH, THAT'S TRUE.
BUT IT'S NOT THAT...

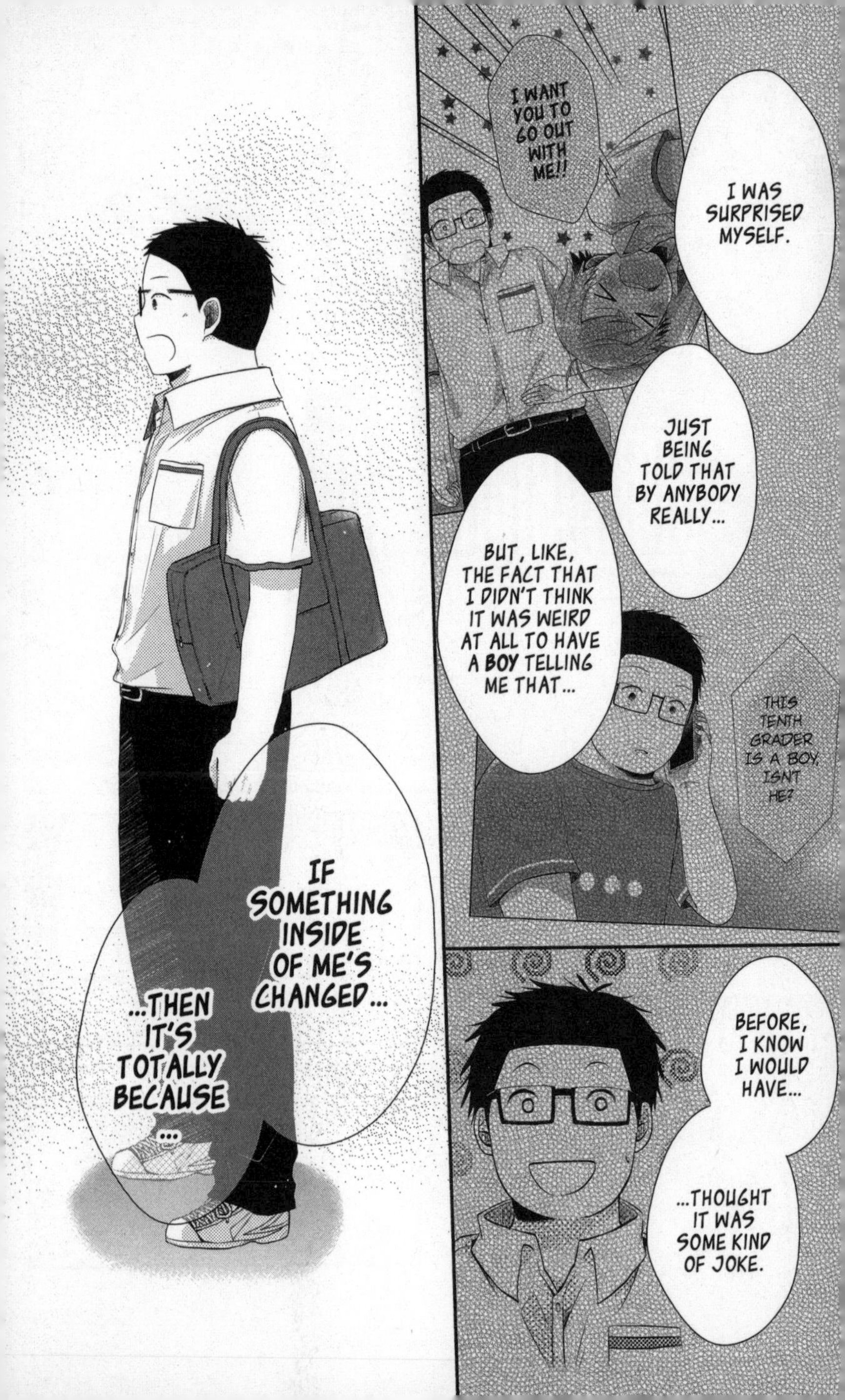
I WANT YOU TO GO OUT WITH ME!!
I WAS SURPRISED MYSELF.
JUST BEING TOLD THAT BY ANYBODY REALLY...
BUT, LIKE, THE FACT THAT I DIDN'T THINK IT WAS WEIRD AT ALL TO HAVE A BOY TELLING ME THAT...
THIS TENTH GRADER IS A BOY, ISN'T HE?
BEFORE, I KNOW I WOULD HAVE...
...THOUGHT IT WAS SOME KIND OF JOKE.
IF SOMETHING INSIDE OF ME'S CHANGED...
...THEN IT'S TOTALLY BECAUSE ...

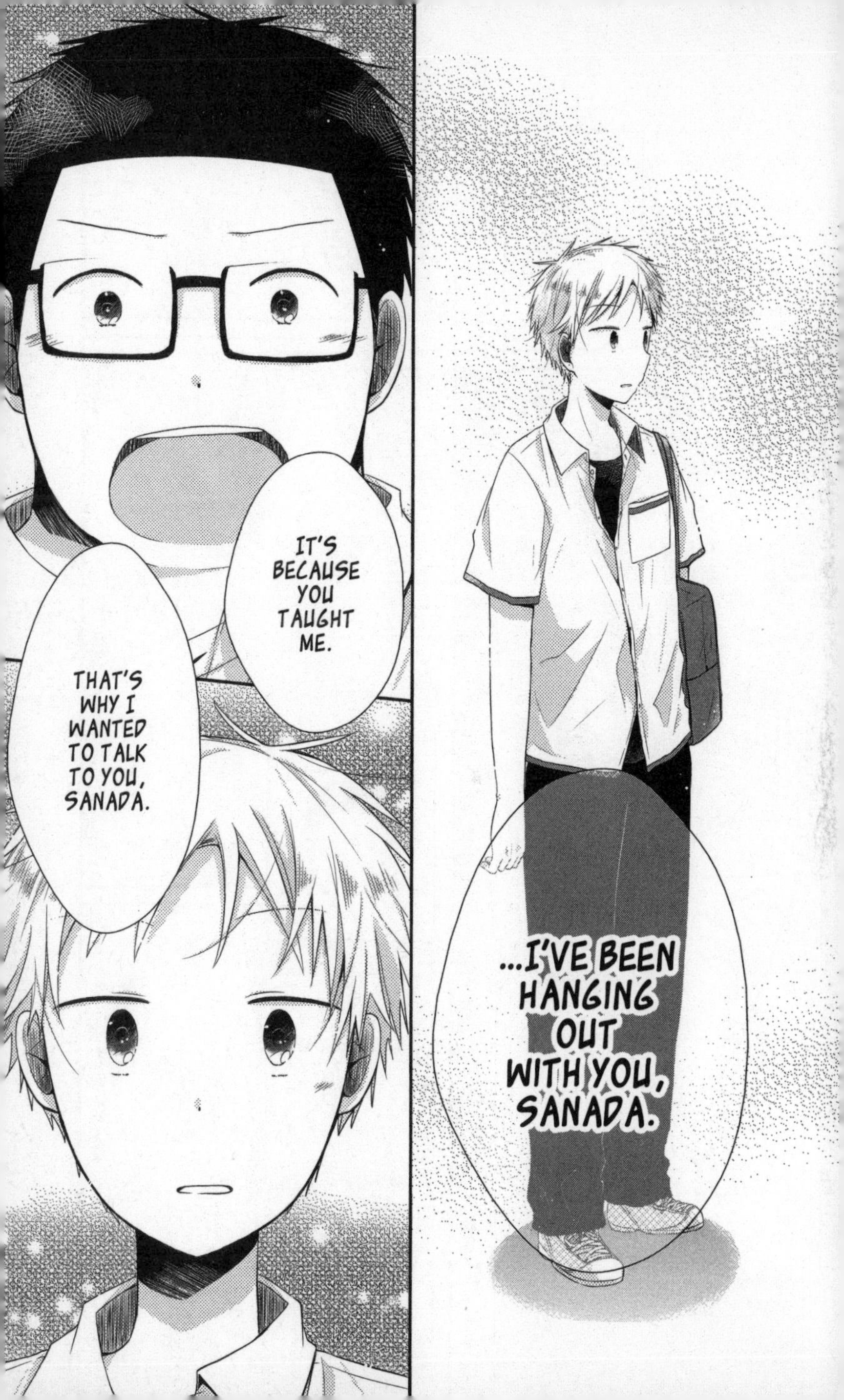
...I'VE BEEN HANGING OUT WITH YOU, SANADA.
IT'S BECAUSE YOU TAUGHT ME.
THAT'S WHY I WANTED TO TALK TO YOU, SANADA.

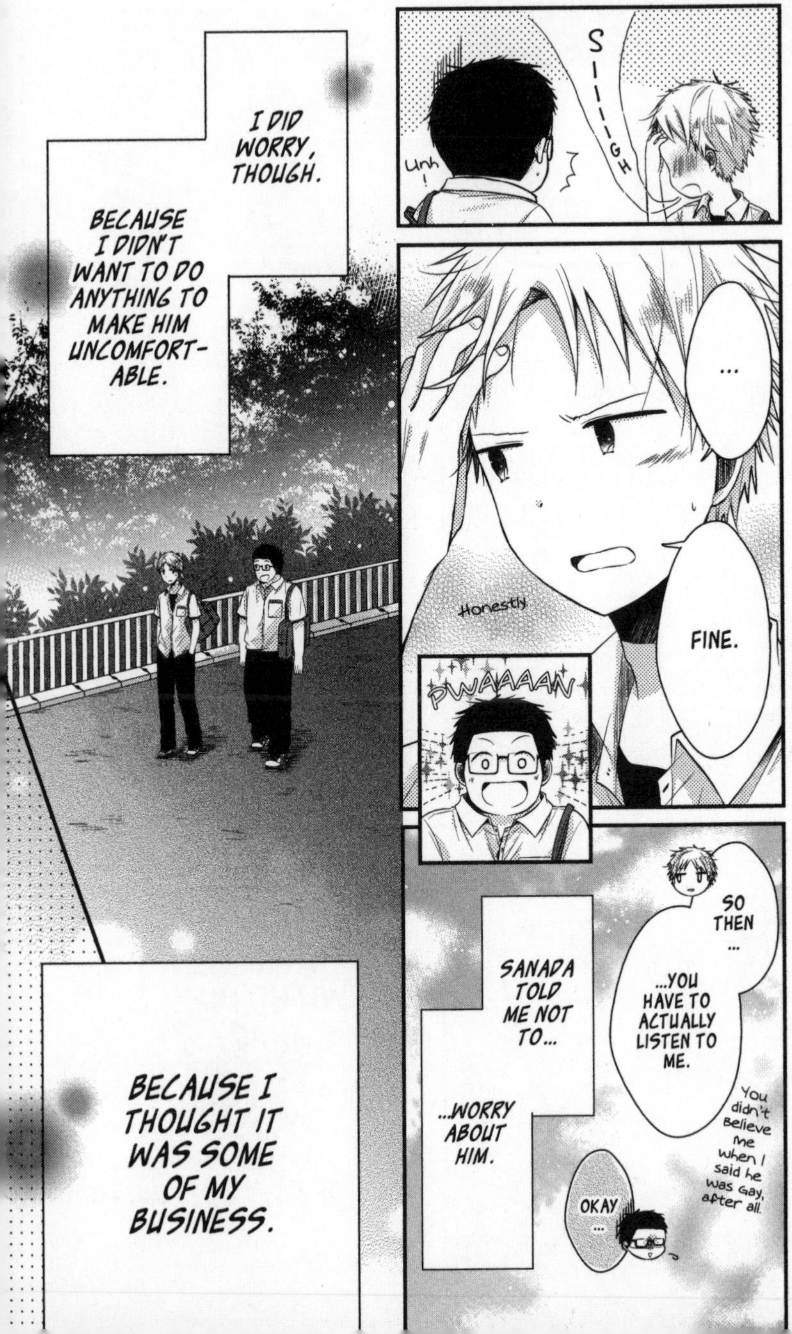
S I I I I G H
Unh!
...
FINE.
Honestly
PWAAAAN
SO THEN...
...YOU HAVE TO ACTUALLY LISTEN TO ME.
You didn't believe me when I said he was gay, after all.
SANADA TOLD ME NOT TO...
OKAY...
...WORRY ABOUT HIM.
I DID WORRY, THOUGH.
BECAUSE I DIDN'T WANT TO DO ANYTHING TO MAKE HIM UNCOMFORT-ABLE.
BECAUSE I THOUGHT IT WAS SOME OF MY BUSINESS.

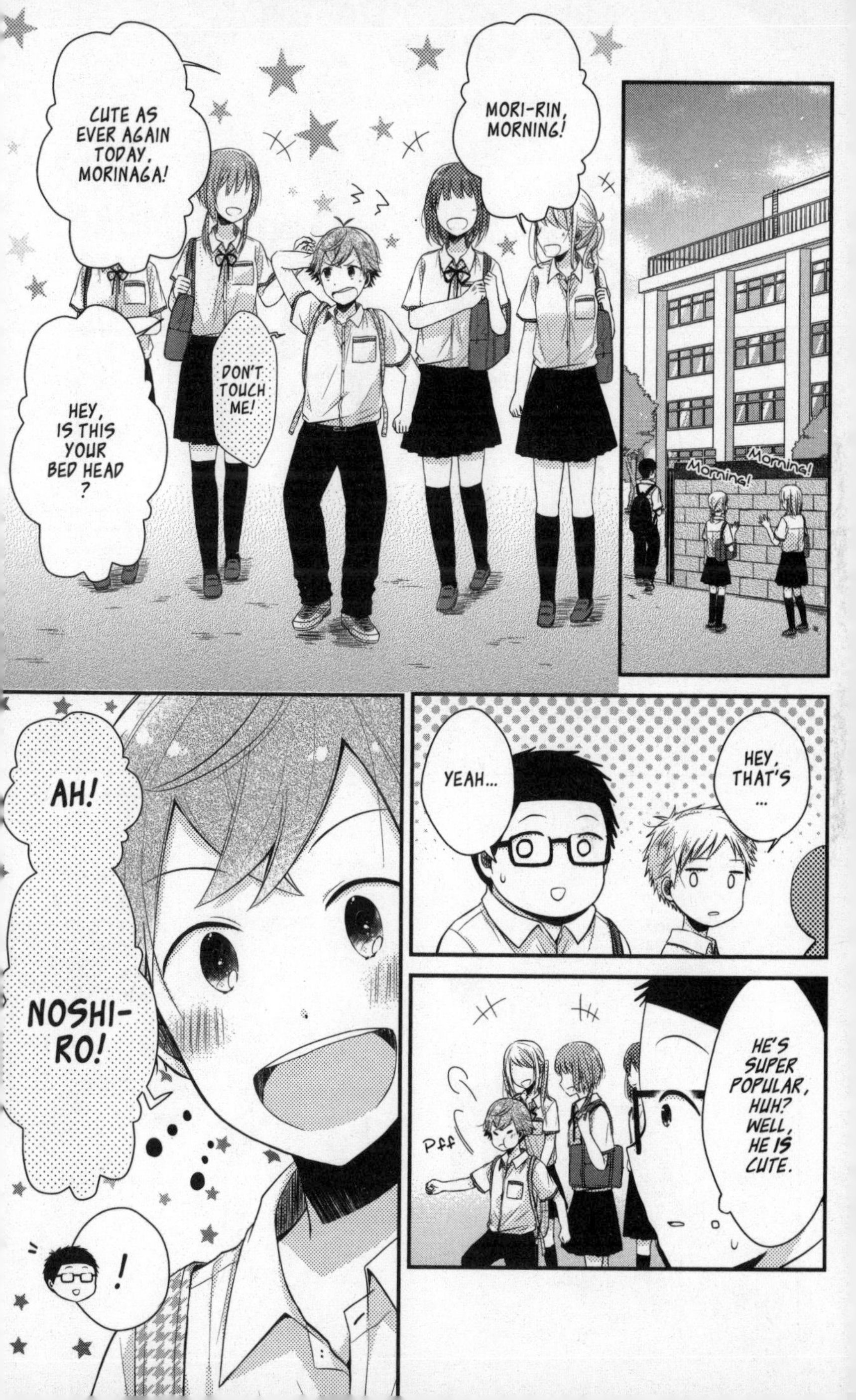

Morning!
Morning!
MORI-RIN, MORNING!
CUTE AS EVER AGAIN TODAY, MORINAGA!
DON'T TOUCH ME!
HEY, IS THIS YOUR BED HEAD?
HEY, THAT'S ...
YEAH...
HE'S SUPER POPULAR, HUH? WELL, HE **IS** CUTE.
Pff
AH!
NOSHI-RO!
!

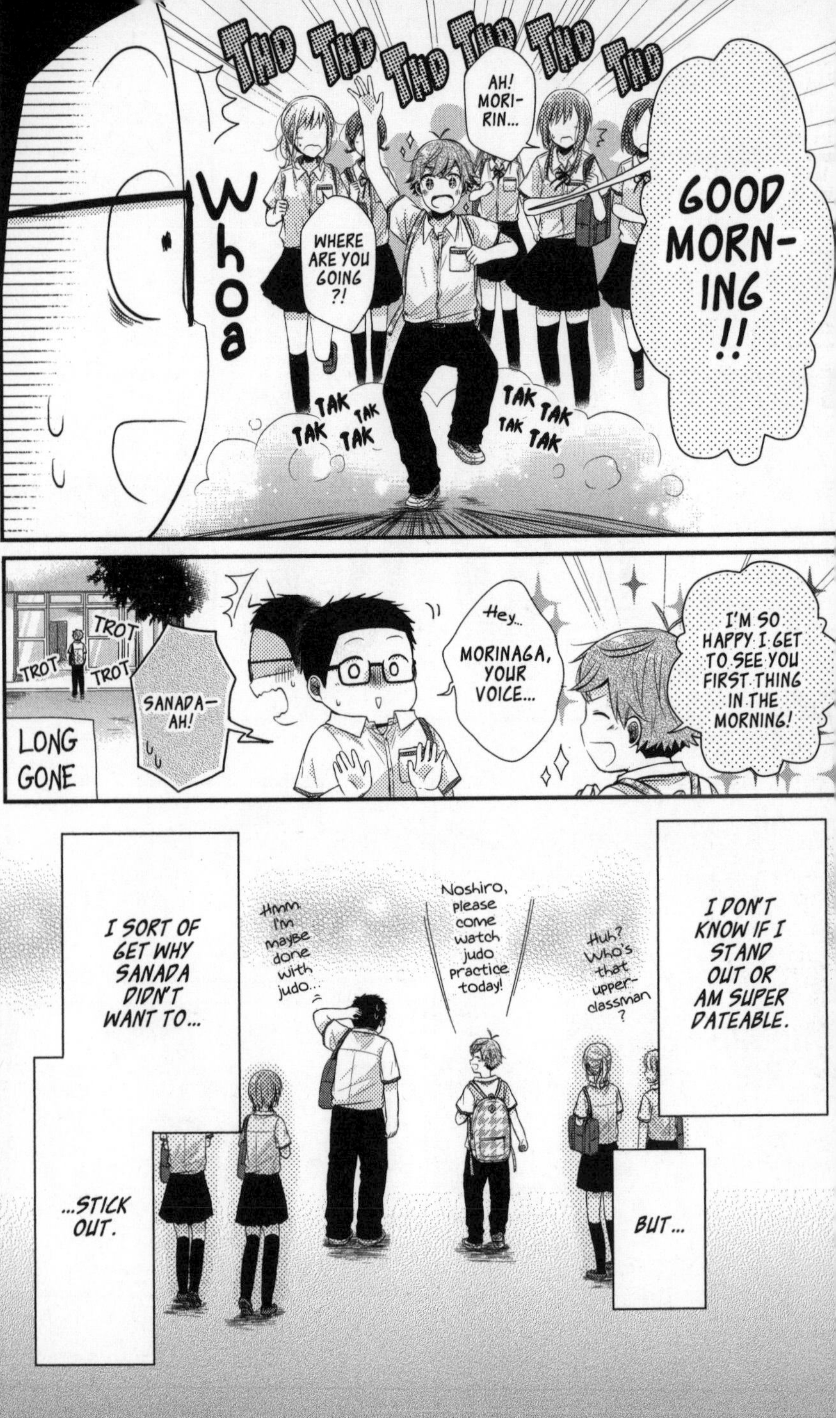
THD THD THD THD THD THD
GOOD MORNING!!
AH! MORI-RIN...
WHERE ARE YOU GOING?!
Whoa
TAK TAK TAK TAK
TAK TAK TAK TAK
I'M SO HAPPY I GET TO SEE YOU FIRST THING IN THE MORNING!
Hey...
MORINAGA, YOUR VOICE...
SANADA-AH!
TROT TROT TROT
LONG GONE
I DON'T KNOW IF I STAND OUT OR AM SUPER DATEABLE.
Huh? Who's that upper-classman?
Noshiro, please come watch judo practice today!
Hmm I'm maybe done with judo...
BUT...
I SORT OF GET WHY SANADA DIDN'T WANT TO...
...STICK OUT.

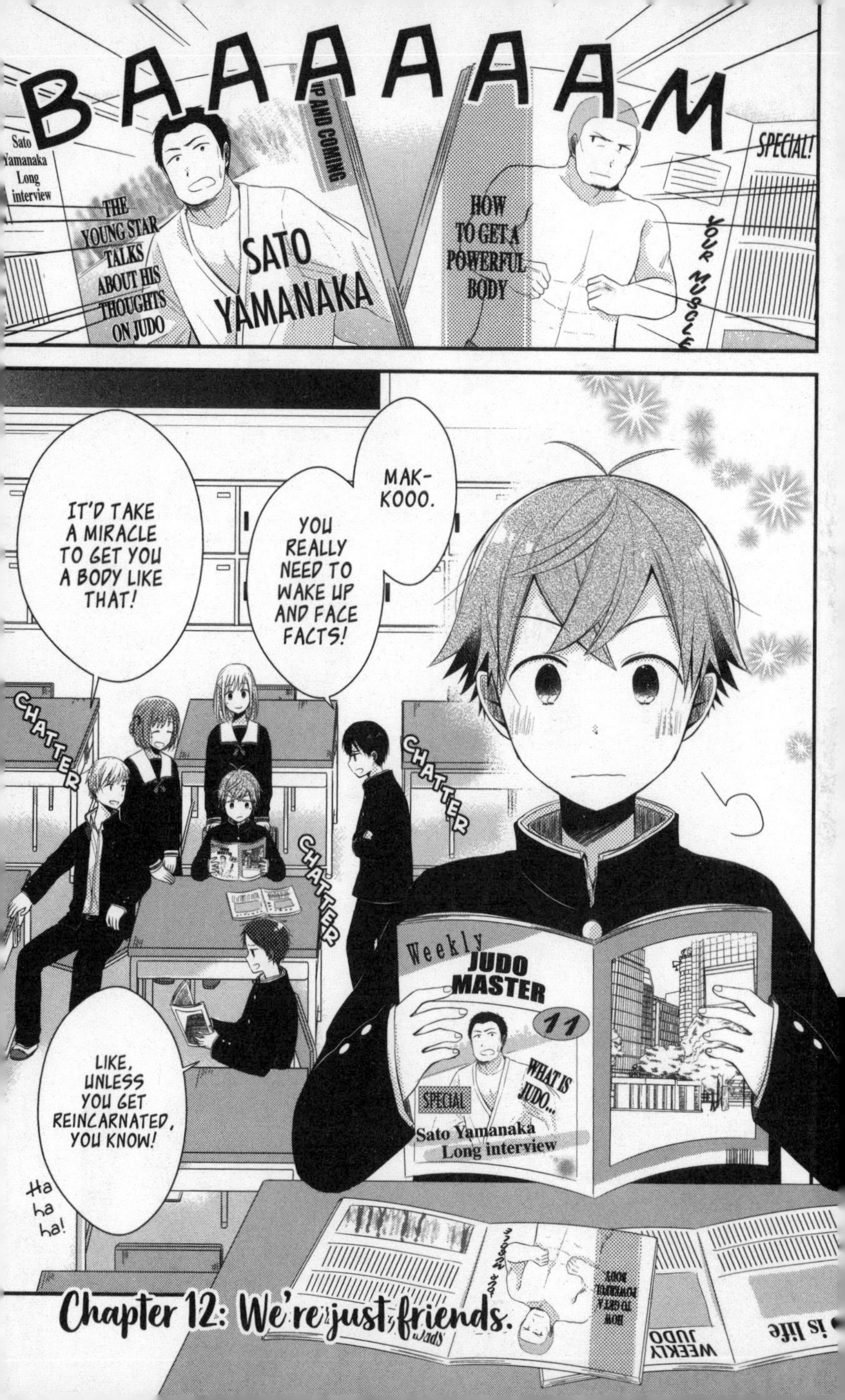
BAAAAAAAM
SPECIAL!
YOUR MUSCLE
HOW TO GET A POWERFUL BODY
UP AND COMING
SATO YAMANAKA
THE YOUNG STAR TALKS ABOUT HIS THOUGHTS ON JUDO
Sato Yamanaka Long interview
Weekly JUDO MASTER
11
WHAT IS JUDO...
SPECIAL
Sato Yamanaka Long interview
MAK-KOOO.
YOU REALLY NEED TO WAKE UP AND FACE FACTS!
IT'D TAKE A MIRACLE TO GET YOU A BODY LIKE THAT!
CHATTER
CHATTER
CHATTER
LIKE, UNLESS YOU GET REINCARNATED, YOU KNOW!
Ha ha ha!
Chapter 12: We're just friends.

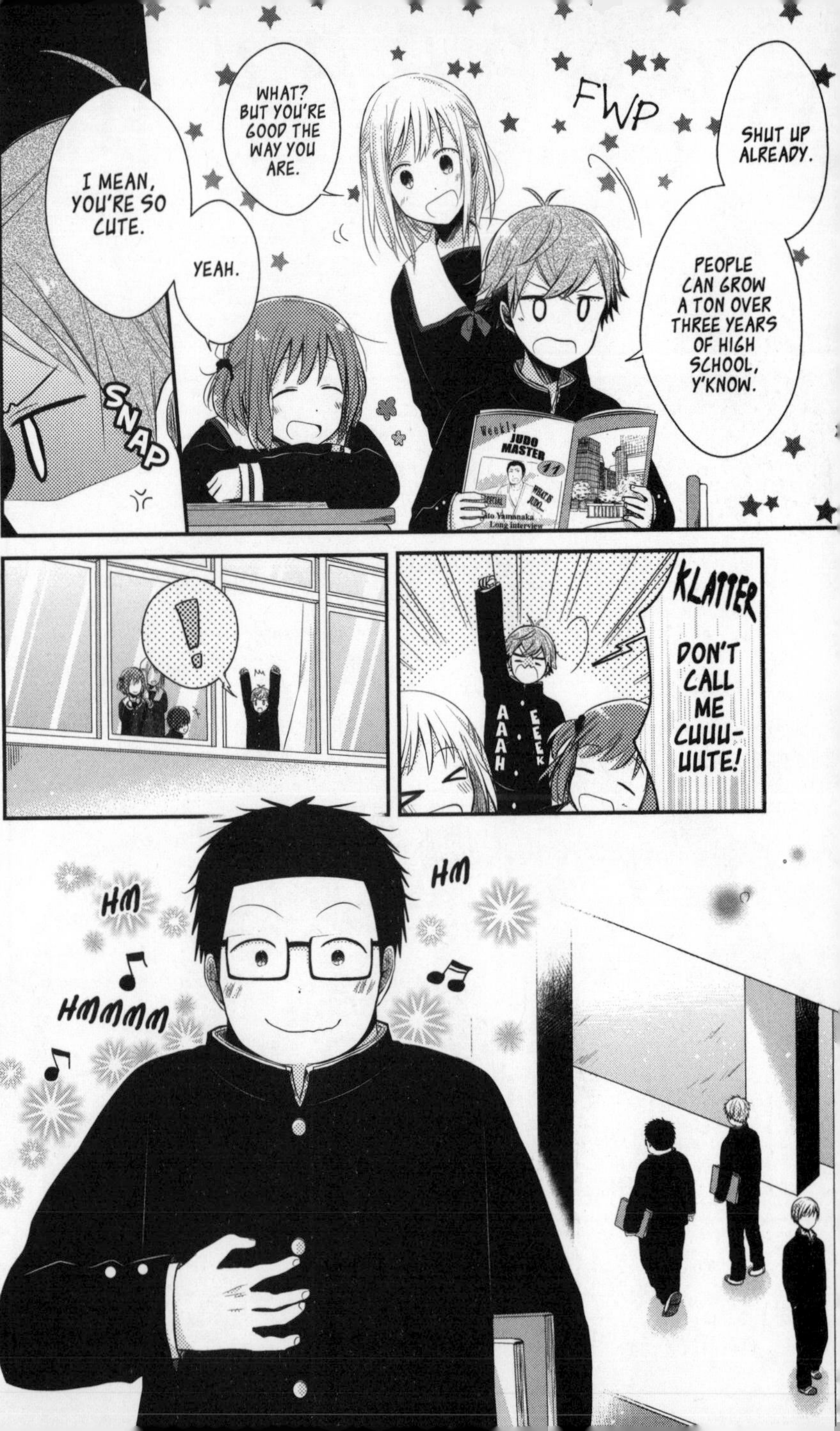
SHUT UP ALREADY.
PEOPLE CAN GROW A TON OVER THREE YEARS OF HIGH SCHOOL, Y'KNOW.
FWP
WHAT? BUT YOU'RE GOOD THE WAY YOU ARE.
I MEAN, YOU'RE SO CUTE.
YEAH.
SNAP
Weekly
JUDO MASTER
11
Long interview
KLATTER
DON'T CALL ME CUUUU-UUTE!
EEEK
AAAH
!
HM
HM
HMMMMM

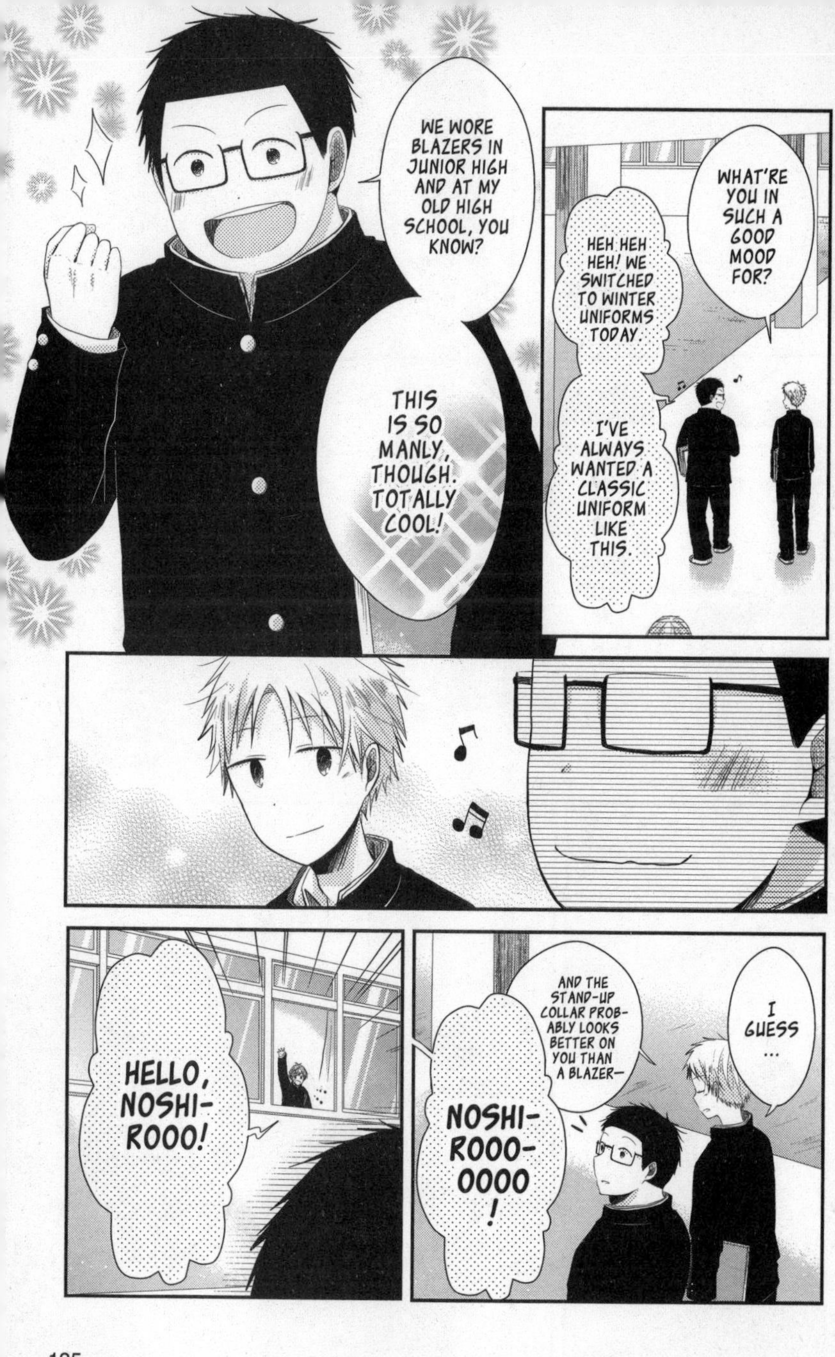
WHAT'RE YOU IN SUCH A GOOD MOOD FOR?
HEH HEH HEH! WE SWITCHED TO WINTER UNIFORMS TODAY.
I'VE ALWAYS WANTED A CLASSIC UNIFORM LIKE THIS.
WE WORE BLAZERS IN JUNIOR HIGH AND AT MY OLD HIGH SCHOOL, YOU KNOW?
THIS IS SO MANLY, THOUGH. TOTALLY COOL!
I GUESS...
AND THE STAND-UP COLLAR PROBABLY LOOKS BETTER ON YOU THAN A BLAZER—
NOSHI-ROOO-OOOO!
HELLO, NOSHI-ROOO!

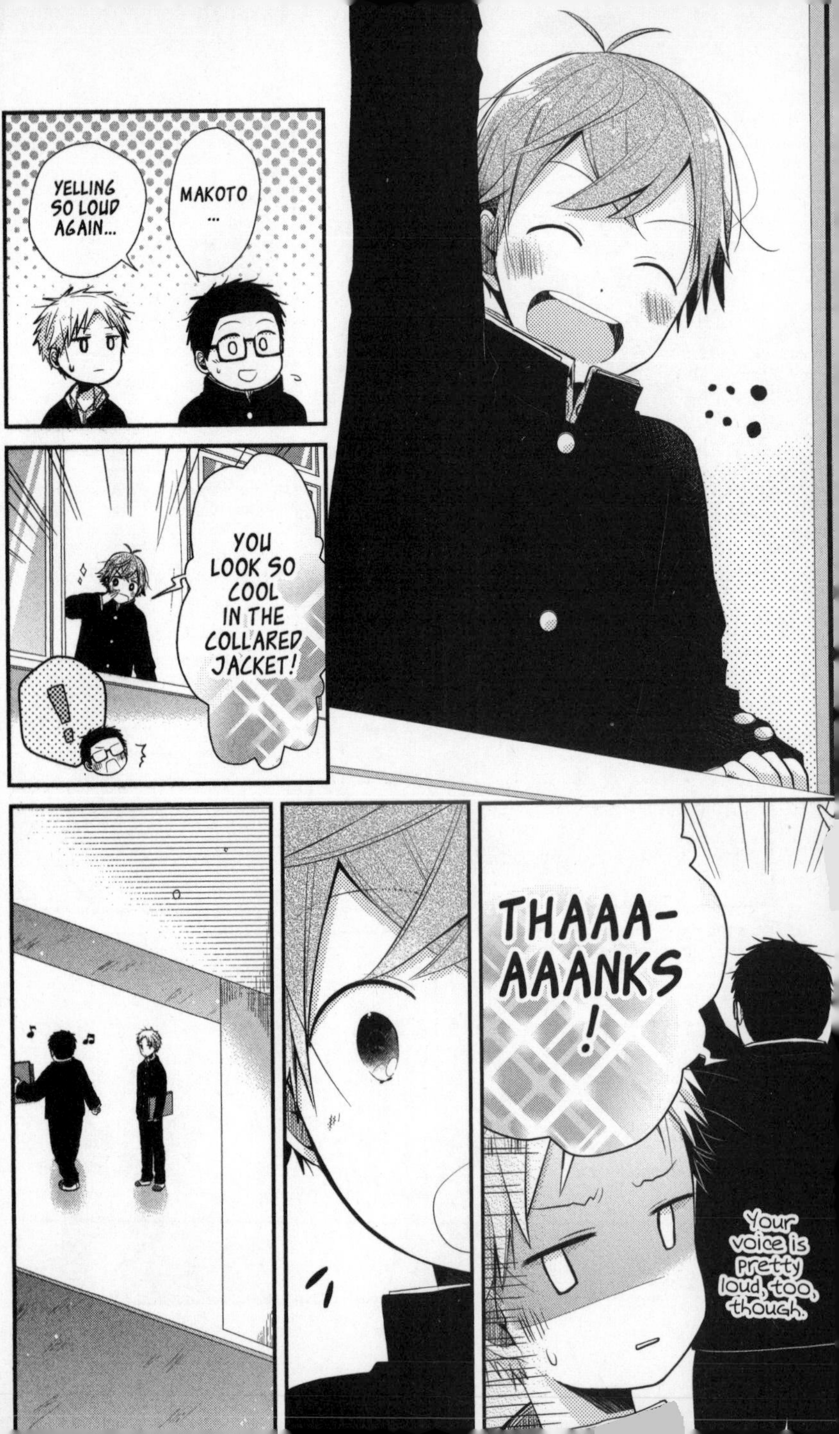
MAKOTO ...
YELLING SO LOUD AGAIN...
YOU LOOK SO COOL IN THE COLLARED JACKET!
!
THAAA-AAANKS!
Your voice is pretty loud, too, though.

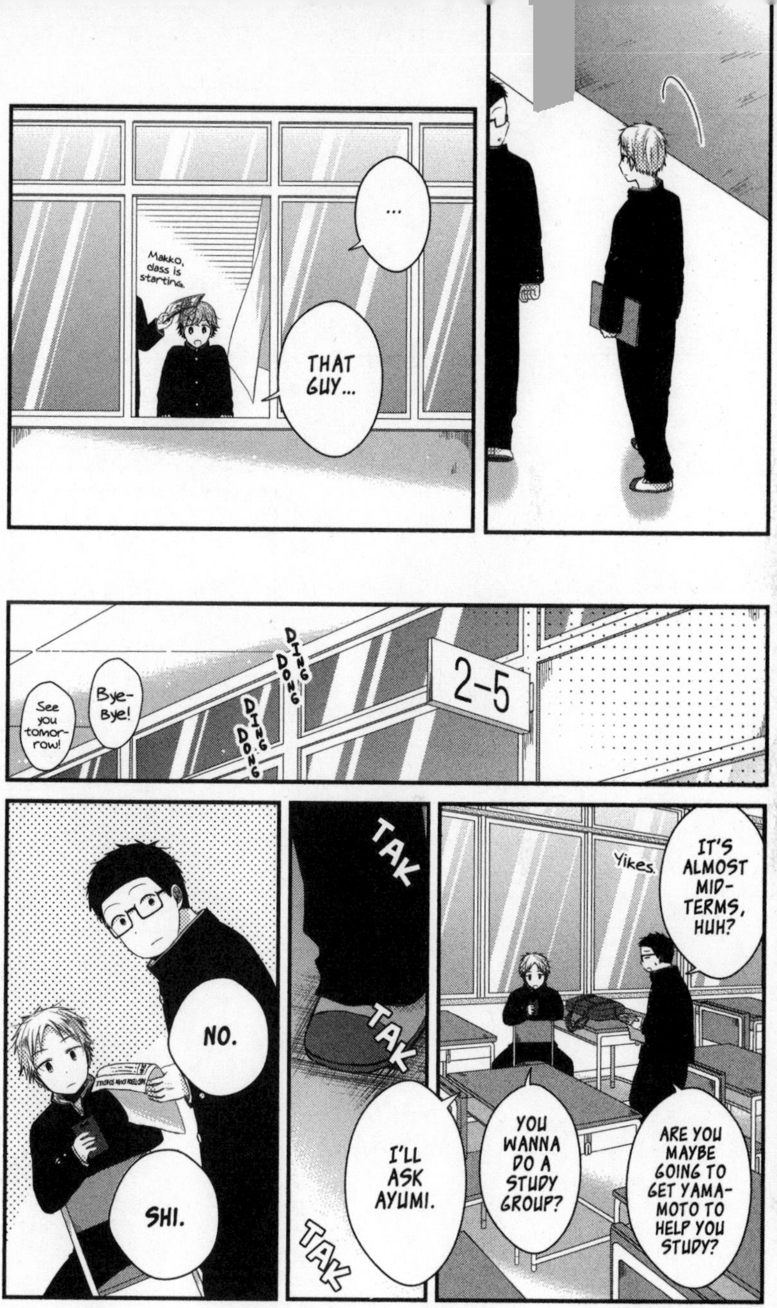
...
THAT GUY...
Makko, class is starting.
DING DONG
DING DONG
Bye-Bye!
See you tomorrow!
IT'S ALMOST MID-TERMS, HUH?
Yikes.
ARE YOU MAYBE GOING TO GET YAMAMOTO TO HELP YOU STUDY?
YOU WANNA DO A STUDY GROUP?
I'LL ASK AYUMI.
TAK
TAK
TAK
NO.
SHI.

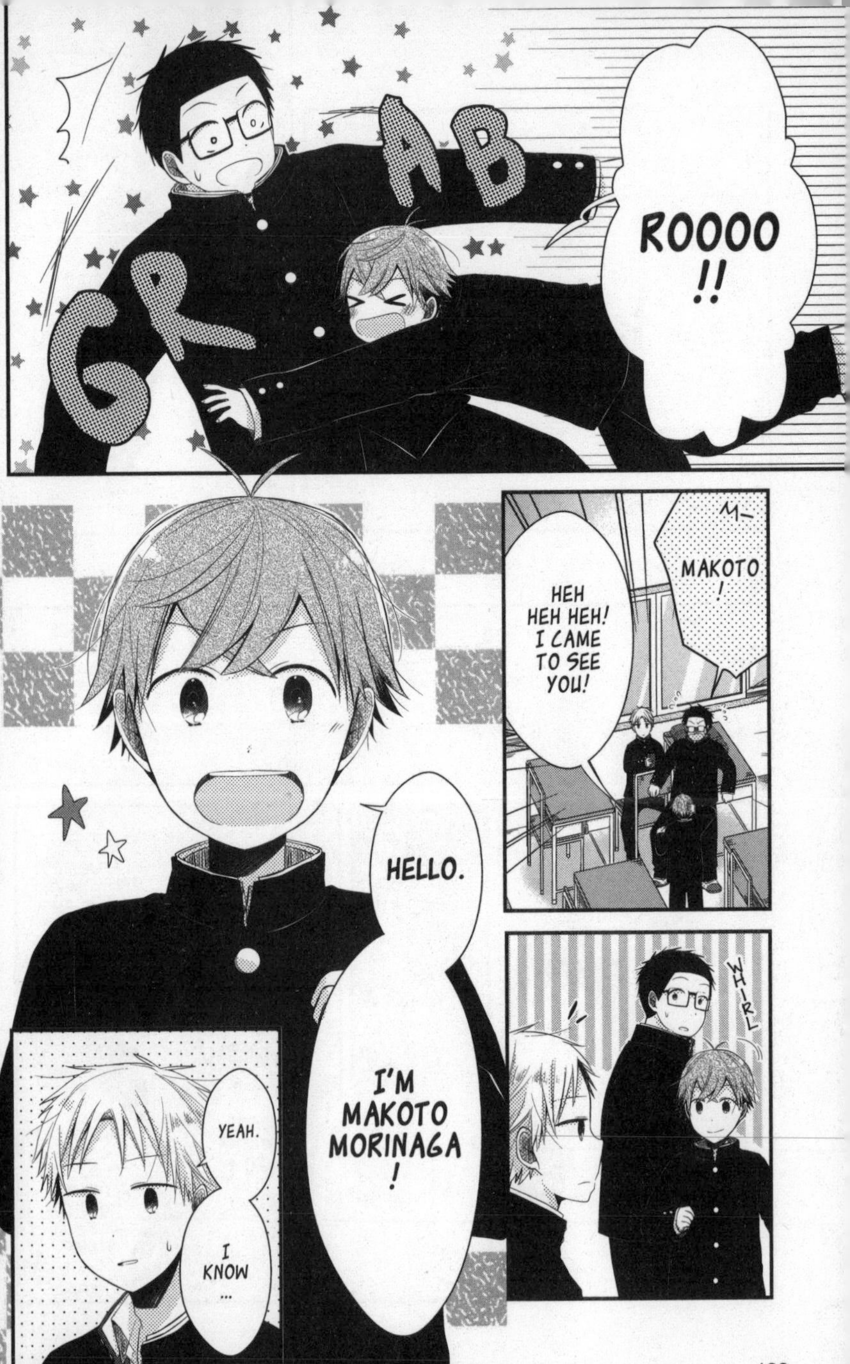
ROOOO !!
GRAB
M-
MAKOTO!
HEH HEH HEH! I CAME TO SEE YOU!
WHIRL
HELLO.
I'M MAKOTO MORINAGA!
YEAH.
I KNOW...

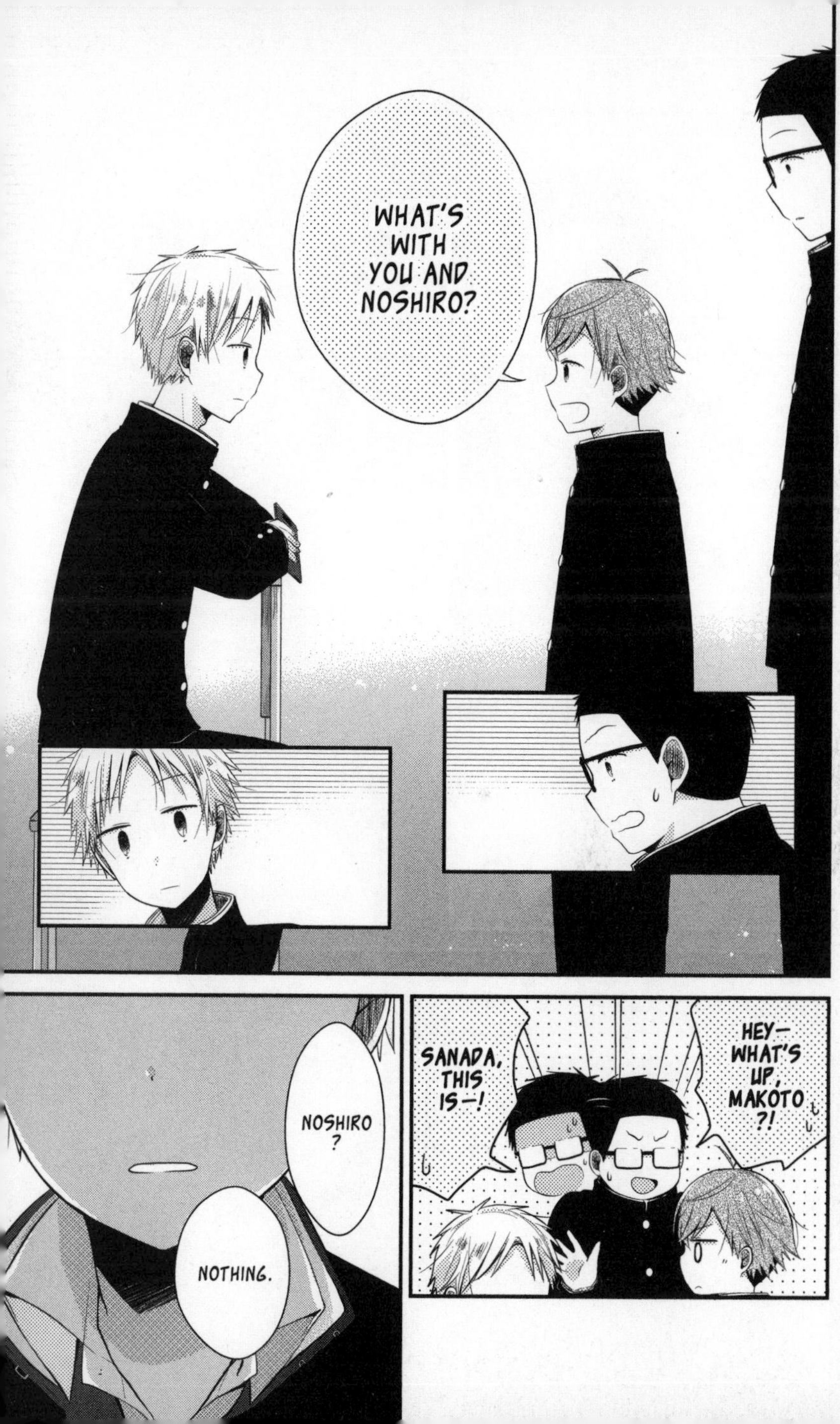
WHAT'S WITH YOU AND NOSHIRO?
HEY— WHAT'S UP, MAKOTO?!
SANADA, THIS IS—!
NOSHIRO?
NOTHING.

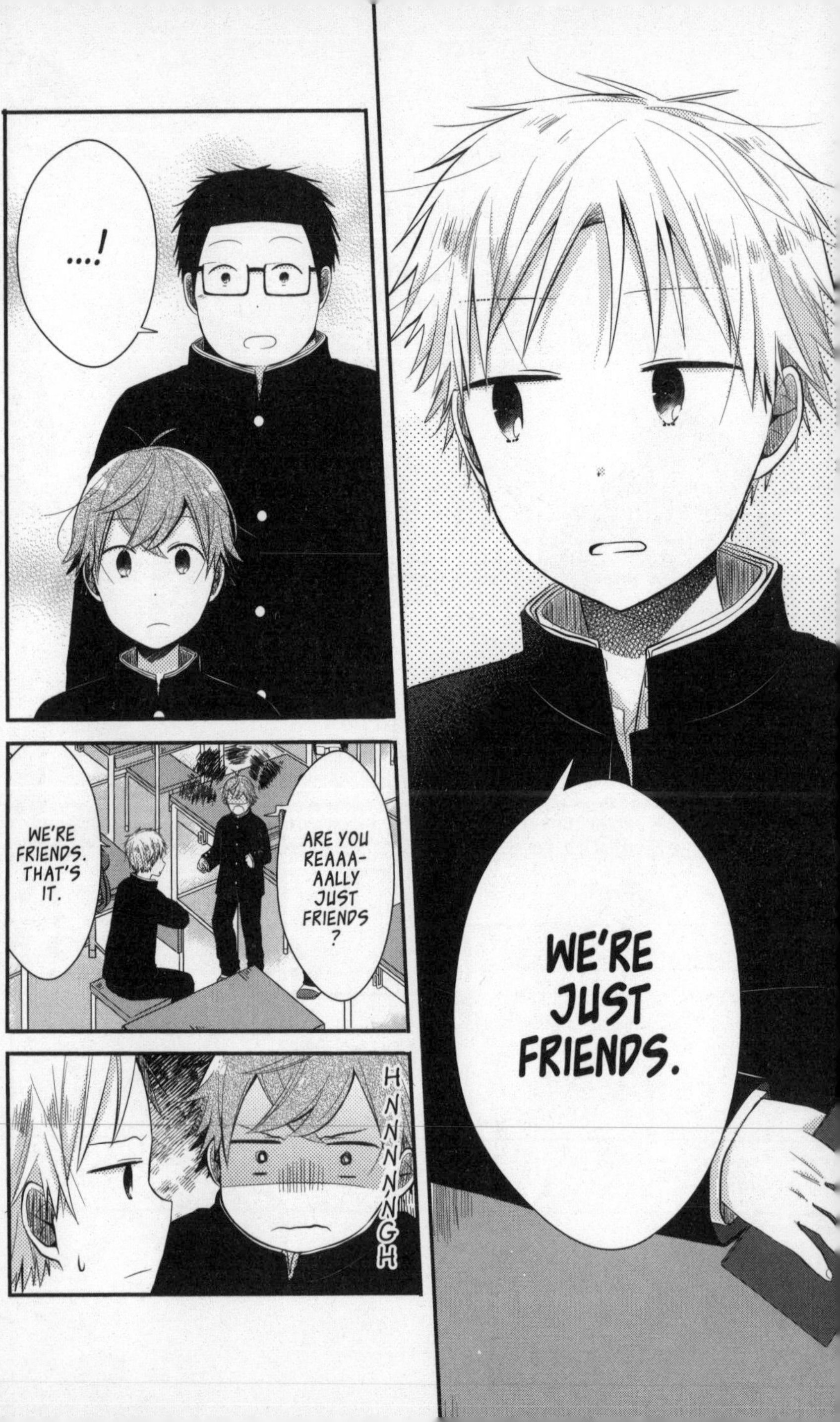
WE'RE JUST FRIENDS.
...!
ARE YOU REAAAAALLY JUST FRIENDS?
WE'RE FRIENDS. THAT'S IT.
HNNNNNGH

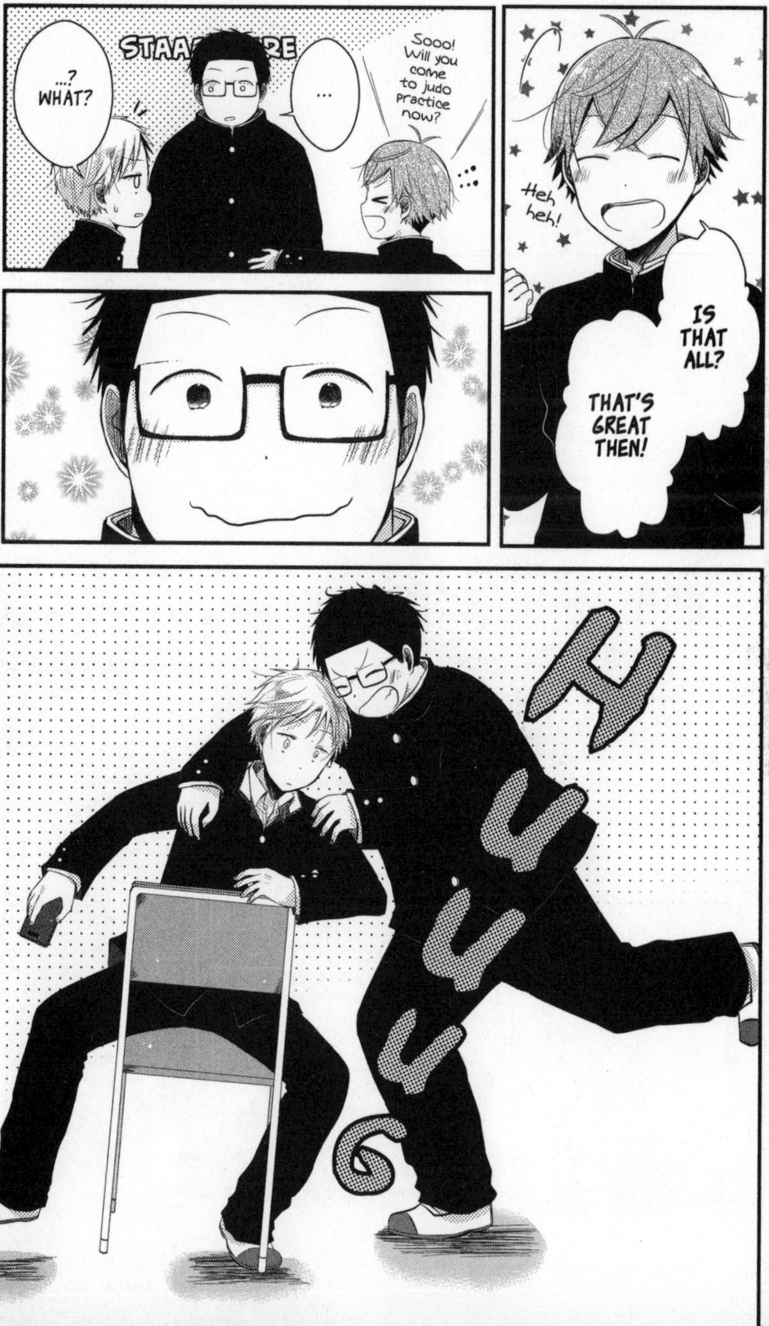
Heh heh!
IS THAT ALL?
THAT'S GREAT THEN!
Sooo! Will you come to judo practice now?
...
STAA
RE
...? WHAT?
HUUUG

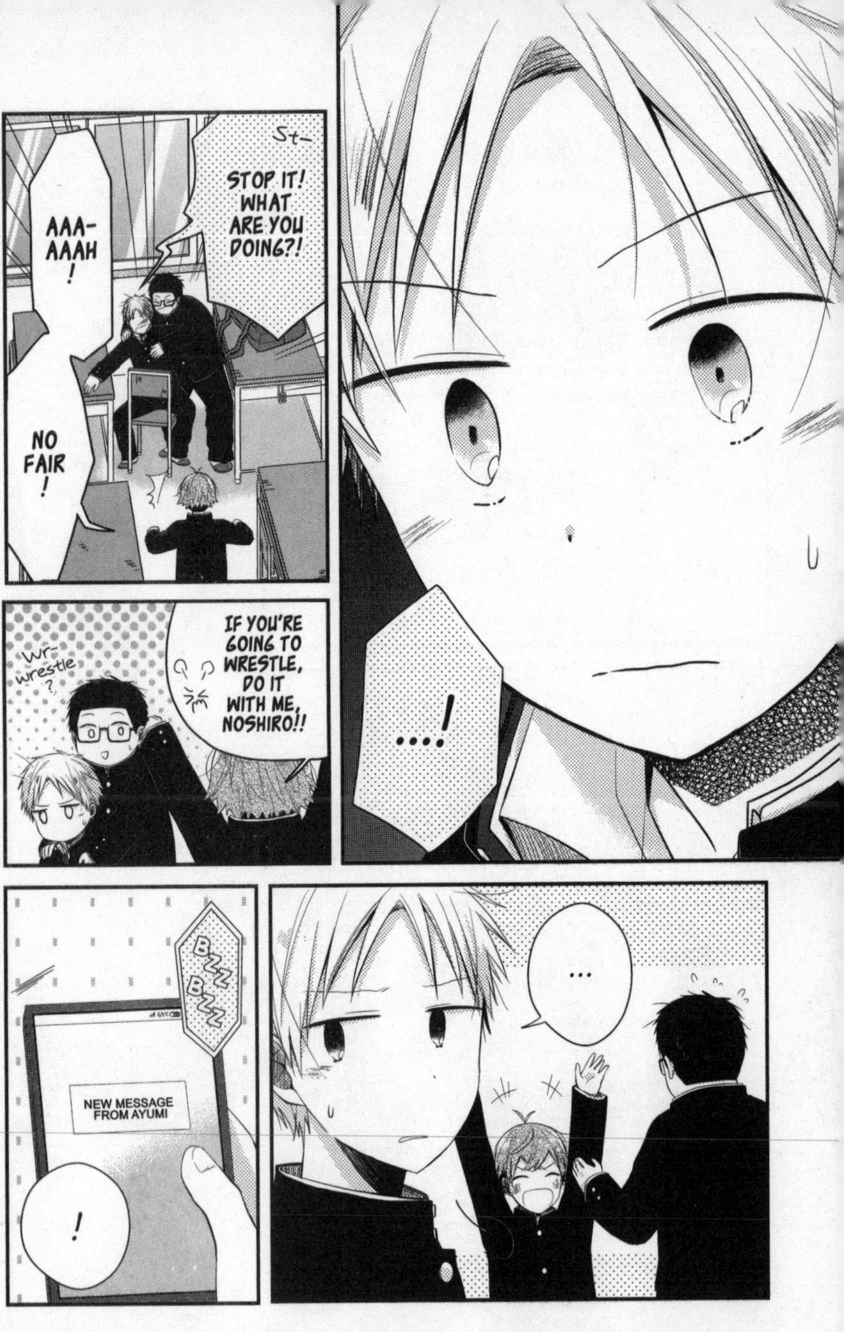
...!
St-
STOP IT! WHAT ARE YOU DOING?!
AAA-AAAH!
NO FAIR!
IF YOU'RE GOING TO WRESTLE, DO IT WITH ME, NOSHIRO!!
Wr-wrestle?
...
BZZ BZZ
NEW MESSAGE FROM AYUMI
!

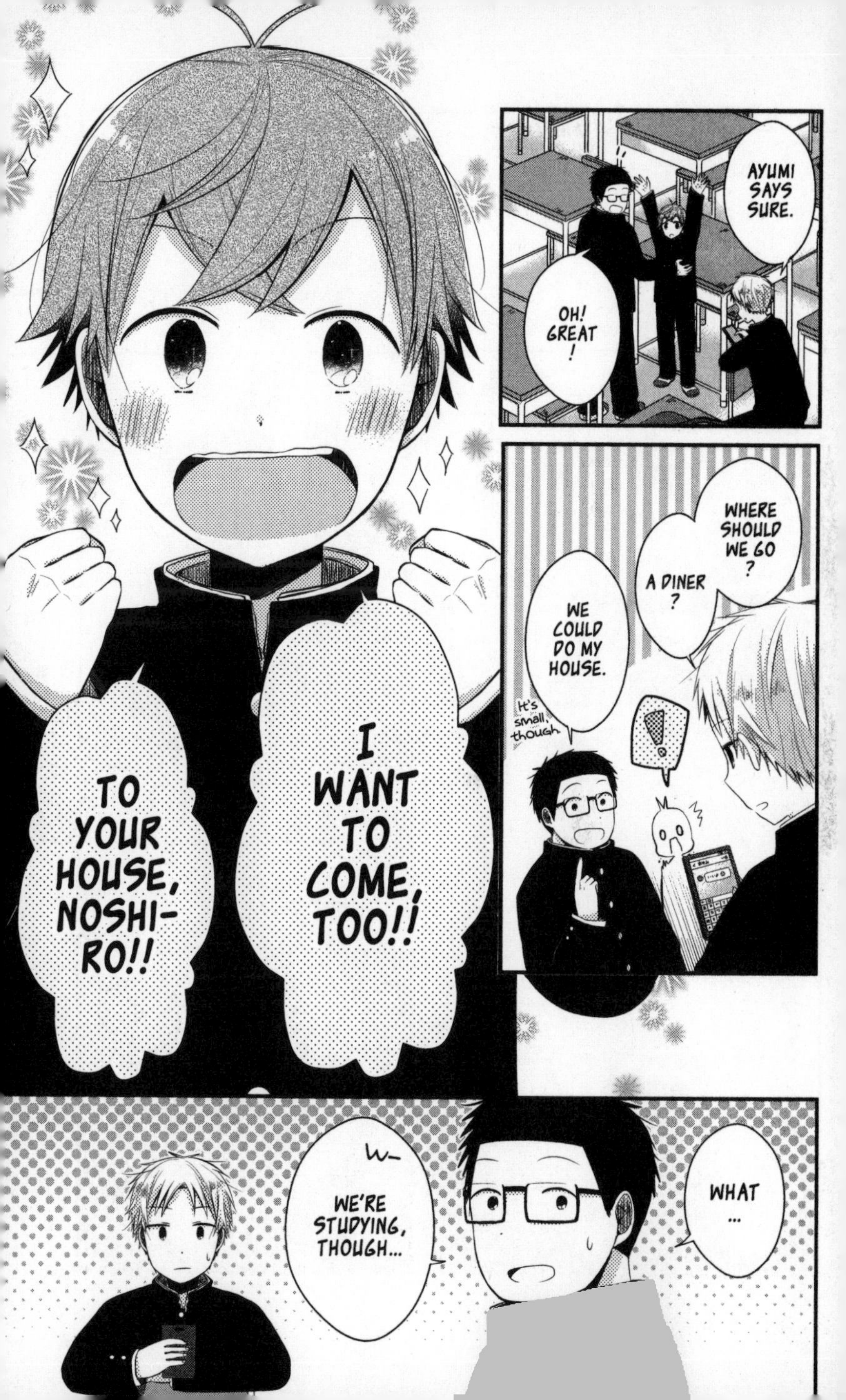
AYUMI SAYS SURE.
OH! GREAT!
WHERE SHOULD WE GO?
A DINER?
WE COULD DO MY HOUSE.
It's small, though.
I WANT TO COME, TOO!!
TO YOUR HOUSE, NOSHIRO!!
WHAT...
W— WE'RE STUDYING, THOUGH...

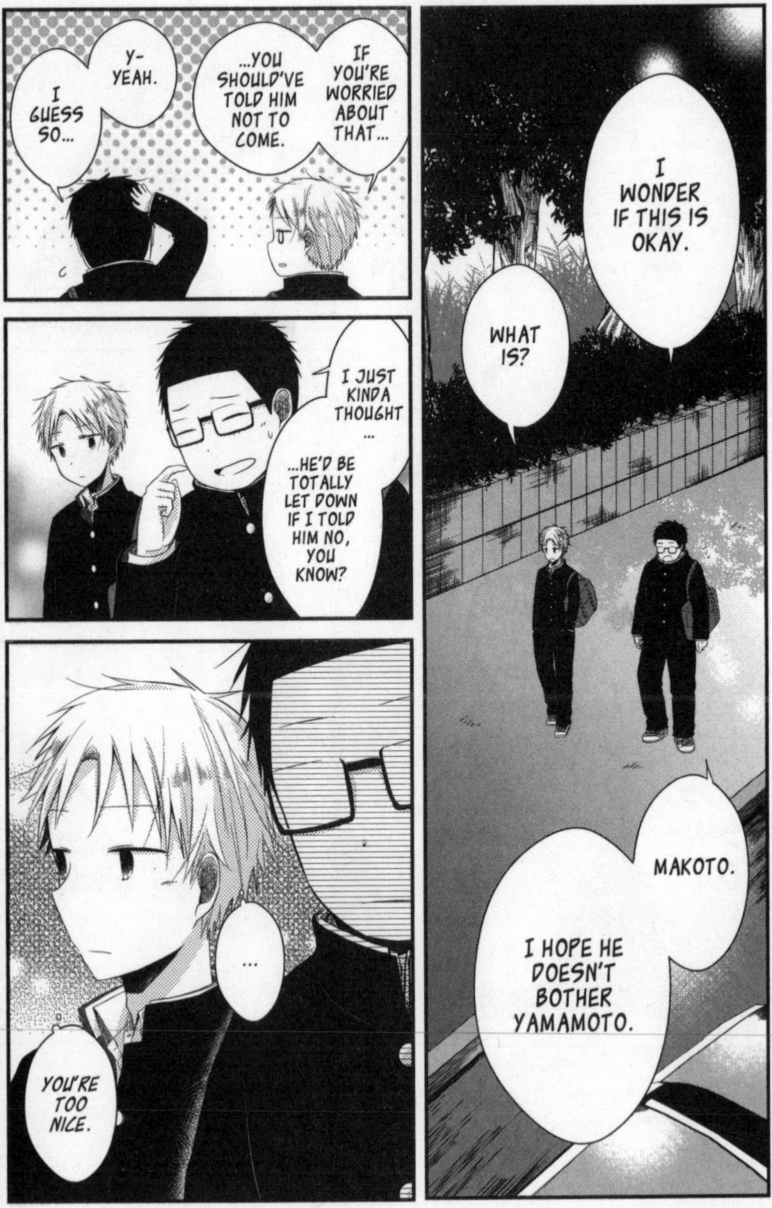
I WONDER IF THIS IS OKAY.
WHAT IS?
MAKOTO.
I HOPE HE DOESN'T BOTHER YAMAMOTO.
IF YOU'RE WORRIED ABOUT THAT...
...YOU SHOULD'VE TOLD HIM NOT TO COME.
Y-YEAH.
I GUESS SO...
I JUST KINDA THOUGHT...
...HE'D BE TOTALLY LET DOWN IF I TOLD HIM NO, YOU KNOW?
...
YOU'RE TOO NICE.

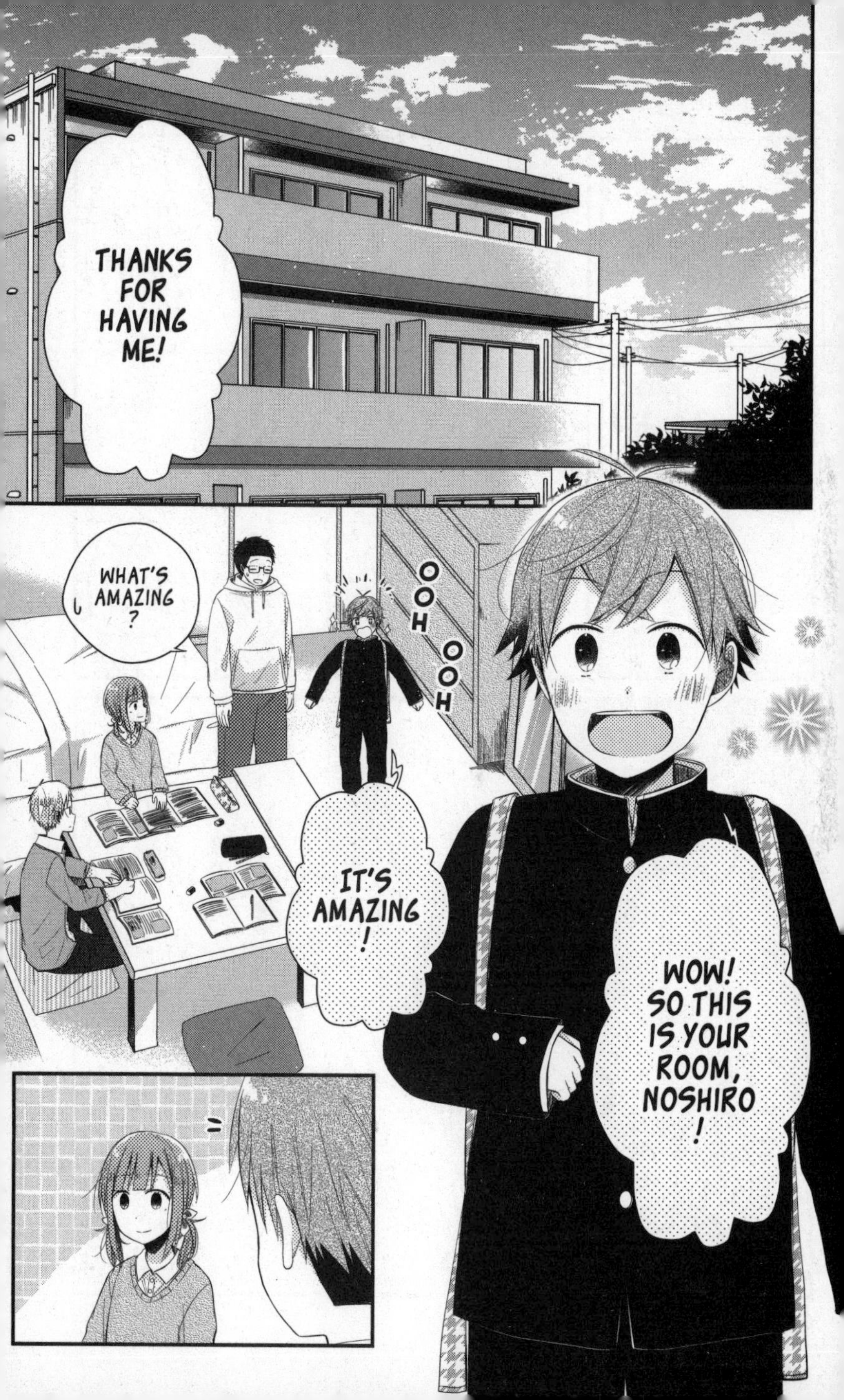
THANKS FOR HAVING ME!
WOW! SO THIS IS YOUR ROOM, NOSHIRO!
OOH OOH
IT'S AMAZING!
WHAT'S AMAZING?

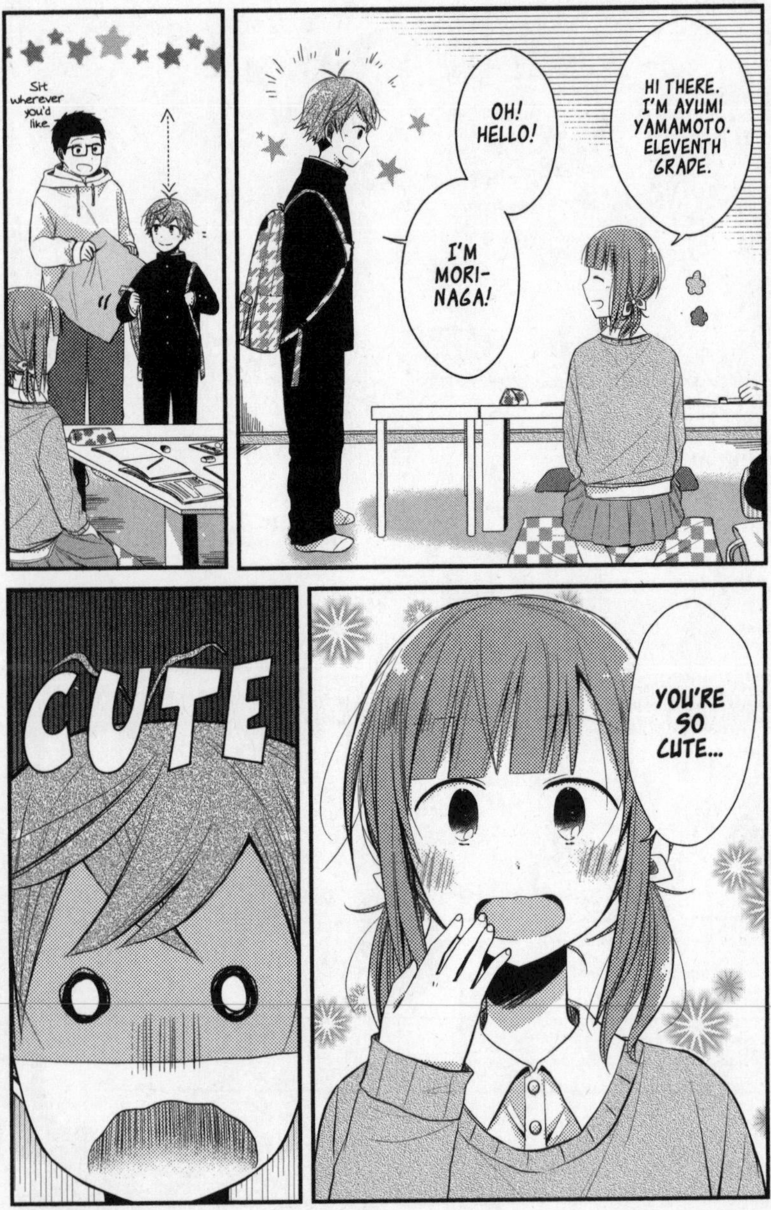
HI THERE. I'M AYUMI YAMAMOTO. ELEVENTH GRADE.
OH! HELLO!
I'M MORI-NAGA!
Sit wherever you'd like
YOU'RE SO CUTE...
CUTE

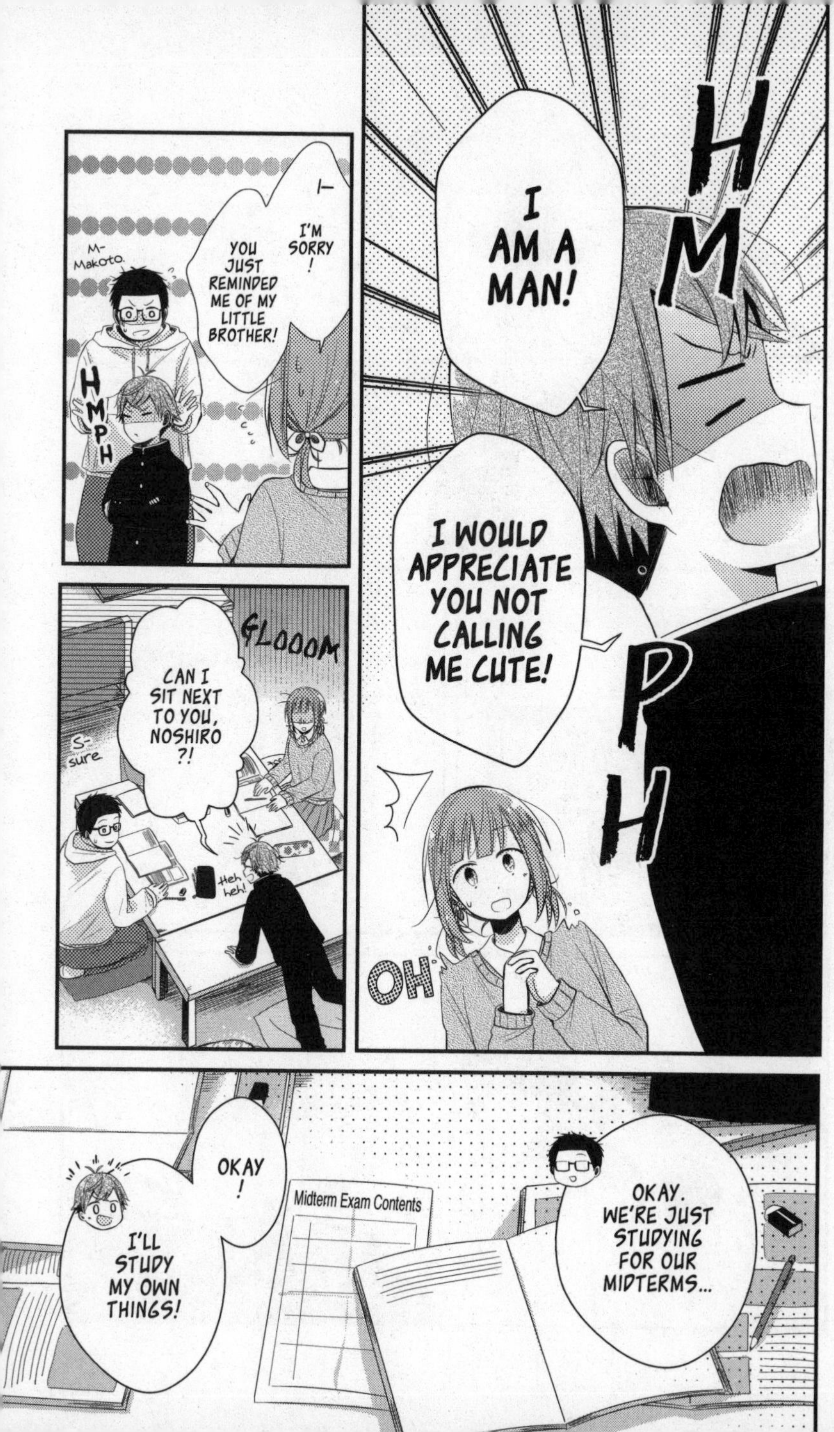
HMPH
I AM A MAN!
I WOULD APPRECIATE YOU NOT CALLING ME CUTE!
OH
I-
I'M SORRY!
YOU JUST REMINDED ME OF MY LITTLE BROTHER!
M-Makoto.
HMPH
GLOOOM
CAN I SIT NEXT TO YOU, NOSHIRO?!
S-sure
Heh heh!
OKAY. WE'RE JUST STUDYING FOR OUR MIDTERMS...
Midterm Exam Contents
OKAY!
I'LL STUDY MY OWN THINGS!

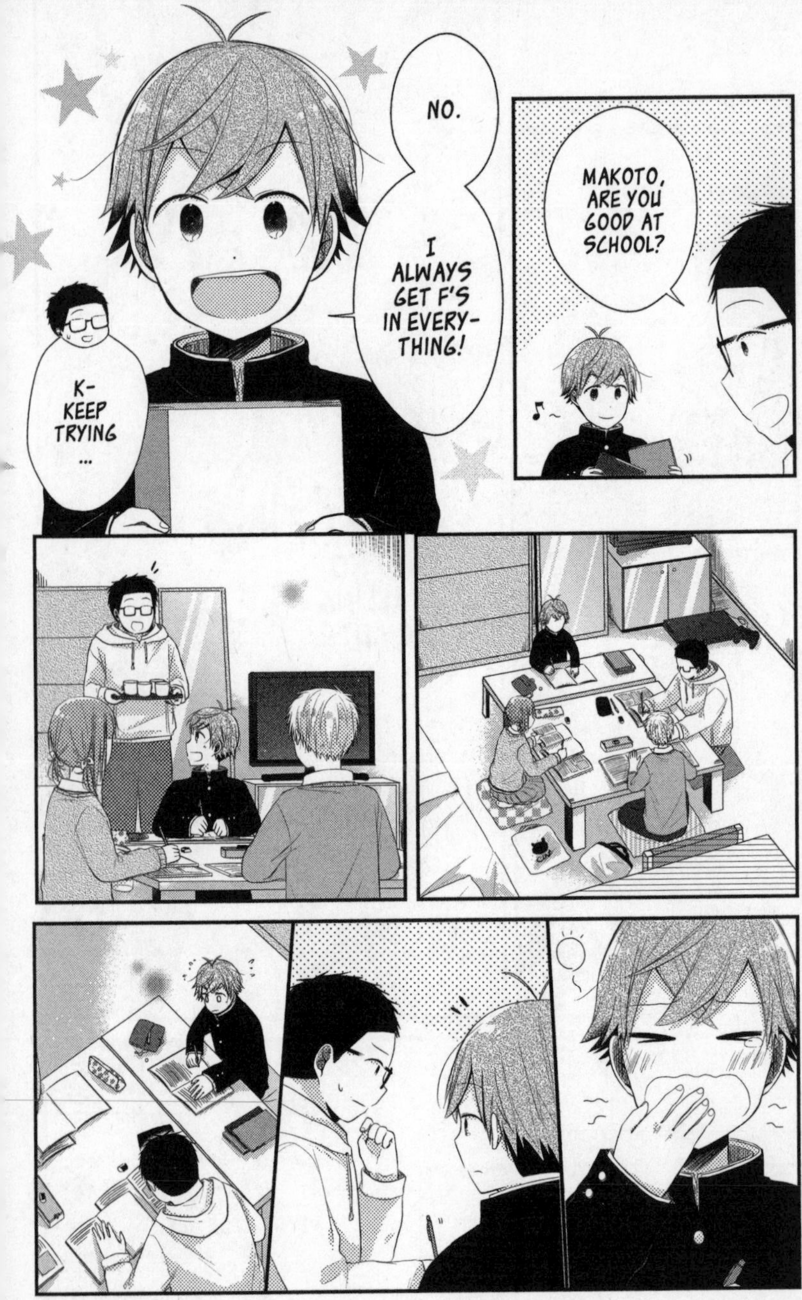
MAKOTO, ARE YOU GOOD AT SCHOOL?
NO.
I ALWAYS GET F'S IN EVERY-THING!
K-KEEP TRYING ...

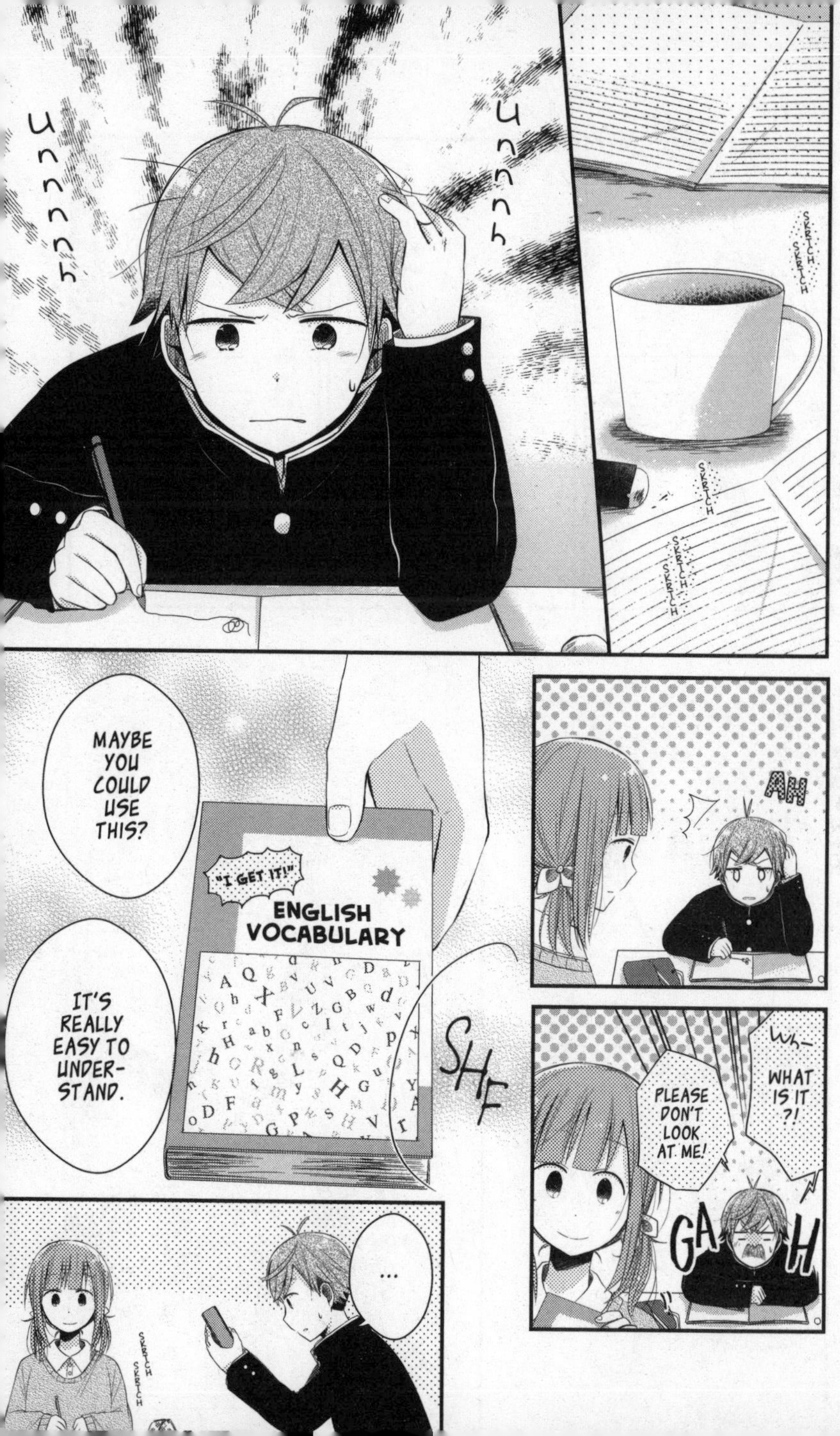
SKRITCH SKRITCH
SKRITCH
SKRITCH SKRITCH
Unnnnh
Unnnnh
AH
Wh- WHAT IS IT?!
PLEASE DON'T LOOK AT ME!
GAH
MAYBE YOU COULD USE THIS?
"I GET IT!"
ENGLISH VOCABULARY
SHF
IT'S REALLY EASY TO UNDER-STAND.
...
SKRITCH SKRITCH

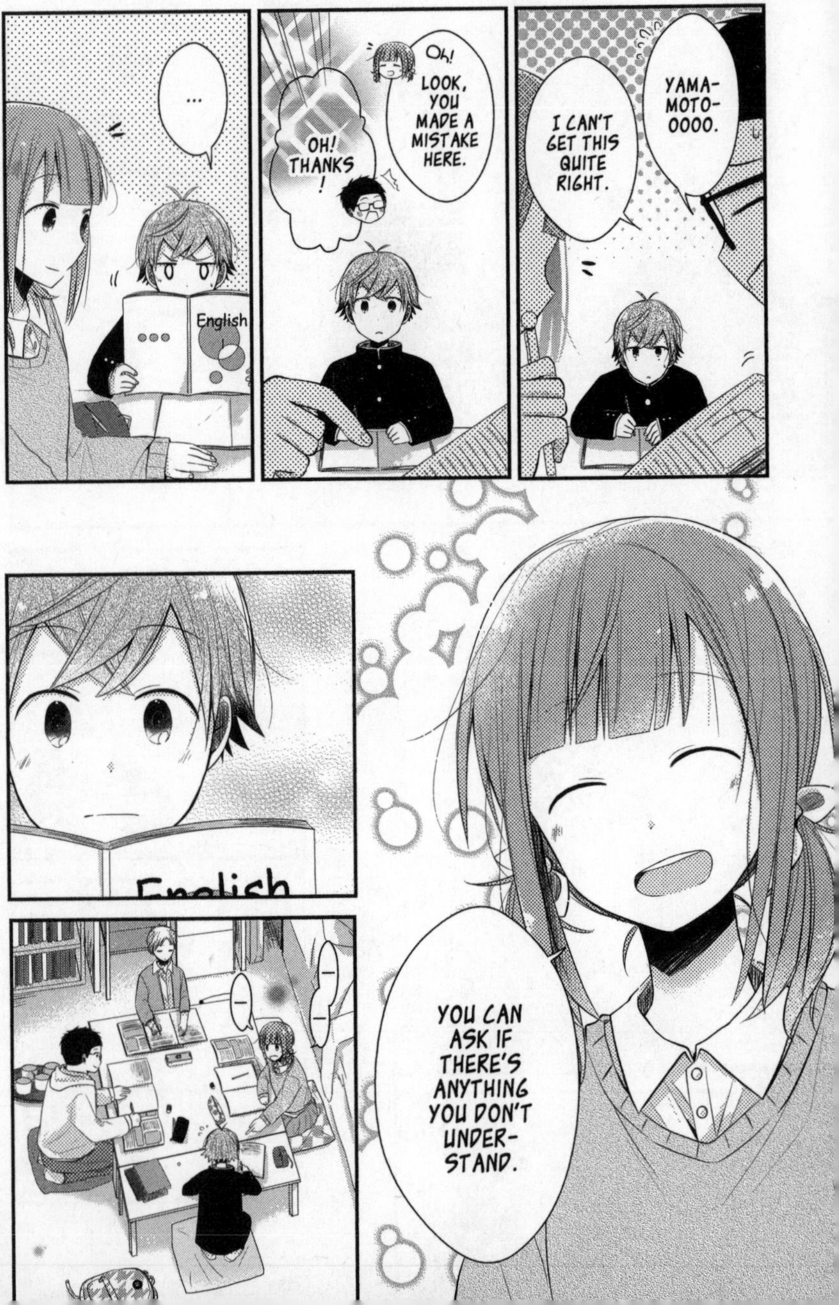
YAMA-MOTO-OOOO.
I CAN'T GET THIS QUITE RIGHT.
Oh! LOOK, YOU MADE A MISTAKE HERE.
OH! THANKS!
...
English
YOU CAN ASK IF THERE'S ANYTHING YOU DON'T UNDER-STAND.
English
—
—

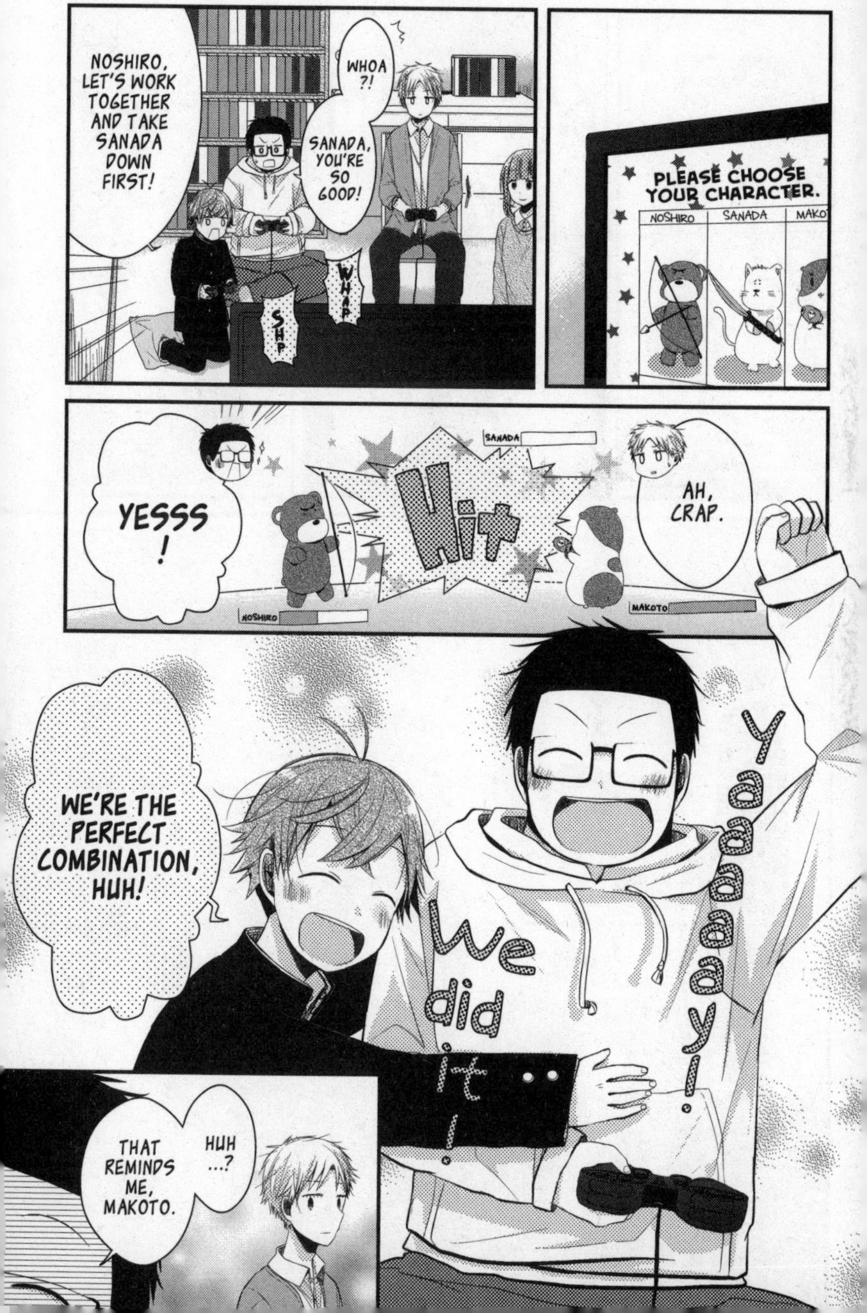
PLEASE CHOOSE YOUR CHARACTER.
NOSHIRO
SANADA
MAKO
WHOA ?!
SANADA, YOU'RE SO GOOD!
WHAP
SHP
NOSHIRO, LET'S WORK TOGETHER AND TAKE SANADA DOWN FIRST!
AH, CRAP.
SANADA
MAKOTO
Hit
NOSHIRO
YESSS!
Yaaaaay!
We did it!
WE'RE THE PERFECT COMBINATION, HUH!
HUH ...?
THAT REMINDS ME, MAKOTO.

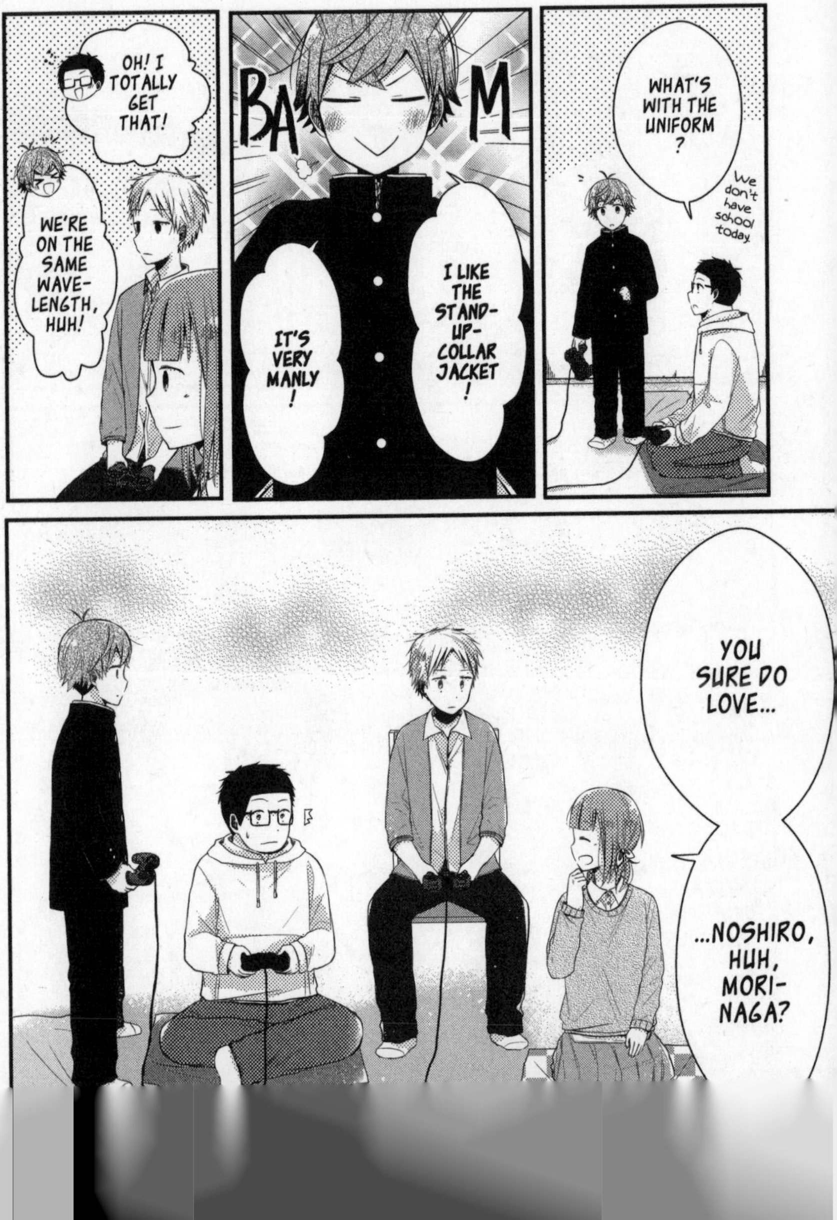
WHAT'S WITH THE UNIFORM?
We don't have school today.
BAM
I LIKE THE STAND-UP-COLLAR JACKET!
IT'S VERY MANLY!
OH! I TOTALLY GET THAT!
WE'RE ON THE SAME WAVE-LENGTH, HUH!
YOU SURE DO LOVE...
...NOSHIRO, HUH, MORI-NAGA?

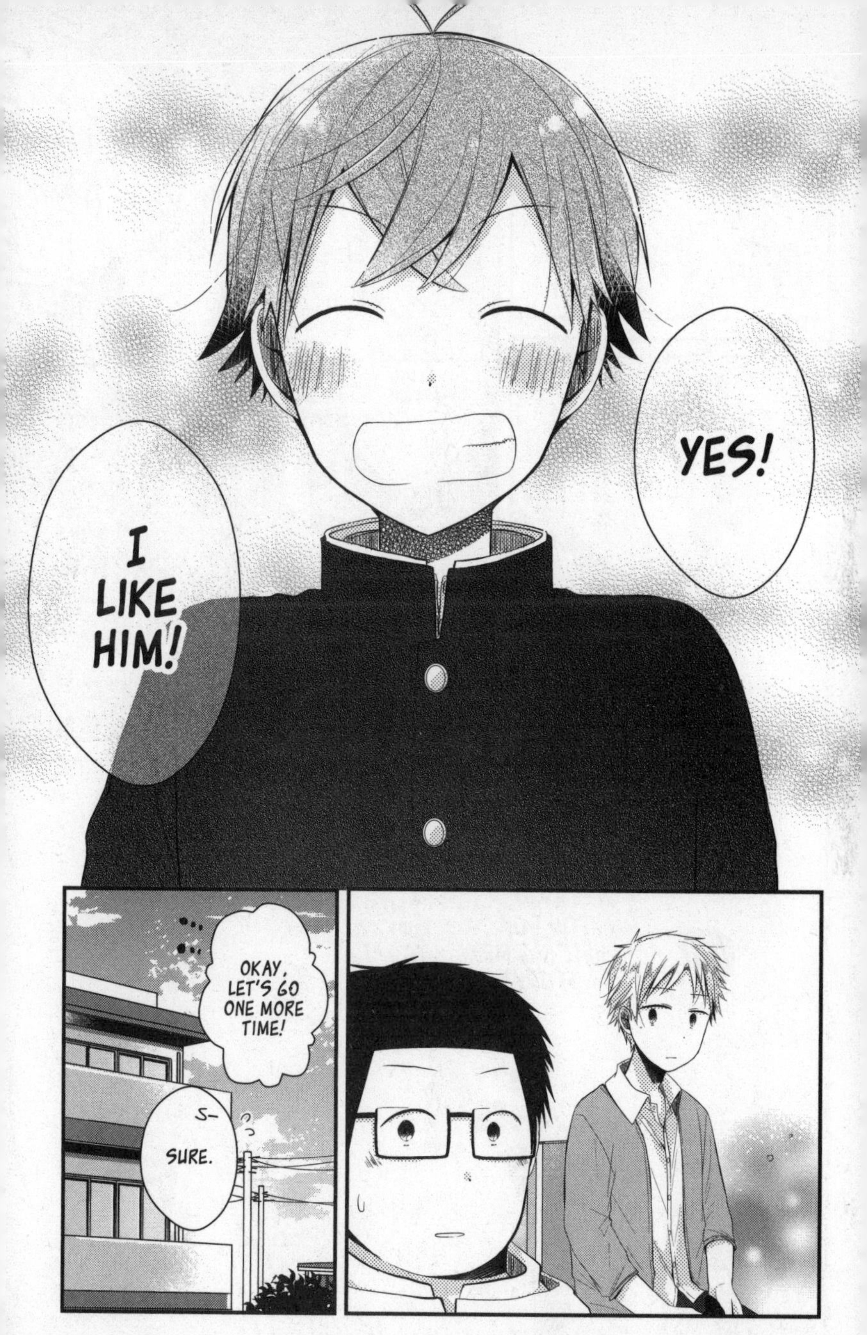
YES!
I LIKE HIM!
OKAY, LET'S GO ONE MORE TIME!
S— SURE.

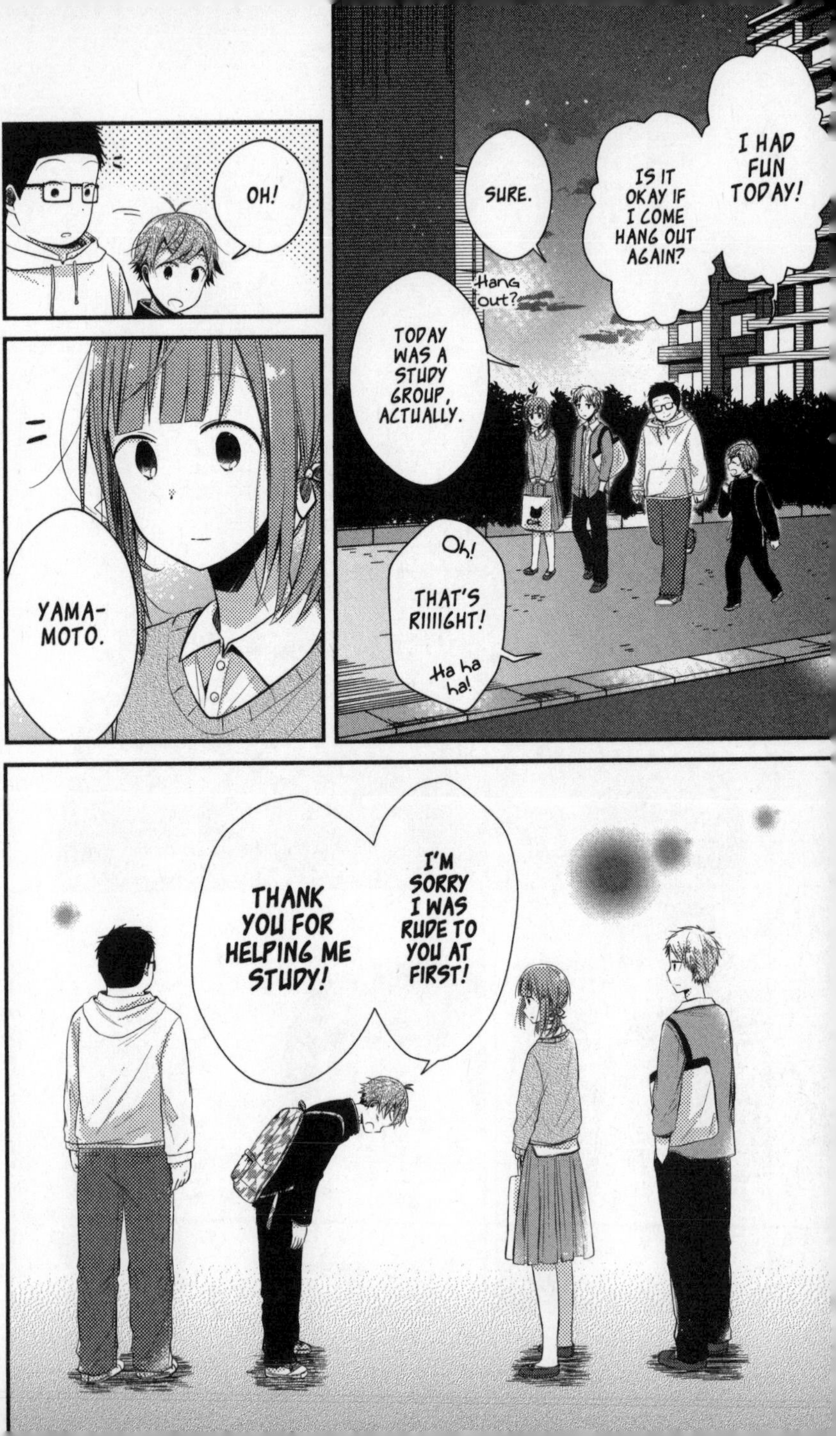
I HAD FUN TODAY!
IS IT OKAY IF I COME HANG OUT AGAIN?
SURE.
Hang out?
TODAY WAS A STUDY GROUP, ACTUALLY.
Oh!
THAT'S RIIIIGHT!
Ha ha ha!
OH!
YAMA-MOTO.
I'M SORRY I WAS RUDE TO YOU AT FIRST!
THANK YOU FOR HELPING ME STUDY!

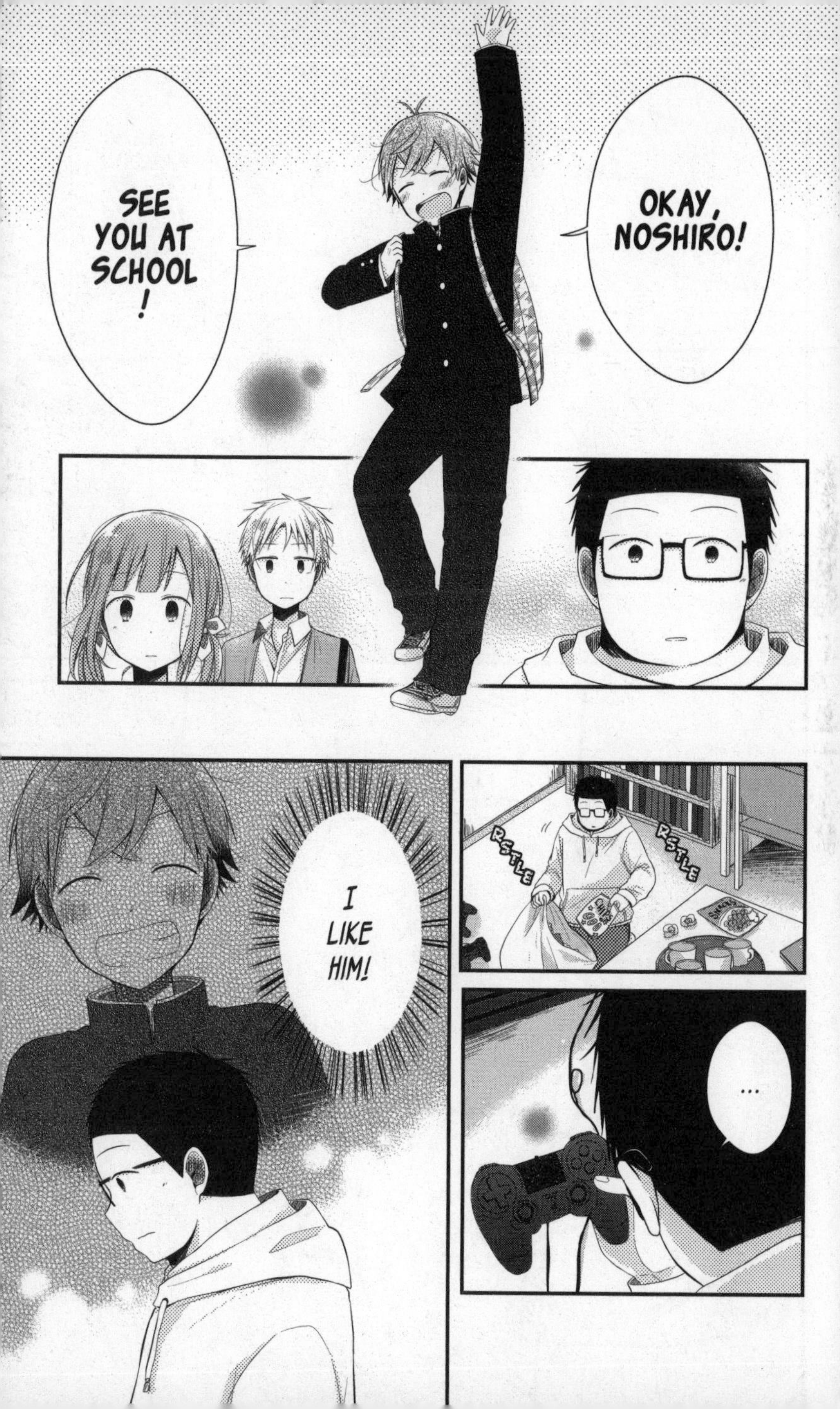
OKAY, NOSHIRO!
SEE YOU AT SCHOOL!
RSTLE
RSTLE
...
I LIKE HIM!

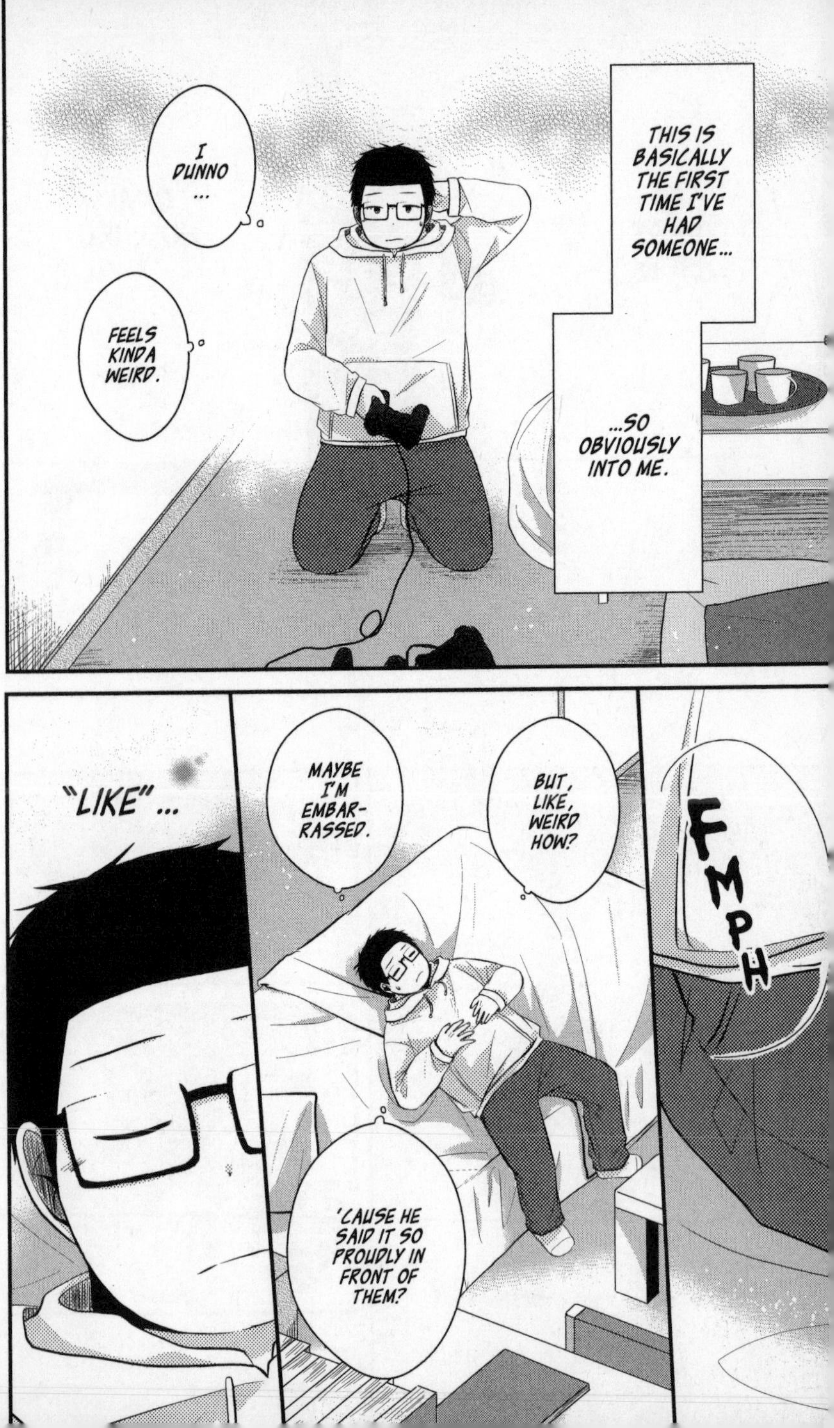
THIS IS BASICALLY THE FIRST TIME I'VE HAD SOMEONE...
...SO OBVIOUSLY INTO ME.
I DUNNO...
FEELS KINDA WEIRD.
FMPH
BUT, LIKE, WEIRD HOW?
MAYBE I'M EMBAR-RASSED.
'CAUSE HE SAID IT SO PROUDLY IN FRONT OF THEM?
"LIKE"...

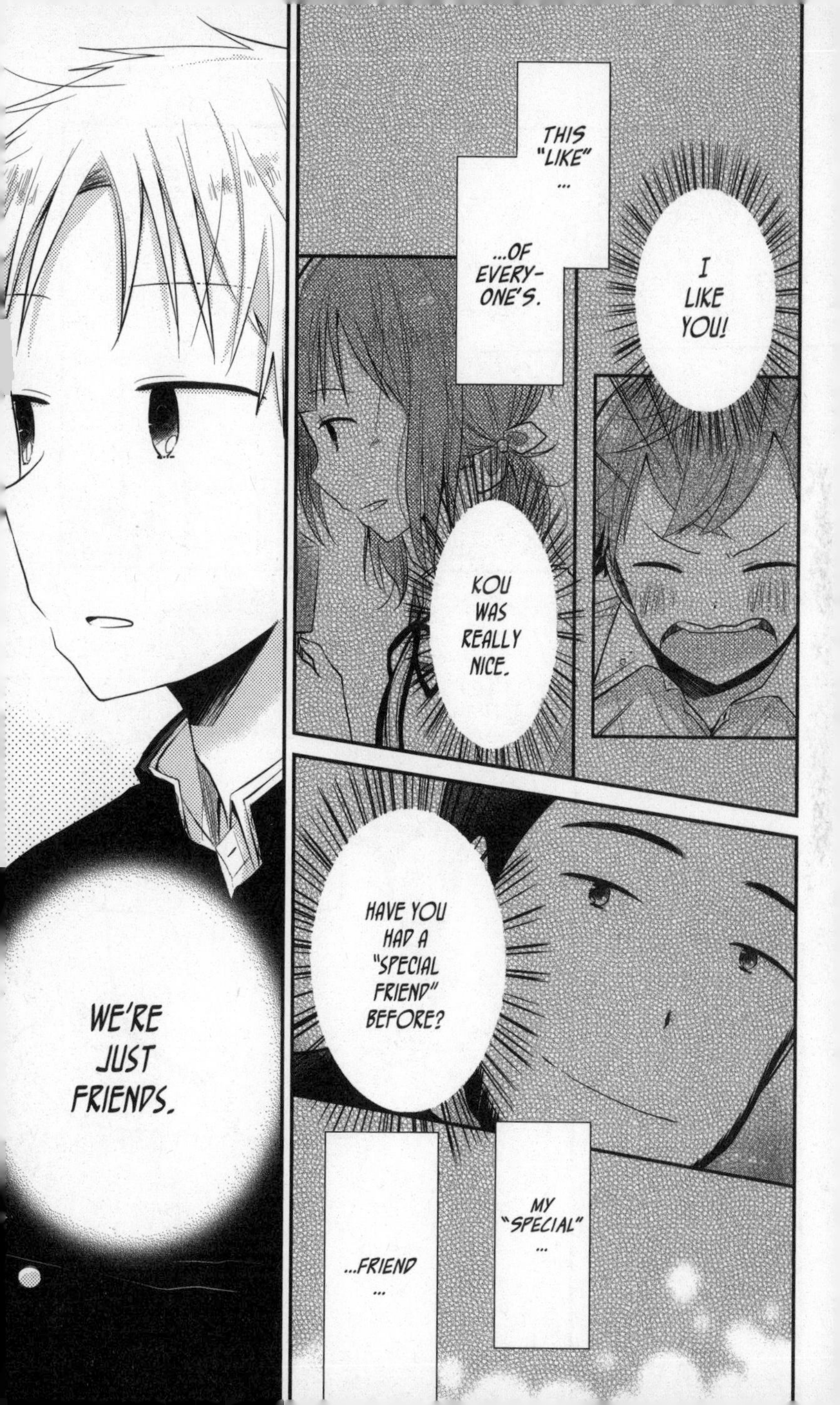

I LIKE YOU!
THIS "LIKE" ...
...OF EVERY-ONE'S.
KOU WAS REALLY NICE.
HAVE YOU HAD A "SPECIAL FRIEND" BEFORE?
MY "SPECIAL" ...
...FRIEND ...
WE'RE JUST FRIENDS.

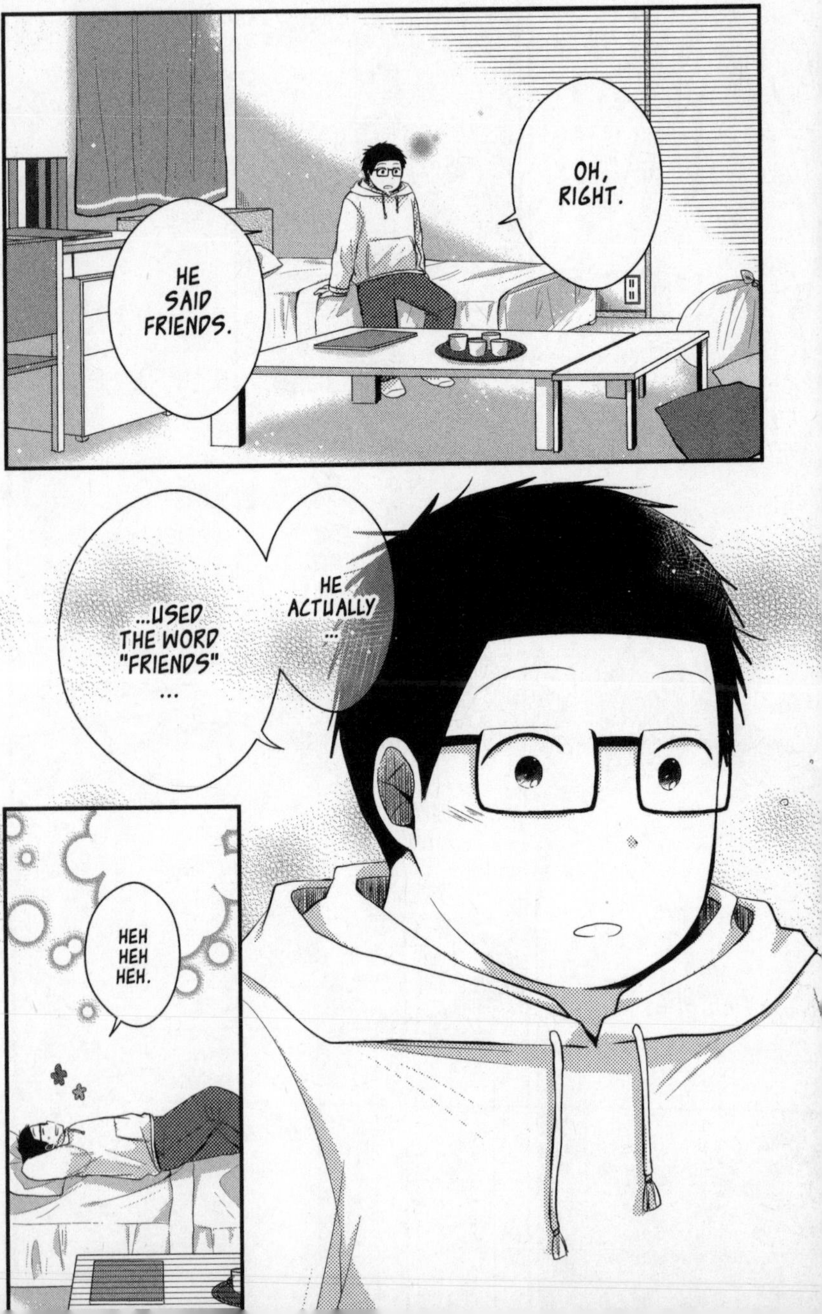
OH, RIGHT.
HE SAID FRIENDS.
HE ACTUALLY...
...USED THE WORD "FRIENDS"...
HEH HEH HEH.

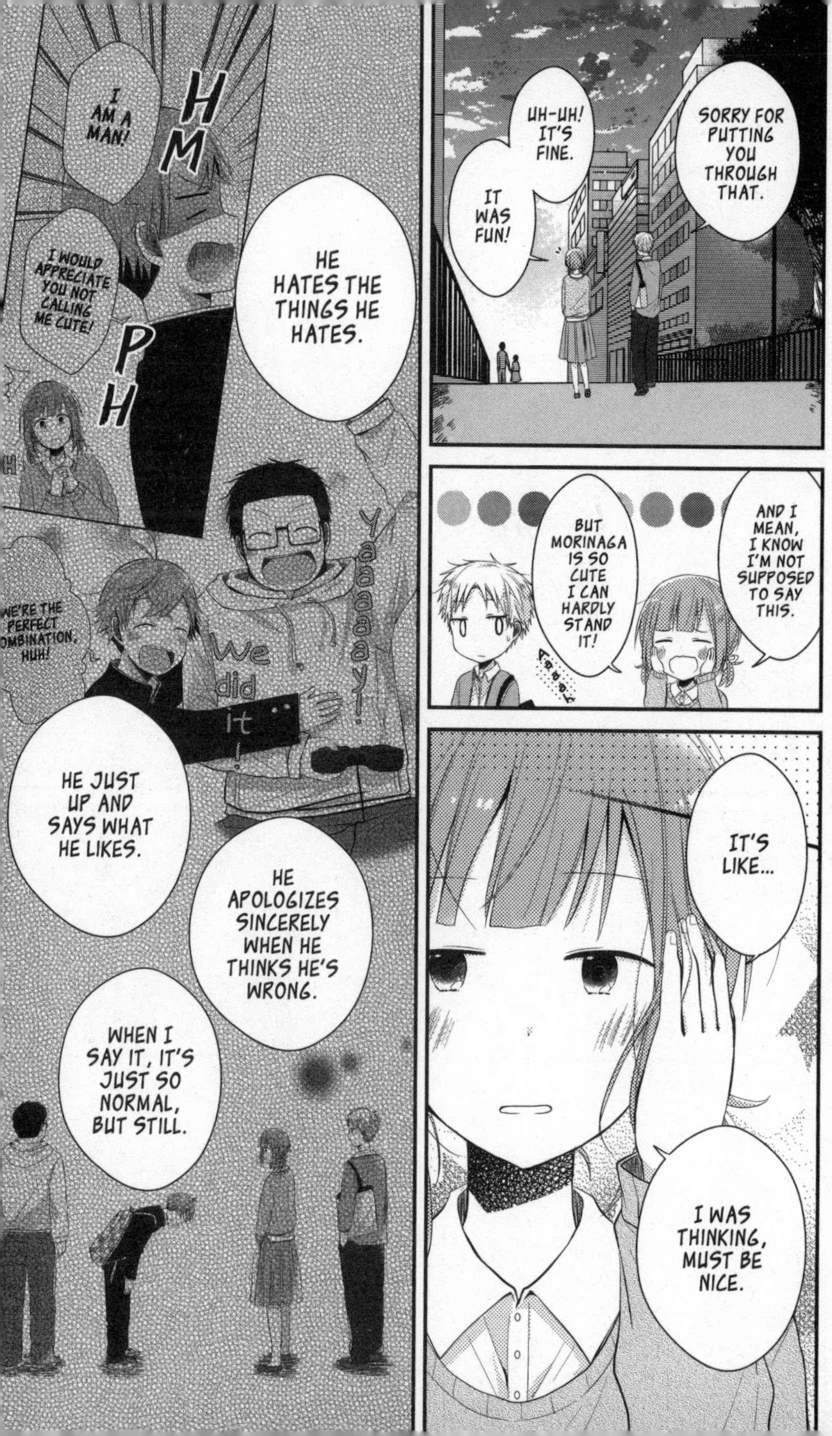
SORRY FOR PUTTING YOU THROUGH THAT.
UH-UH! IT'S FINE.
IT WAS FUN!
AND I MEAN, I KNOW I'M NOT SUPPOSED TO SAY THIS.
BUT MORINAGA IS SO CUTE I CAN HARDLY STAND IT!
IT'S LIKE...
I WAS THINKING, MUST BE NICE.
HE HATES THE THINGS HE HATES.
HM
I AM A MAN!
PH
I WOULD APPRECIATE YOU NOT CALLING ME CUTE!
Yaaaaaay!
We did it!
WE'RE THE PERFECT OMBINATION, HUH!
HE JUST UP AND SAYS WHAT HE LIKES.
HE APOLOGIZES SINCERELY WHEN HE THINKS HE'S WRONG.
WHEN I SAY IT, IT'S JUST SO NORMAL, BUT STILL.

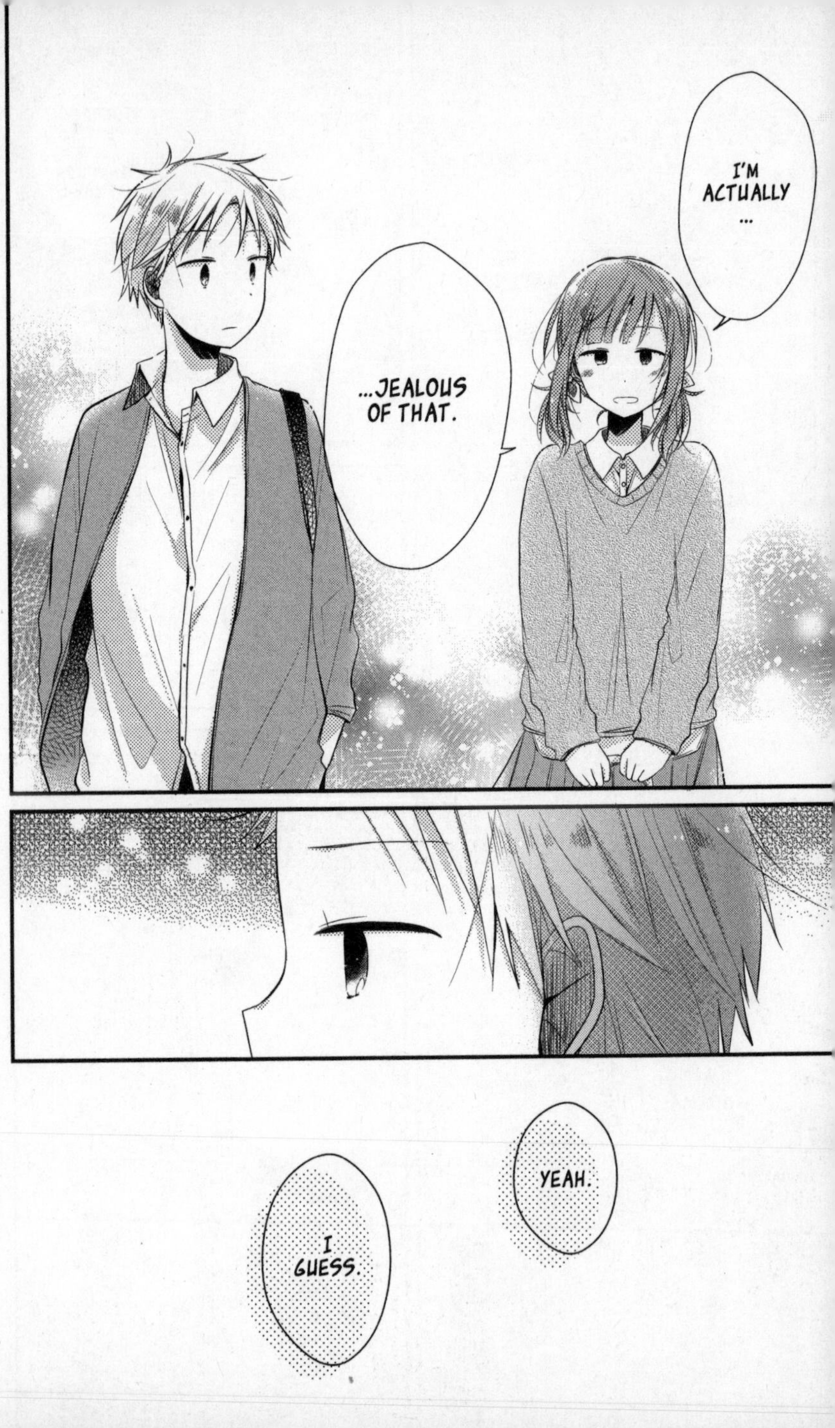
I'M ACTUALLY ...
...JEALOUS OF THAT.
YEAH.
I GUESS.

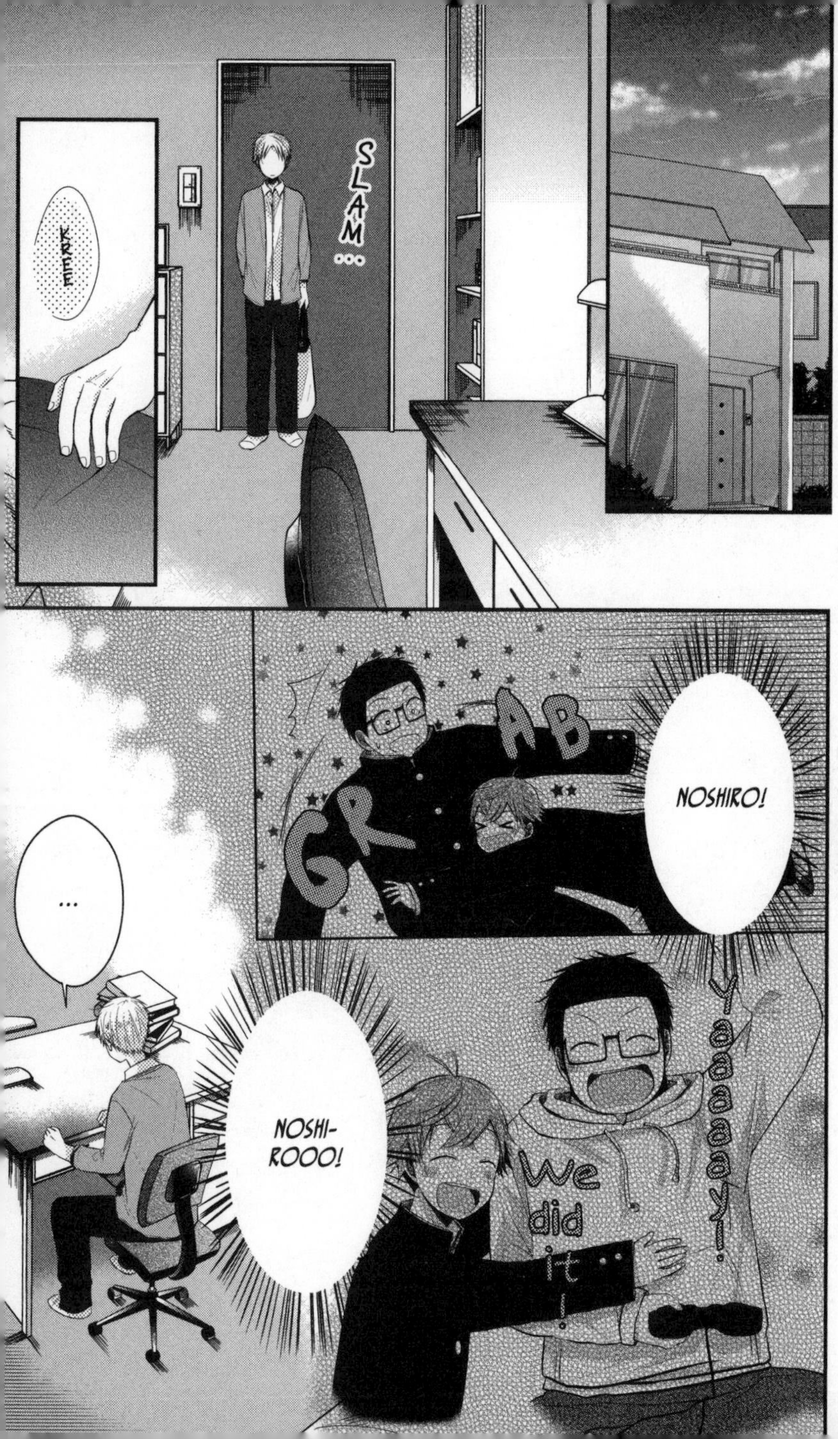

SLAM...
KREE
NOSHIRO!
GRAB
Yaaaaaaay!
We did it!
NOSHI-ROOO!
...

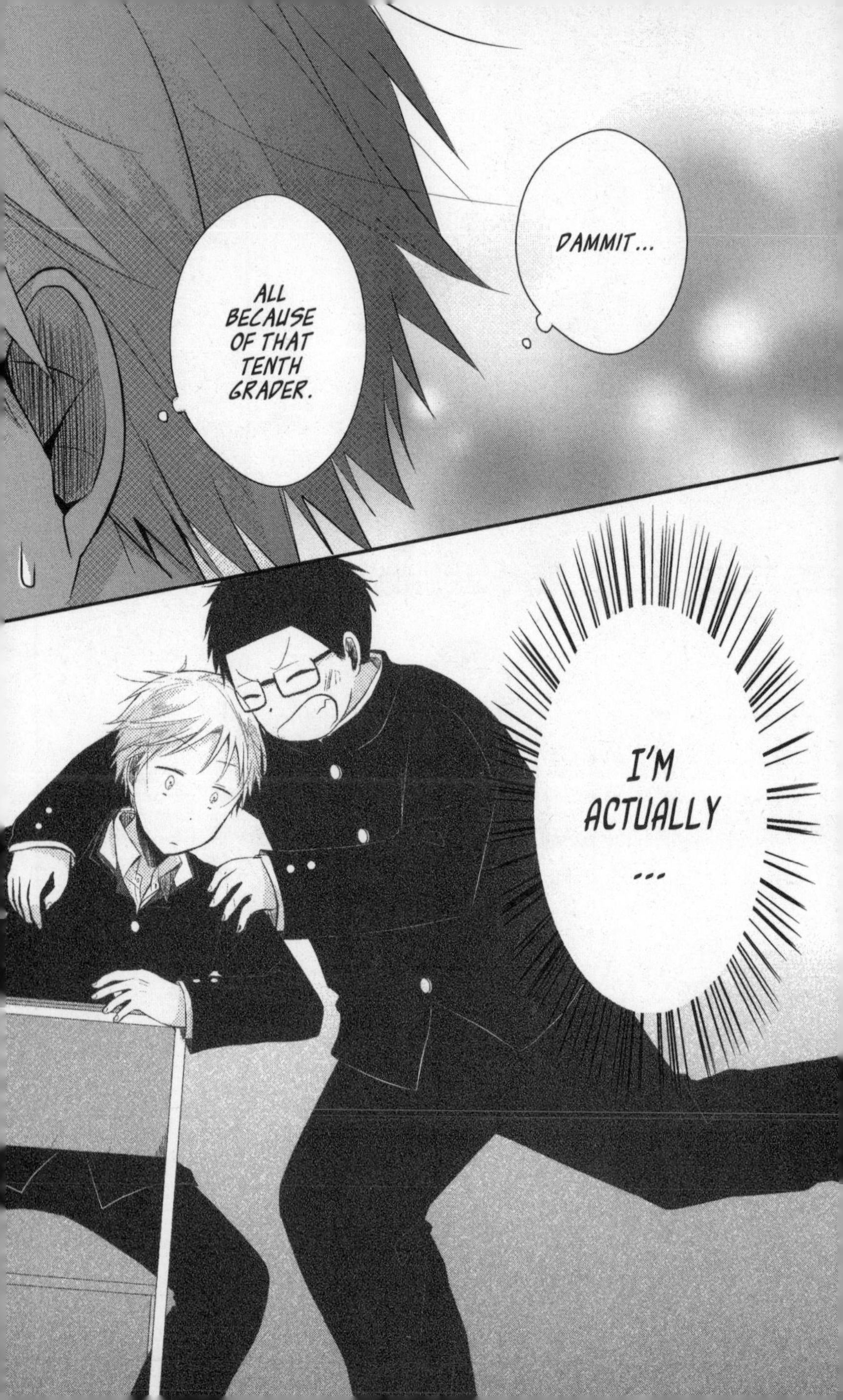
DAMMIT...
ALL BECAUSE OF THAT TENTH GRADER.
I'M ACTUALLY ...

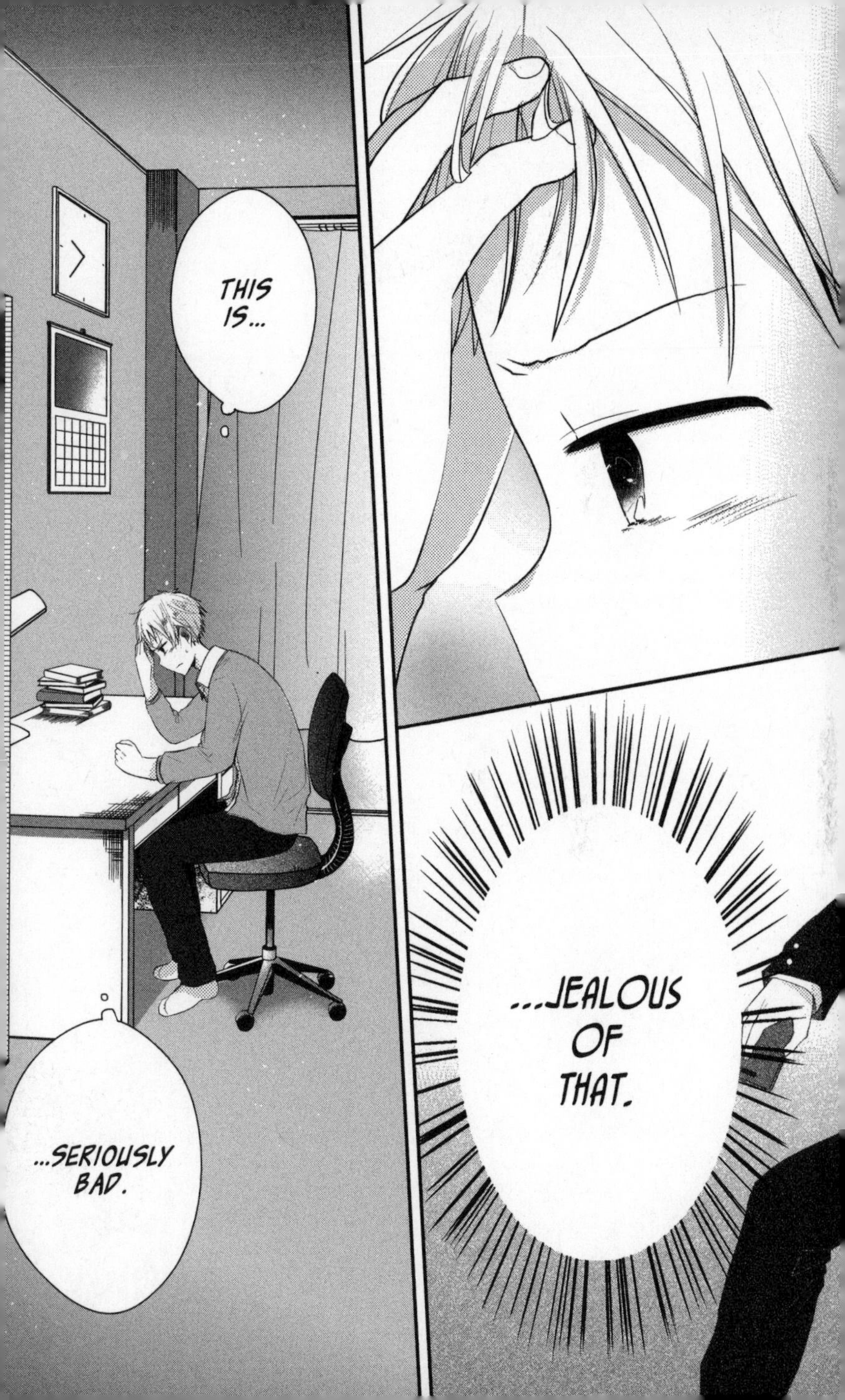
...JEALOUS OF THAT.
THIS IS...
...SERIOUSLY BAD.

That Blue
Sky Feeling

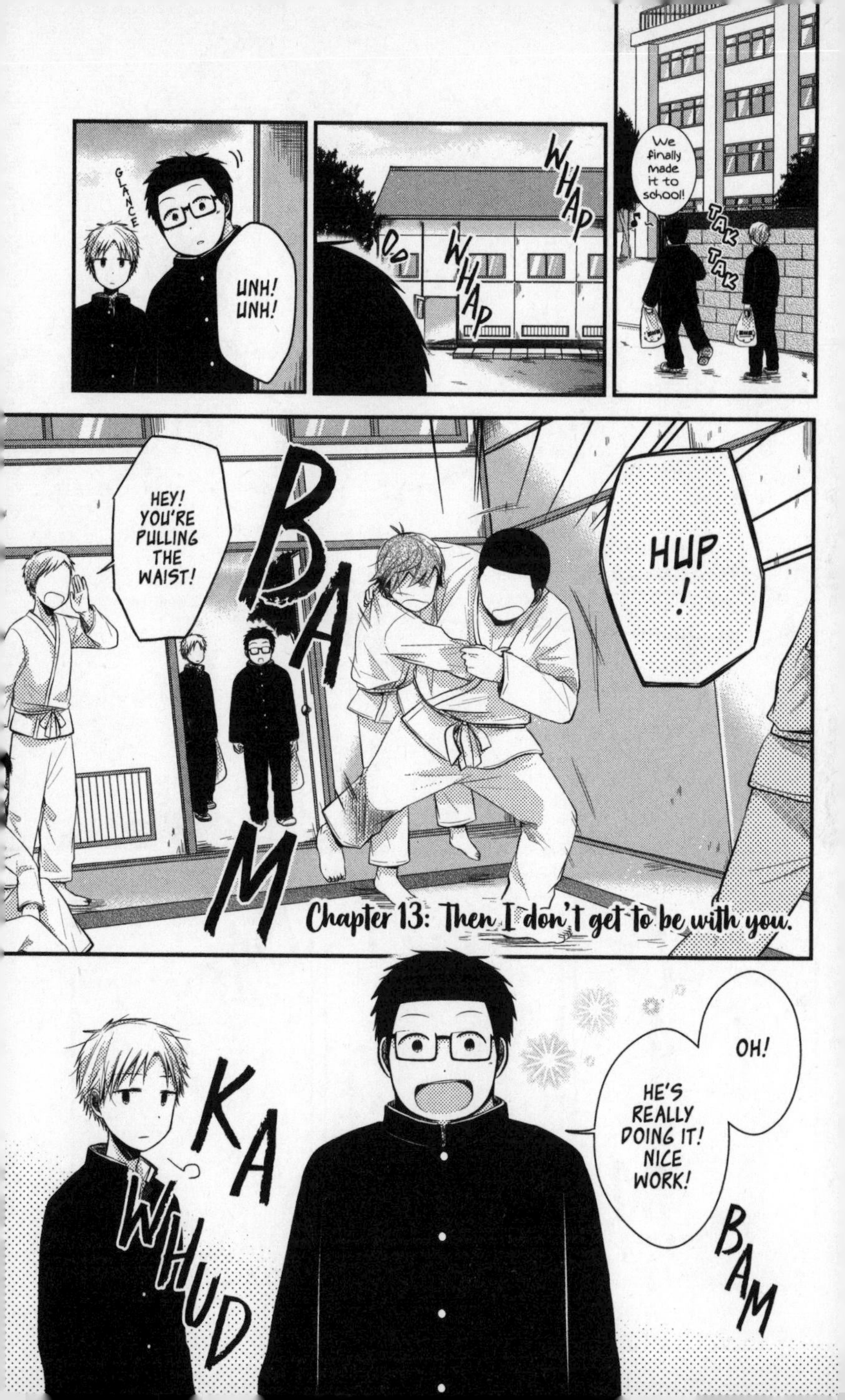
We finally made it to school!
TAK TAK
WHAP WHAP
GLANCE
UNH! UNH!
HUP!
BAM
HEY! YOU'RE PULLING THE WAIST!
Chapter 13: Then I don't get to be with you.
OH!
HE'S REALLY DOING IT! NICE WORK!
BAM
KA WHUD

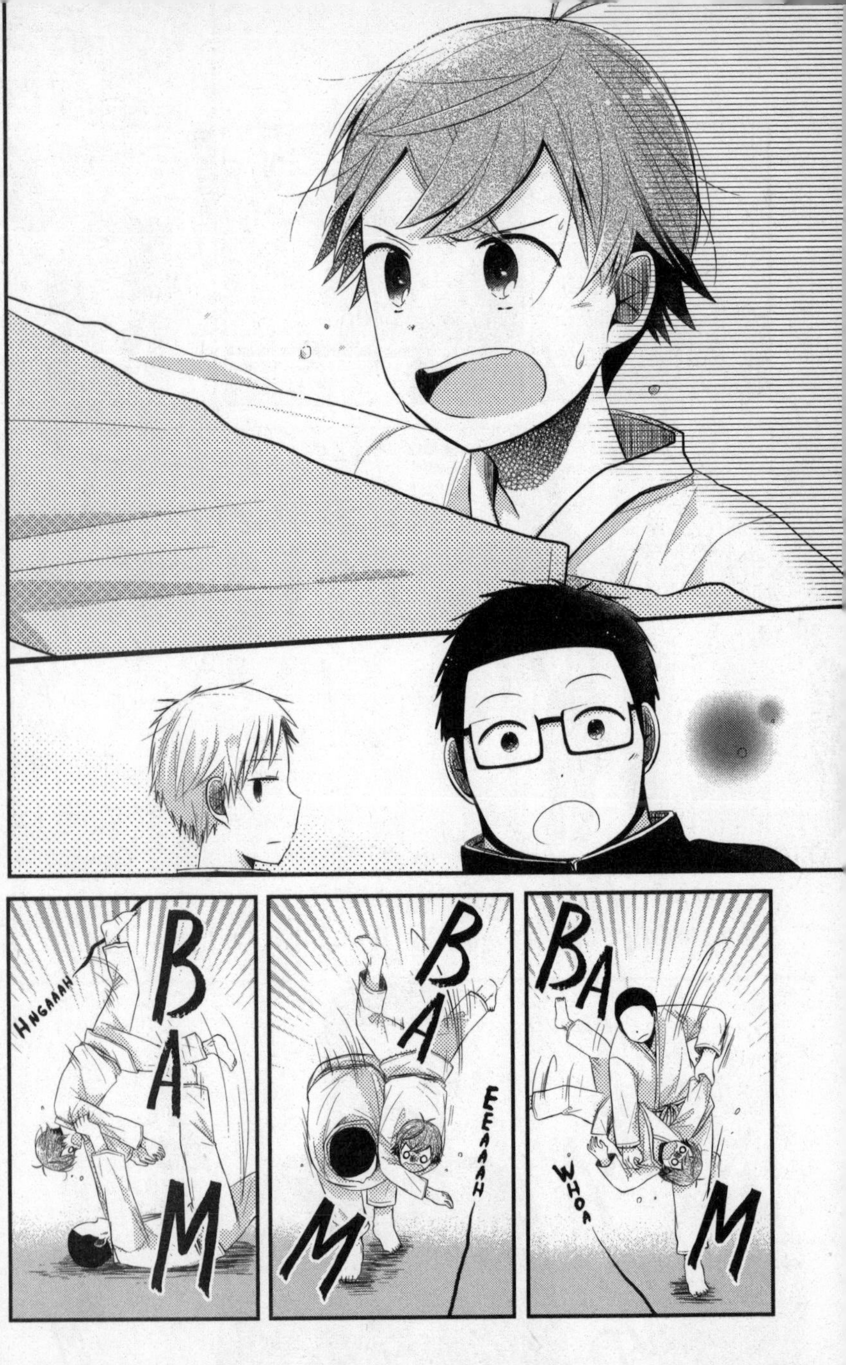
BAM
WHOA
BAM
EEAAAAH
BAM
HNGAAAH

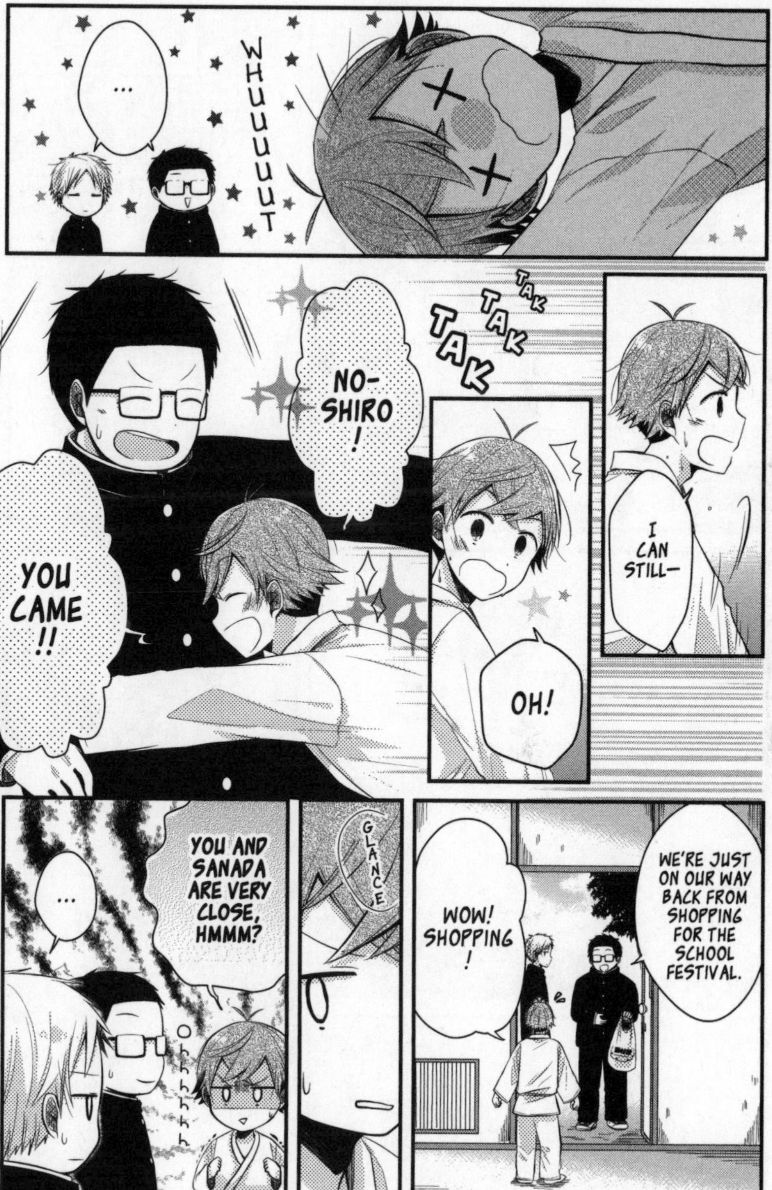
WHUUUUUT
...
I CAN STILL—
TAK TAK TAK
OH!
NO-SHIRO!
YOU CAME!!
WE'RE JUST ON OUR WAY BACK FROM SHOPPING FOR THE SCHOOL FESTIVAL.
WOW! SHOPPING!
GLANCE
YOU AND SANADA ARE VERY CLOSE, HMMM?
...
Ohhhhhh

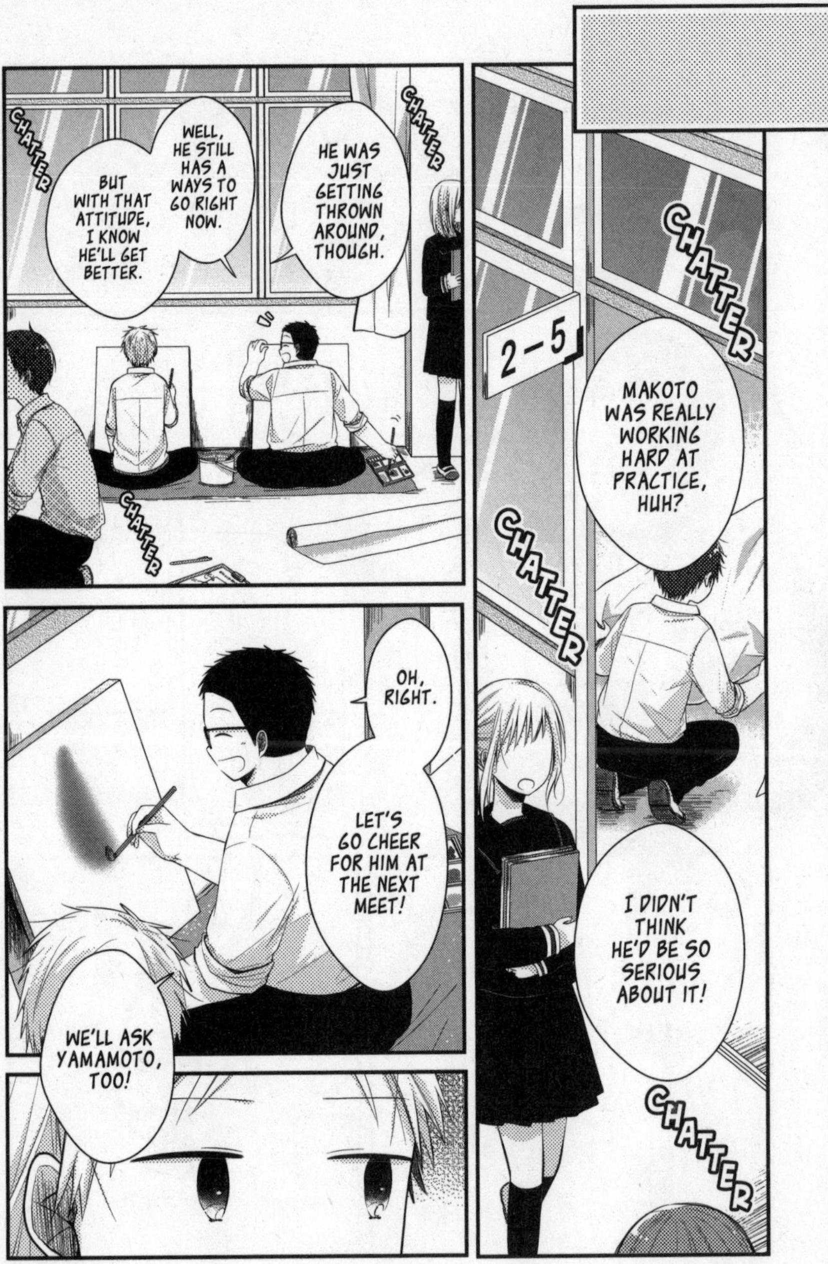
CHATTER
2-5
MAKOTO WAS REALLY WORKING HARD AT PRACTICE, HUH?
CHATTER
I DIDN'T THINK HE'D BE SO SERIOUS ABOUT IT!
CHATTER
CHATTER
HE WAS JUST GETTING THROWN AROUND, THOUGH.
WELL, HE STILL HAS A WAYS TO GO RIGHT NOW.
BUT WITH THAT ATTITUDE, I KNOW HE'LL GET BETTER.
CHATTER
CHATTER
OH, RIGHT.
LET'S GO CHEER FOR HIM AT THE NEXT MEET!
WE'LL ASK YAMAMOTO, TOO!

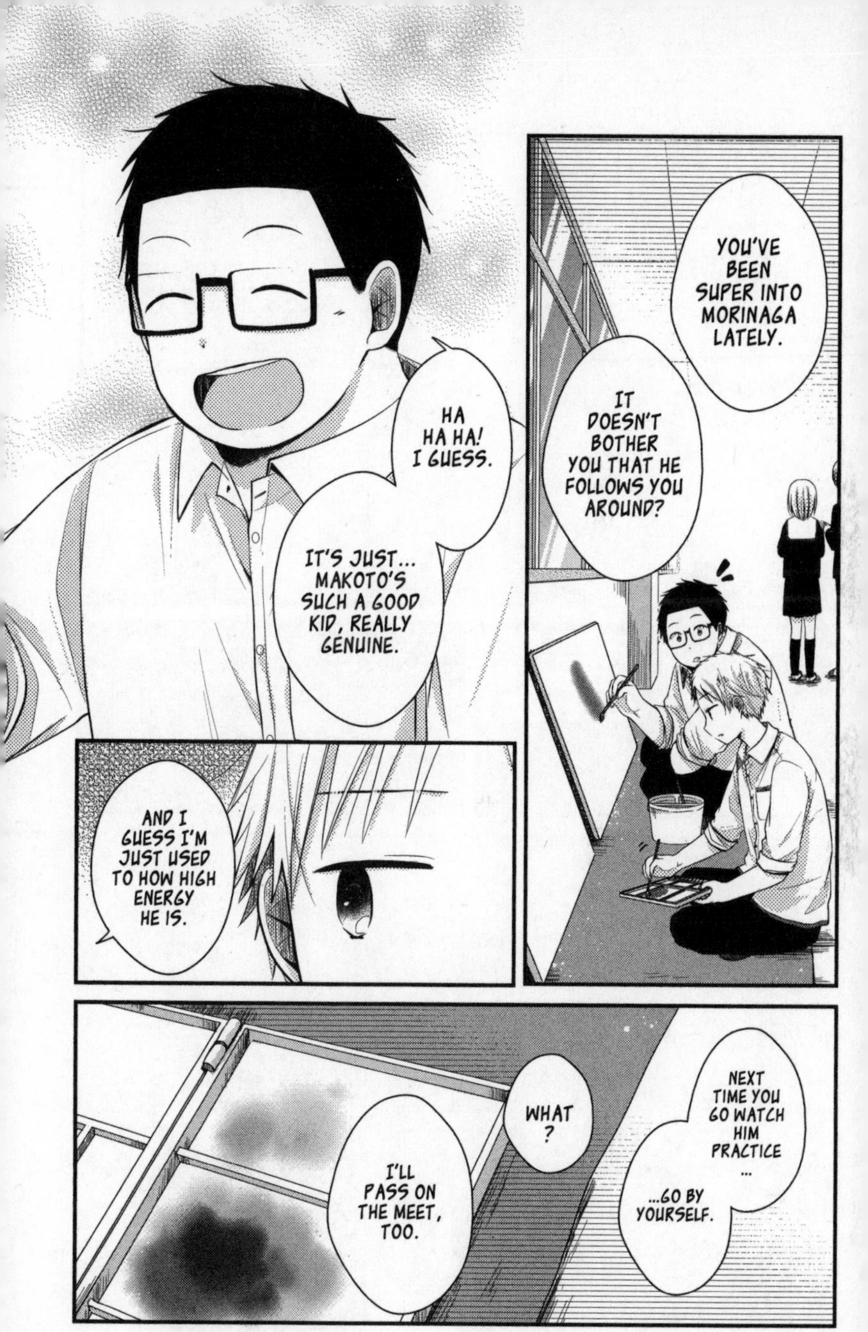
YOU'VE BEEN SUPER INTO MORINAGA LATELY.
IT DOESN'T BOTHER YOU THAT HE FOLLOWS YOU AROUND?
HA HA HA! I GUESS.
IT'S JUST... MAKOTO'S SUCH A GOOD KID, REALLY GENUINE.
AND I GUESS I'M JUST USED TO HOW HIGH ENERGY HE IS.
NEXT TIME YOU GO WATCH HIM PRACTICE ...
...GO BY YOURSELF.
WHAT?
I'LL PASS ON THE MEET, TOO.

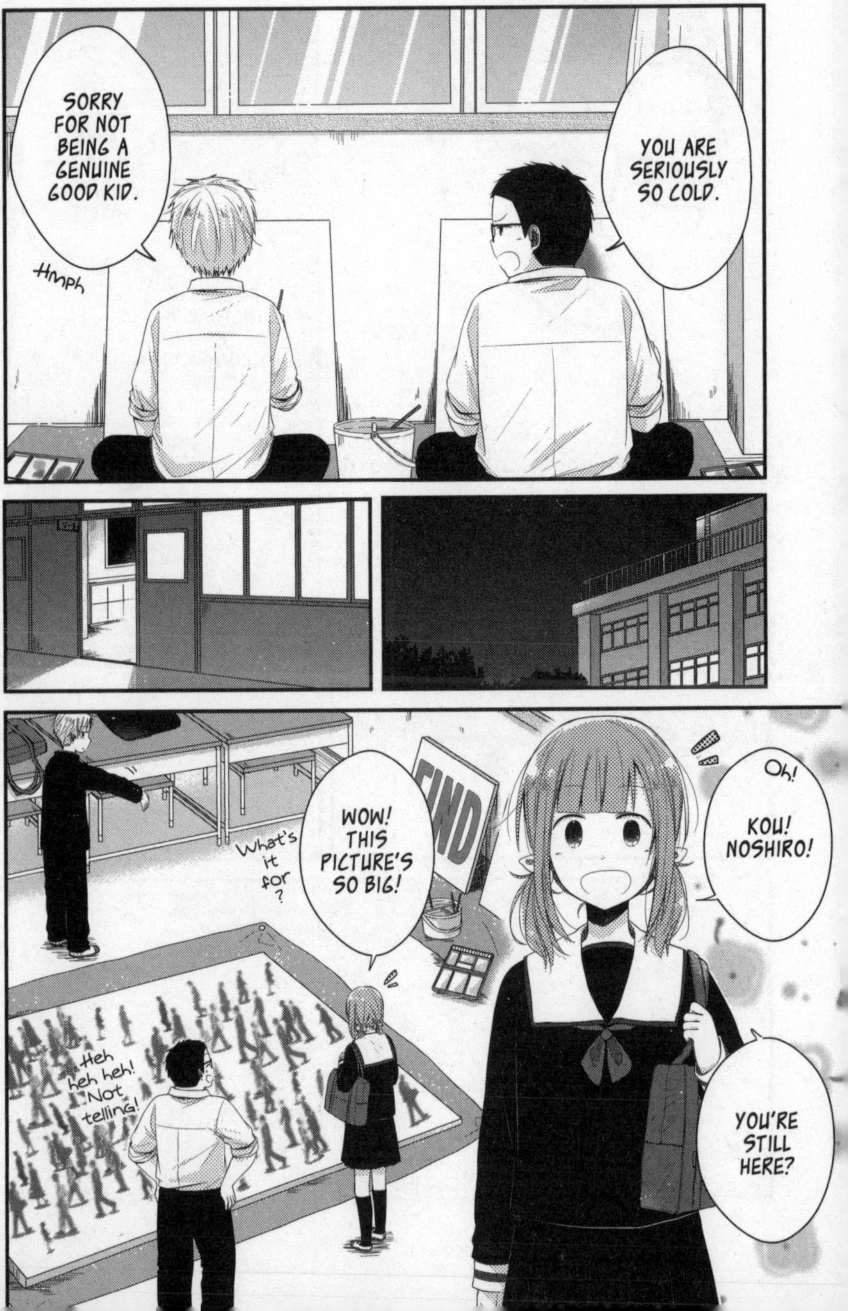
YOU ARE SERIOUSLY SO COLD.
SORRY FOR NOT BEING A GENUINE GOOD KID.
Hmph
Oh!
KOU! NOSHIRO!
YOU'RE STILL HERE?
WOW! THIS PICTURE'S SO BIG!
What's it for?
Heh heh heh! Not telling!

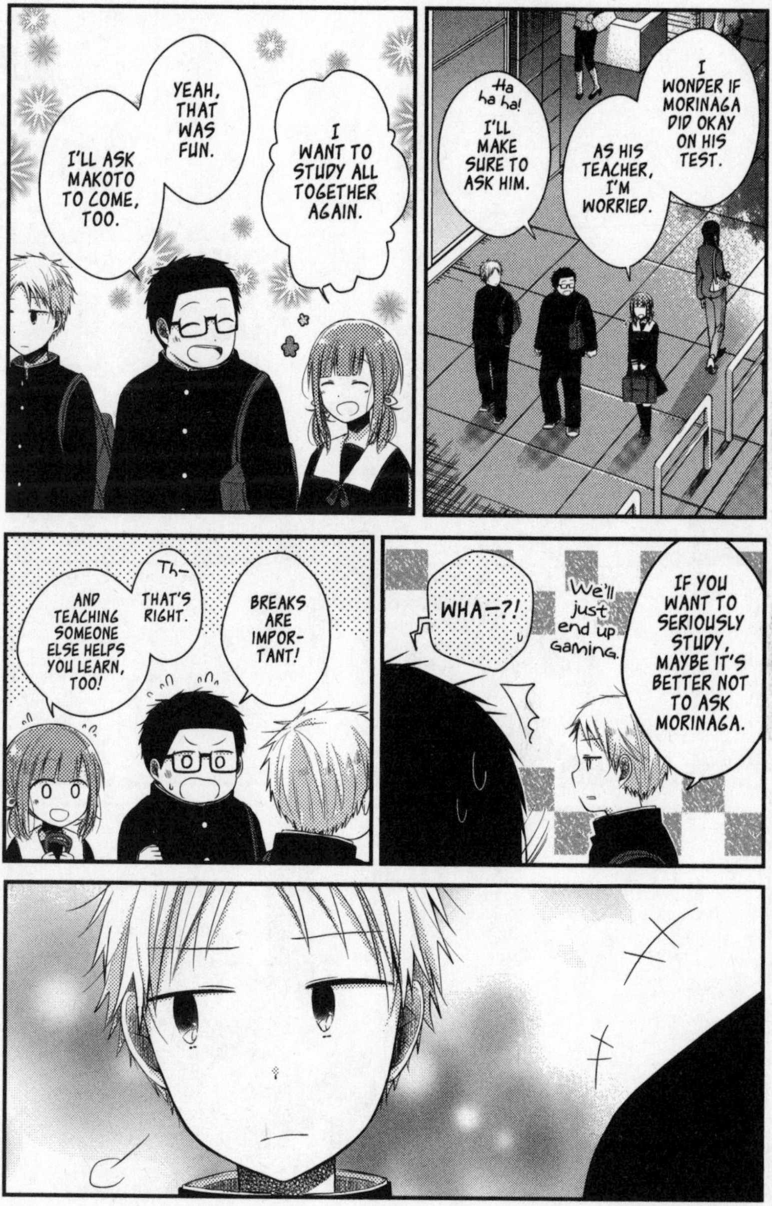
I WONDER IF MORINAGA DID OKAY ON HIS TEST.
AS HIS TEACHER, I'M WORRIED.
Ha ha ha! I'LL MAKE SURE TO ASK HIM.
I WANT TO STUDY ALL TOGETHER AGAIN.
YEAH, THAT WAS FUN.
I'LL ASK MAKOTO TO COME, TOO.
IF YOU WANT TO SERIOUSLY STUDY, MAYBE IT'S BETTER NOT TO ASK MORINAGA.
We'll just end up gaming.
WHA—?!
BREAKS ARE IMPOR-TANT!
Th— THAT'S RIGHT.
AND TEACHING SOMEONE ELSE HELPS YOU LEARN, TOO!

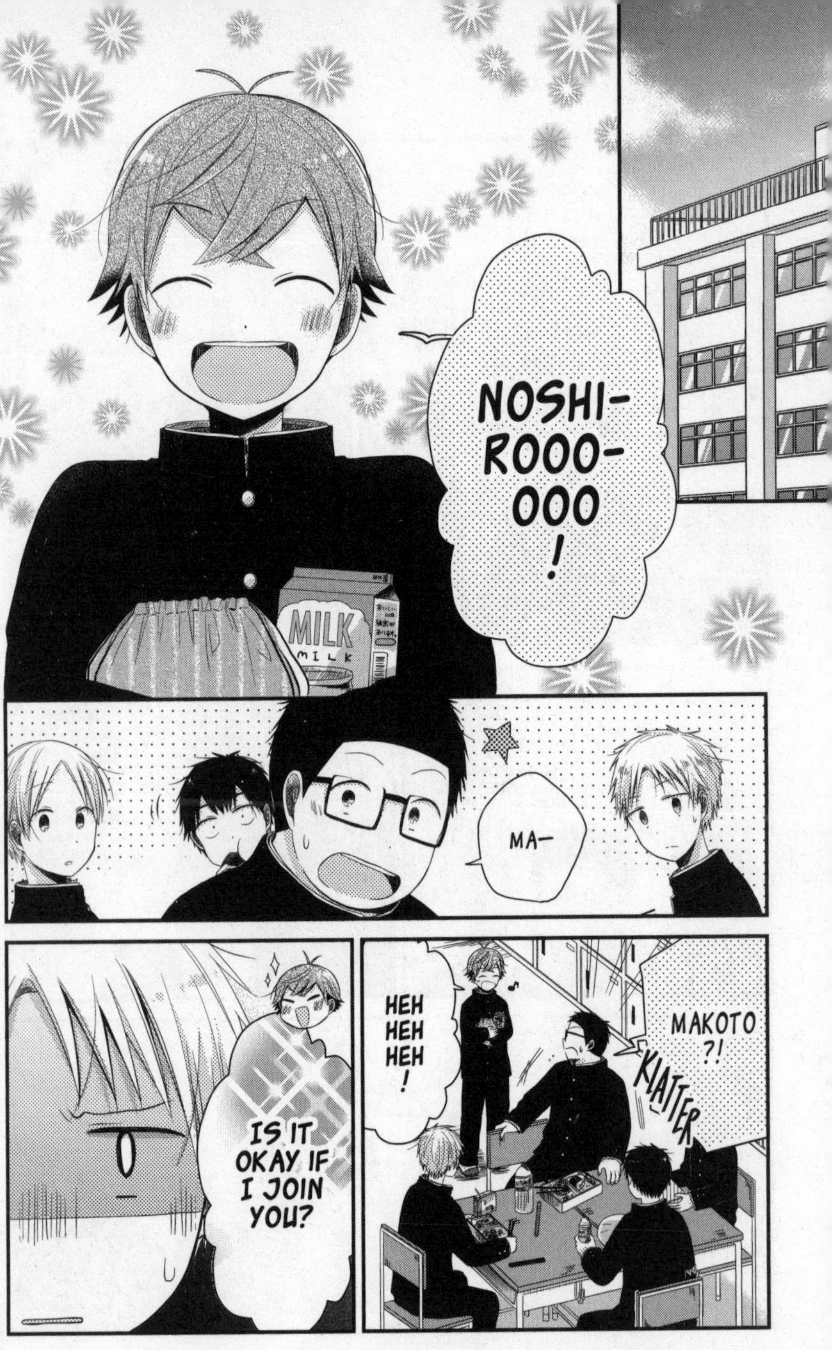
NOSHI-ROOO-OOO!
MILK
MILK
MA—
MAKOTO?!
KLATTER
HEH HEH HEH!
IS IT OKAY IF I JOIN YOU?

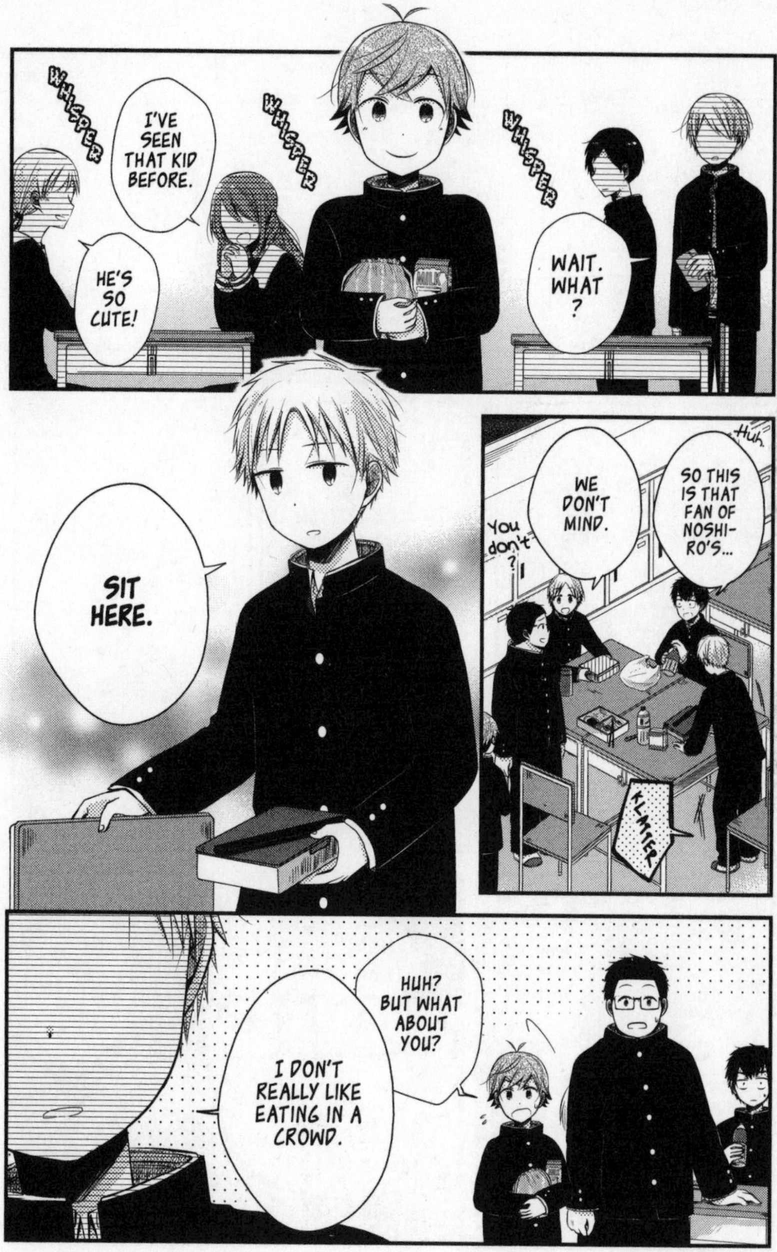
WHISPER
WAIT. WHAT?
WHISPER
WHISPER
I'VE SEEN THAT KID BEFORE.
HE'S SO CUTE!
Huh.
SO THIS IS THAT FAN OF NOSHIRO'S...
WE DON'T MIND.
You don't?
KLATTER
SIT HERE.
HUH? BUT WHAT ABOUT YOU?
I DON'T REALLY LIKE EATING IN A CROWD.

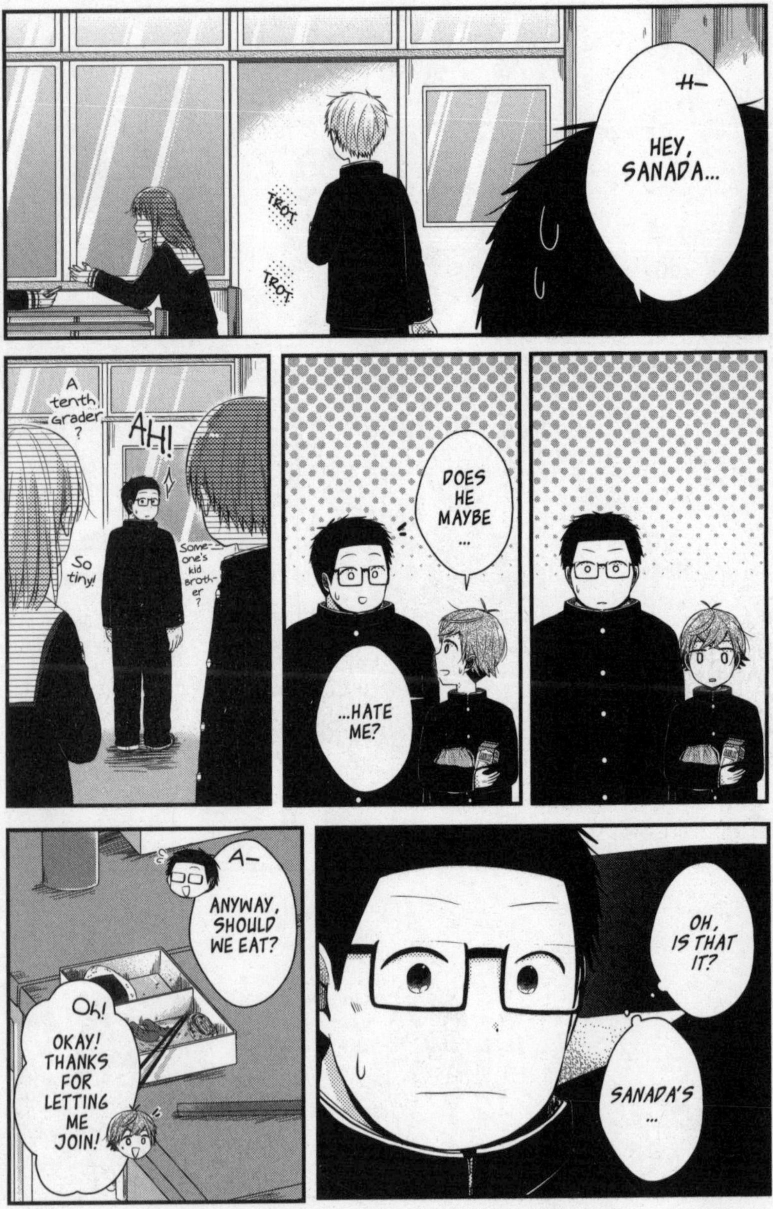
H—
HEY, SANADA...
TROT
TROT
DOES HE MAYBE ...
...HATE ME?
AH!
A tenth grader?
Some-one's kid broth-er?
So tiny!
OH, IS THAT IT?
SANADA'S ...
A—
ANYWAY, SHOULD WE EAT?
Oh!
OKAY! THANKS FOR LETTING ME JOIN!

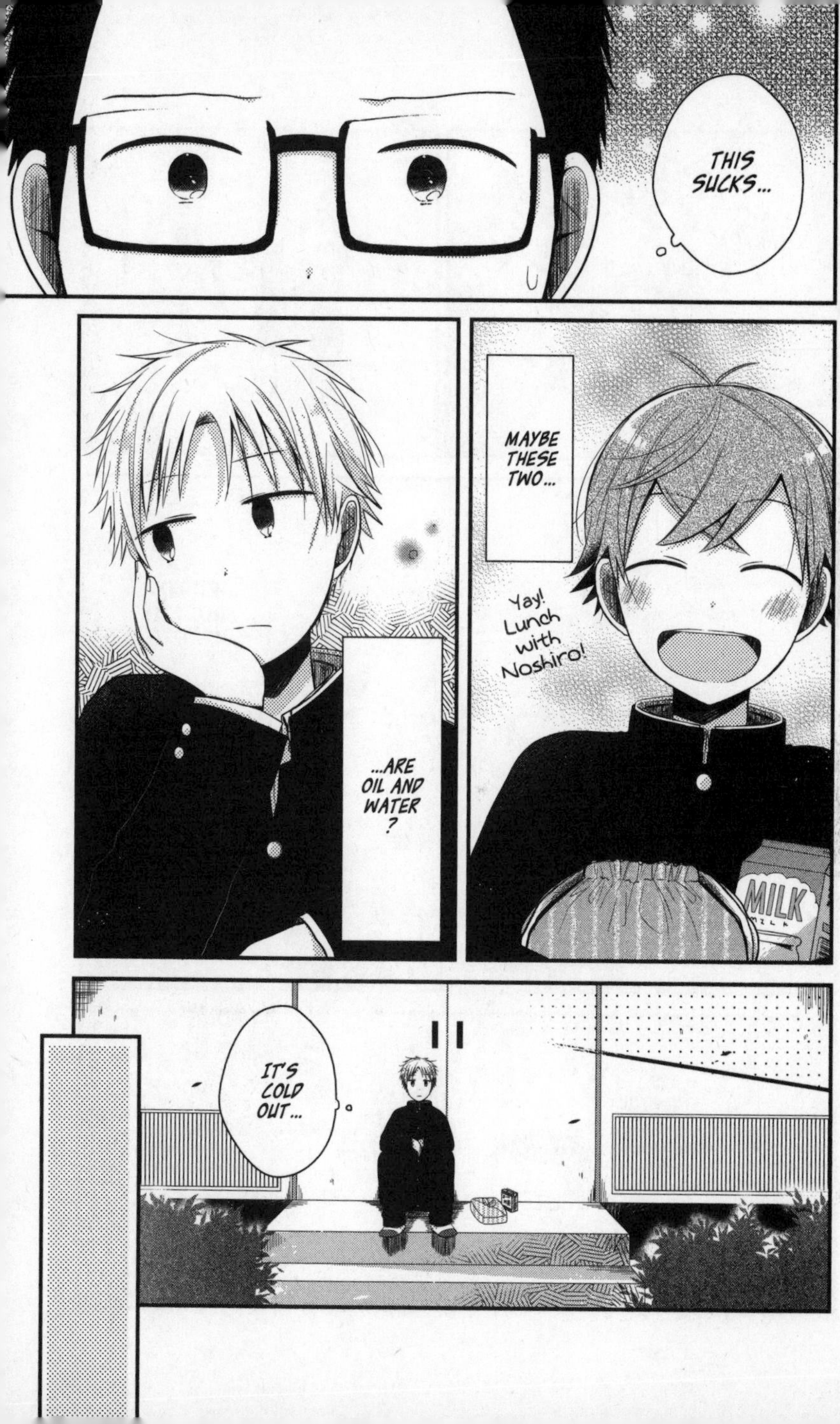
THIS SUCKS...
MAYBE THESE TWO...
Yay! Lunch with Noshiro!
...ARE OIL AND WATER?
MILK
IT'S COLD OUT...

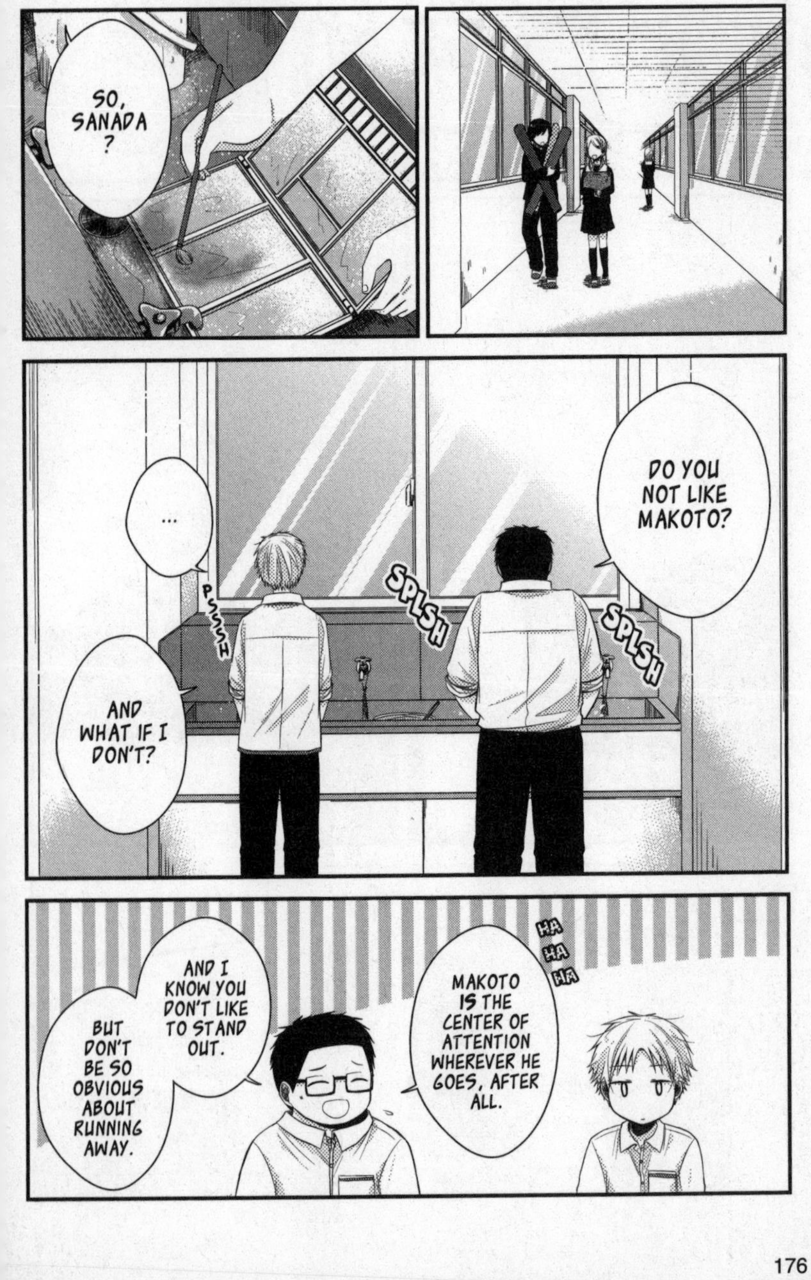
SO, SANADA?
DO YOU NOT LIKE MAKOTO?
SPLSH
SPLSH
PSSSH
...
AND WHAT IF I DON'T?
HA HA HA
MAKOTO IS THE CENTER OF ATTENTION WHEREVER HE GOES, AFTER ALL.
AND I KNOW YOU DON'T LIKE TO STAND OUT.
BUT DON'T BE SO OBVIOUS ABOUT RUNNING AWAY.

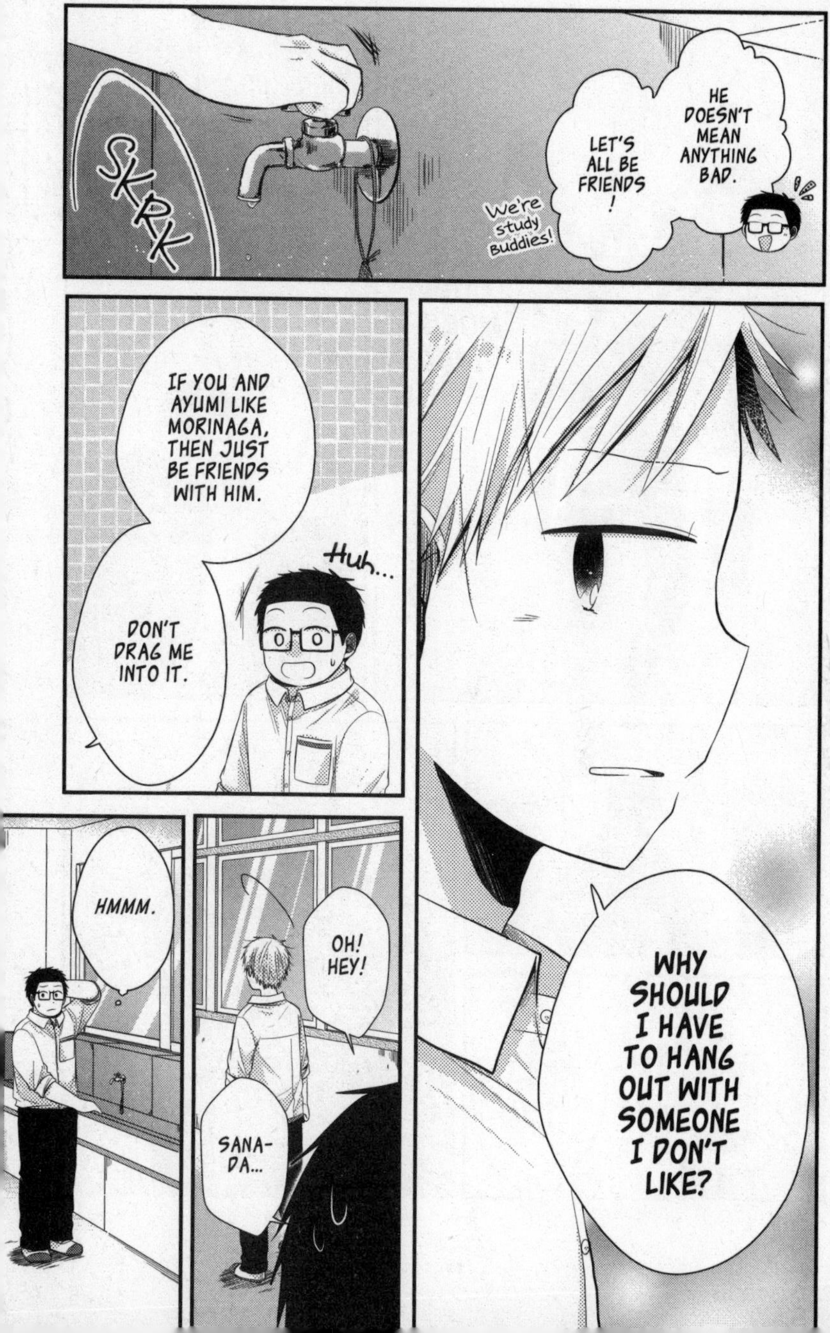
HE DOESN'T MEAN ANYTHING BAD.
LET'S ALL BE FRIENDS!
We're study Buddies!
SKRK
WHY SHOULD I HAVE TO HANG OUT WITH SOMEONE I DON'T LIKE?
IF YOU AND AYUMI LIKE MORINAGA, THEN JUST BE FRIENDS WITH HIM.
Huh...
DON'T DRAG ME INTO IT.
OH! HEY!
SANA-DA...
HMMM.

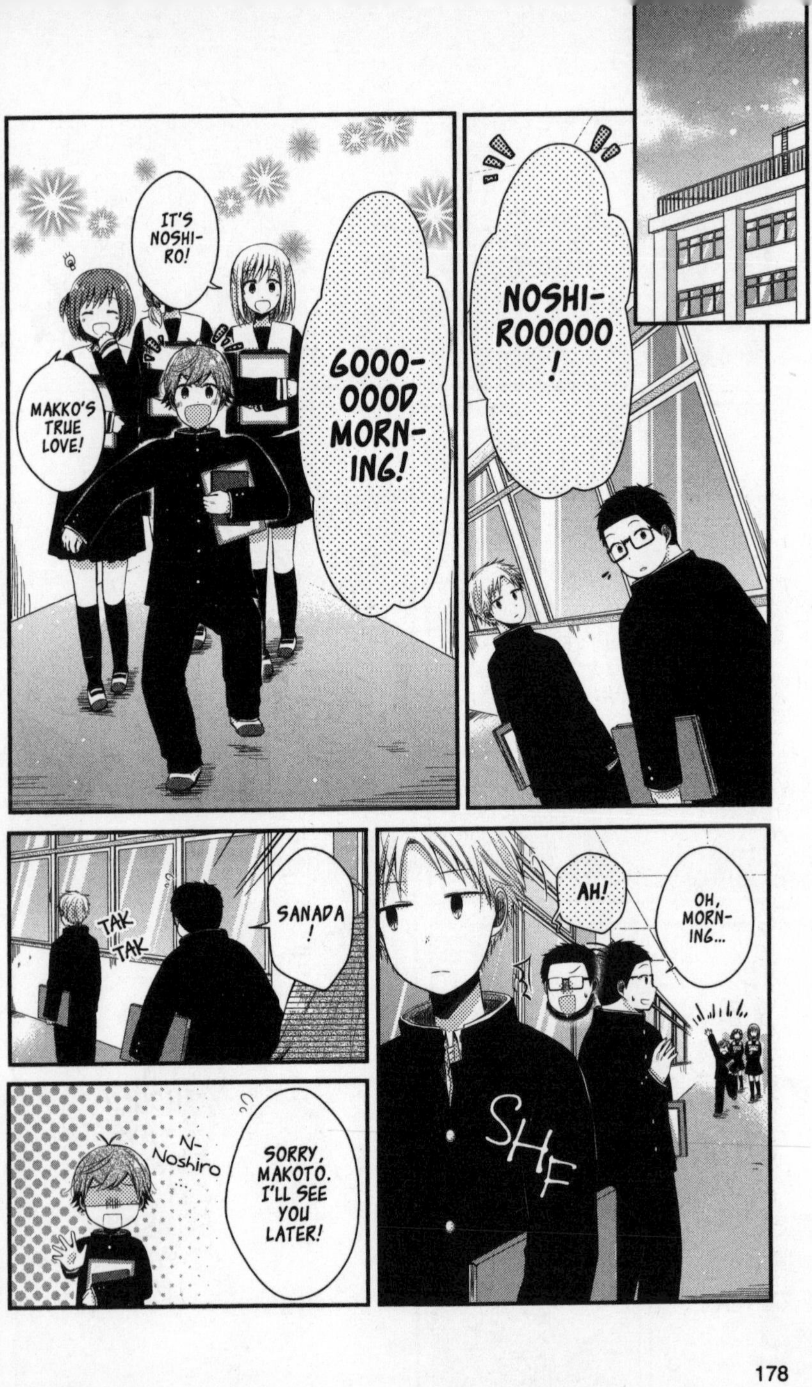
NOSHI-ROOOOO!
GOOO-OOOD MORN-ING!
IT'S NOSHI-RO!
MAKKO'S TRUE LOVE!
OH, MORN-ING...
AH!
SHF
SANADA!
TAK TAK
SORRY, MAKOTO. I'LL SEE YOU LATER!
N-Noshiro...

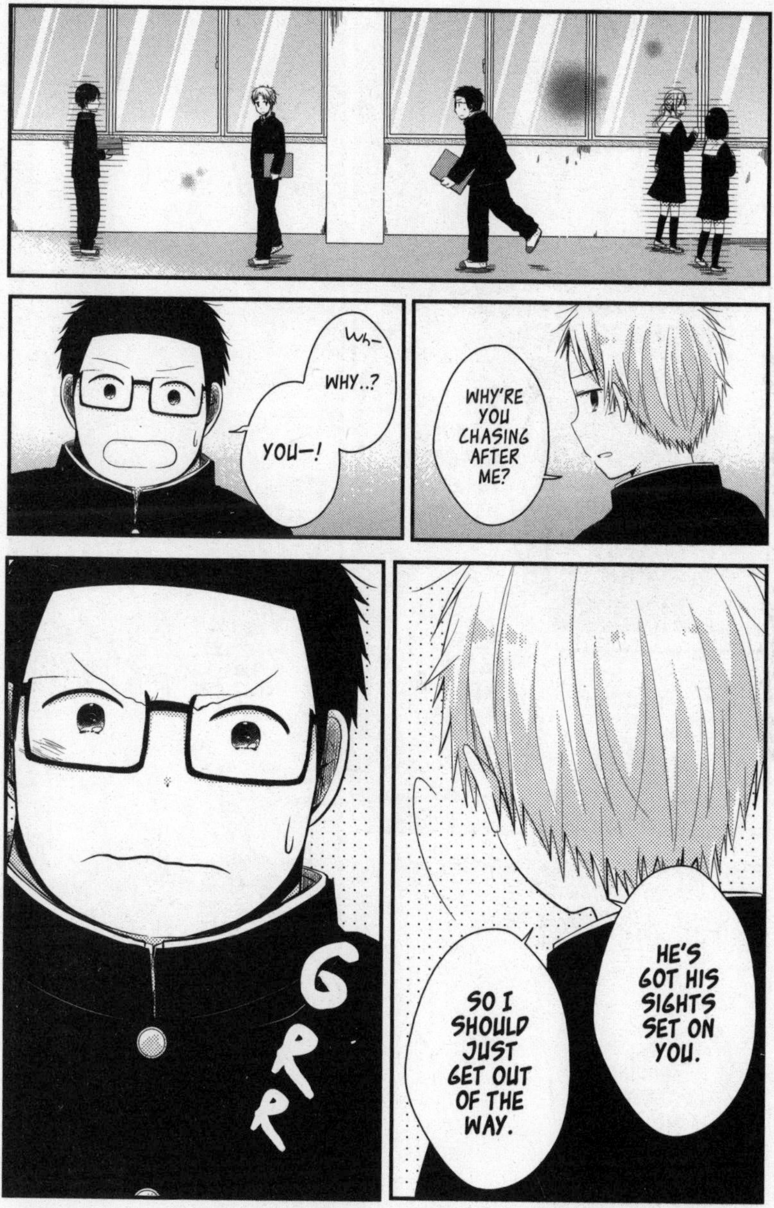
WHY'RE YOU CHASING AFTER ME?
Wh-
WHY..?
YOU—!
HE'S GOT HIS SIGHTS SET ON YOU.
SO I SHOULD JUST GET OUT OF THE WAY.
GRRR

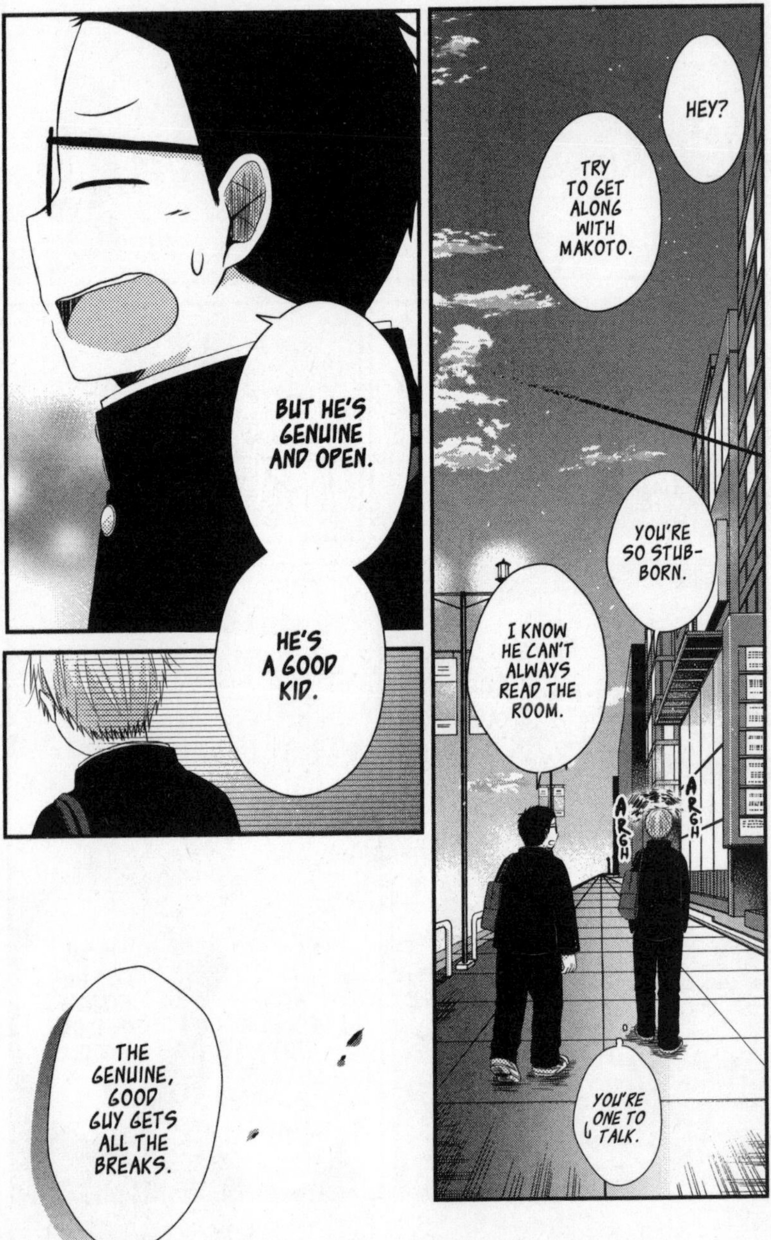
HEY?
TRY TO GET ALONG WITH MAKOTO.
YOU'RE SO STUB-BORN.
I KNOW HE CAN'T ALWAYS READ THE ROOM.
ARGH
ARGH
YOU'RE ONE TO TALK.
BUT HE'S GENUINE AND OPEN.
HE'S A GOOD KID.
THE GENUINE, GOOD GUY GETS ALL THE BREAKS.

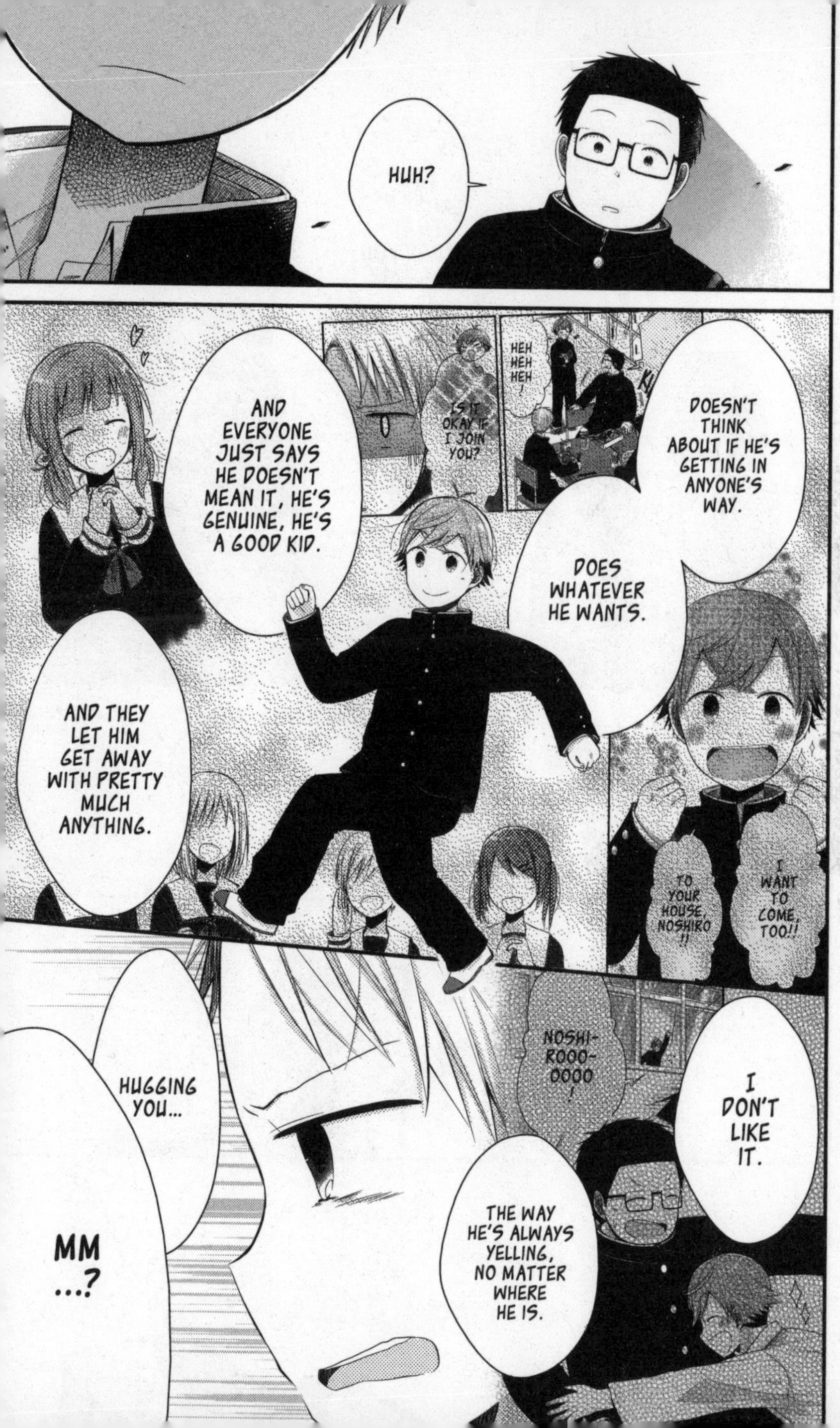
HUH?
DOESN'T THINK ABOUT IF HE'S GETTING IN ANYONE'S WAY.
HEH HEH HEH!
IS IT OKAY IF I JOIN YOU?
DOES WHATEVER HE WANTS.
I WANT TO COME, TOO!!
TO YOUR HOUSE, NOSHIRO!!
AND EVERYONE JUST SAYS HE DOESN'T MEAN IT, HE'S GENUINE, HE'S A GOOD KID.
AND THEY LET HIM GET AWAY WITH PRETTY MUCH ANYTHING.
I DON'T LIKE IT.
NOSHI-ROOO-OOOO!
THE WAY HE'S ALWAYS YELLING, NO MATTER WHERE HE IS.
HUGGING YOU...
MM ...?

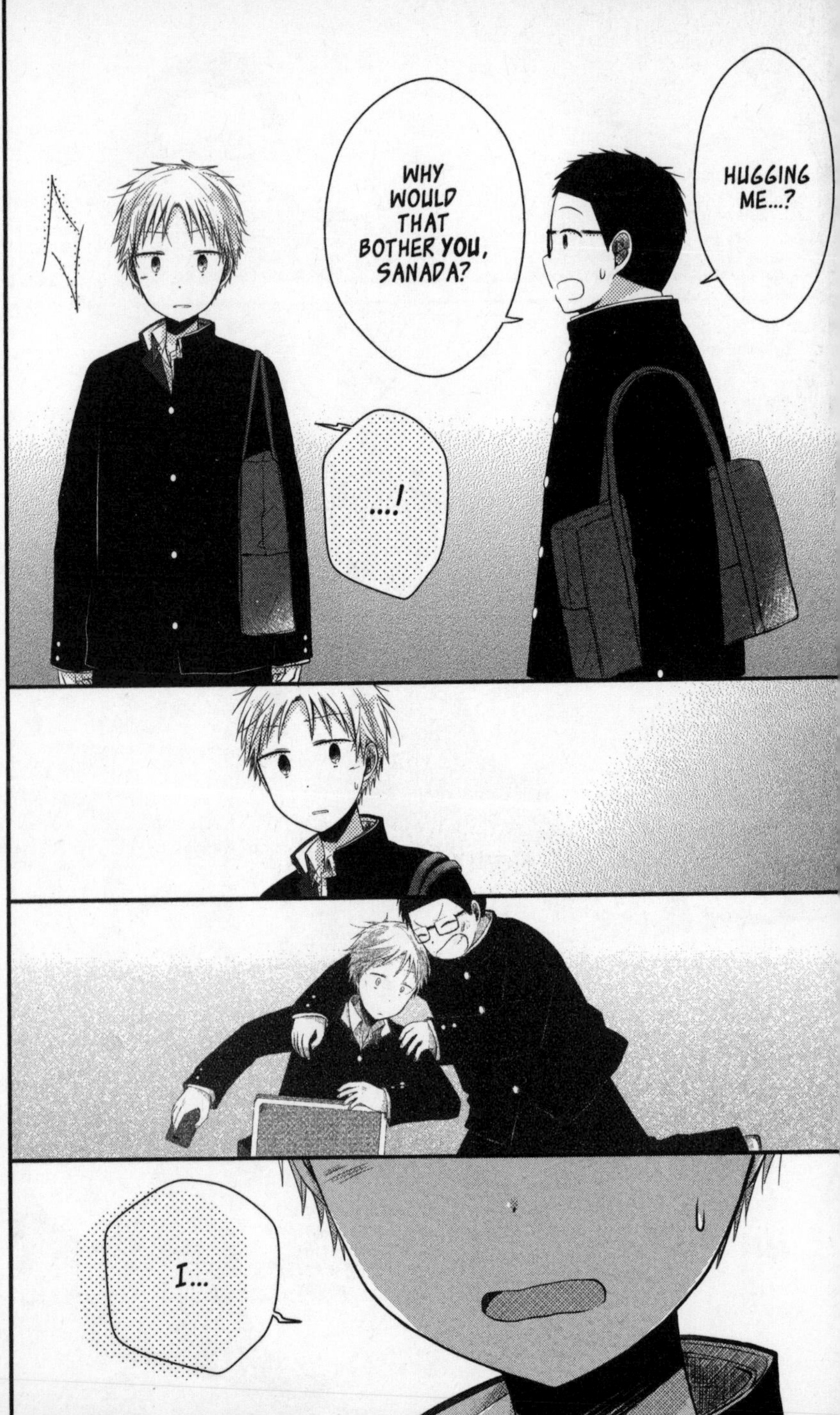
HUGGING ME...?
WHY WOULD THAT BOTHER YOU, SANADA?
...!
I...

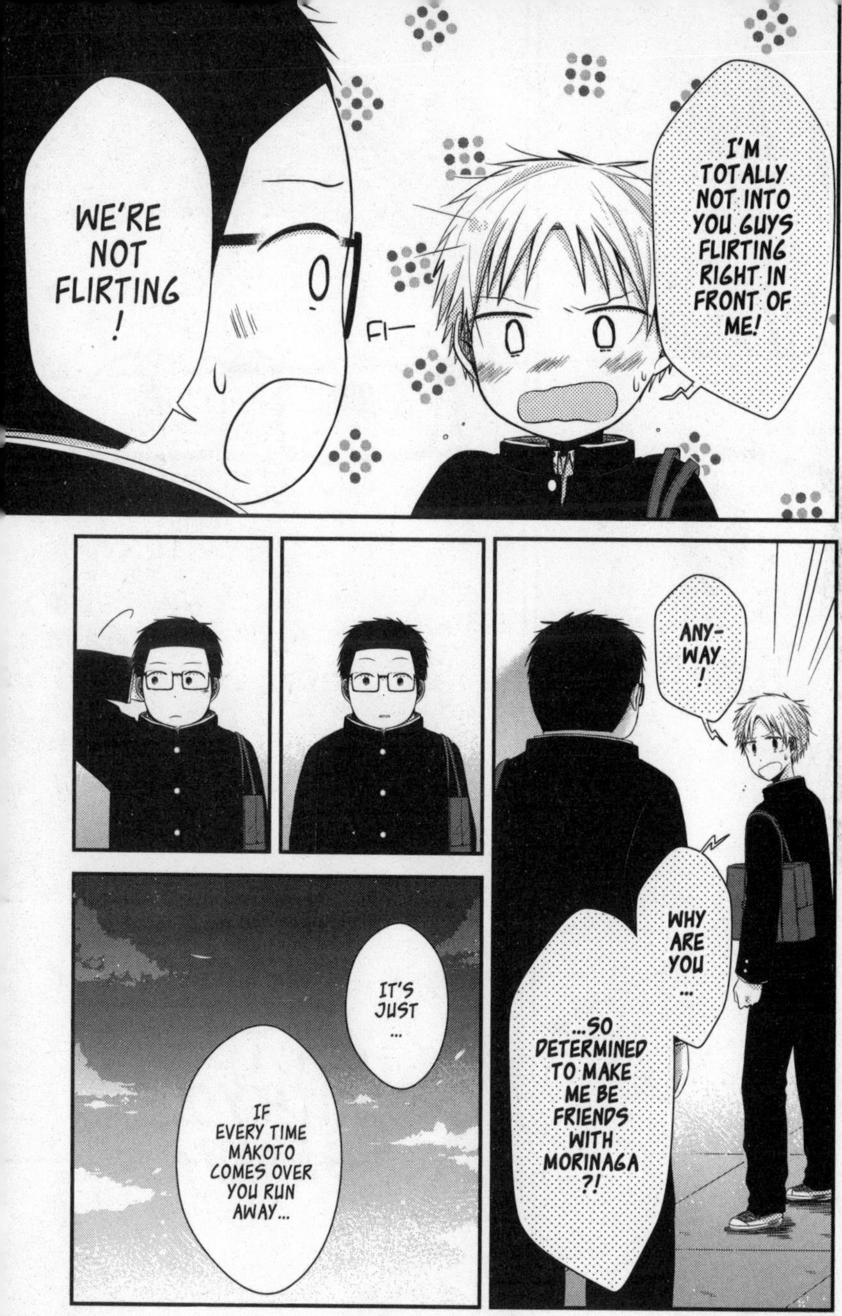
I'M TOTALLY NOT INTO YOU GUYS FLIRTING RIGHT IN FRONT OF ME!
WE'RE NOT FLIRTING!
FI—
ANY-WAY!
WHY ARE YOU...
...SO DETERMINED TO MAKE ME BE FRIENDS WITH MORINAGA?!
IT'S JUST...
IF EVERY TIME MAKOTO COMES OVER YOU RUN AWAY...

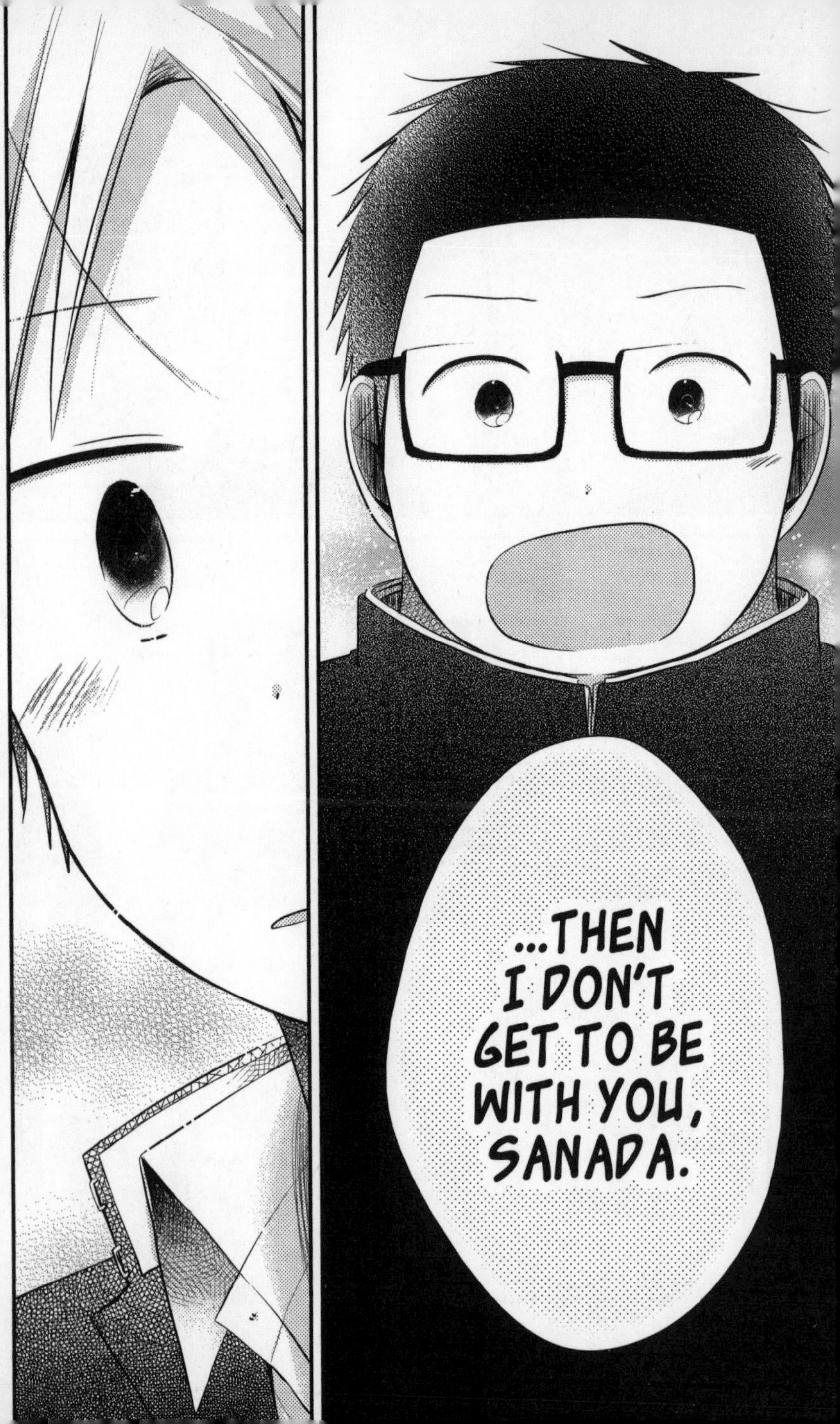
...THEN I DON'T GET TO BE WITH YOU, SANADA.

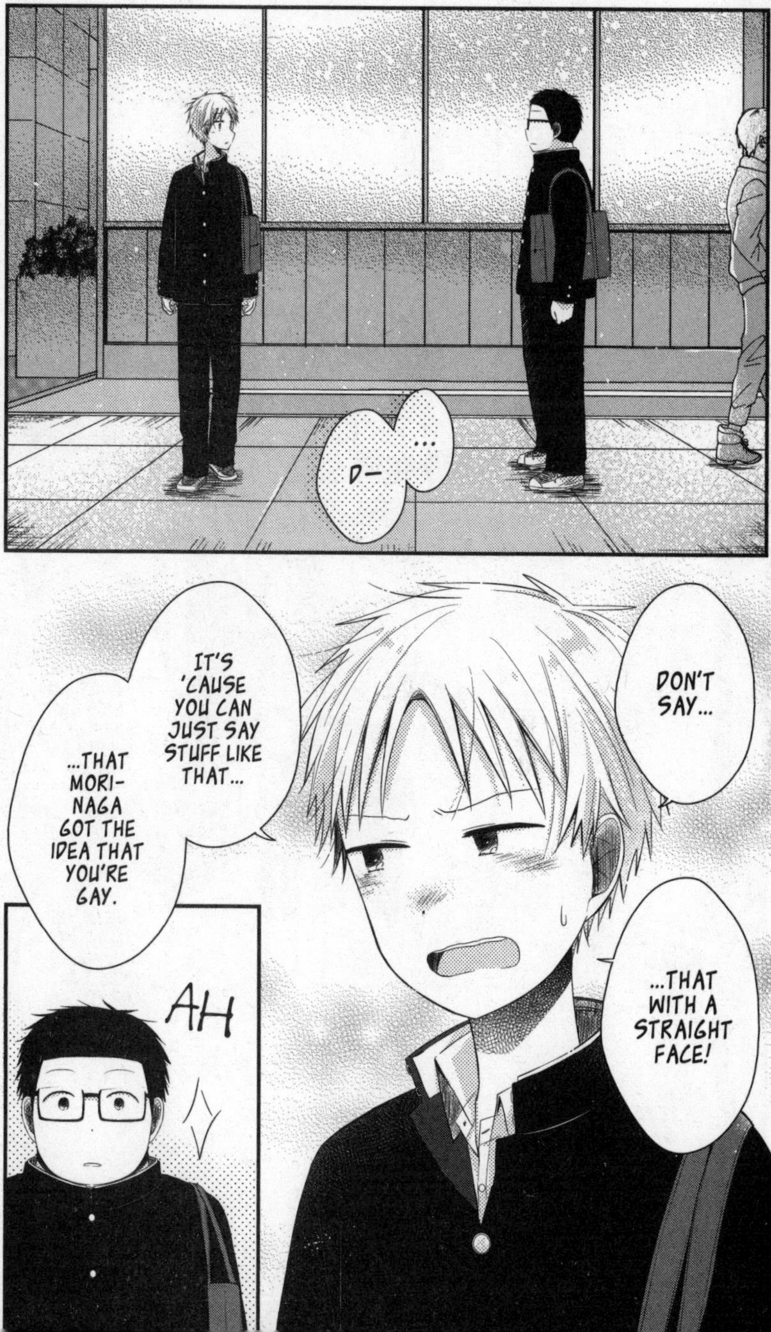
...
D—
DON'T SAY...
...THAT WITH A STRAIGHT FACE!
IT'S 'CAUSE YOU CAN JUST SAY STUFF LIKE THAT...
...THAT MORINAGA GOT THE IDEA THAT YOU'RE GAY.
AH

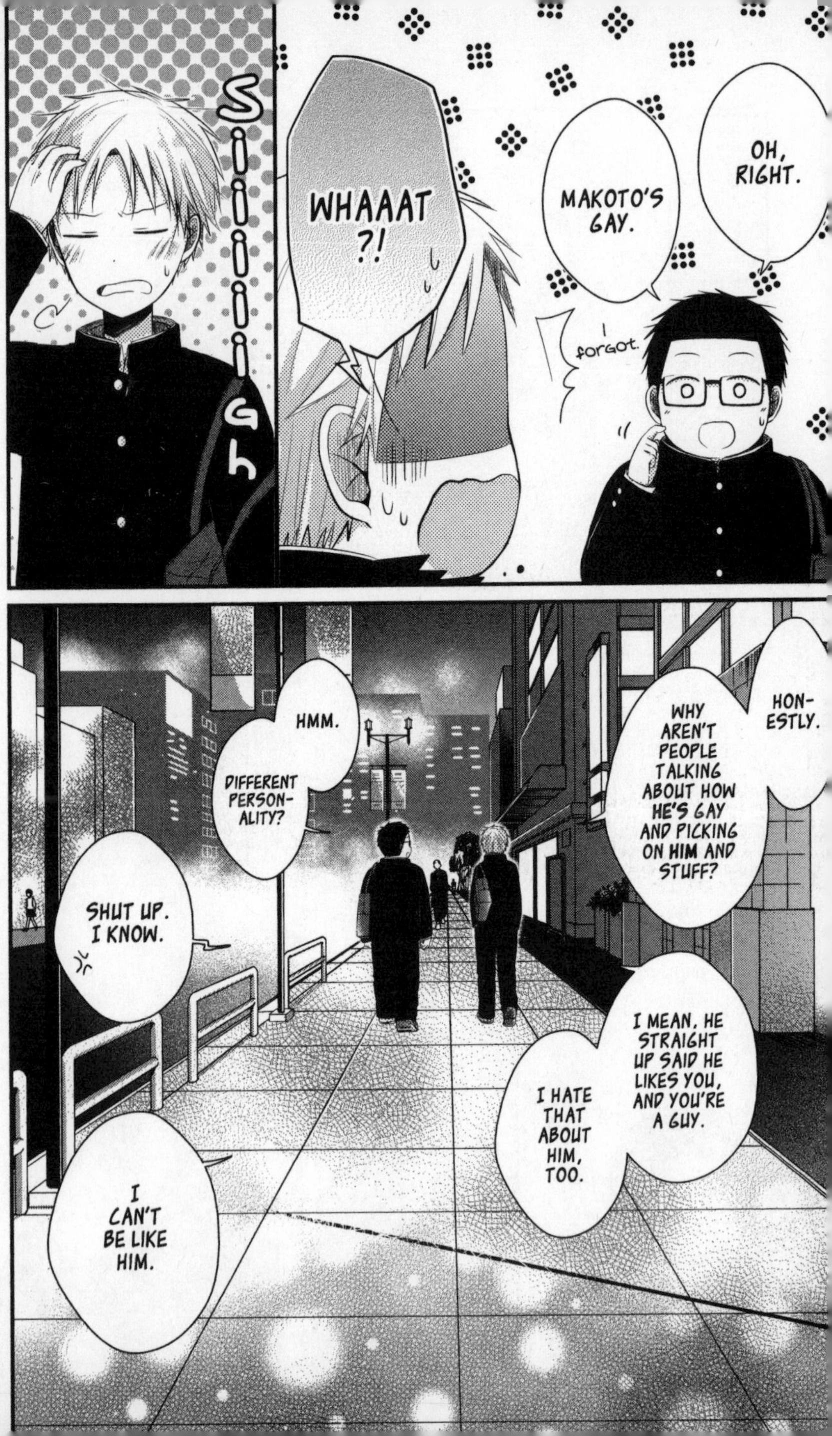
OH, RIGHT.
MAKOTO'S GAY.
I forgot.
WHAAAT ?!
Siiiiiiigh
HON-ESTLY.
WHY AREN'T PEOPLE TALKING ABOUT HOW HE'S GAY AND PICKING ON HIM AND STUFF?
HMM.
DIFFERENT PERSON-ALITY?
I MEAN, HE STRAIGHT UP SAID HE LIKES YOU, AND YOU'RE A GUY.
I HATE THAT ABOUT HIM, TOO.
SHUT UP. I KNOW.
I CAN'T BE LIKE HIM.

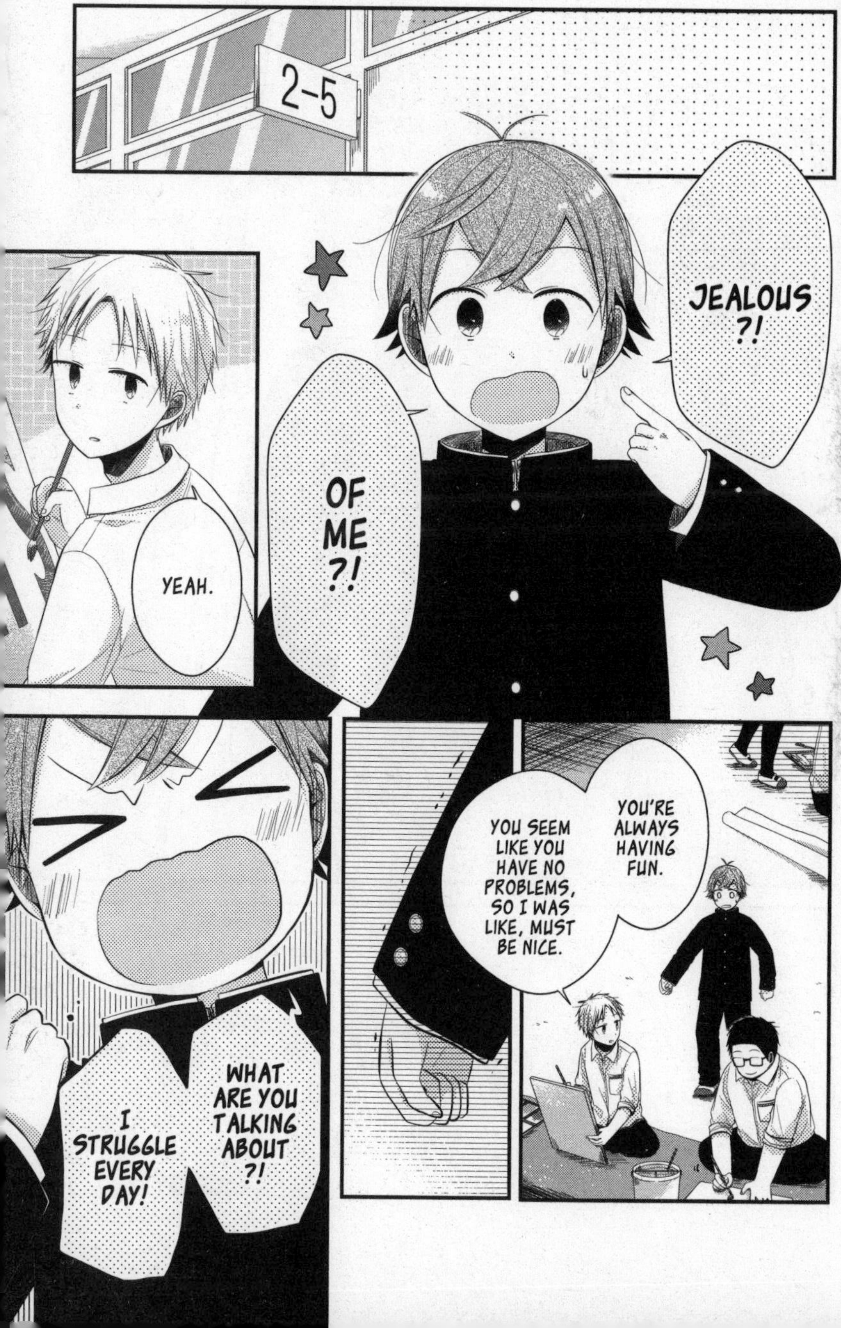
2-5
JEALOUS ?!
OF ME ?!
YEAH.
YOU'RE ALWAYS HAVING FUN.
YOU SEEM LIKE YOU HAVE NO PROBLEMS, SO I WAS LIKE, MUST BE NICE.
WHAT ARE YOU TALKING ABOUT ?!
I STRUGGLE EVERY DAY!

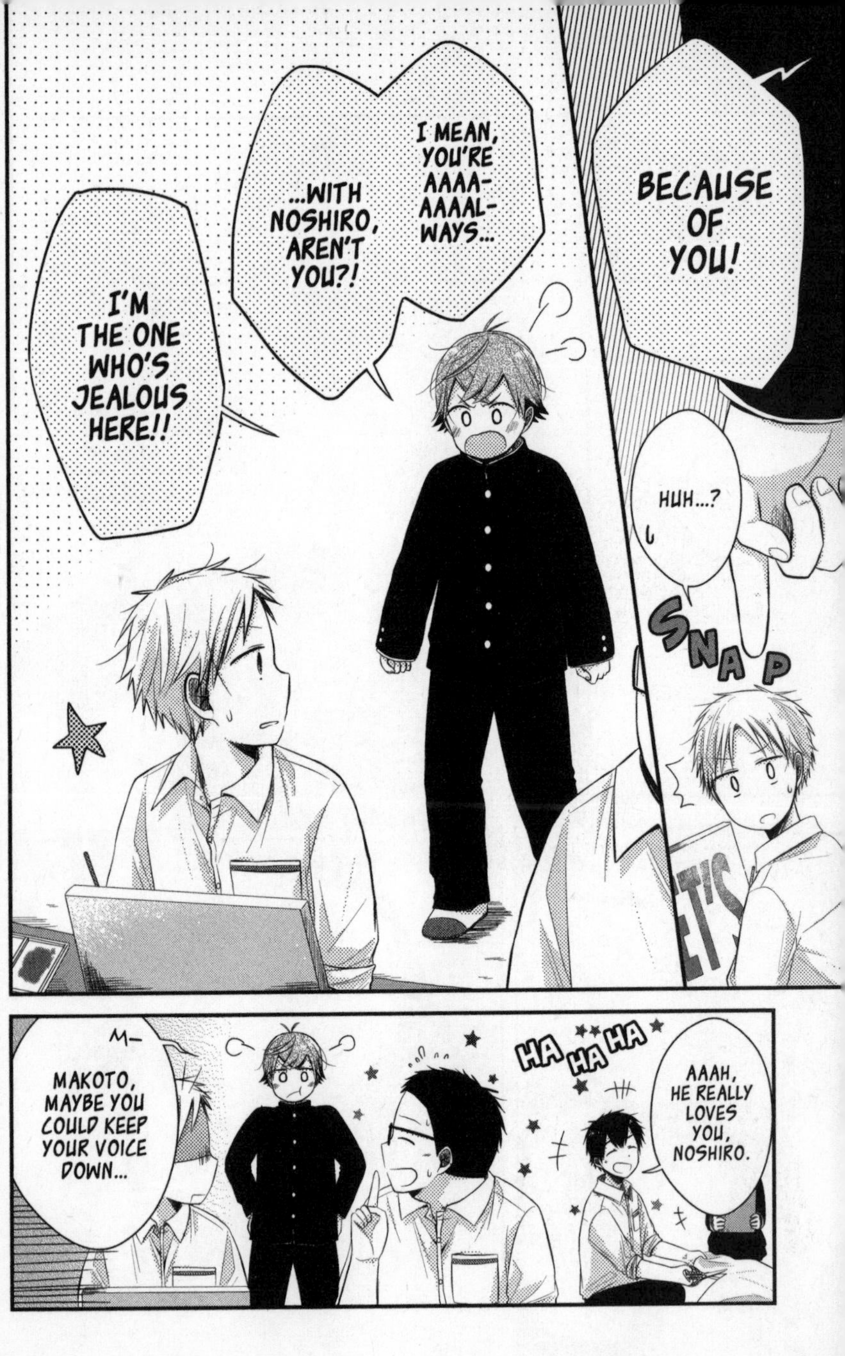
BECAUSE OF YOU!
HUH...?
SNAP
I MEAN, YOU'RE AAAA-AAAAL-WAYS...
...WITH NOSHIRO, AREN'T YOU?!
I'M THE ONE WHO'S JEALOUS HERE!!
AAAH, HE REALLY LOVES YOU, NOSHIRO.
HA HA HA
M— MAKOTO, MAYBE YOU COULD KEEP YOUR VOICE DOWN...

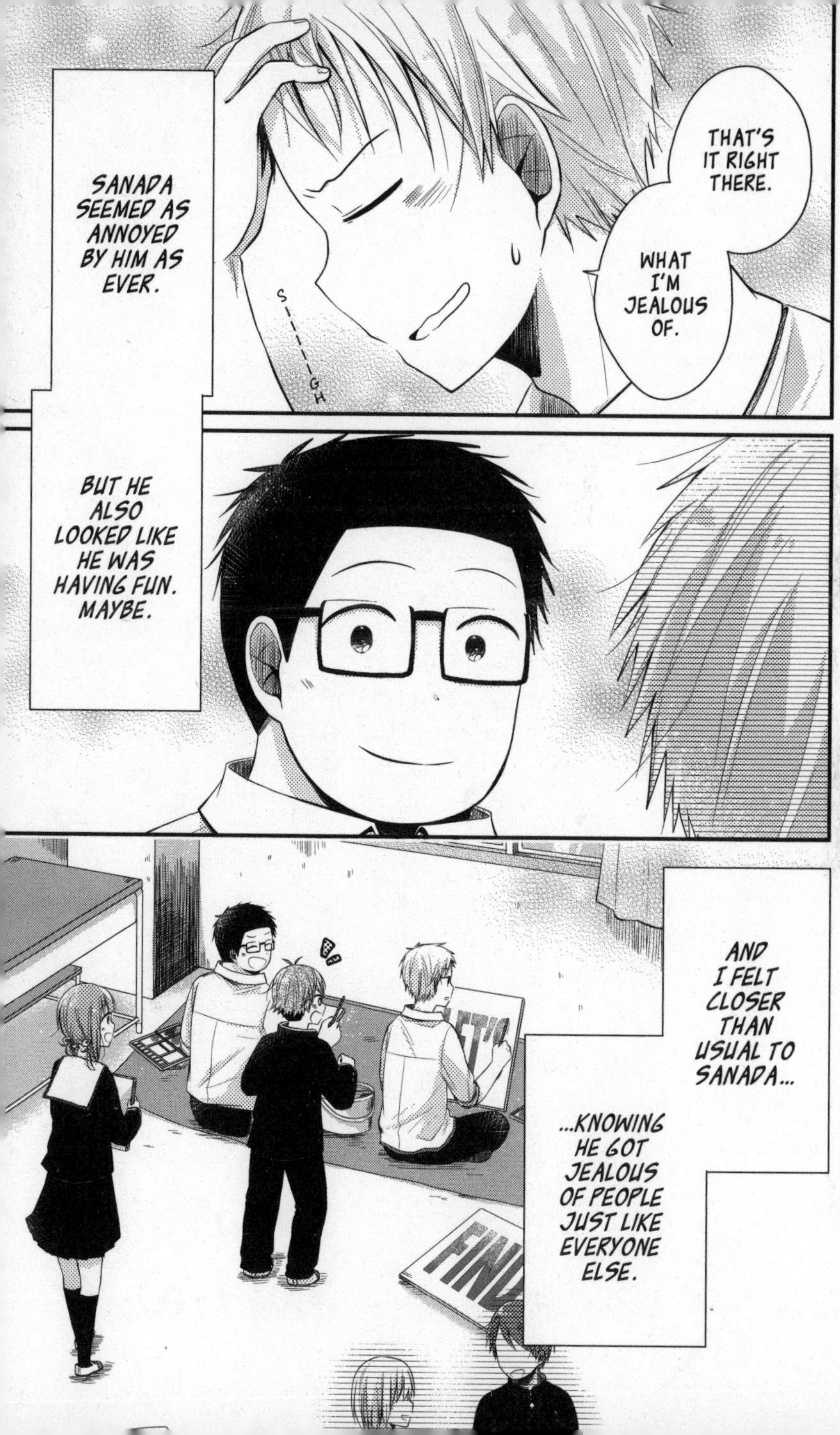
THAT'S IT RIGHT THERE.
WHAT I'M JEALOUS OF.
SIGH
SANADA SEEMED AS ANNOYED BY HIM AS EVER.
BUT HE ALSO LOOKED LIKE HE WAS HAVING FUN. MAYBE.
AND I FELT CLOSER THAN USUAL TO SANADA...
...KNOWING HE GOT JEALOUS OF PEOPLE JUST LIKE EVERYONE ELSE.

That Blue
Sky Feeling

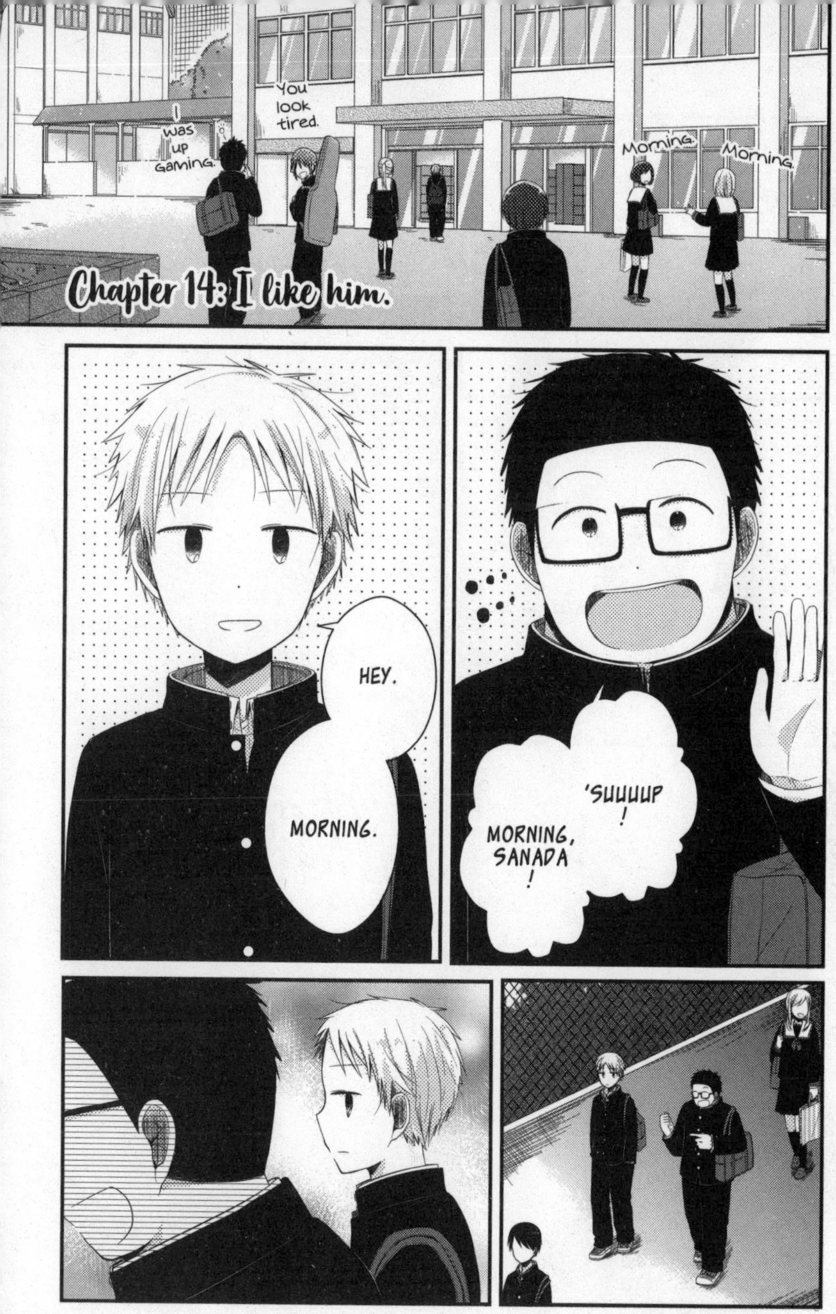
Morning.
Morning.
You look tired.
I was up gaming.
Chapter 14: I like him.
'SUUUUP! MORNING, SANADA!
HEY. MORNING.

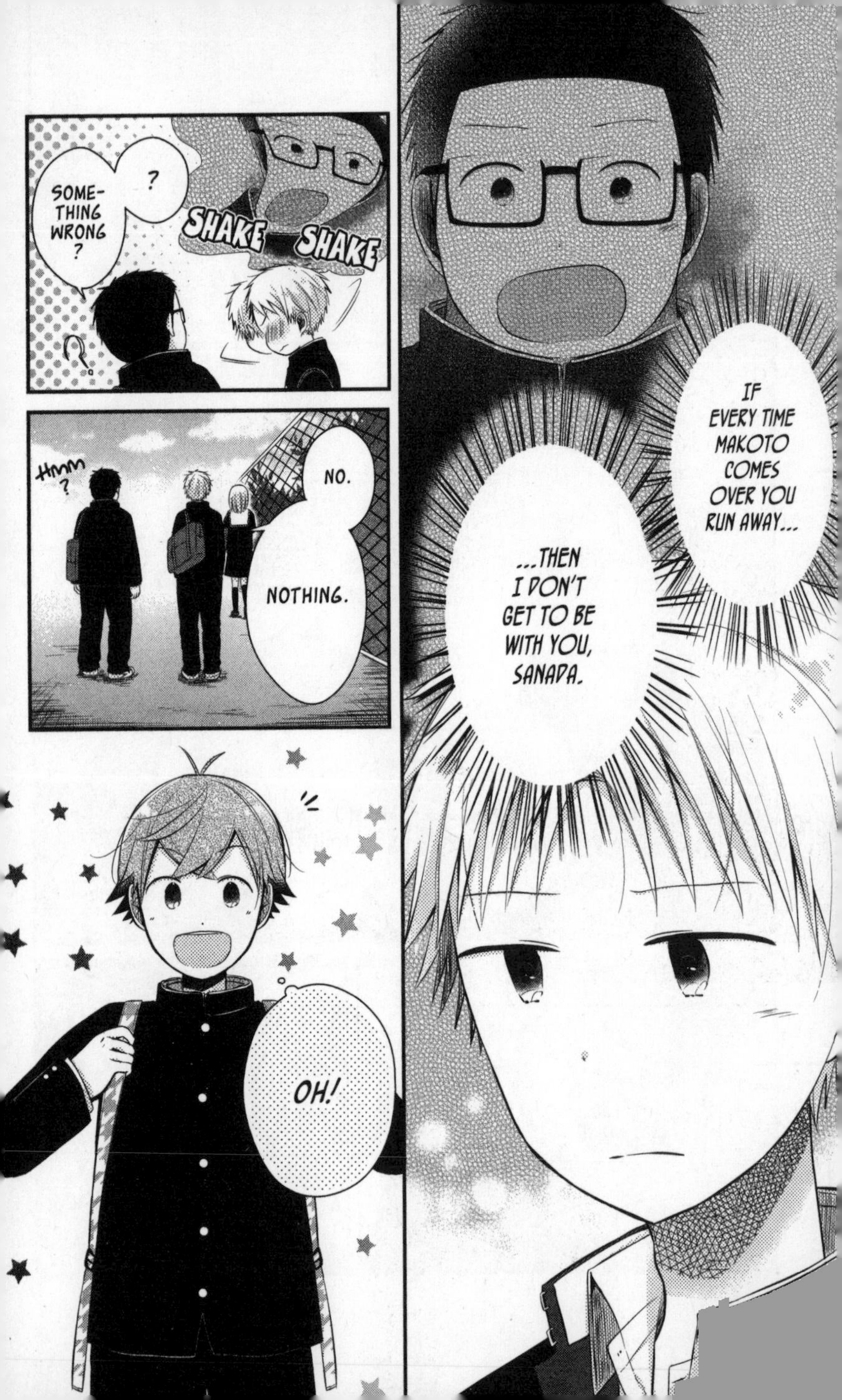
IF EVERY TIME MAKOTO COMES OVER YOU RUN AWAY...
...THEN I DON'T GET TO BE WITH YOU, SANADA.
SHAKE
SHAKE
?
SOME-THING WRONG?
NO.
NOTHING.
Hmm?
OH!

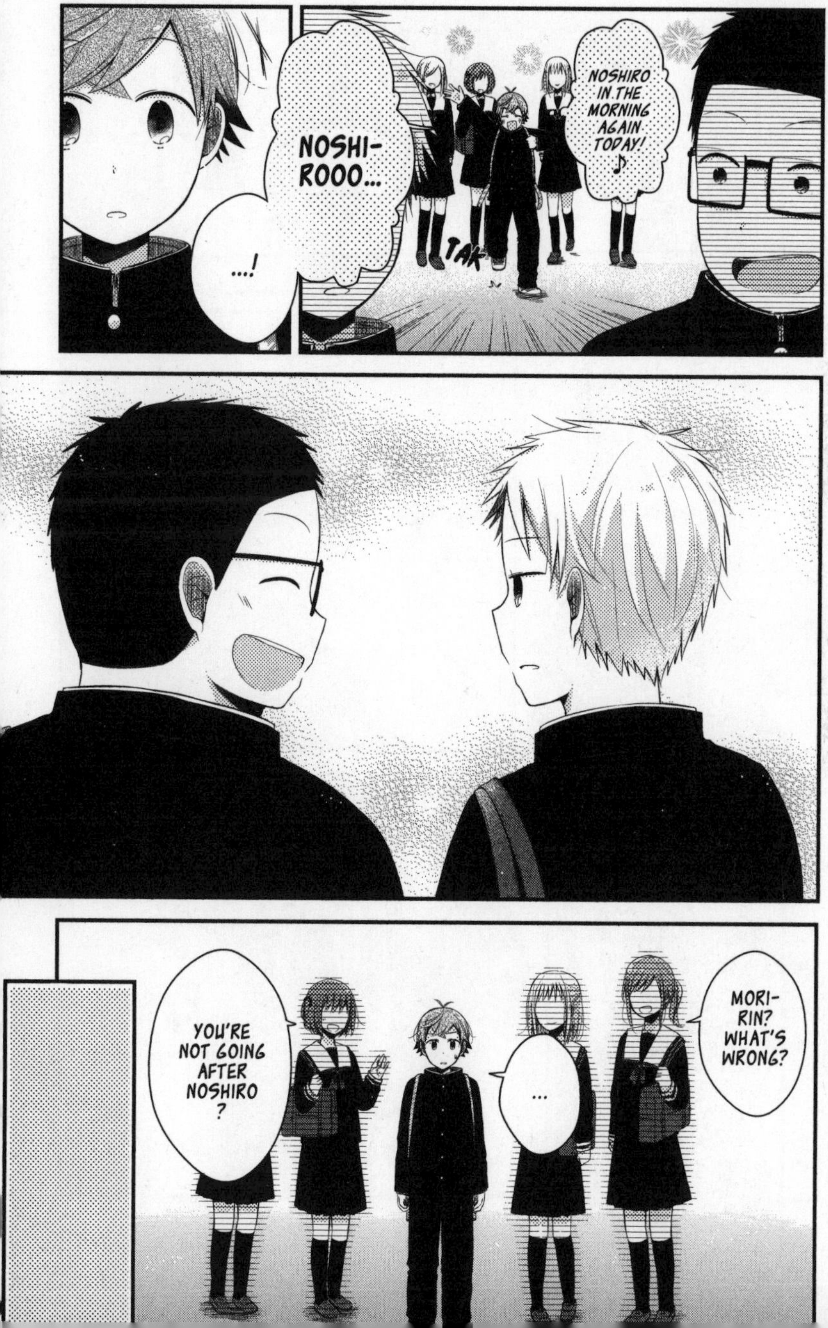
NOSHIRO IN THE MORNING AGAIN TODAY! ♪
NOSHI-ROOO...
TAK
...!
MORI-RIN? WHAT'S WRONG?
...
YOU'RE NOT GOING AFTER NOSHIRO?

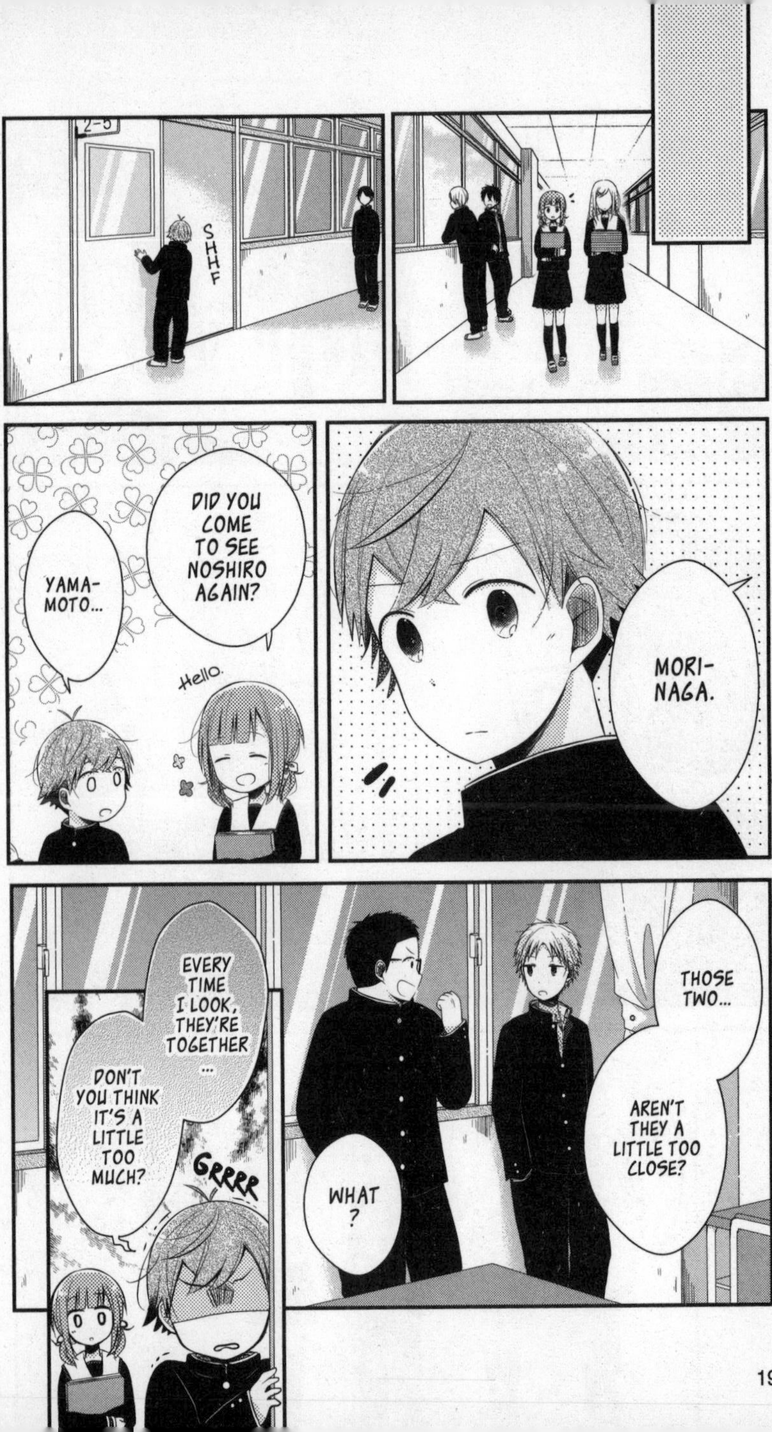
SHHF
MORI-NAGA.
DID YOU COME TO SEE NOSHIRO AGAIN?
YAMA-MOTO...
Hello.
THOSE TWO...
AREN'T THEY A LITTLE TOO CLOSE?
WHAT?
EVERY TIME I LOOK, THEY'RE TOGETHER...
DON'T YOU THINK IT'S A LITTLE TOO MUCH?
GRRRR

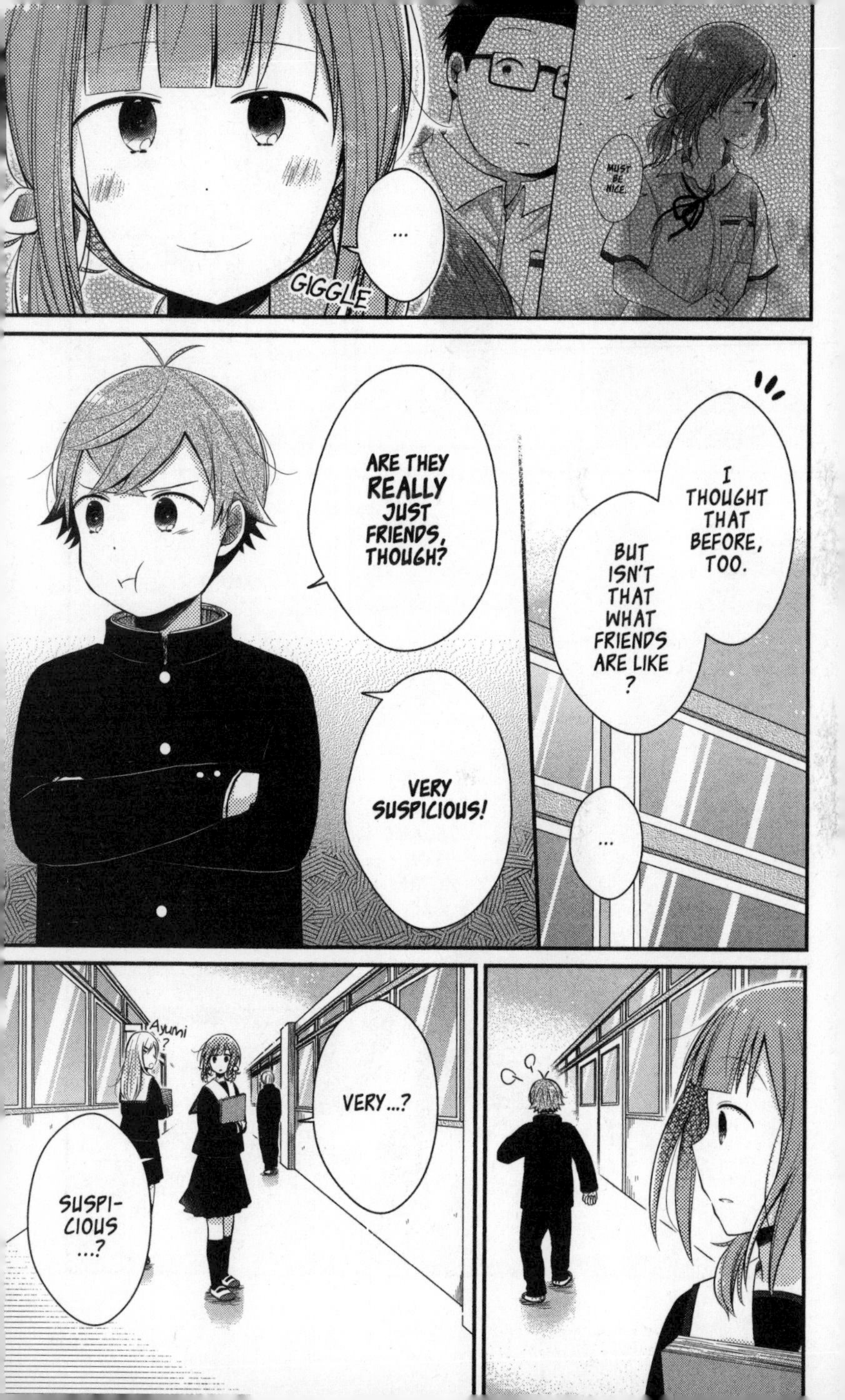
MUST BE NICE.
...
GIGGLE
I THOUGHT THAT BEFORE, TOO.
BUT ISN'T THAT WHAT FRIENDS ARE LIKE?
...
ARE THEY REALLY JUST FRIENDS, THOUGH?
VERY SUSPICIOUS!
Ayumi?
VERY...?
SUSPI-CIOUS...?

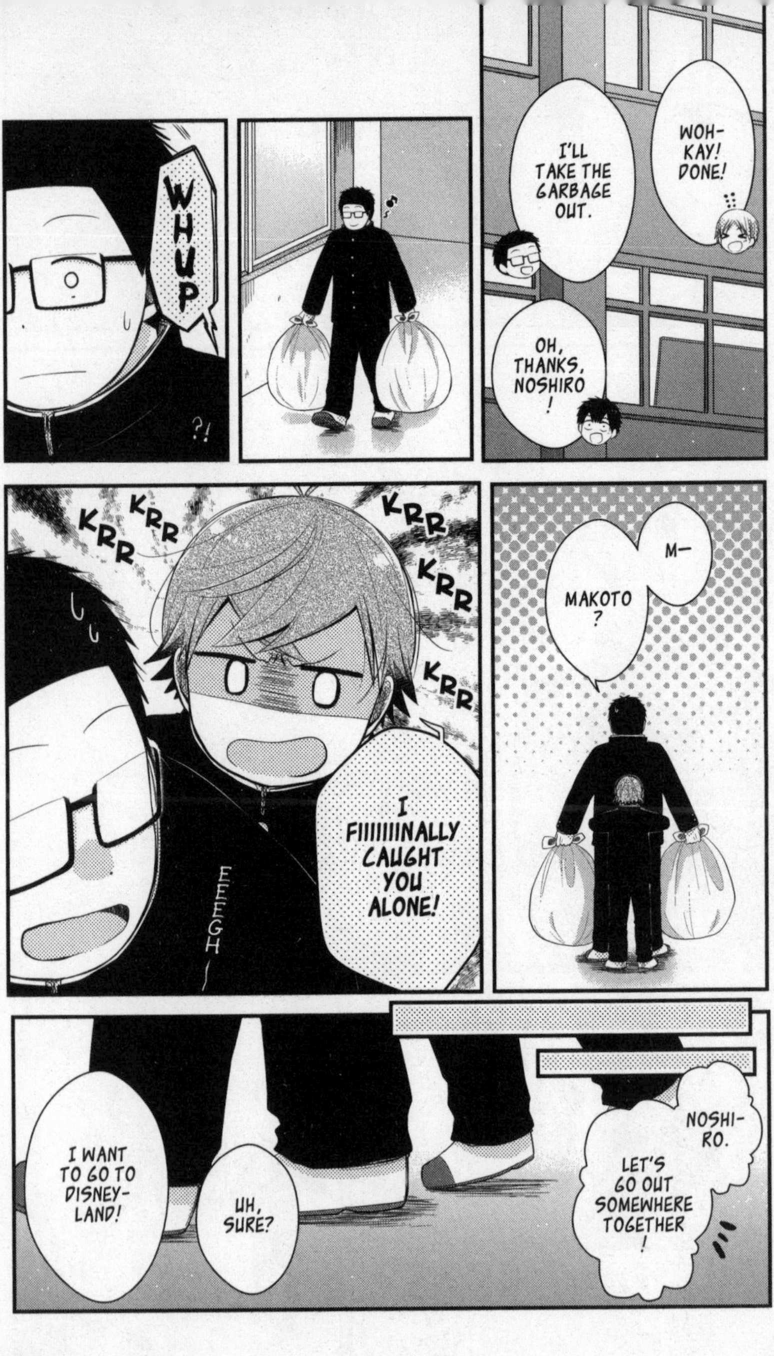
WOH-KAY! DONE!
I'LL TAKE THE GARBAGE OUT.
OH, THANKS, NOSHIRO!
WHUP
?!
M—
MAKOTO?
KRR KRR
KRR
KRR
KRR
KRR
I FIIIIIIINALLY CAUGHT YOU ALONE!
EEEGH~
NOSHIRO.
LET'S GO OUT SOMEWHERE TOGETHER!
UH, SURE?
I WANT TO GO TO DISNEY-LAND!

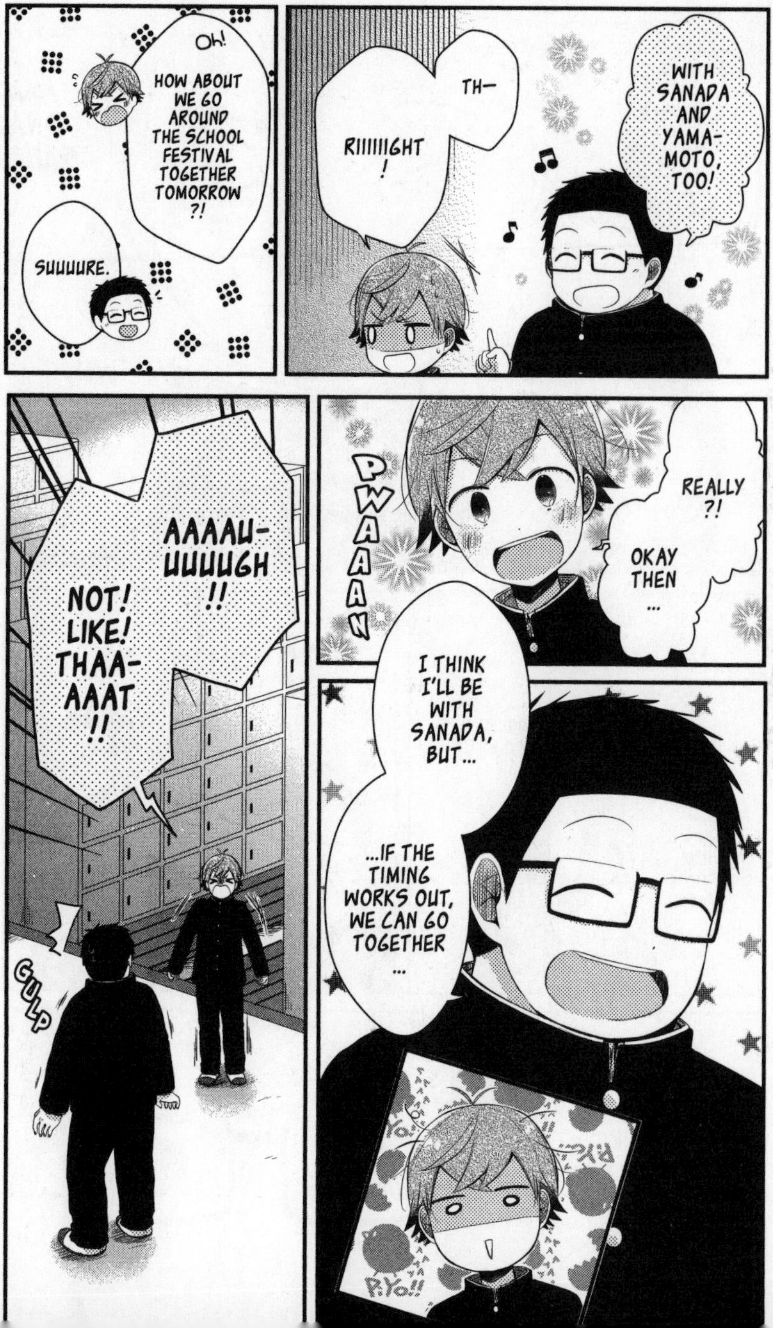
WITH SANADA AND YAMAMOTO, TOO!
TH—
RIIIIIIGHT!
Oh!
HOW ABOUT WE GO AROUND THE SCHOOL FESTIVAL TOGETHER TOMORROW?!
SUUUURE.
REALLY?!
OKAY THEN...
PWAAAAN
I THINK I'LL BE WITH SANADA, BUT...
...IF THE TIMING WORKS OUT, WE CAN GO TOGETHER...
PiYo!!
AAAAUUUUUGH!!
NOT! LIKE! THAAAAT!!
GULP

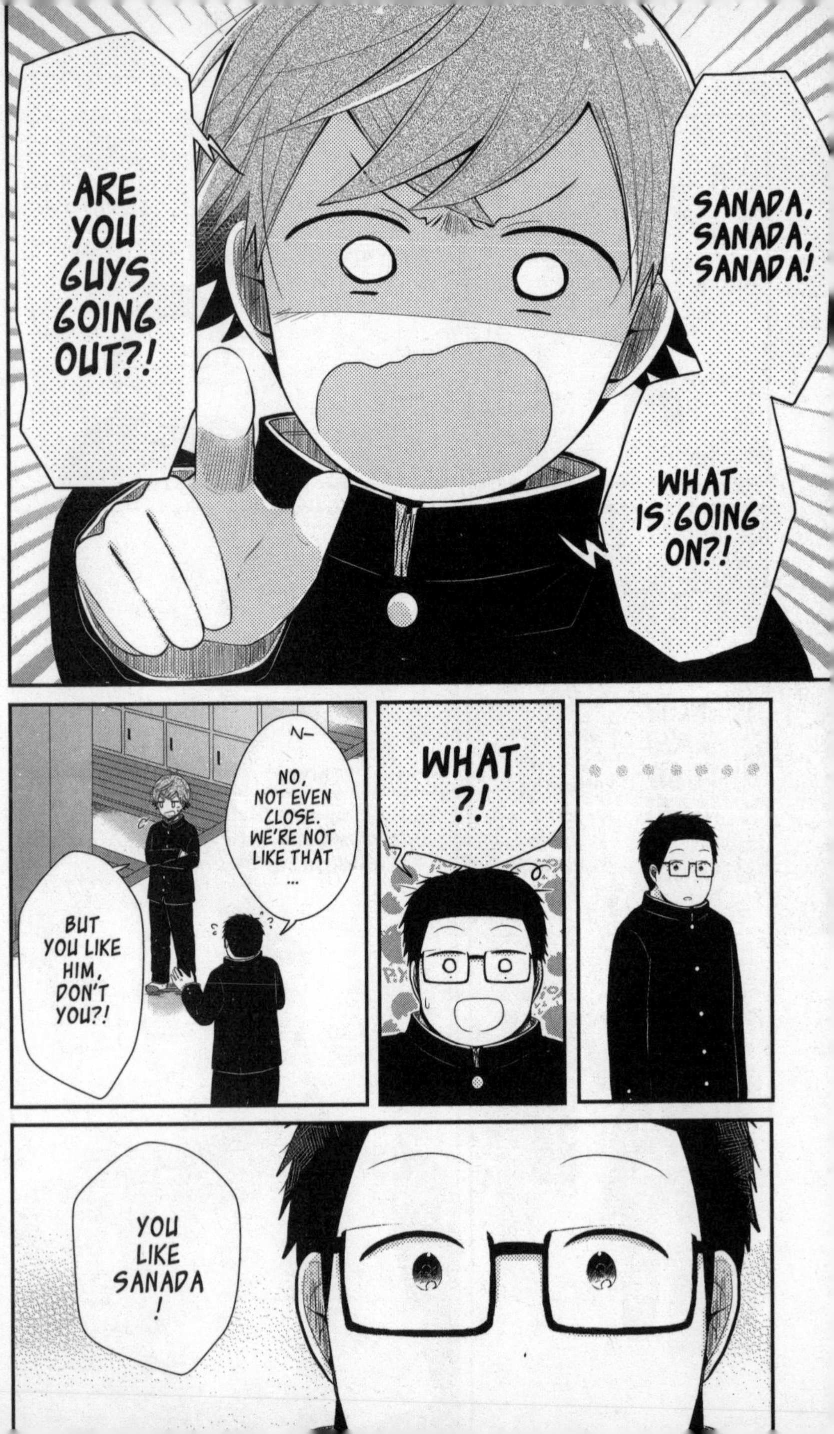
SANADA, SANADA, SANADA!
WHAT IS GOING ON?!
ARE YOU GUYS GOING OUT?!
• • • • • •
WHAT?!
N— NO, NOT EVEN CLOSE. WE'RE NOT LIKE THAT...
BUT YOU LIKE HIM, DON'T YOU?!
YOU LIKE SANADA!

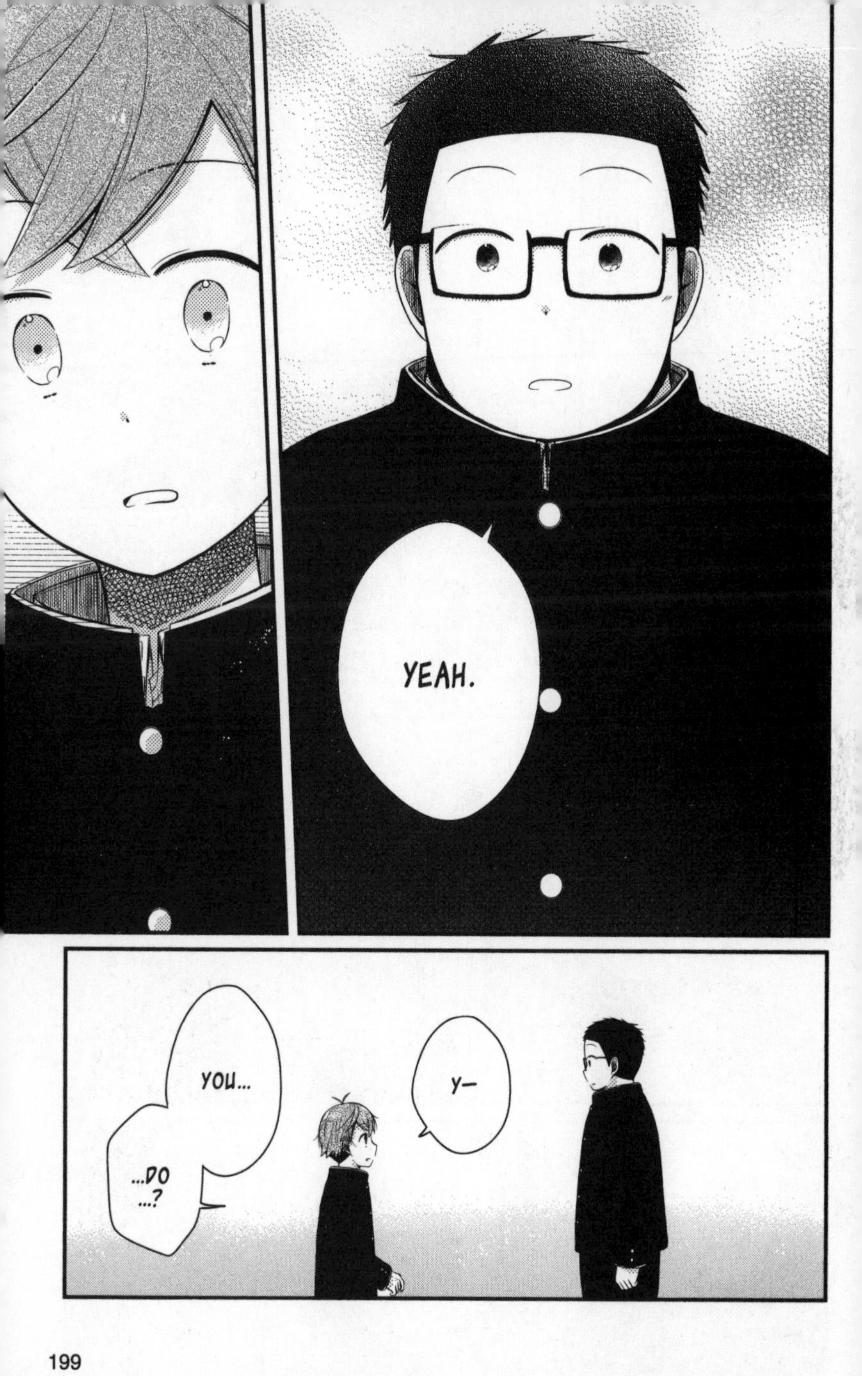
YEAH.
Y—
YOU...
...DO ...?

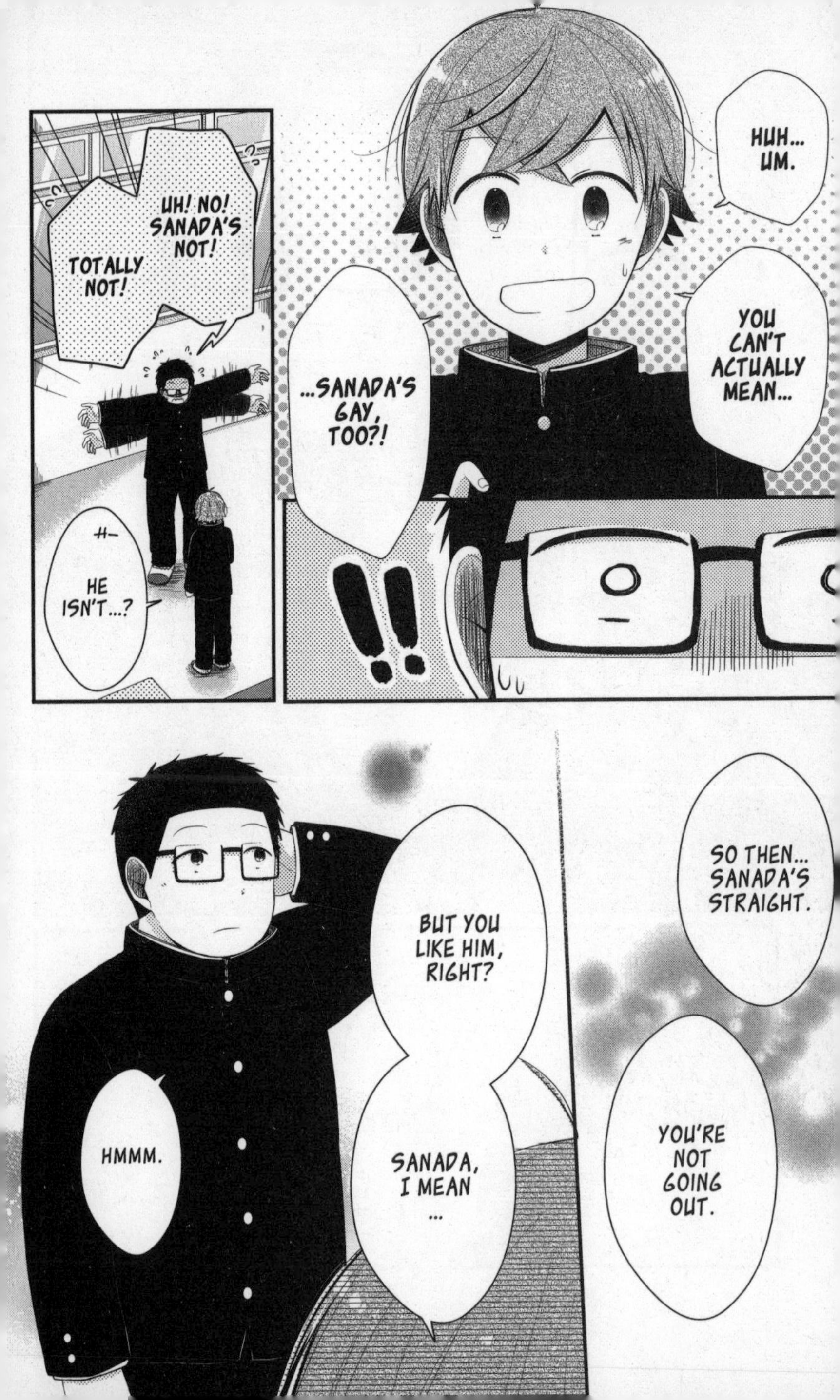
HUH... UM.
YOU CAN'T ACTUALLY MEAN...
...SANADA'S GAY, TOO?!
!!
UH! NO! SANADA'S NOT!
TOTALLY NOT!
H- HE ISN'T...?
SO THEN... SANADA'S STRAIGHT.
YOU'RE NOT GOING OUT.
BUT YOU LIKE HIM, RIGHT?
SANADA, I MEAN ...
HMMM.

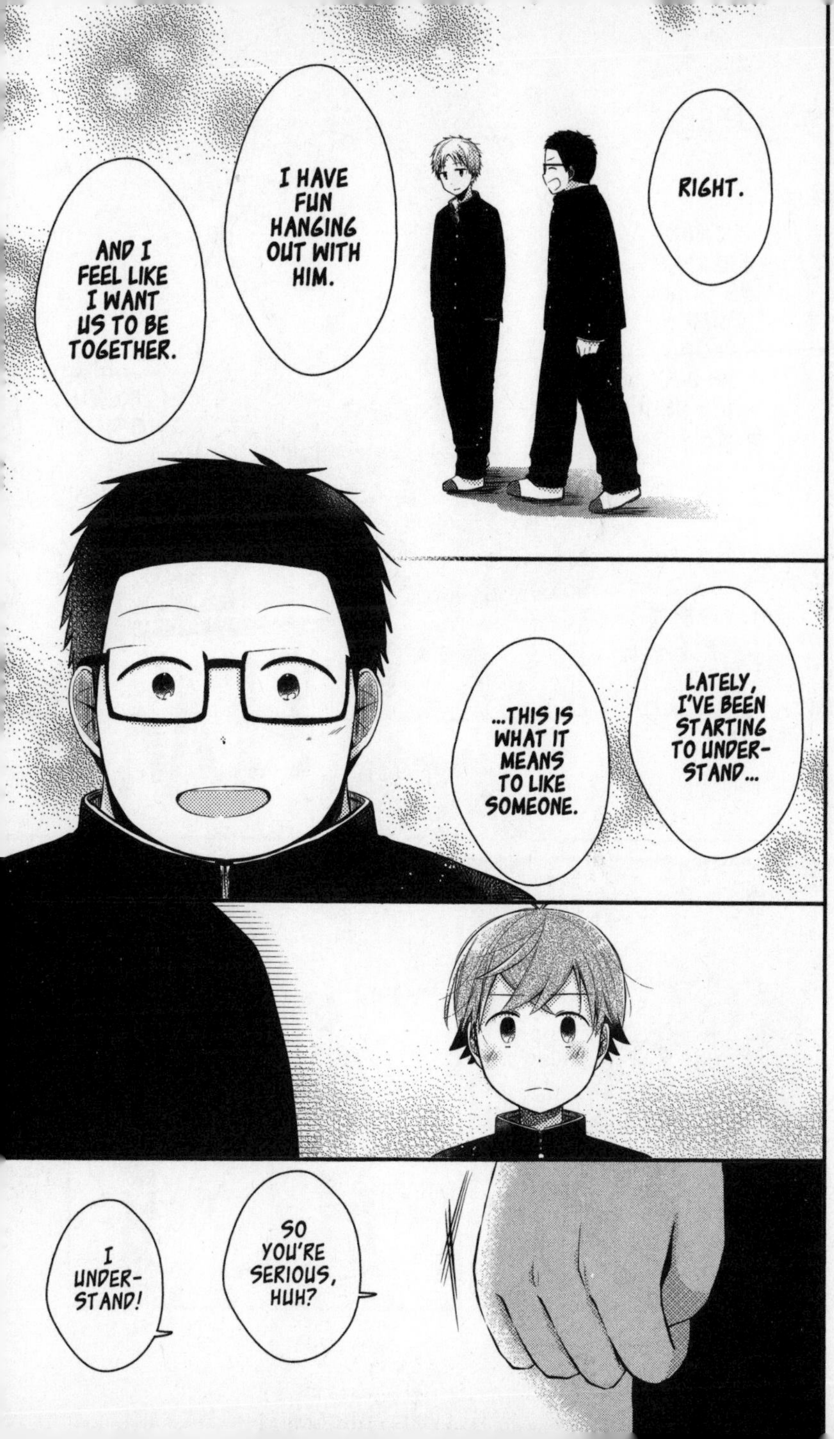
RIGHT.
I HAVE FUN HANGING OUT WITH HIM.
AND I FEEL LIKE I WANT US TO BE TOGETHER.
LATELY, I'VE BEEN STARTING TO UNDER-STAND...
...THIS IS WHAT IT MEANS TO LIKE SOMEONE.
SO YOU'RE SERIOUS, HUH?
I UNDER-STAND!

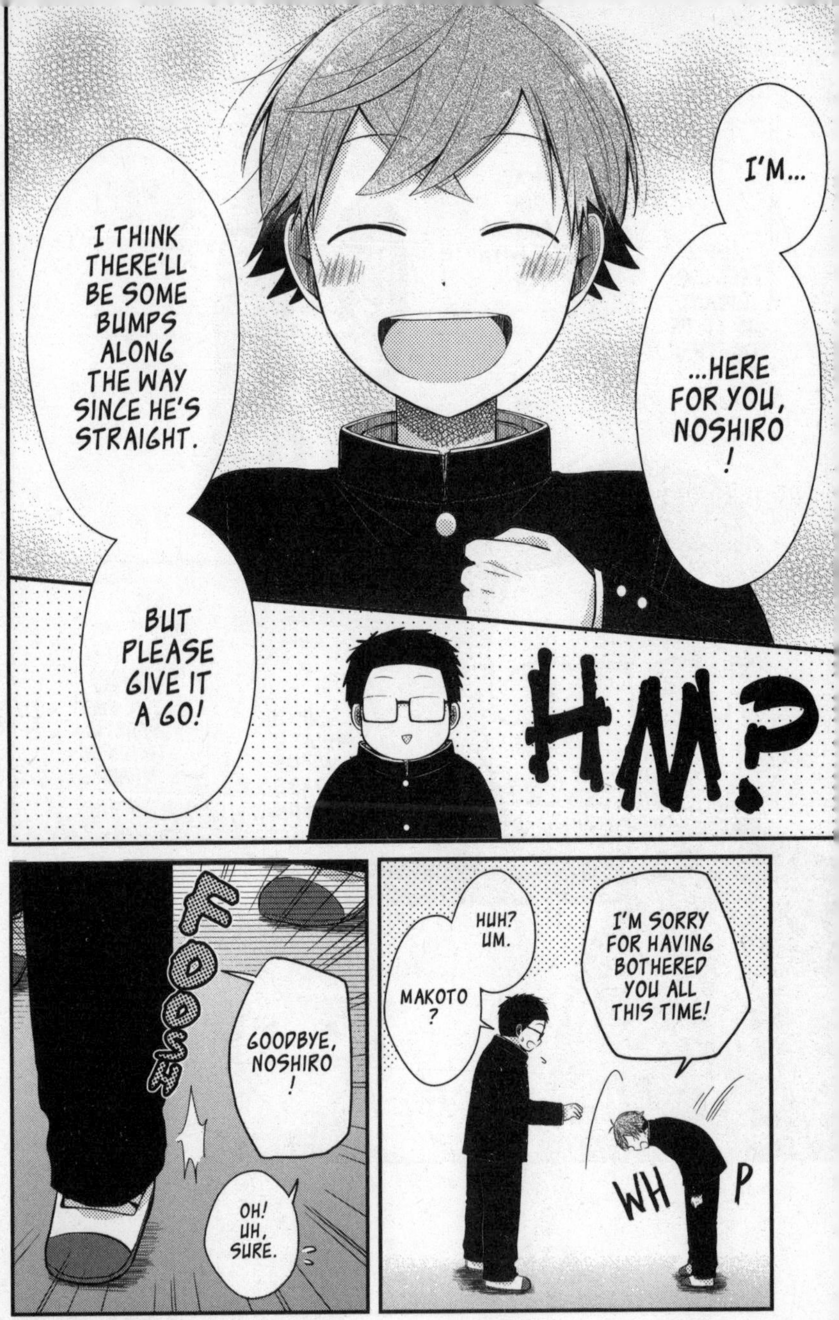
I'M...
...HERE FOR YOU, NOSHIRO!
I THINK THERE'LL BE SOME BUMPS ALONG THE WAY SINCE HE'S STRAIGHT.
BUT PLEASE GIVE IT A GO!
HM?
I'M SORRY FOR HAVING BOTHERED YOU ALL THIS TIME!
WH P
HUH? UM.
MAKOTO?
FOOSH
GOODBYE, NOSHIRO!
OH! UH, SURE.

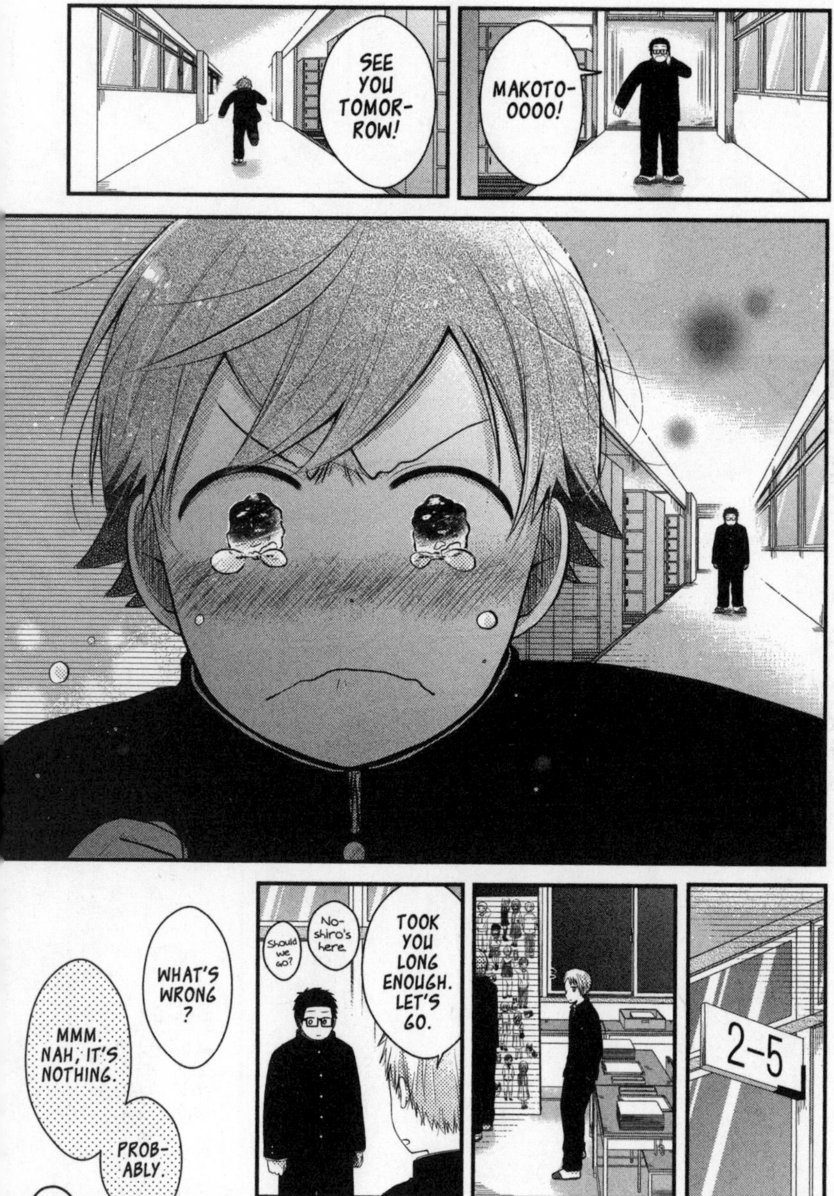
MAKOTO-OOOO!
SEE YOU TOMOR-ROW!
2-5
TOOK YOU LONG ENOUGH. LET'S GO.
No-shiro's here
Should we go?
WHAT'S WRONG?
MMM. NAH, IT'S NOTHING.
PROB-ABLY.
?

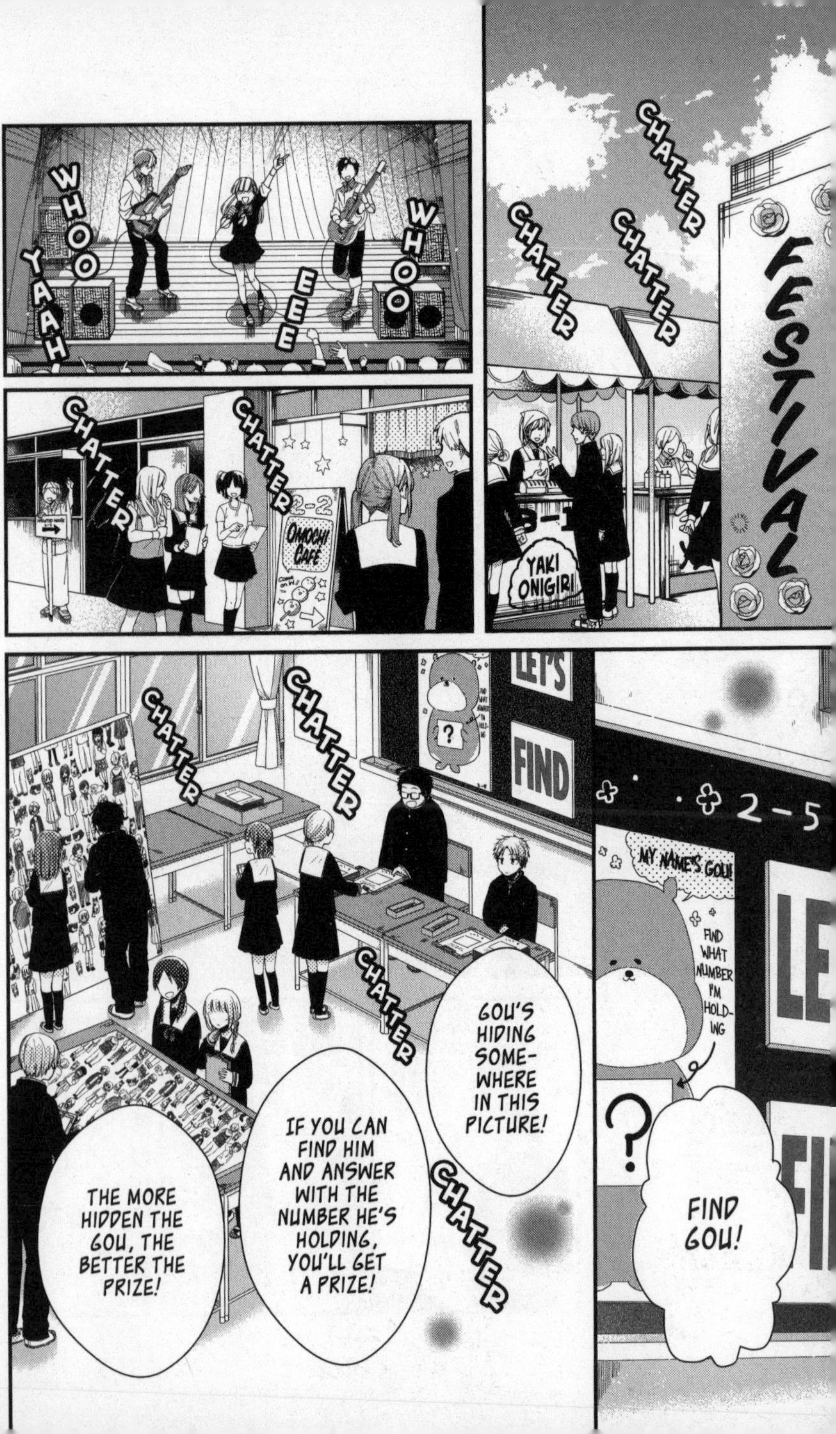
CHATTER
CHATTER
CHATTER
FESTIVAL
YAKI ONIGIRI
WHOO
EEE
WHOO
YAAH
CHATTER
CHATTER
2-2
OMOCHI CAFÉ
2-5
MY NAME'S GOU!
FIND WHAT NUMBER I'M HOLD-ING
FIND GOU!
LET'S
FIND
CHATTER
CHATTER
GOU'S HIDING SOME-WHERE IN THIS PICTURE!
CHATTER
IF YOU CAN FIND HIM AND ANSWER WITH THE NUMBER HE'S HOLDING, YOU'LL GET A PRIZE!
CHATTER
THE MORE HIDDEN THE GOU, THE BETTER THE PRIZE!

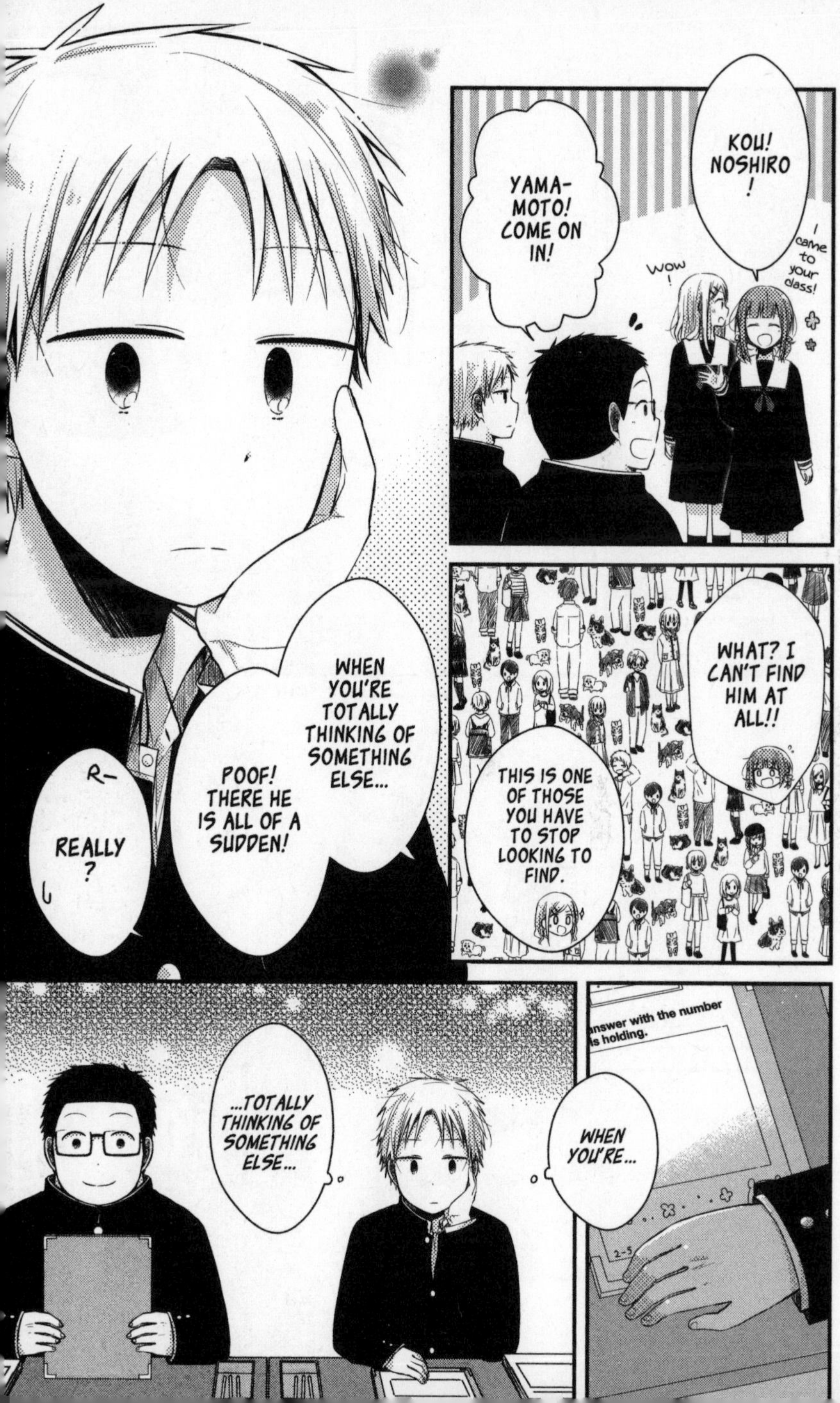
KOU! NOSHIRO!
I came to your class!
YAMA-MOTO! COME ON IN!
Wow!
WHAT? I CAN'T FIND HIM AT ALL!!
THIS IS ONE OF THOSE YOU HAVE TO STOP LOOKING TO FIND.
WHEN YOU'RE TOTALLY THINKING OF SOMETHING ELSE...
POOF! THERE HE IS ALL OF A SUDDEN!
R— REALLY?
nswer with the number
s holding.
WHEN YOU'RE...
...TOTALLY THINKING OF SOMETHING ELSE...

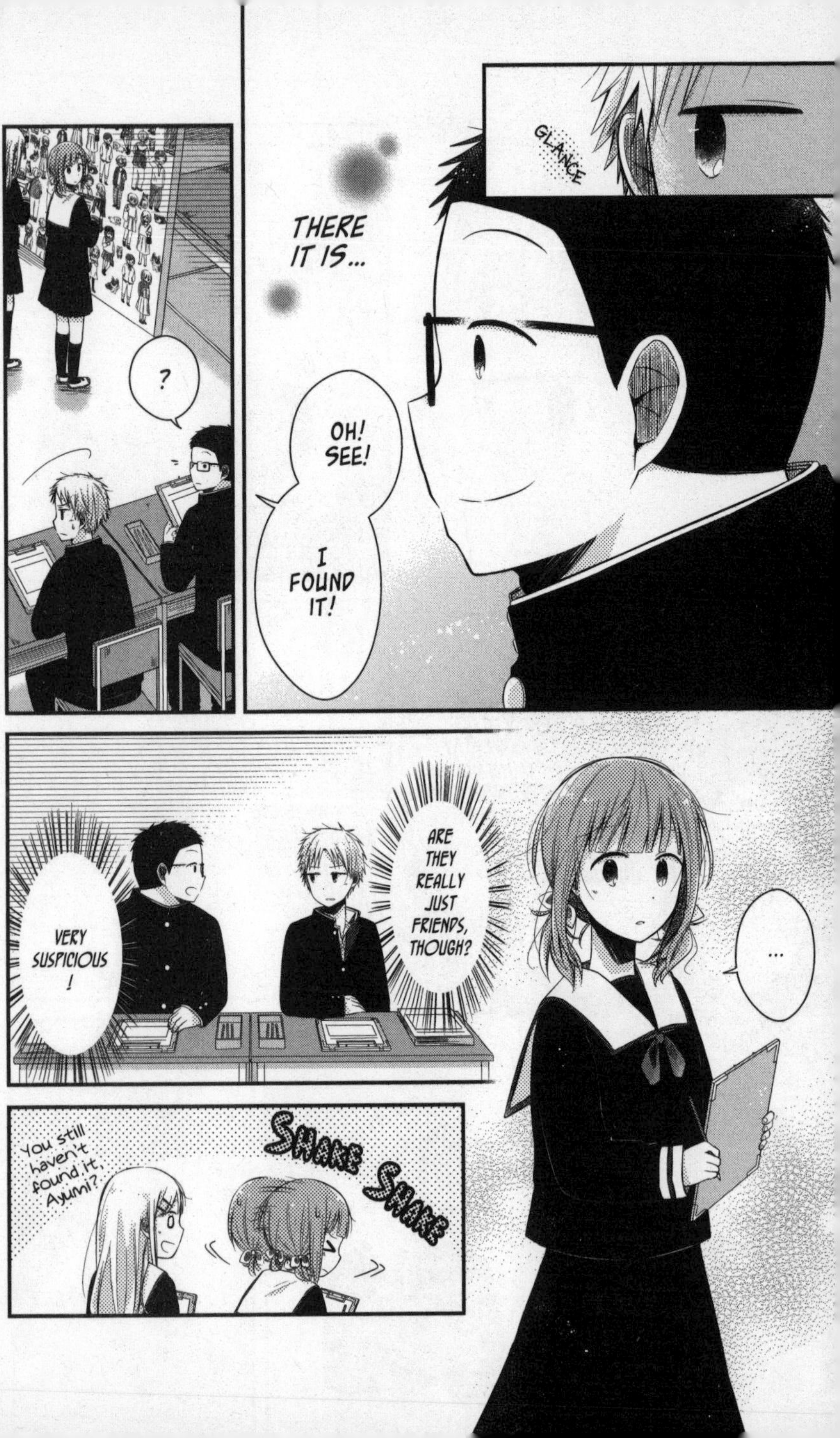
GLANCE
THERE IT IS...
OH! SEE!
I FOUND IT!
?
...
ARE THEY REALLY JUST FRIENDS, THOUGH?
VERY SUSPICIOUS!
SHAKE SHAKE
You still haven't found it, Ayumi?

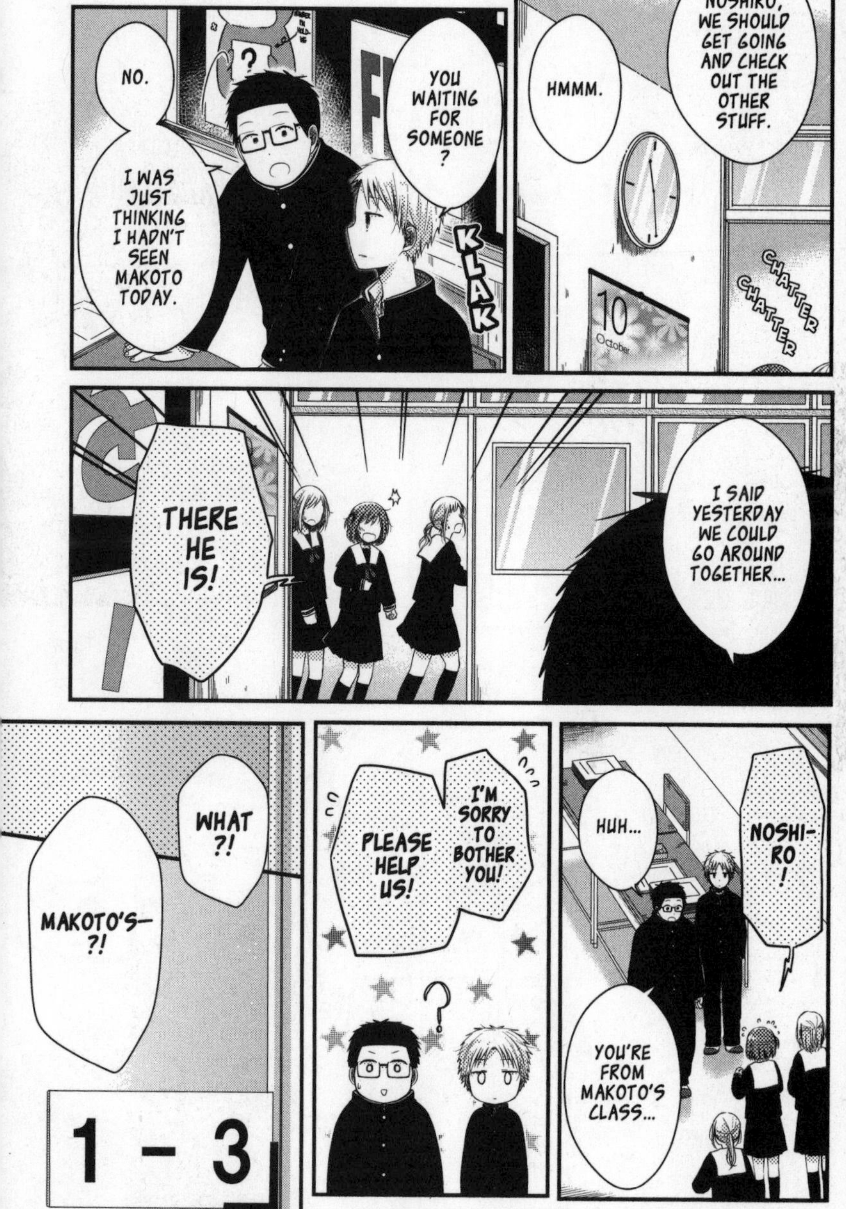
NOSHIRO, WE SHOULD GET GOING AND CHECK OUT THE OTHER STUFF.
HMMM.
CHATTER CHATTER
10 October
YOU WAITING FOR SOMEONE?
KLAK
NO.
I WAS JUST THINKING I HADN'T SEEN MAKOTO TODAY.
I SAID YESTERDAY WE COULD GO AROUND TOGETHER...
THERE HE IS!
NOSHI-RO!
HUH...
YOU'RE FROM MAKOTO'S CLASS...
I'M SORRY TO BOTHER YOU!
PLEASE HELP US!
WHAT?!
MAKOTO'S—?!
1-3

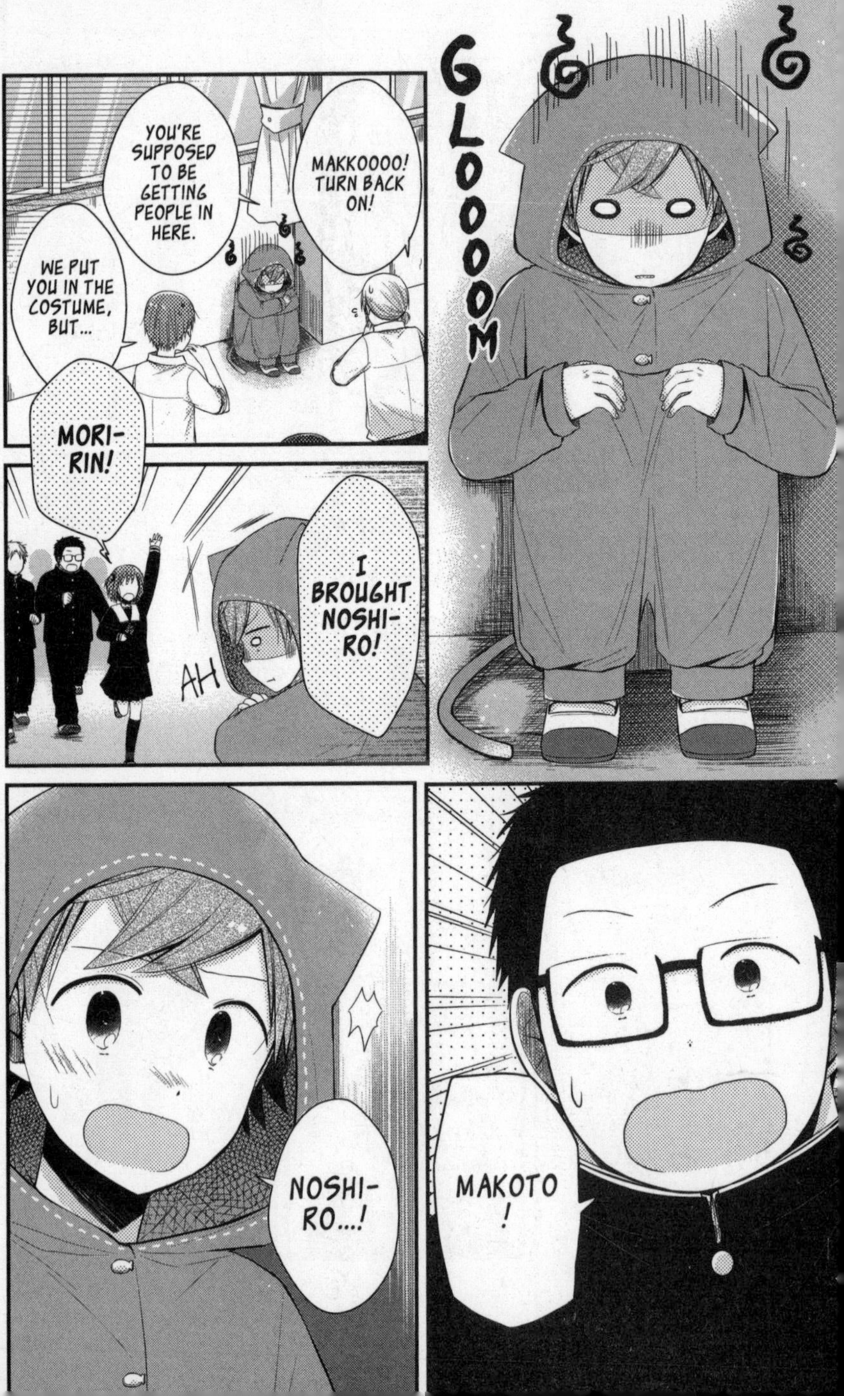
GLOOOOM
MAKKOOOO! TURN BACK ON!
YOU'RE SUPPOSED TO BE GETTING PEOPLE IN HERE.
WE PUT YOU IN THE COSTUME, BUT...
MORI-RIN!
I BROUGHT NOSHIRO!
AH
MAKOTO!
NOSHIRO...!

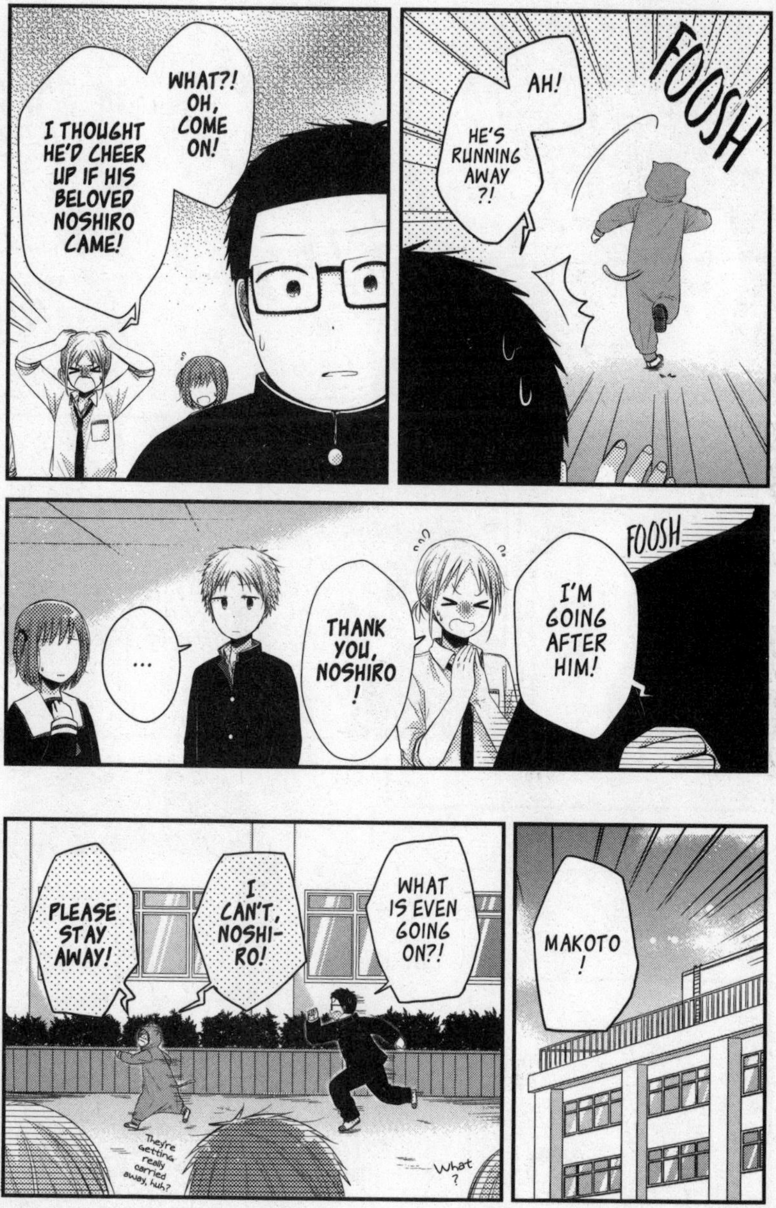
FOOSH
AH!
HE'S RUNNING AWAY?!
WHAT?! OH, COME ON!
I THOUGHT HE'D CHEER UP IF HIS BELOVED NOSHIRO CAME!
FOOSH
I'M GOING AFTER HIM!
THANK YOU, NOSHIRO!
...
MAKOTO!
WHAT IS EVEN GOING ON?!
I CAN'T, NOSHIRO!
PLEASE STAY AWAY!
What?
They're getting really carried away, huh?

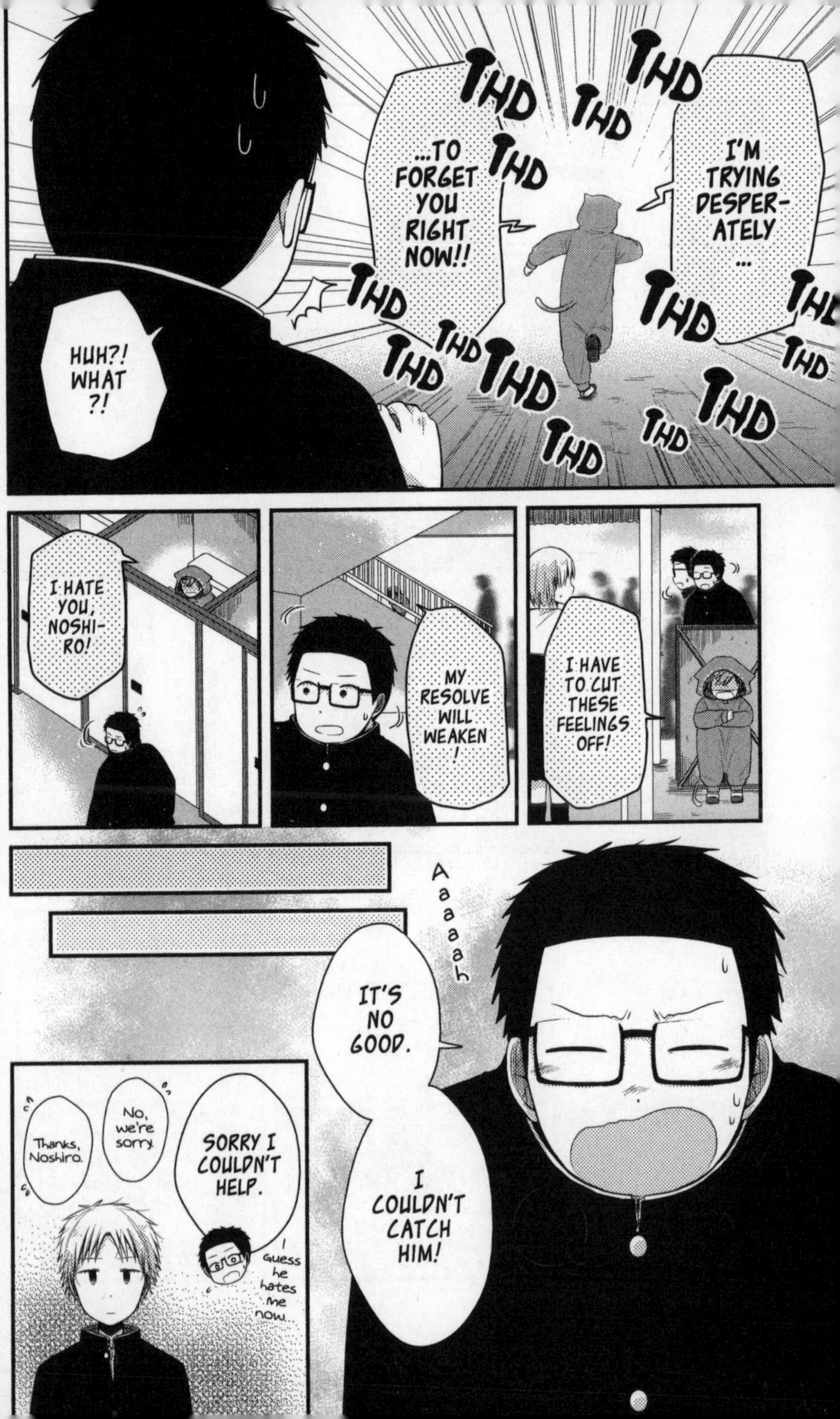
I'M TRYING DESPERATELY...
...TO FORGET YOU RIGHT NOW!!
THD THD THD THD
THD THD THD THD THD THD THD THD THD
HUH?! WHAT?!
I HAVE TO CUT THESE FEELINGS OFF!
MY RESOLVE WILL WEAKEN!
I HATE YOU, NOSHIRO!
Aaaaah
IT'S NO GOOD.
I COULDN'T CATCH HIM!
SORRY I COULDN'T HELP.
No, we're sorry.
Thanks, Noshiro.
I guess he hates me now...

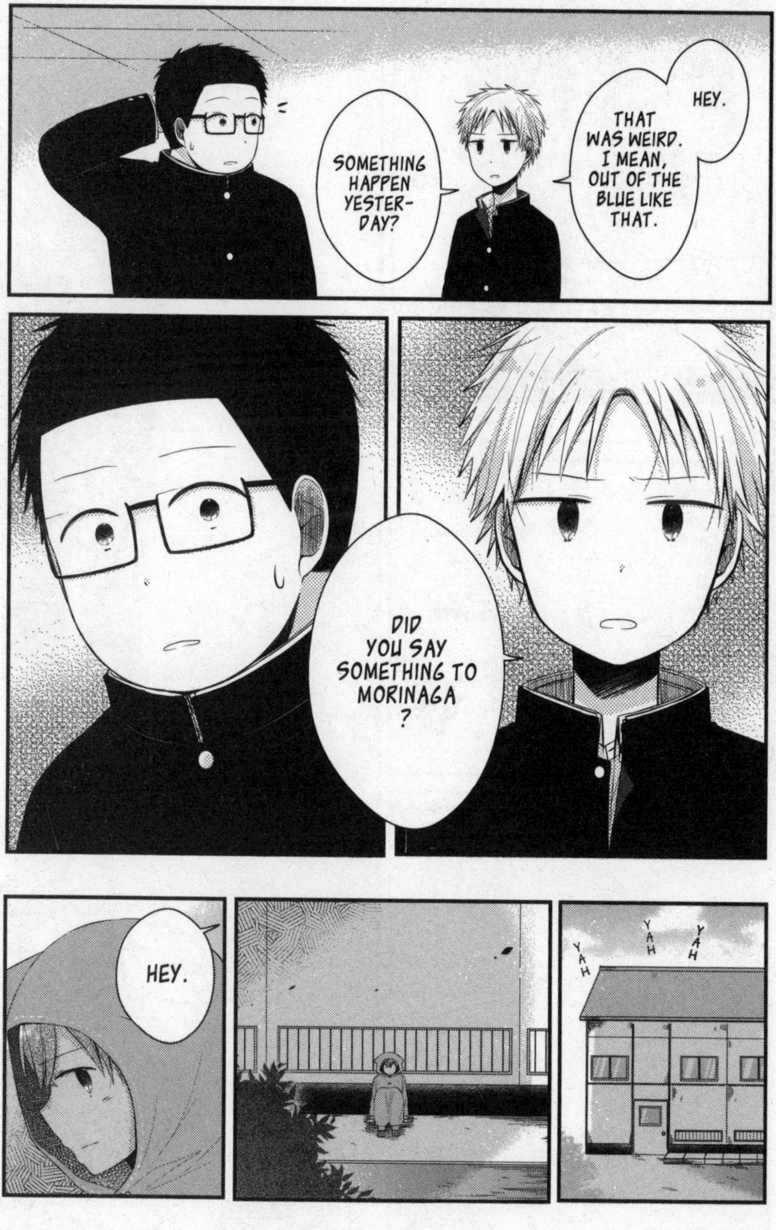
HEY.
THAT WAS WEIRD. I MEAN, OUT OF THE BLUE LIKE THAT.
SOMETHING HAPPEN YESTER-DAY?
DID YOU SAY SOMETHING TO MORINAGA?
YAH YAH YAH
HEY.

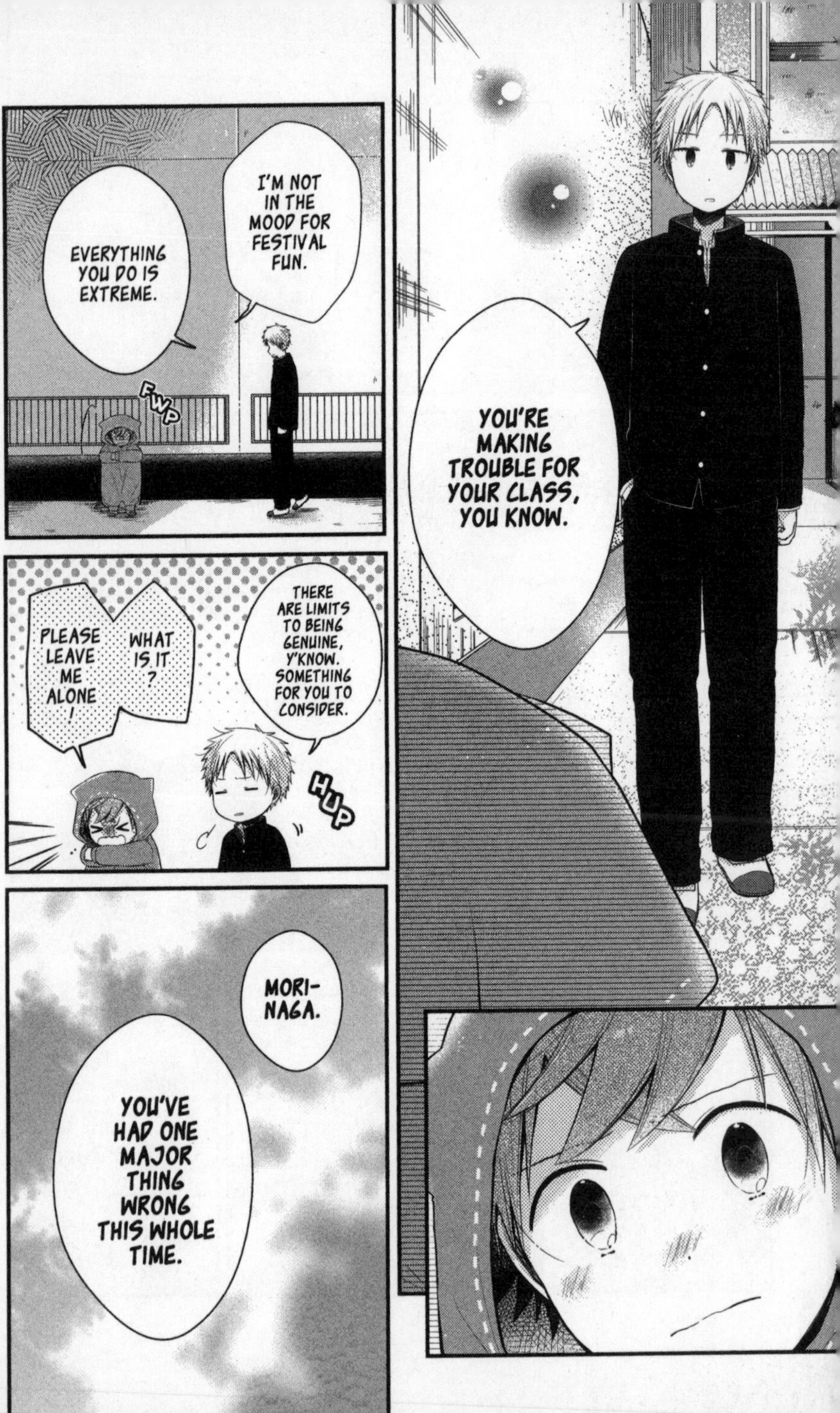
YOU'RE MAKING TROUBLE FOR YOUR CLASS, YOU KNOW.
I'M NOT IN THE MOOD FOR FESTIVAL FUN.
EVERYTHING YOU DO IS EXTREME.
FWP
THERE ARE LIMITS TO BEING GENUINE, Y'KNOW. SOMETHING FOR YOU TO CONSIDER.
WHAT IS IT?
PLEASE LEAVE ME ALONE!
HUP
MORI-NAGA.
YOU'VE HAD ONE MAJOR THING WRONG THIS WHOLE TIME.

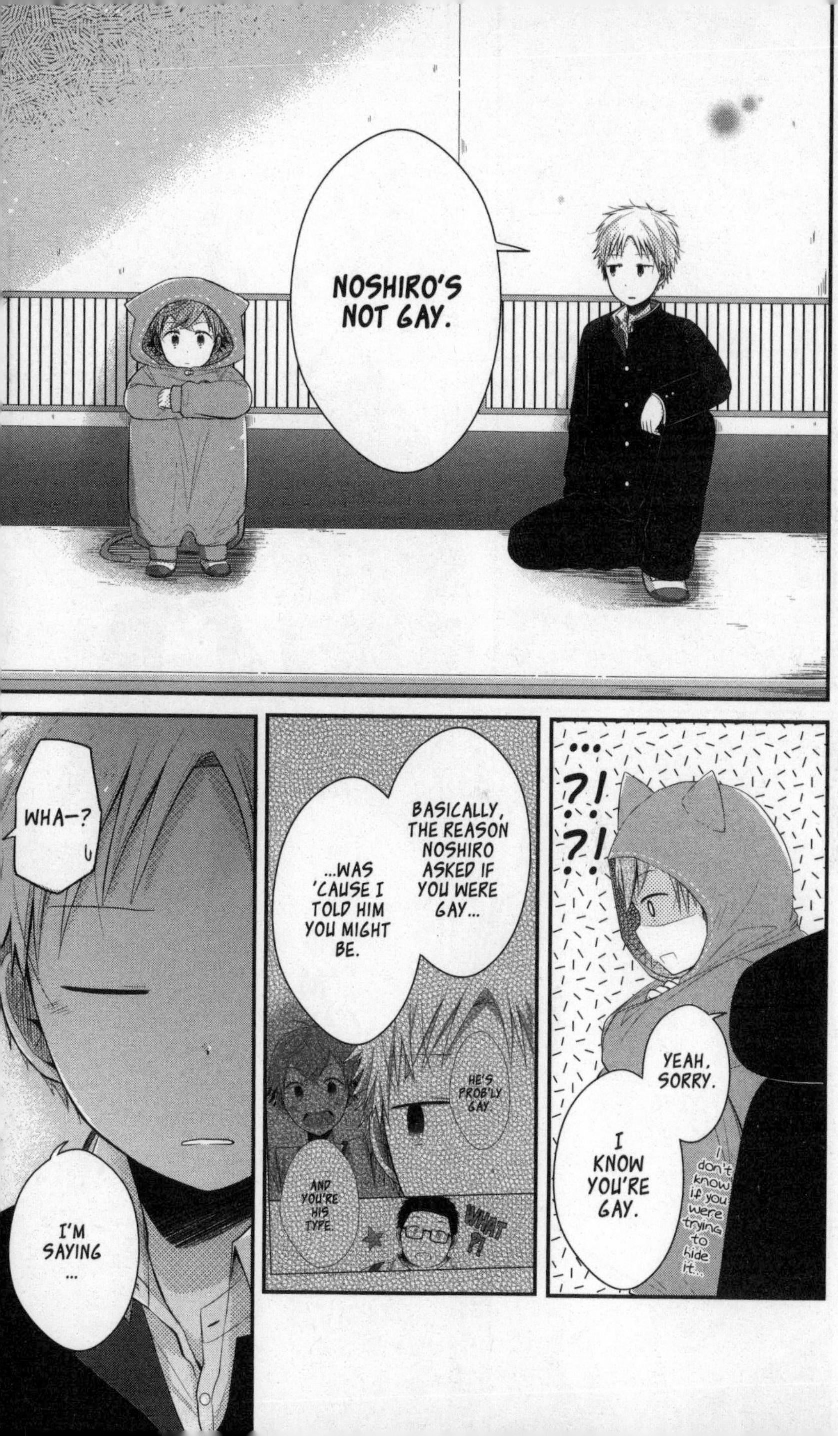
NOSHIRO'S NOT GAY.
...?!?!
YEAH, SORRY.
I KNOW YOU'RE GAY.
I don't know if you were trying to hide it...
BASICALLY, THE REASON NOSHIRO ASKED IF YOU WERE GAY...
...WAS 'CAUSE I TOLD HIM YOU MIGHT BE.
HE'S PROB'LY GAY.
AND YOU'RE HIS TYPE.
WHAT?!
WHA—?
I'M SAYING ...

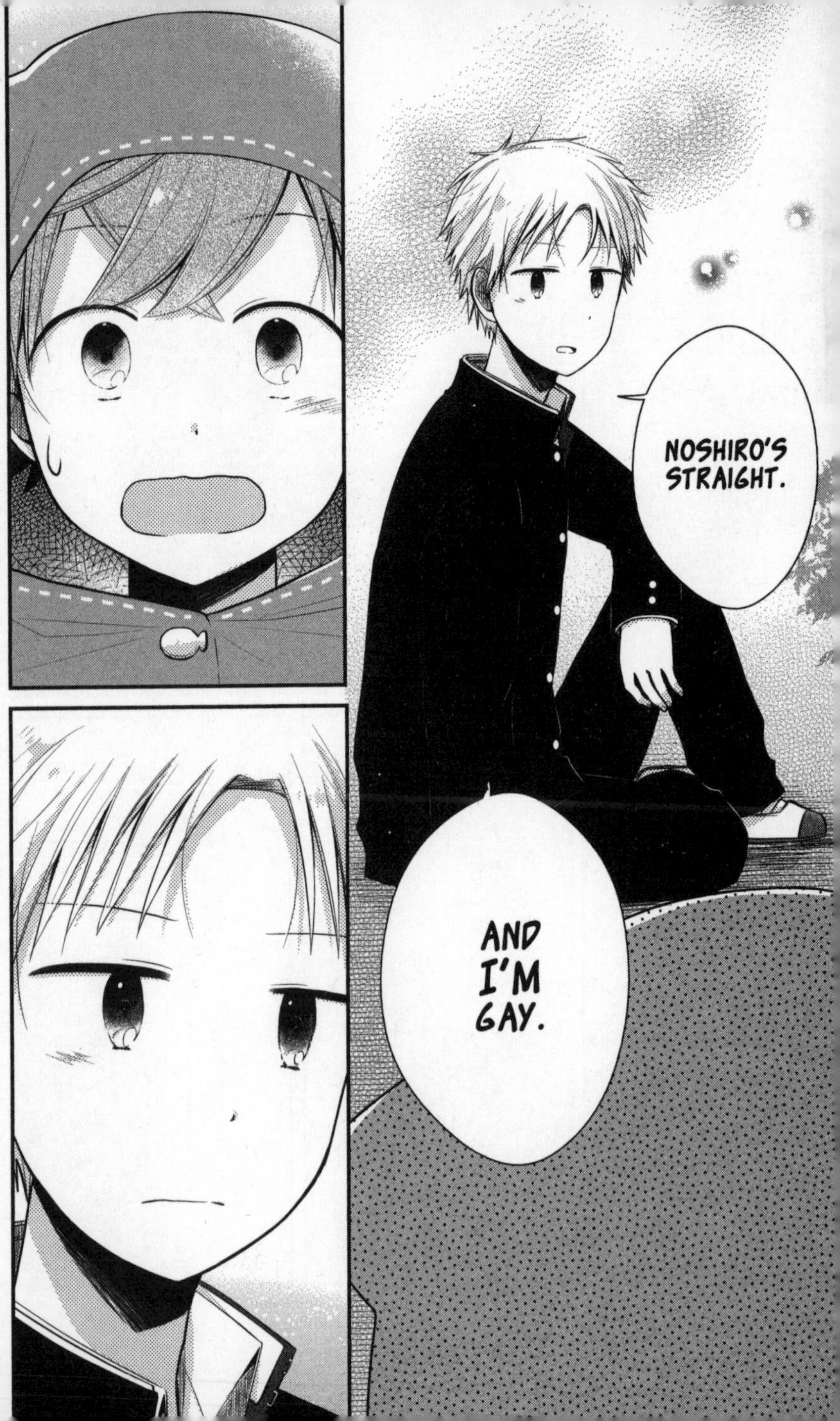
NOSHIRO'S STRAIGHT.
AND I'M GAY.

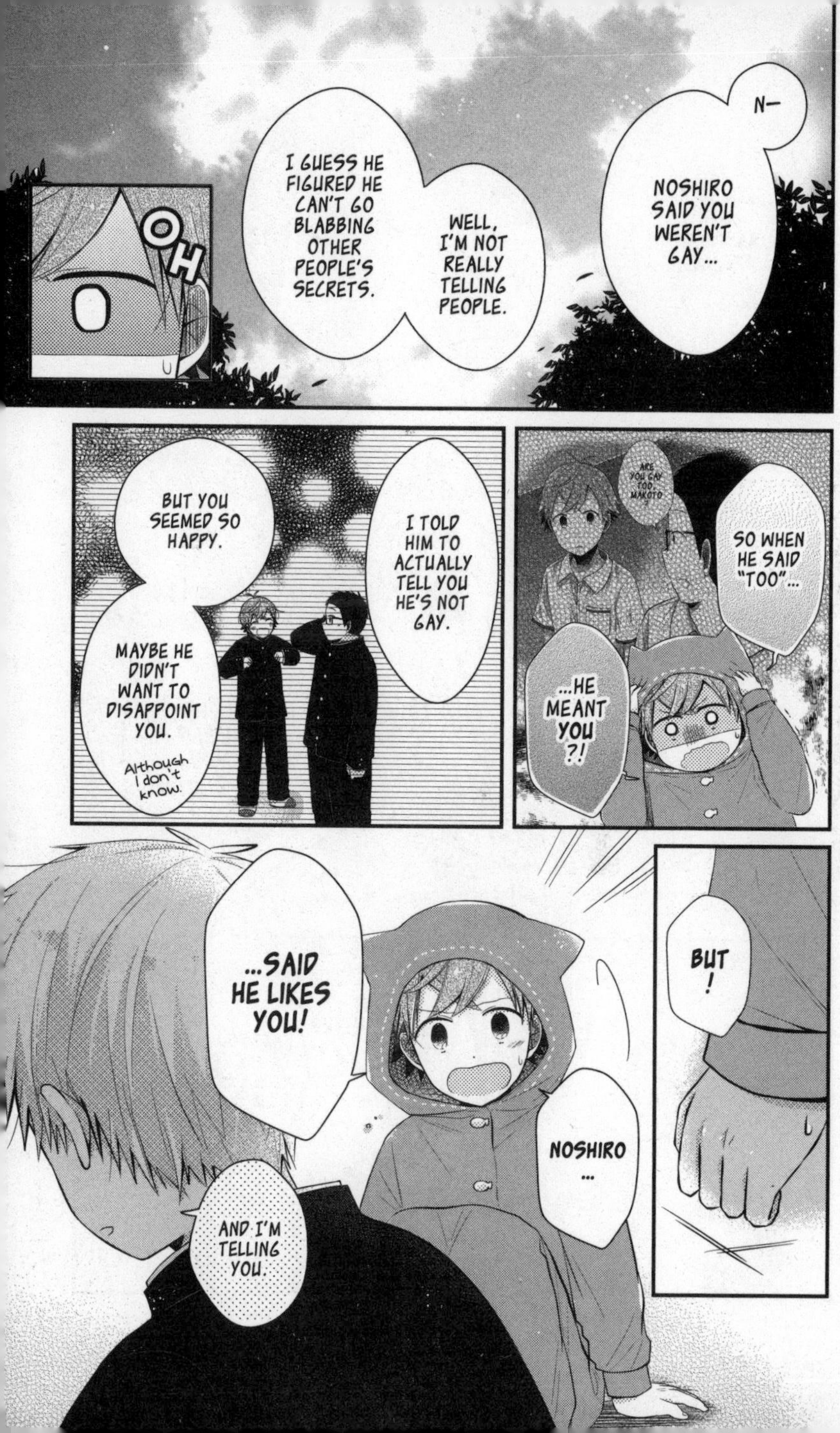
N—
NOSHIRO SAID YOU WEREN'T GAY...
WELL, I'M NOT REALLY TELLING PEOPLE.
I GUESS HE FIGURED HE CAN'T GO BLABBING OTHER PEOPLE'S SECRETS.
OH
ARE YOU GAY TOO, MAKOTO?
SO WHEN HE SAID "TOO"...
...HE MEANT YOU?!
I TOLD HIM TO ACTUALLY TELL YOU HE'S NOT GAY.
BUT YOU SEEMED SO HAPPY.
MAYBE HE DIDN'T WANT TO DISAPPOINT YOU.
Although I don't know.
BUT!
NOSHIRO...
...SAID HE LIKES YOU!
AND I'M TELLING YOU.

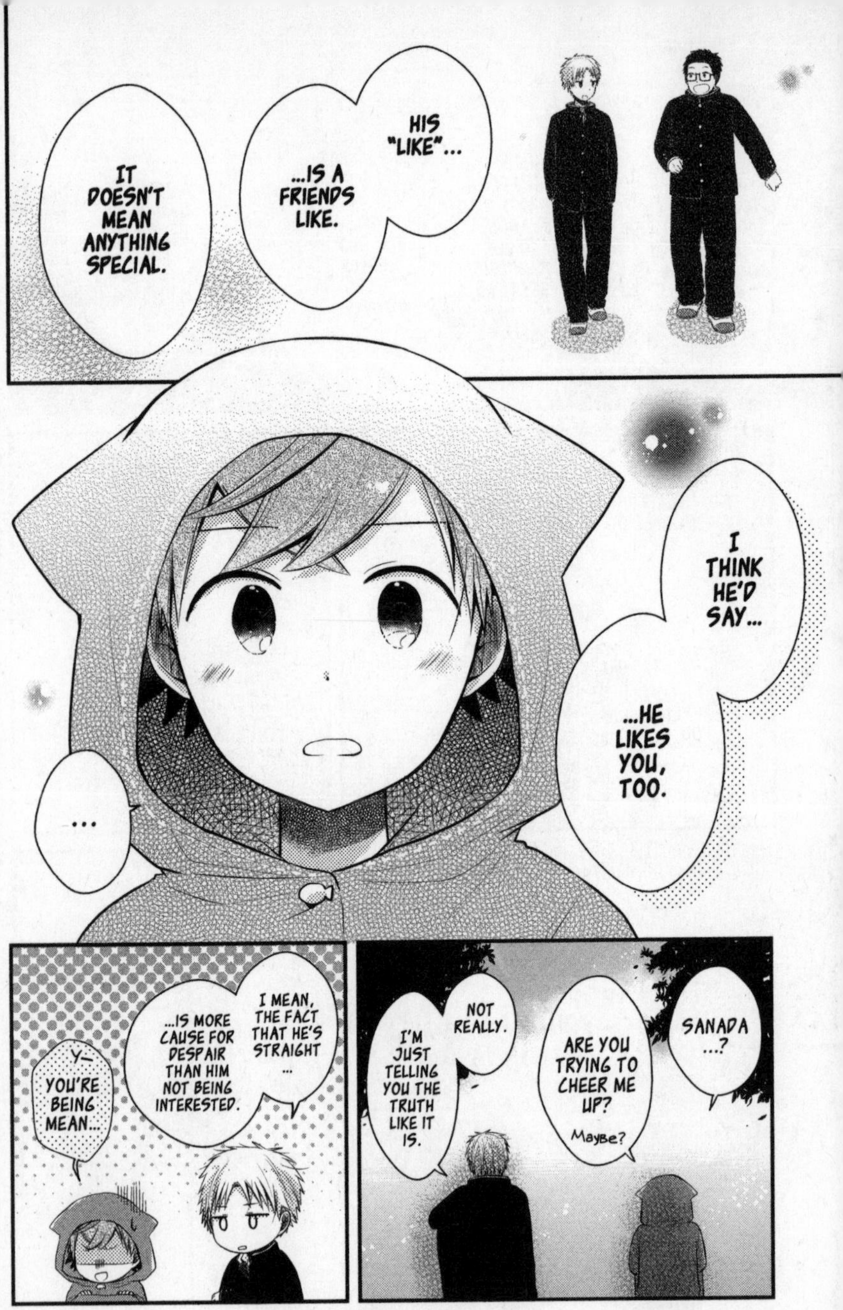
HIS "LIKE"...
...IS A FRIENDS LIKE.
IT DOESN'T MEAN ANYTHING SPECIAL.
I THINK HE'D SAY...
...HE LIKES YOU, TOO.
...
SANADA ...?
ARE YOU TRYING TO CHEER ME UP?
Maybe?
NOT REALLY.
I'M JUST TELLING YOU THE TRUTH LIKE IT IS.
I MEAN, THE FACT THAT HE'S STRAIGHT ...
...IS MORE CAUSE FOR DESPAIR THAN HIM NOT BEING INTERESTED.
Y— YOU'RE BEING MEAN...

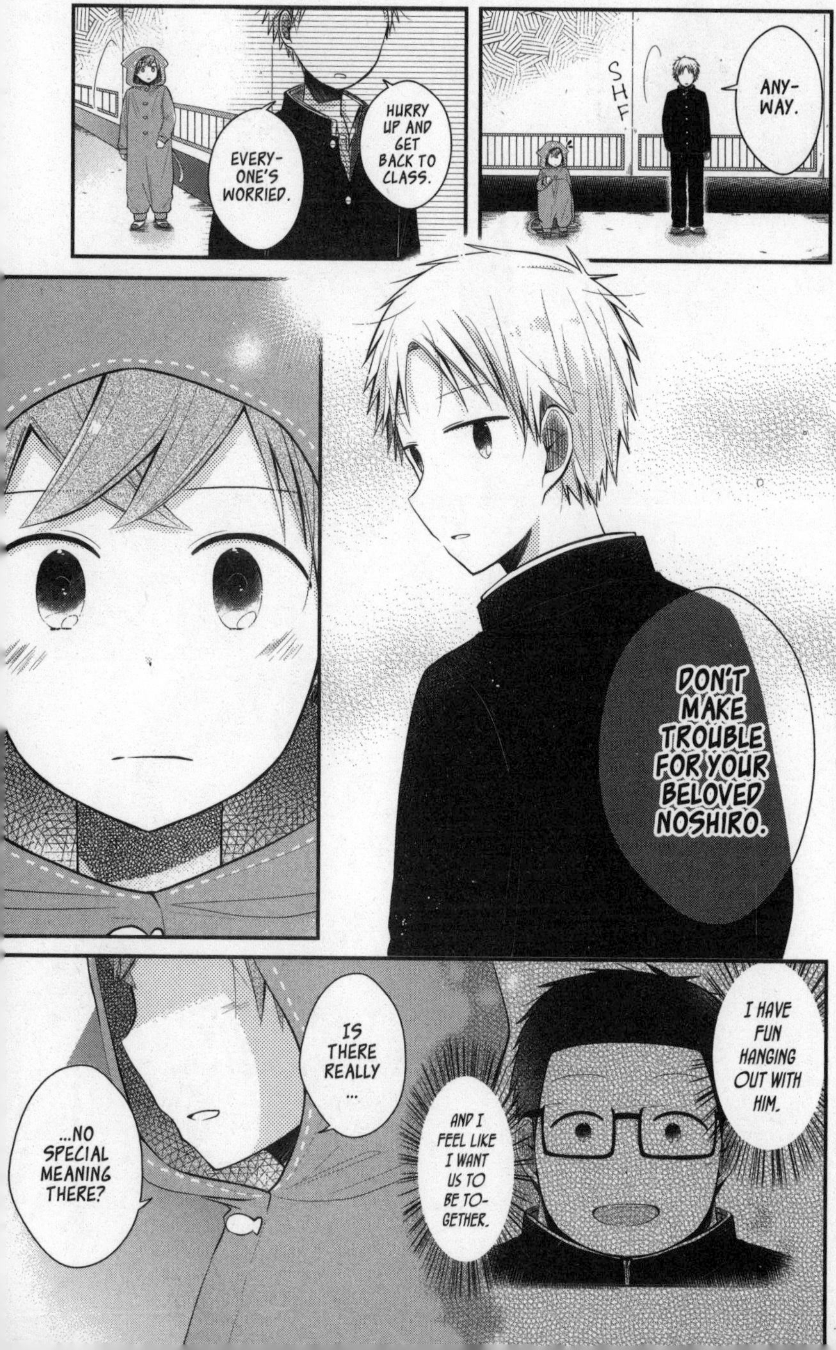
ANY-WAY.
SHF
HURRY UP AND GET BACK TO CLASS.
EVERY-ONE'S WORRIED.
DON'T MAKE TROUBLE FOR YOUR BELOVED NOSHIRO.
I HAVE FUN HANGING OUT WITH HIM.
AND I FEEL LIKE I WANT US TO BE TO-GETHER.
IS THERE REALLY...
...NO SPECIAL MEANING THERE?

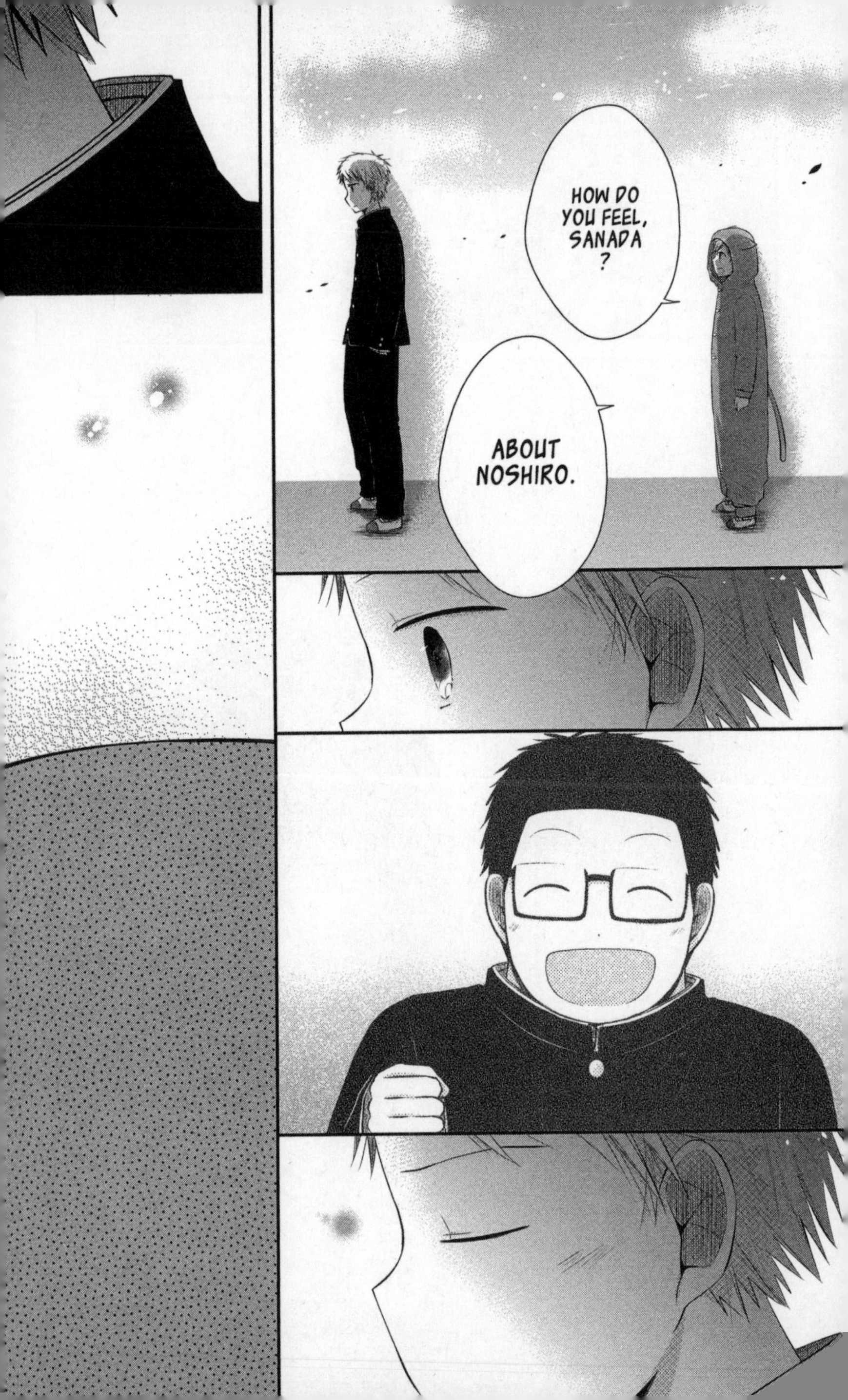
HOW DO YOU FEEL, SANADA ?
ABOUT NOSHIRO.

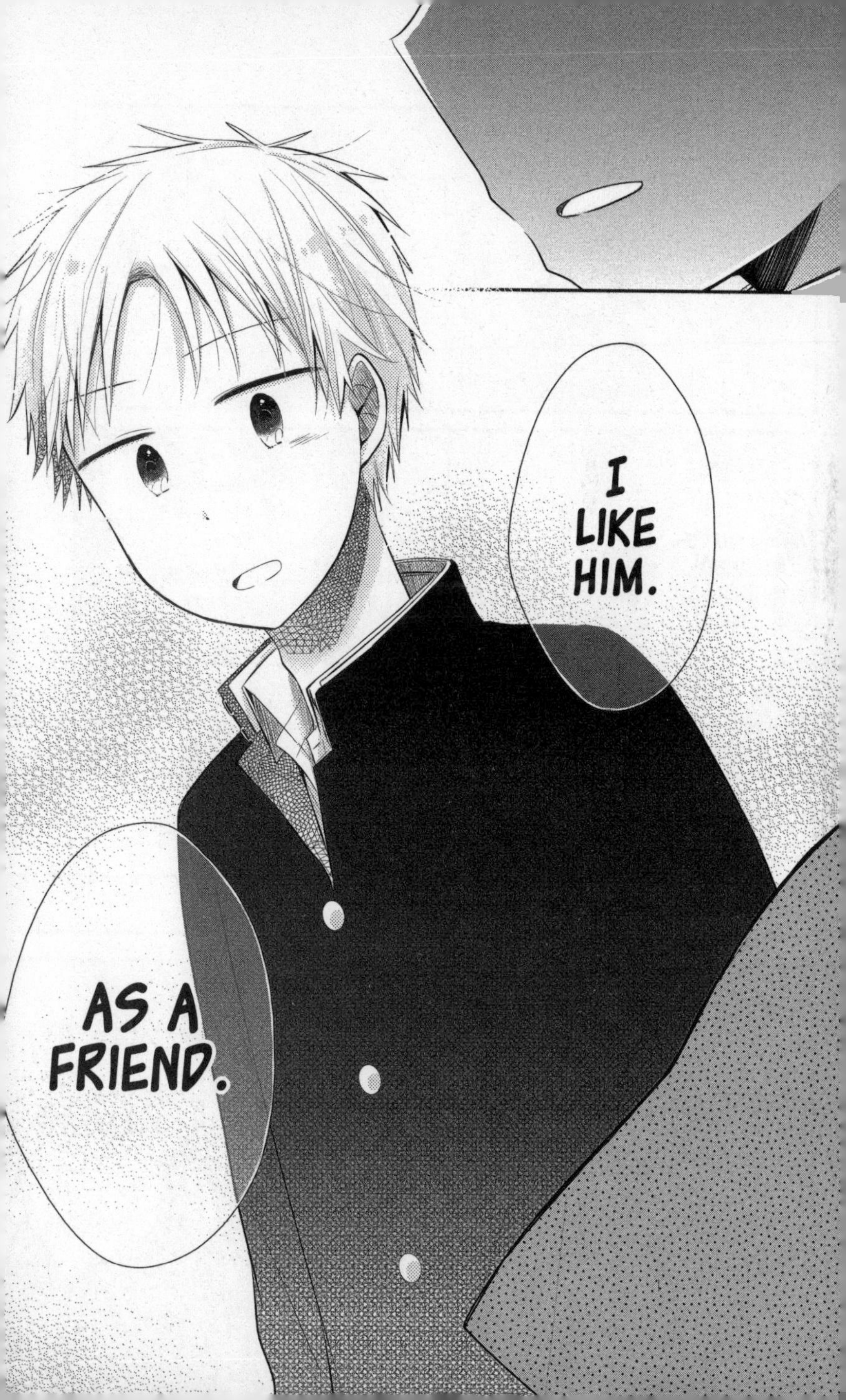
I LIKE HIM.
AS A FRIEND.

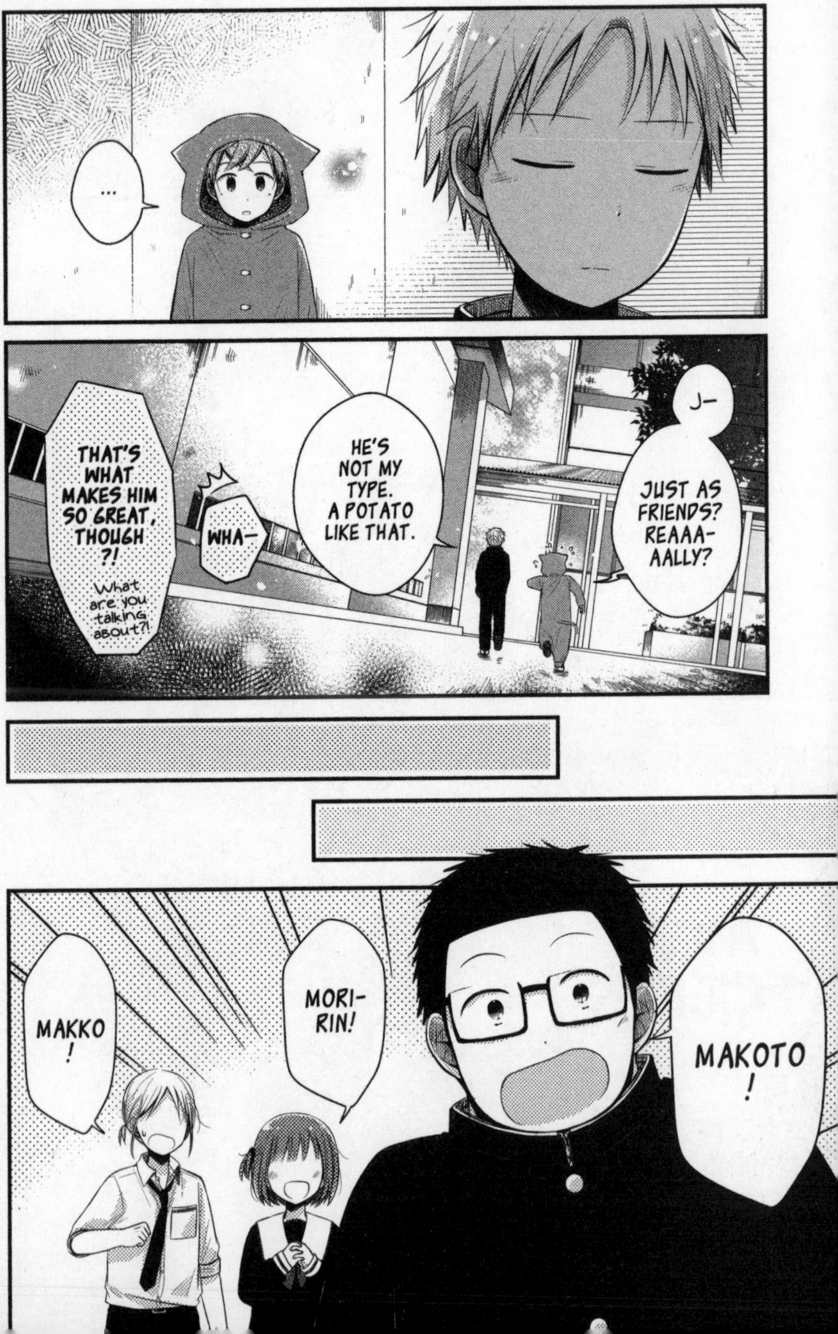
...
J—
JUST AS FRIENDS? REAAAA-AALLY?
HE'S NOT MY TYPE. A POTATO LIKE THAT.
WHA—
THAT'S WHAT MAKES HIM SO GREAT, THOUGH?!
What are you talking about?!
MAKOTO!
MORI-RIN!
MAKKO!

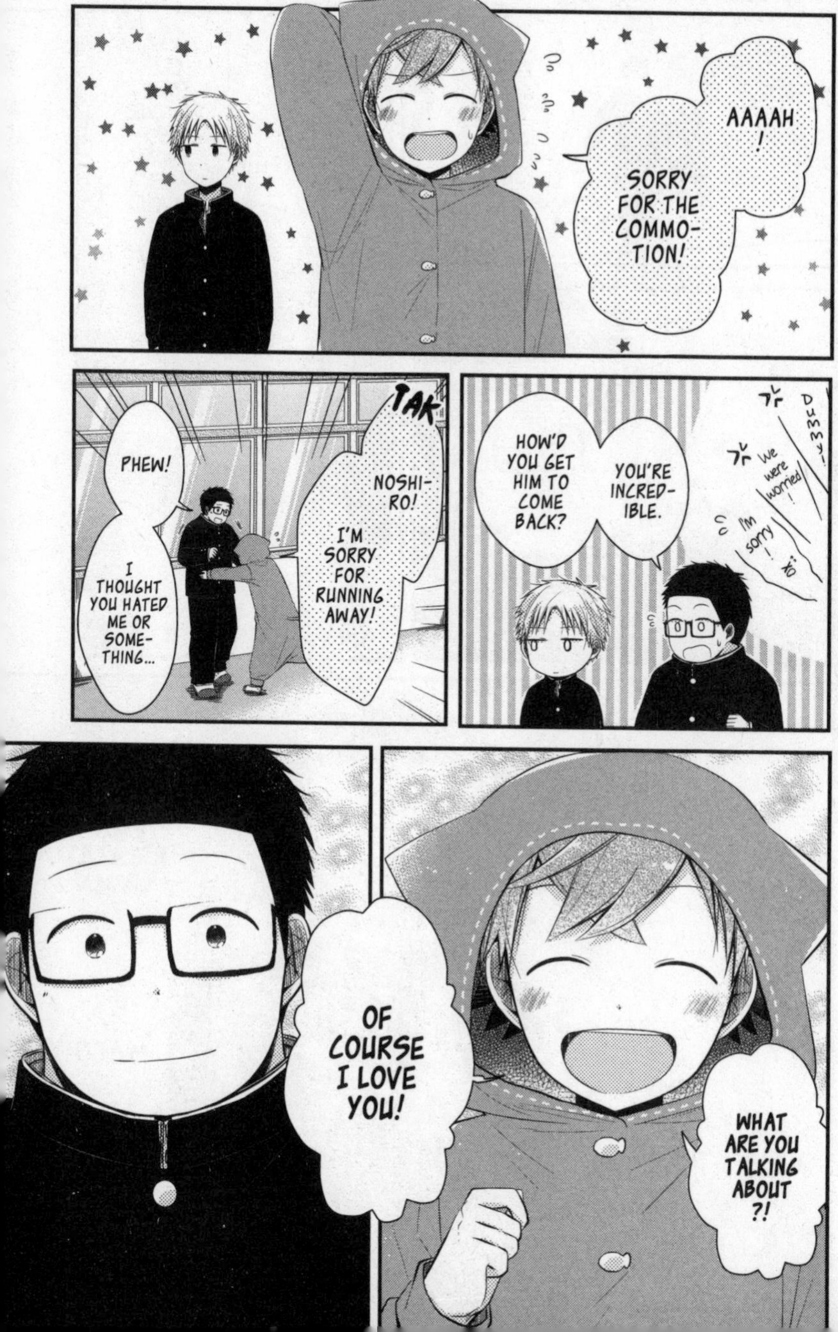
AAAAH!
SORRY FOR THE COMMOTION!
DUMMY!
We were worried!
I'm sorry!
XO
YOU'RE INCREDIBLE.
HOW'D YOU GET HIM TO COME BACK?
TAK
NOSHIRO!
I'M SORRY FOR RUNNING AWAY!
PHEW!
I THOUGHT YOU HATED ME OR SOMETHING...
OF COURSE I LOVE YOU!
WHAT ARE YOU TALKING ABOUT?!

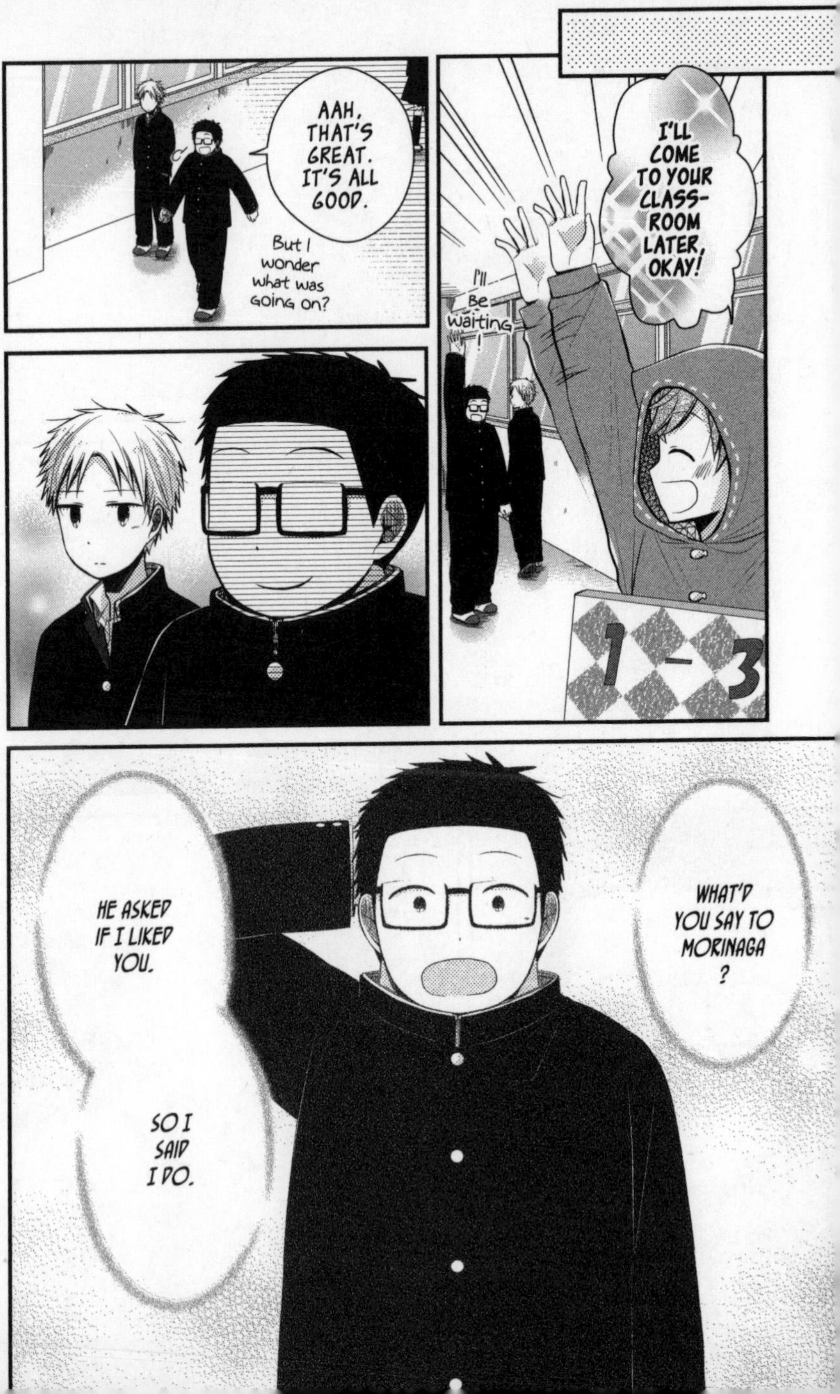
I'LL COME TO YOUR CLASS-ROOM LATER, OKAY!
I'll Be waiting!
AAH, THAT'S GREAT. IT'S ALL GOOD.
But I wonder what was going on?
WHAT'D YOU SAY TO MORINAGA?
HE ASKED IF I LIKED YOU.
SO I SAID I DO.

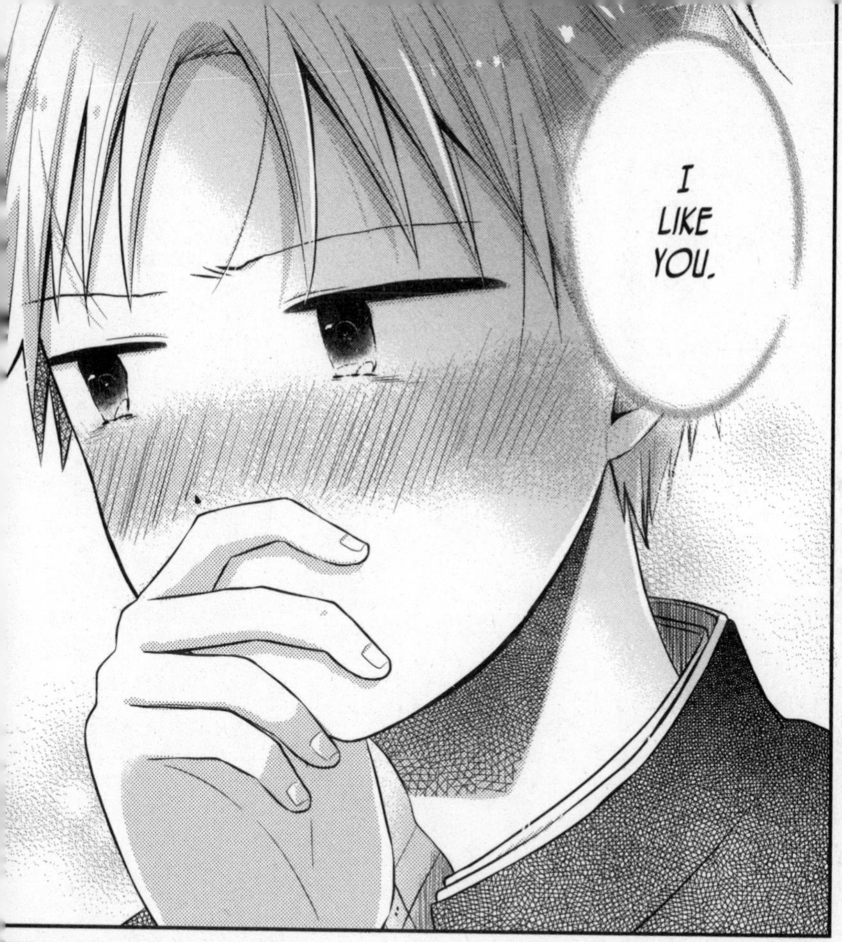
I LIKE YOU.

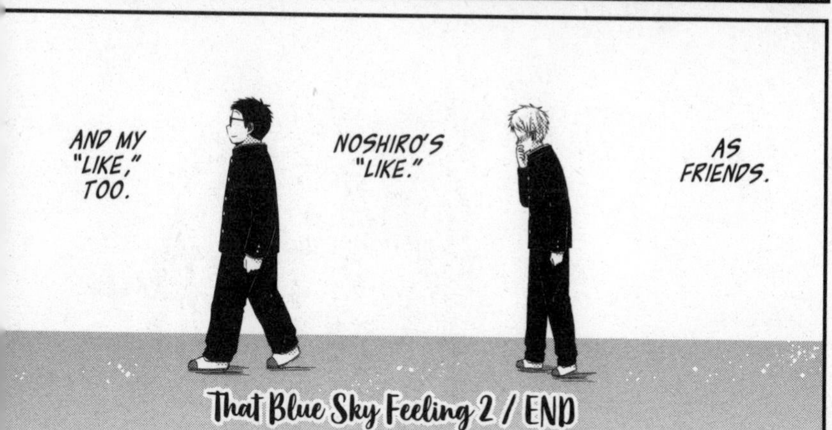
AS FRIENDS.
NOSHIRO'S "LIKE."
AND MY "LIKE," TOO.
That Blue Sky Feeling 2 / END

That Blue
Sky Feeling

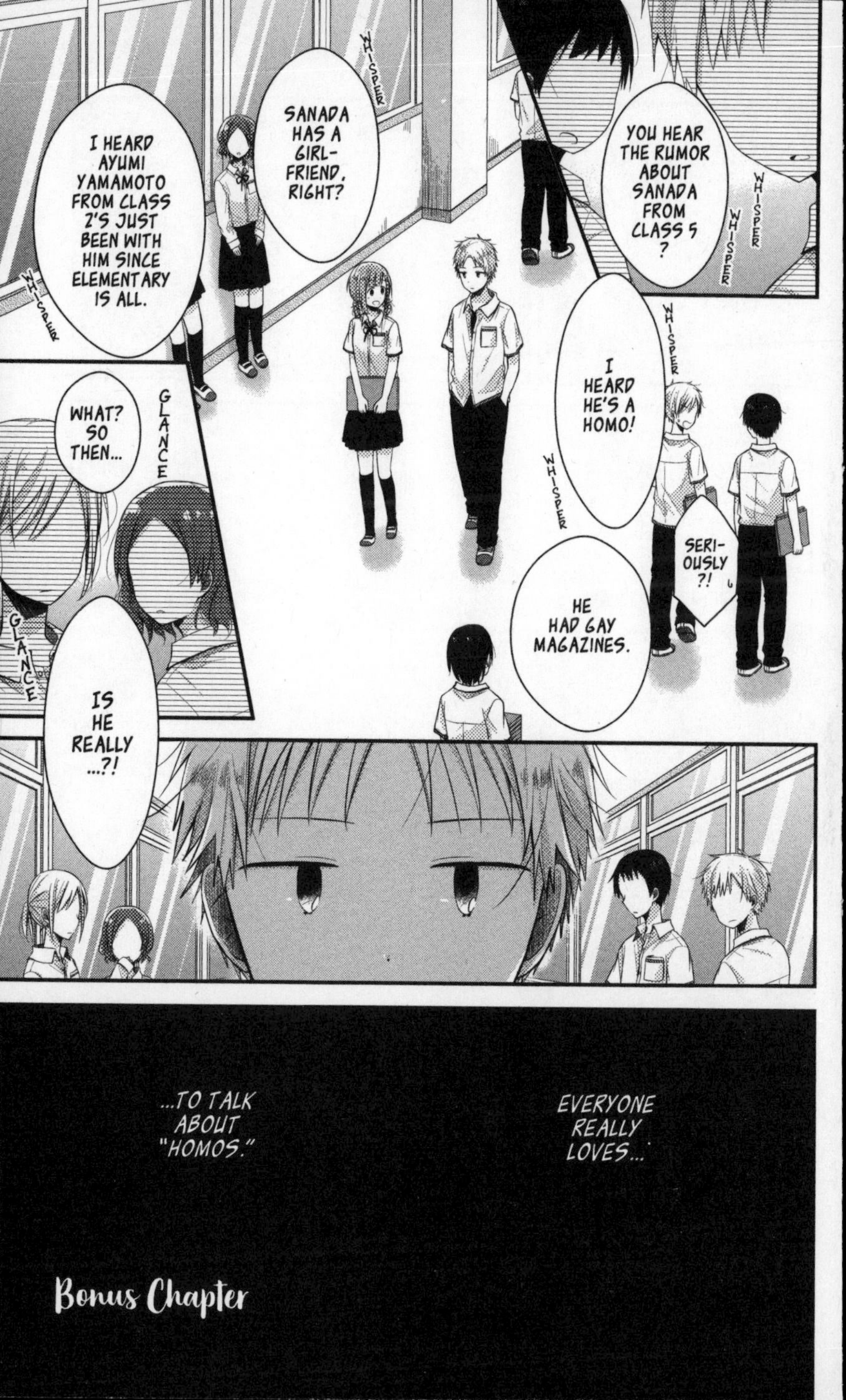
YOU HEAR THE RUMOR ABOUT SANADA FROM CLASS 5?
WHISPER WHISPER
I HEARD HE'S A HOMO!
WHISPER
WHISPER
SERI-OUSLY?!
HE HAD GAY MAGAZINES.
WHISPER
SANADA HAS A GIRL-FRIEND, RIGHT?
I HEARD AYUMI YAMAMOTO FROM CLASS 2'S JUST BEEN WITH HIM SINCE ELEMENTARY IS ALL.
WHISPER
GLANCE
WHAT? SO THEN...
GLANCE
IS HE REALLY...?!
EVERYONE REALLY LOVES...
...TO TALK ABOUT "HOMOS."
Bonus Chapter

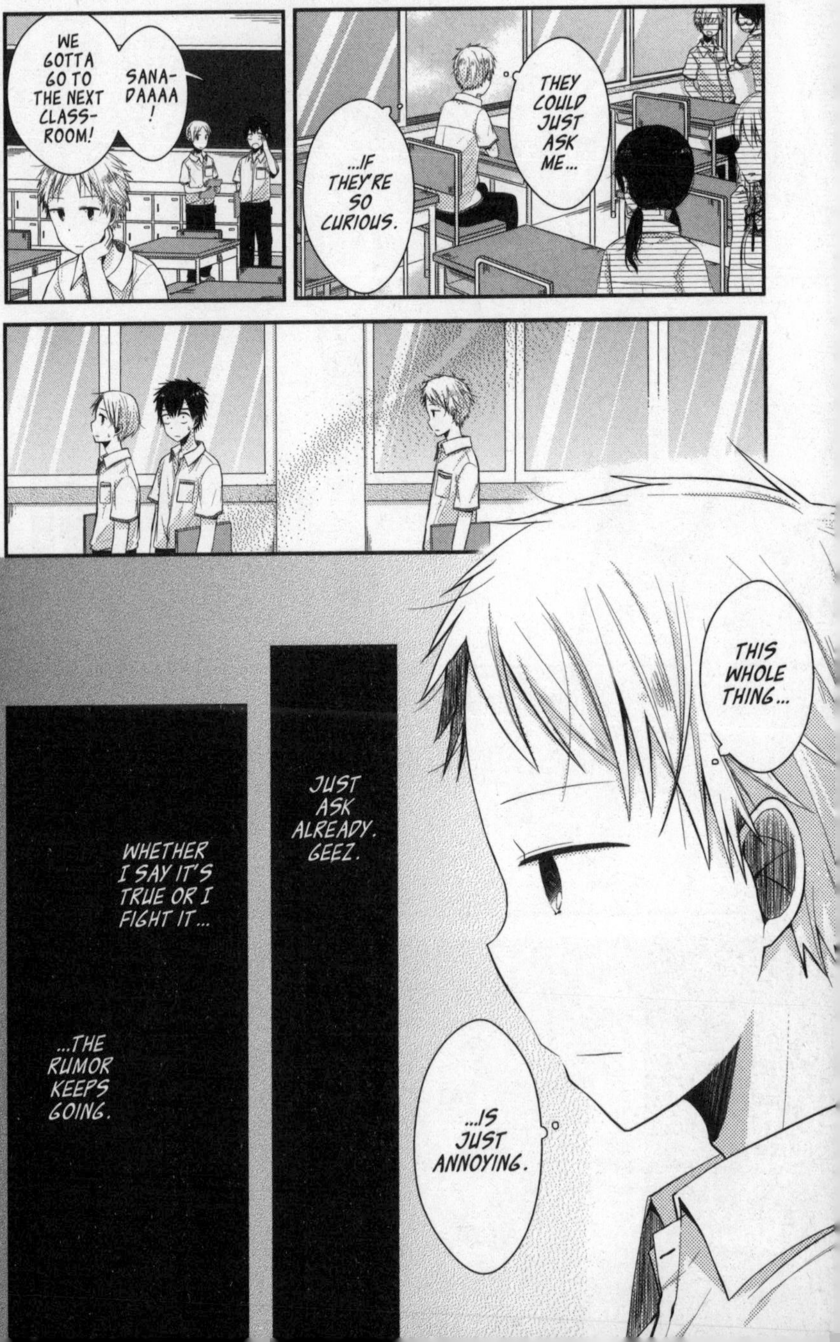
THEY COULD JUST ASK ME...
...IF THEY'RE SO CURIOUS.
SANA-DAAAA!
WE GOTTA GO TO THE NEXT CLASSROOM!
THIS WHOLE THING...
...IS JUST ANNOYING.
JUST ASK ALREADY. GEEZ.
WHETHER I SAY IT'S TRUE OR I FIGHT IT...
...THE RUMOR KEEPS GOING.

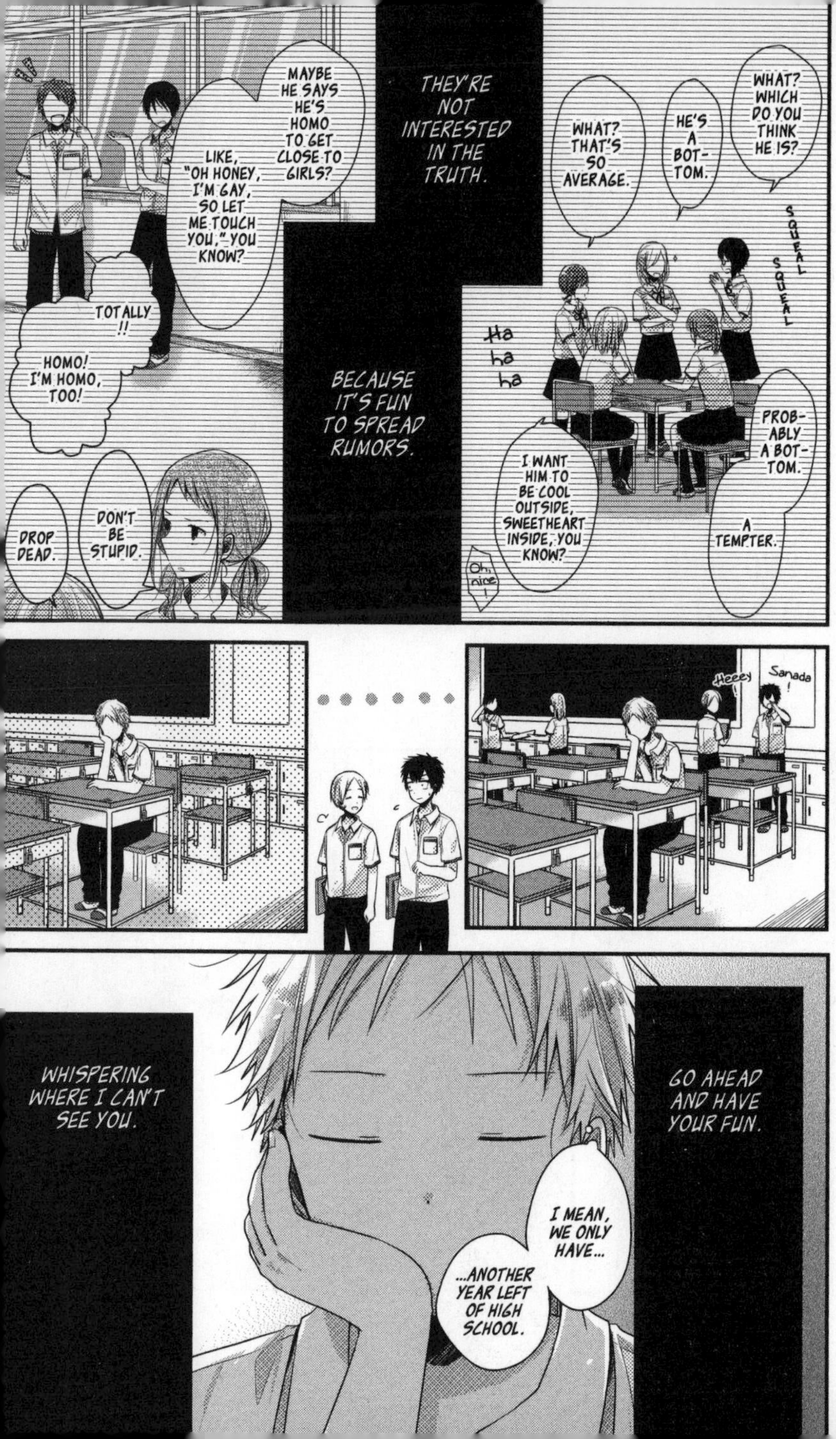
WHAT? WHICH DO YOU THINK HE IS?
HE'S A BOT-TOM.
WHAT? THAT'S SO AVERAGE.
SQUEAL SQUEAL
Ha ha ha
PROB-ABLY A BOT-TOM.
A TEMPTER.
I WANT HIM TO BE COOL OUTSIDE, SWEETHEART INSIDE, YOU KNOW?
Oh, nice!
THEY'RE NOT INTERESTED IN THE TRUTH.
BECAUSE IT'S FUN TO SPREAD RUMORS.
MAYBE HE SAYS HE'S HOMO TO GET CLOSE TO GIRLS?
LIKE, "OH HONEY, I'M GAY, SO LET ME TOUCH YOU," YOU KNOW?
TOTALLY!!
HOMO! I'M HOMO, TOO!
DON'T BE STUPID.
DROP DEAD.
Sanada!
Heeey!
......
GO AHEAD AND HAVE YOUR FUN.
I MEAN, WE ONLY HAVE...
...ANOTHER YEAR LEFT OF HIGH SCHOOL.
WHISPERING WHERE I CAN'T SEE YOU.

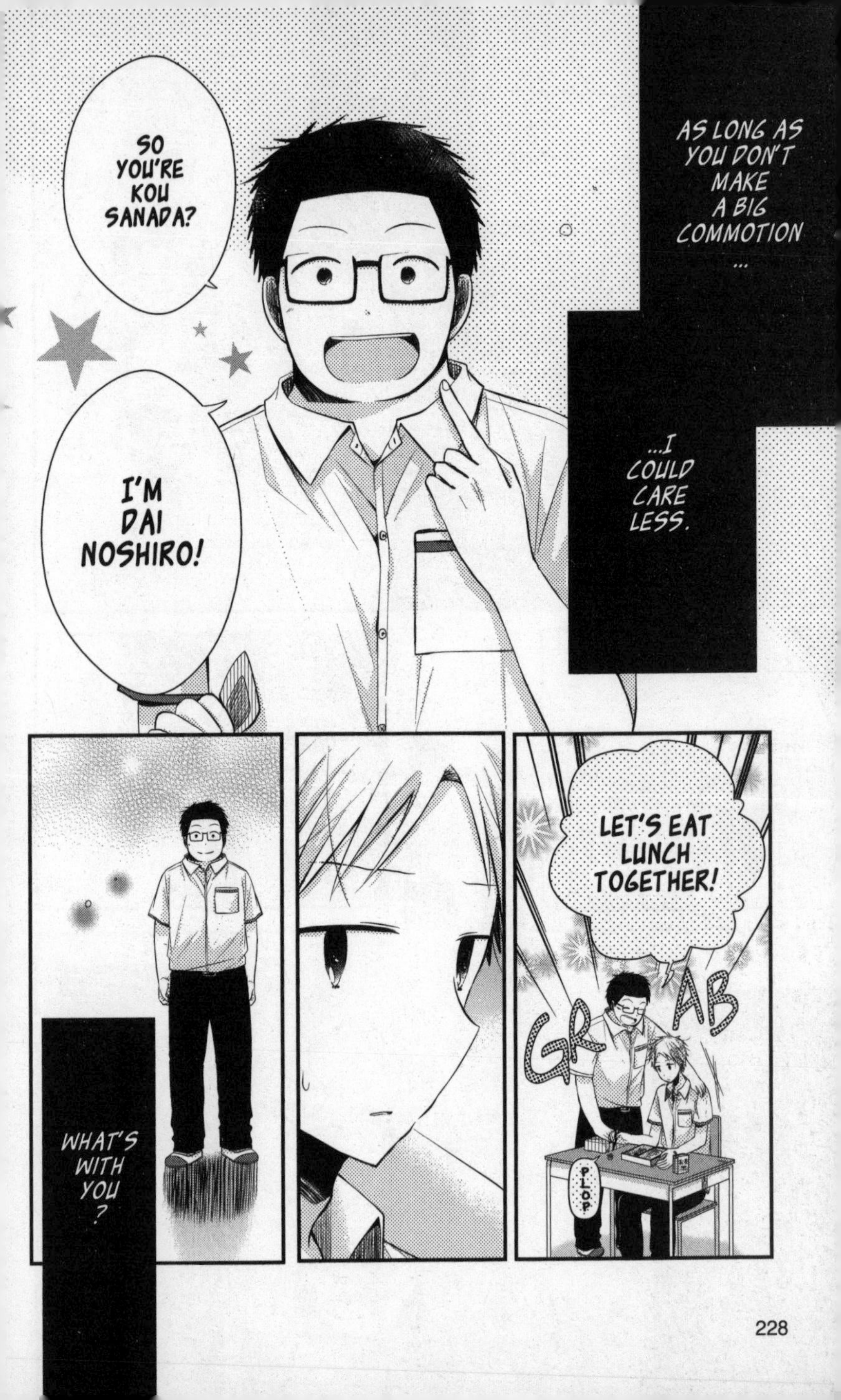
AS LONG AS YOU DON'T MAKE A BIG COMMOTION...
SO YOU'RE KOU SANADA?
...I COULD CARE LESS.
I'M DAI NOSHIRO!
LET'S EAT LUNCH TOGETHER!
GRAB
PLOP
WHAT'S WITH YOU?

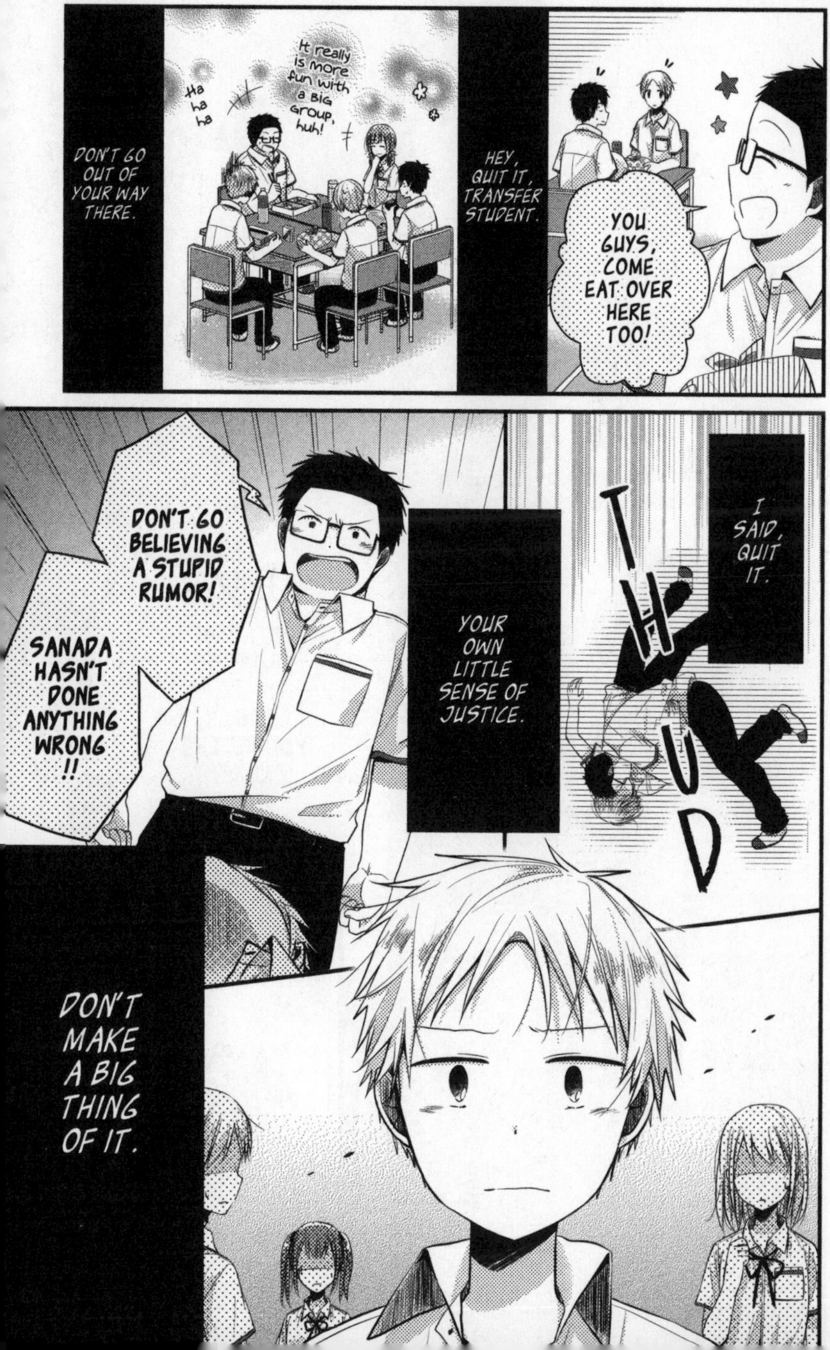
YOU GUYS, COME EAT OVER HERE TOO!
HEY, QUIT IT, TRANSFER STUDENT.
It really is more fun with a big group, huh!
Ha ha ha
DON'T GO OUT OF YOUR WAY THERE.
I SAID, QUIT IT.
THUD
YOUR OWN LITTLE SENSE OF JUSTICE.
DON'T GO BELIEVING A STUPID RUMOR!
SANADA HASN'T DONE ANYTHING WRONG!!
DON'T MAKE A BIG THING OF IT.

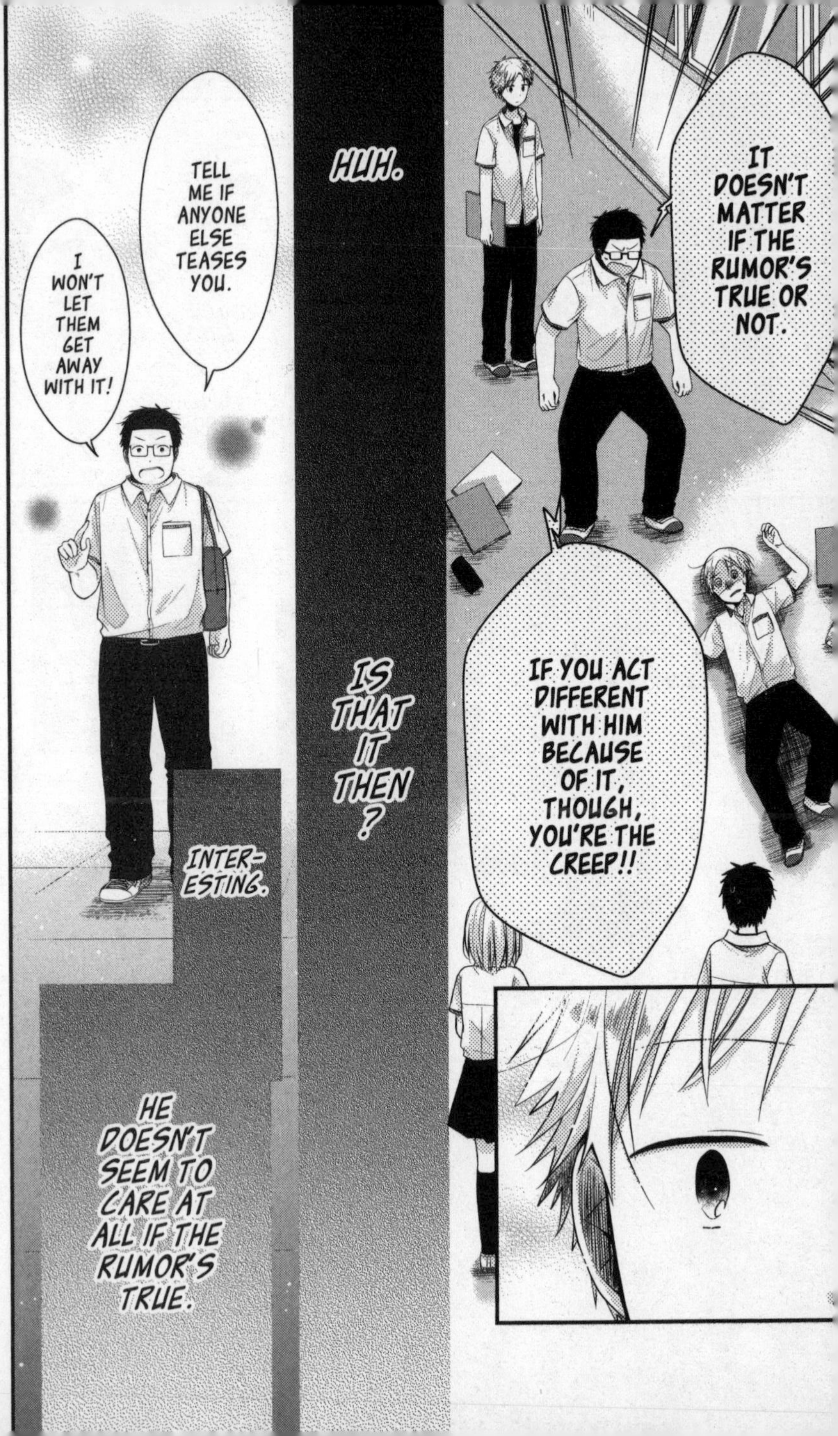
IT DOESN'T MATTER IF THE RUMOR'S TRUE OR NOT.
IF YOU ACT DIFFERENT WITH HIM BECAUSE OF IT, THOUGH, YOU'RE THE CREEP!!
HUH.
IS THAT IT THEN?
TELL ME IF ANYONE ELSE TEASES YOU.
I WON'T LET THEM GET AWAY WITH IT!
INTER-ESTING.
HE DOESN'T SEEM TO CARE AT ALL IF THE RUMOR'S TRUE.

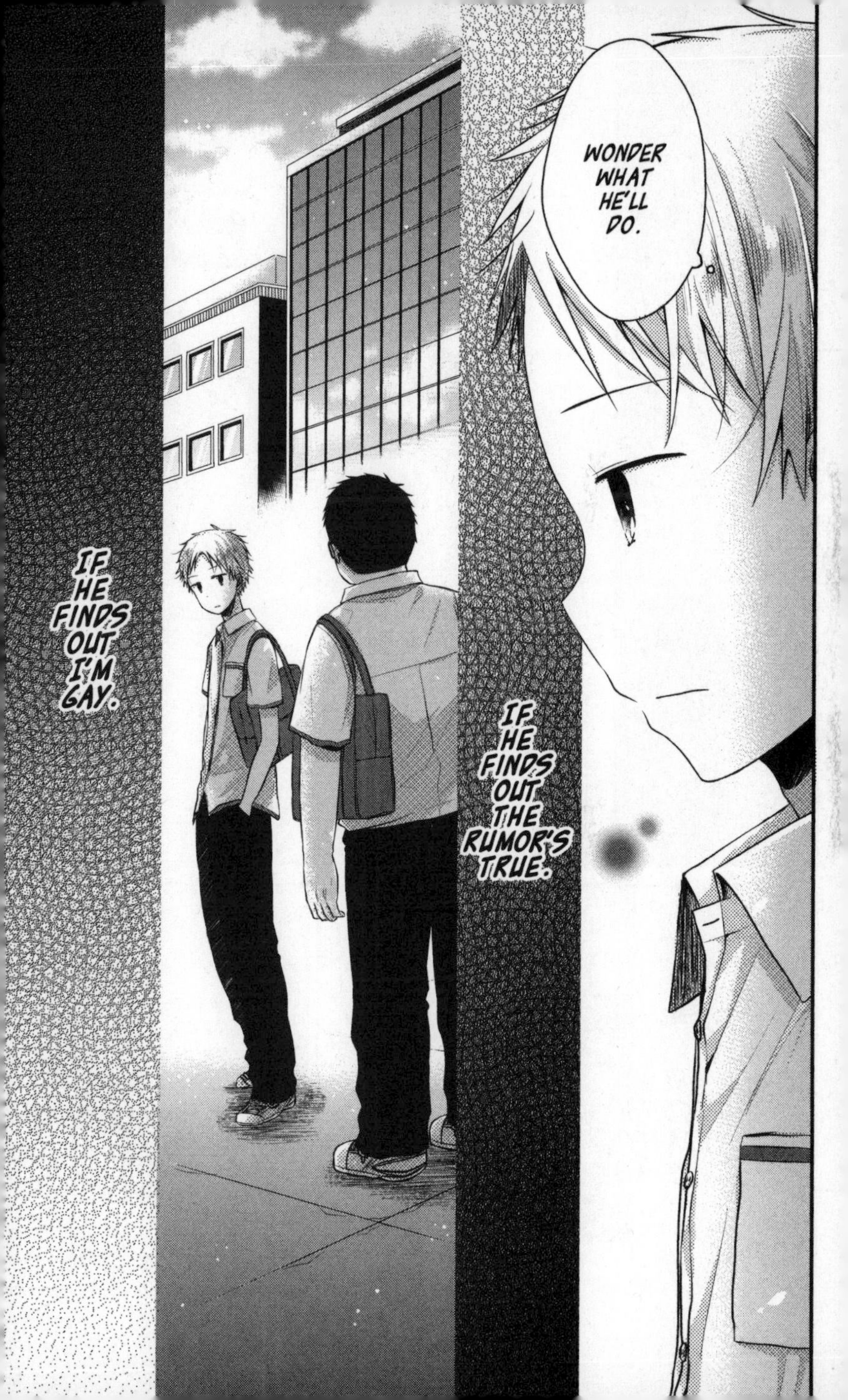
WONDER WHAT HE'LL DO.
IF HE FINDS OUT THE RUMOR'S TRUE.
IF HE FINDS OUT I'M GAY.

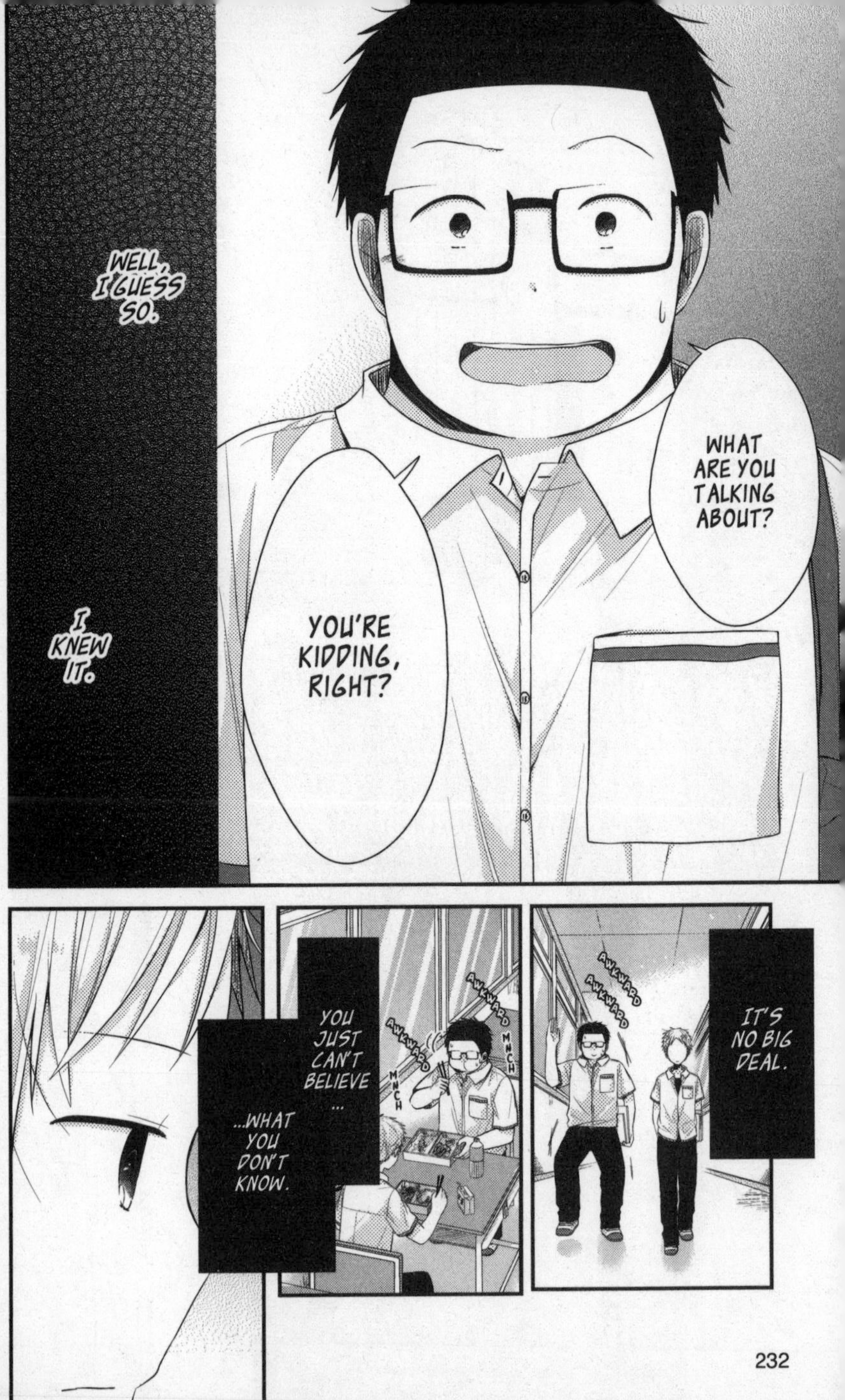
WHAT ARE YOU TALKING ABOUT?
YOU'RE KIDDING, RIGHT?
WELL, I GUESS SO.
I KNEW IT.
IT'S NO BIG DEAL.
AWKWARD
AWKWARD
YOU JUST CAN'T BELIEVE...
AWKWARD
MNCH
MNCH
...WHAT YOU DON'T KNOW.

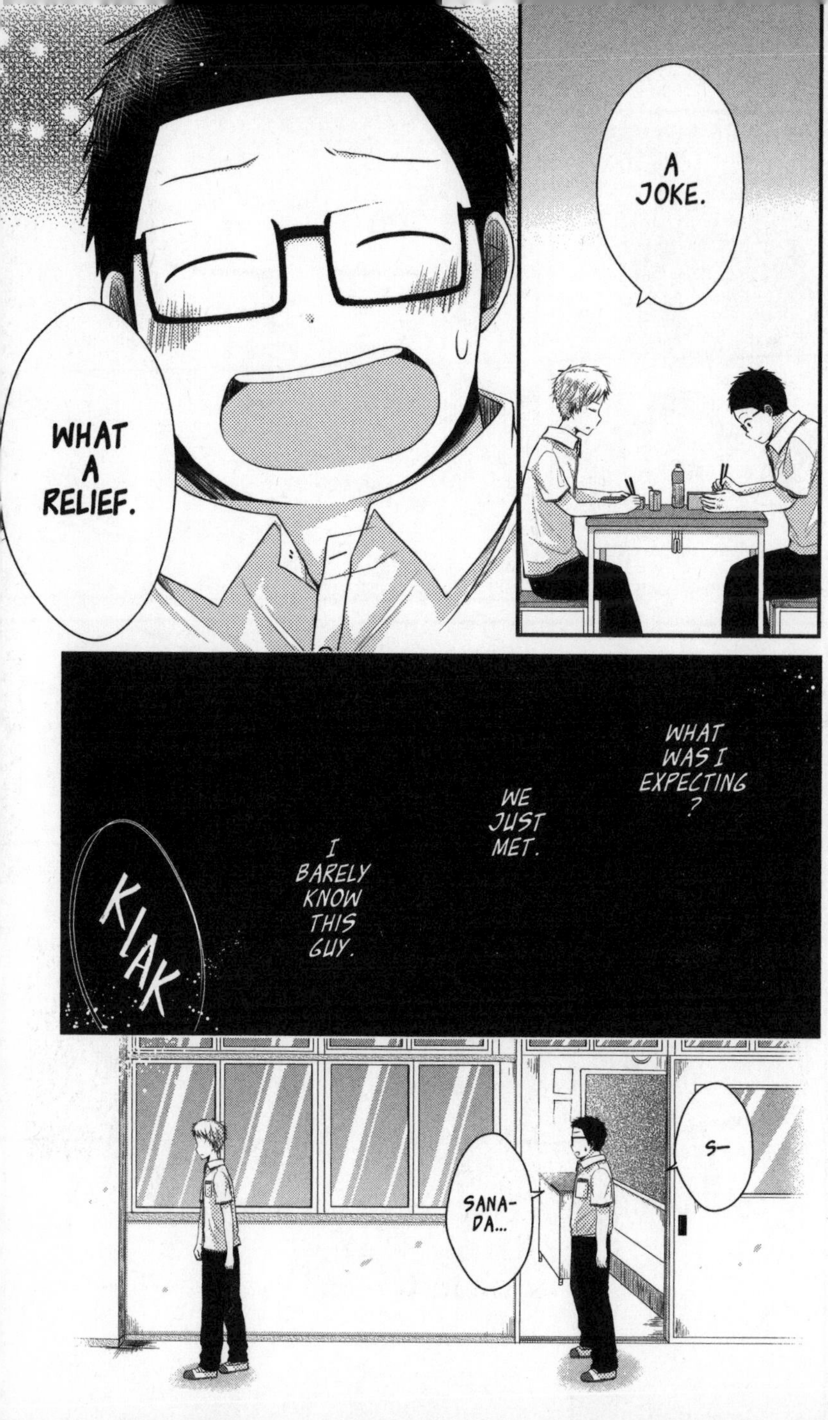
A JOKE.
WHAT A RELIEF.
WHAT WAS I EXPECTING?
WE JUST MET.
I BARELY KNOW THIS GUY.
KLAK
S—
SANA-DA...

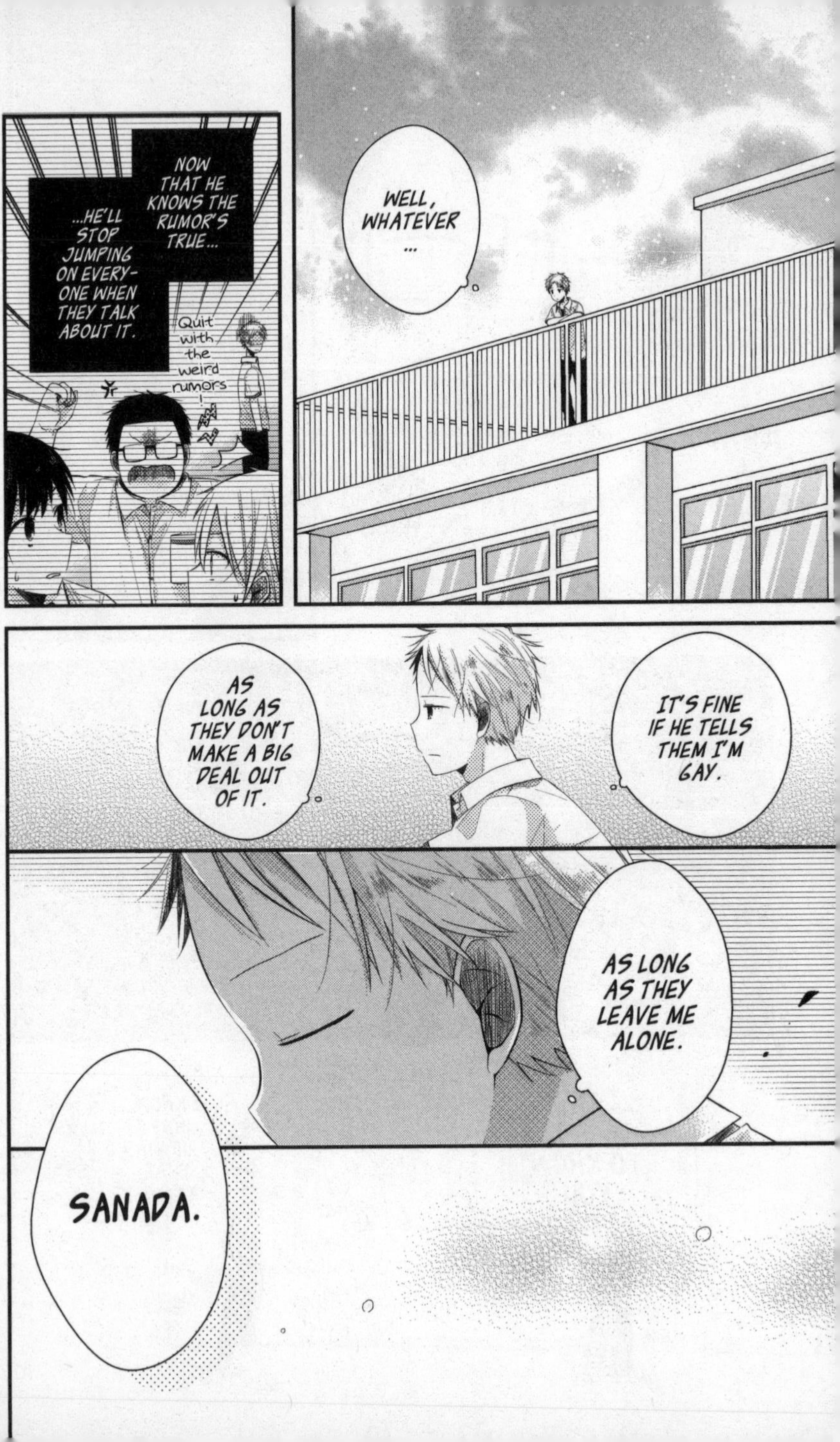
WELL, WHATEVER ...
NOW THAT HE KNOWS THE RUMOR'S TRUE...
...HE'LL STOP JUMPING ON EVERYONE WHEN THEY TALK ABOUT IT.
Quit with the weird rumors!
IT'S FINE IF HE TELLS THEM I'M GAY.
AS LONG AS THEY DON'T MAKE A BIG DEAL OUT OF IT.
AS LONG AS THEY LEAVE ME ALONE.
SANADA.

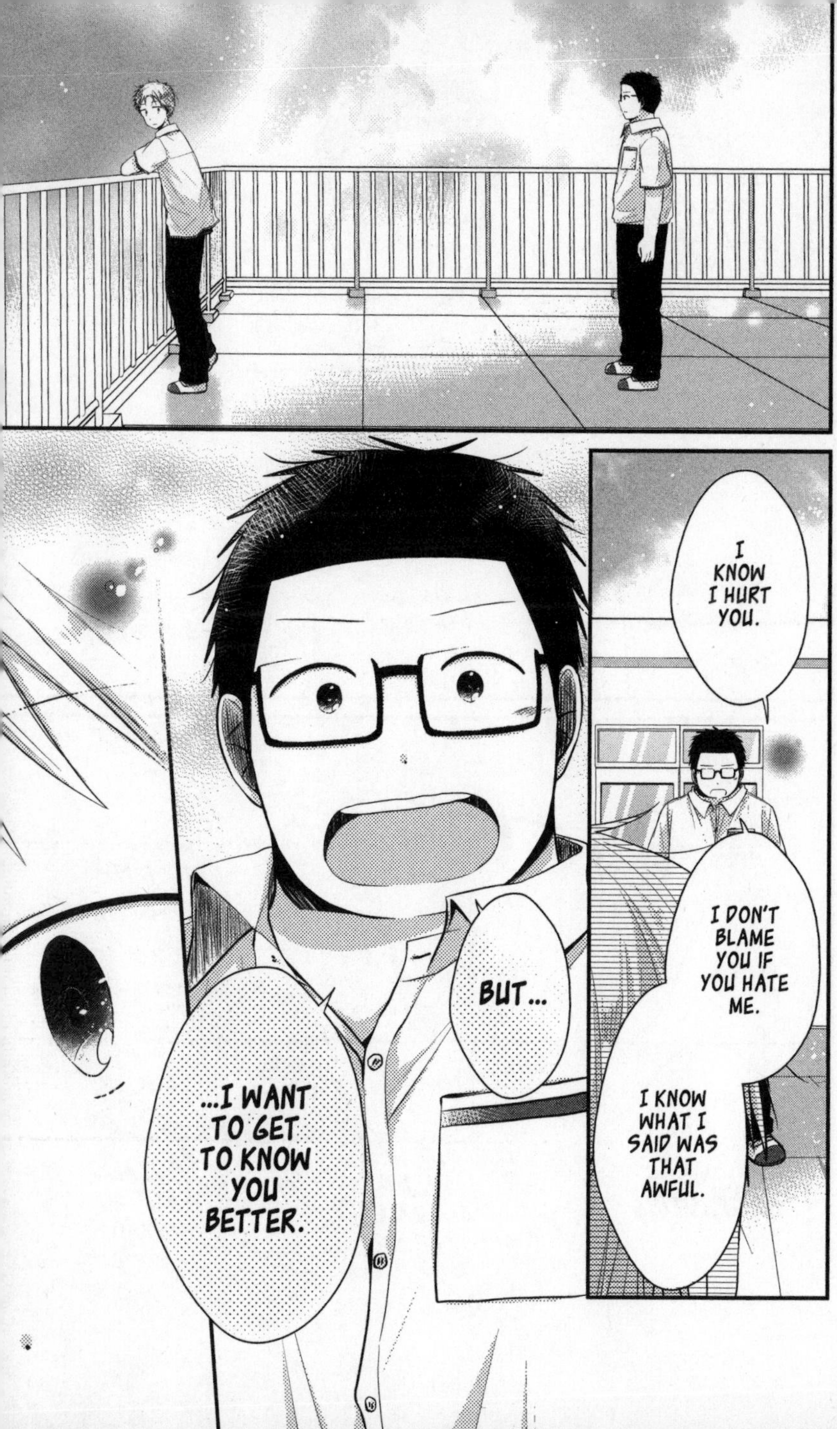
I KNOW I HURT YOU.
I DON'T BLAME YOU IF YOU HATE ME.
I KNOW WHAT I SAID WAS THAT AWFUL.
BUT...
...I WANT TO GET TO KNOW YOU BETTER.

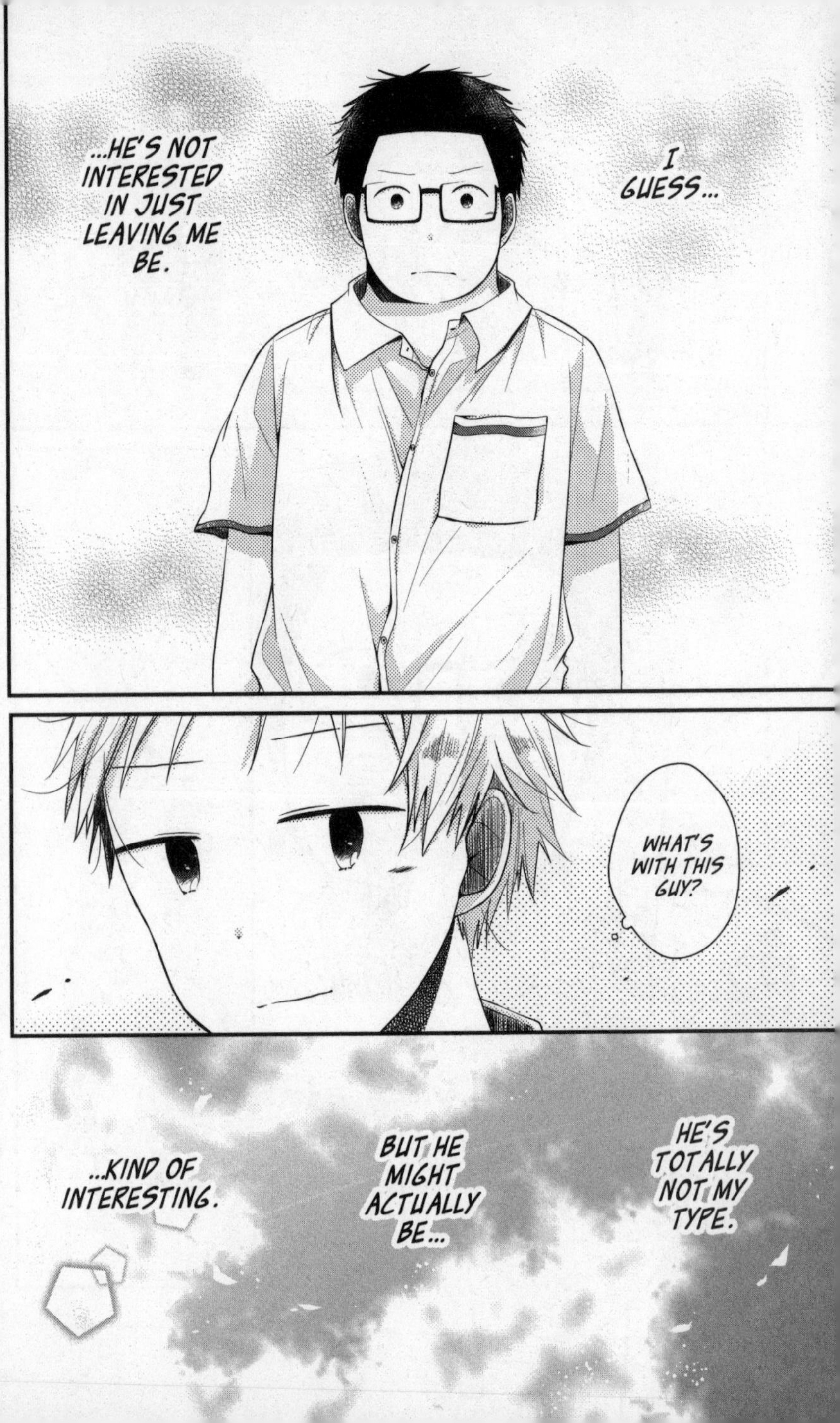
I GUESS...
...HE'S NOT INTERESTED IN JUST LEAVING ME BE.
WHAT'S WITH THIS GUY?
HE'S TOTALLY NOT MY TYPE.
BUT HE MIGHT ACTUALLY BE...
...KIND OF INTERESTING.

CHANGES IN THE REMAKE VERSION NO. 2

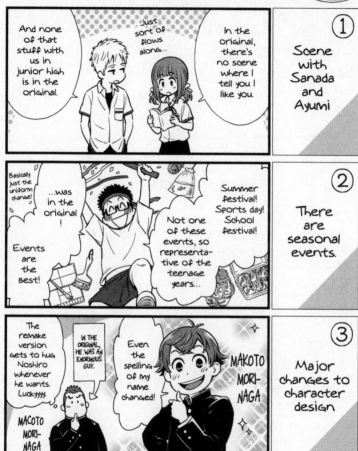

1
Scene with Sanada and Ayumi

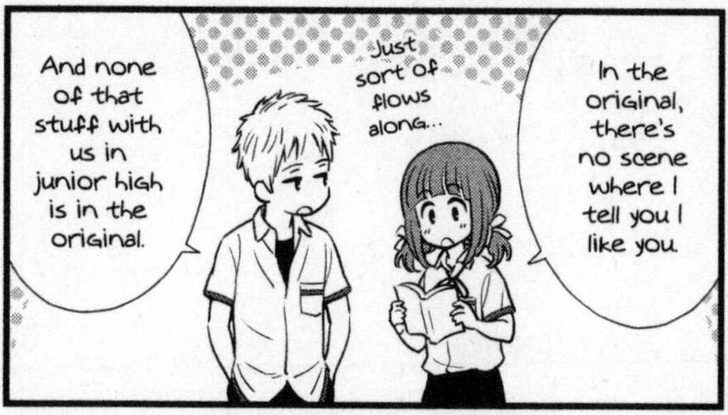
In the original, there's no scene where I tell you I like you.
Just sort of flows along...
And none of that stuff with us in junior high is in the original.

2
There are seasonal events.

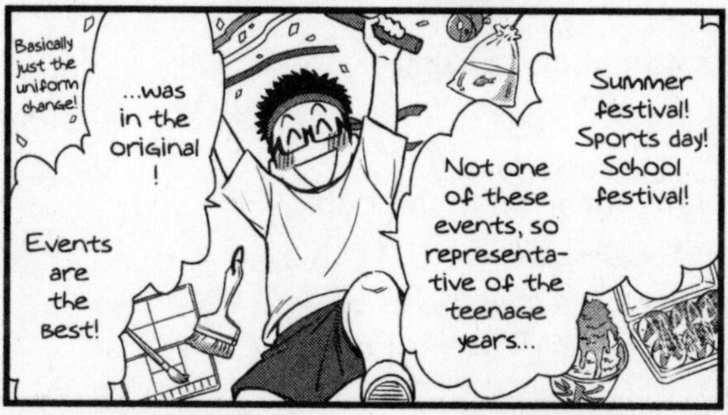
Summer festival! Sports day! School festival!
Not one of these events, so representative of the teenage years...
...was in the original !
Basically just the uniform change!
Events are the best!

3
Major changes to character design

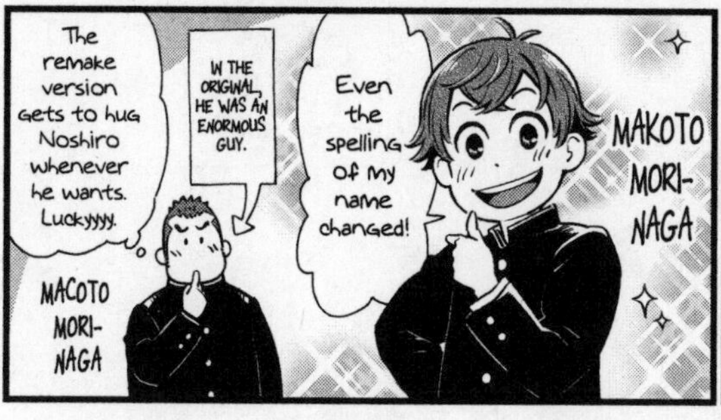
MAKOTO MORI-NAGA
Even the spelling of my name changed!
IN THE ORIGINAL, HE WAS AN ENORMOUS GUY.
The remake version gets to hug Noshiro whenever he wants. Luckyyyy.
MACOTO MORI-NAGA

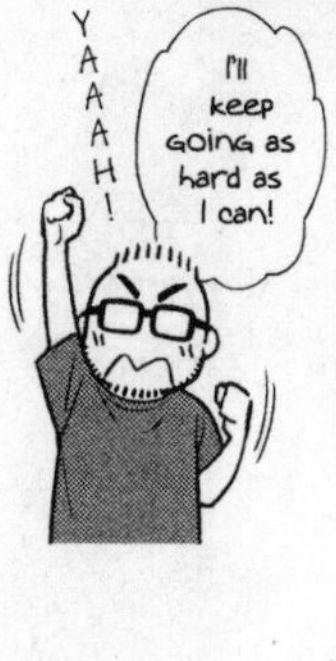
YAAAH!
I'll keep going as hard as I can!

Volume 2!

The differences between the new *Blue Sky* and the original keep piling up.
I get to see new sides to Noshiro and the other characters, and I personally am surprised andjealous and happy.
I hope you'll watch over and cheer them on whatever road they end up going down in the future, too!

~Okura

Special Thanks

Story: Okura

Editor

Assistants

Hina
Takiue
Kamaboko Sazaki

Friends, family,
everyone involved in the book

All the readers
supporting us

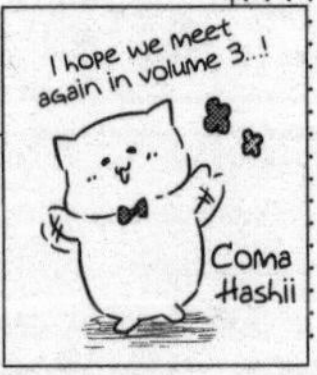
I hope we meet again in volume 3...!
Coma Hashii

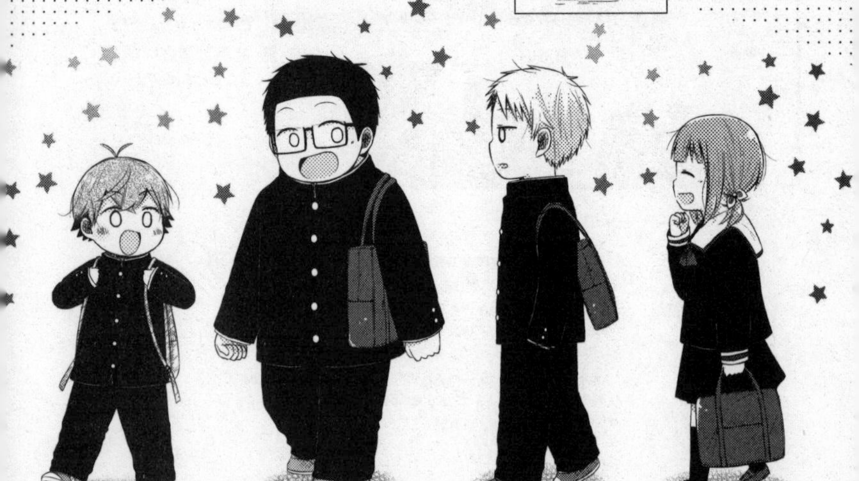

About the Authors

That Blue Sky Feeling is Okura and Coma Hashii's first manga series and is based on writer Okura's original webcomic.

Okura

Realize things you never noticed before. Think about things you never thought of before. Let one thought after another wander through your mind. I hope that this work can help readers to do just that.

Coma Hashii

It's been a little over a year since we started the series! The time has passed in the blink of an eye. I have basically no memories of doing the work. But I do hope you enjoy this second volume!

That Blue Sky Feeling
Vol. 2
VIZ Media Edition

STORY BY
Okura
ART BY
Coma Hashii

Translation/Jocelyne Allen
Lettering/Joanna Estep
Design/Yukiko Whitley
Editor/Joel Enos

SORAIRO FLUTTER vol. 2
© 2018 Okura, Coma Hashii/SQUARE ENIX CO., LTD.
First published in Japan in 2018 by SQUARE ENIX CO., LTD.
English translation rights arranged with SQUARE ENIX CO., LTD.
and VIZ Media, LLC.
English translation © 2019 SQUARE ENIX CO., LTD.

The stories, characters and incidents mentioned in this
publication are entirely fictional.

No portion of this book may be reproduced or transmitted in
any form or by any means without written permission from
the copyright holders.

Printed in the U.S.A.

Published by VIZ Media, LLC
P.O. Box 77010
San Francisco, CA 94107

10 9 8 7 6 5 4 3 2 1
First printing, March 2019

VIZ MEDIA
viz.com

RATED
T
TEEN

PARENTAL ADVISORY
THAT BLUE SKY FEELING is rated T for Teen and
is recommended for ages 13 and up. Contains
suggestive themes.